DATE DUE

*f*P

THE FREE PRESS

New York   London   Toronto   Sydney   Singapore

LEARNING DISABILITIES: A TO Z

A Parent's Complete Guide to Learning Disabilities from Preschool to Adulthood

CORINNE SMITH, PH.D.
LISA STRICK

ƒP

THE FREE PRESS
A Division of Simon & Schuster Inc.
1230 Avenue of the Americas
New York, NY 10020

THE FREE PRESS and colophon are trademarks
of Simon & Schuster Inc.

Manufactured in the United States of America

10   9   8   7   6   5   4   3   2   1

Library of Congress Cataloging-in-Publication Data

Smith, Corinne Roth.
    Learning disabilities : A to Z : a parent's complete guide to
learning disabilities from preschool to adulthood / Corinne Smith,
Lisa Strick.
      p.   cm.
    Includes index.
    ISBN 0–684–82738–7
    1. Learning disabilities—United States.   2. Learning disabled
children—Education—United States.   I. Strick, Lisa W.   II. Title.
LC4705.S62   1997
371.92'6—dc21   97-12489
                                                  CIP

To our children

Benjamin and Eli

Juli and Rachael

CONTENTS

PART IV: A QUALITY LIFE

11. Strategies for Promoting Personal Success   257

12. Looking Forward to the Future   323

    Appendixes:

A. Benchmarks of Normal Development   365

B. Common Assessment Measures   375

C. The Development of Reading, Writing, and Math Skills   386

D. Resource List   392

    Index   399

    Acknowledgments   408

Part I

UNDERSTANDING LEARNING DISABILITIES

1

WHAT ARE
LEARNING DISABILITIES?

◆ Brian's first-grade teacher describes him as "a human pinball machine." He never walks; he bolts. He leaves his desk every few minutes to sharpen his pencil, get more paper, look in on the class gerbils. He can't seem to resist commenting on everything he sees. Brian's classmates find his restlessness and interruptions annoying, but neither punishments nor rewards have produced any lasting change in his behavior. On his mid-term report, Brian's teacher writes: "Brian is bright and enthusiastic, but he needs to settle down. He is falling behind because he just won't pay attention."

◆ Eleven-year-old Aisha is quiet and shy. She works hard, but her progress in school has always been slow. Now in fifth grade, she is more than a year behind her peers in both math and reading. Her teachers do not believe Aisha is smart enough to keep up with the class, and they have reduced their expectations of her. Aisha's parents say she grasps ideas well enough at home, and they are puzzled by her slow academic progress. They are also worried about the fact that Aisha is becoming increasingly withdrawn: she has no friends, and she spends most of her free time alone watching television.

◆ Frank has been put on notice that he is failing eighth grade, and he will have to repeat it if he does not start handing in his assignments and stop cutting classes. He has been in trouble for other things this year: fighting, vandalism, and (most recently) showing up at a school dance drunk. Frank says he doesn't care if he fails—he plans to quit school at sixteen, so he's just "doing time" until then. All but one of Frank's teachers find him hostile and uncooperative. The teacher who runs the computer lab says Frank is attentive and capable; he even helps others who don't know what to do.

◆ A popular tenth-grader, Joel has enjoyed sports since he was in elementary school. He has earned places on the high school wrestling, track, and baseball teams. He is also active in student government and sells advertising for the school yearbook. His grades, however, are mostly C's and D's. Joel's teachers complain that his homework is careless, sloppy, and incomplete; his handwriting is unreadable. "Maybe if he weren't so involved in extracurricular activities, he'd be able to focus on his work," Joel's history teacher comments. "He'll never get into college if he doesn't start making an effort!"

It can be easy to make assumptions about students like these. Brian is immature and lacks self-control. Aisha is a child who is slow intellectually. Frank has a "bad attitude" and emotional problems. Joel needs to overcome his lack of academic motivation.

If you take a closer look, however, a very different picture emerges:

◆ Brian's wandering mind and restless drive to keep moving frustrate him and his family even more than they do his teacher, but this behavior is beyond his control. He lacks the ability to plan ahead and "screen out" distractions, so he can't concentrate no matter how hard he tries. Brian also cannot regulate his impulses to investigate and comment on anything he notices that is new. At the end of each day he is exhausted from responding to all the sights and sounds that swirl around him, yet he can't "turn himself off" until he falls asleep (which is a struggle in itself).

◆ A psychologist found that Aisha's intelligence is in the gifted range. She must struggle to keep up with less able peers because she has difficulty making sense out of written symbols. The psychologist told Aisha's parents that Aisha has become depressed as a result of her school problems. "She sees herself as a total failure," he said.

◆ Frank started avoiding classes and homework to hide the trouble he has understanding either verbal directions or very much of what he reads. Brighter than average, he is successful in learning situations that do not call for extensive use of language. Junior high, however, does not provide him with many opportunities of that kind. Frank feels like a misfit and longs to escape the endless failure and criticism that he faces in school.

◆ Joel's success as an athlete masks his poor fine motor coordination. Difficulty controlling his hands makes it extremely hard for Joel to manipulate a pen or pencil (he is also "all thumbs" when it comes to chores like washing dishes or setting the table). Joel is a conscientious student and understands class material, but he finds it virtually impossible to express what he knows when he is required to write it down.

All of these students have *learning disabilities*, neurological handicaps that affect the brain's ability to understand, remember, or communicate information. Once believed to be rare, learning disabilities are now believed to affect at least 5 percent of the population, or more than 12 million Americans. Many authorities feel that the number of individuals affected is actually much higher, and experts agree that many children are not doing as well as they could in school because of disabilities which have not been identified. Year after year, many of these youngsters are erroneously pegged as slow-witted, insolent, or lazy. They are constantly being urged to shape up or knuckle down by anxious adults concerned about their academic performance. When the usual tactics of reward and punishment fail, parents and teachers become frustrated—but no one is more frustrated than the students themselves. "The most depressing words in the English language have got to be 'Just try harder,'" says a student whose disabilities were finally identified in high school. "I *was* trying, but because I wasn't *succeeding* nobody believed me."

Although learning disabilities have become the focus of more intense research in recent years, they are still poorly understood by the general public. Information about learning disabilities has been so slow to "trickle down" that misconceptions abound even among teachers and other education professionals. The confusion is not hard to understand. For one thing, the term *learning disability* refers not to a single disorder but to a broad range of handicaps that can affect any area of academic performance. Only rarely can they be traced to a simple cause: many different things can impair brain function, and these children's physiological problems are often complicated to some degree by their home and school environments. Learning disabilities can be divided into general types, but since they

often occur in combinations—and also vary tremendously in severity—it can be very hard to see what students grouped under this label
have in common.

In fact, learning disabilities are often so subtle that these children
do not seem handicapped at all. Many children with learning disabilities have intelligences in the average to superior range, and what is
usually most obvious about them is that they are able (even exceptionally so) in some areas. How can a kid know everything there is to
know about dinosaurs at the age of four, but still be unable to learn
the alphabet? How can a student who reads three years beyond her
grade level turn in written work that is incomprehensible? How can
a child read a paragraph aloud flawlessly and not remember its contents five minutes later? No wonder these students are so often accused of being inattentive, uncooperative, or unmotivated!

This discrepancy between what it seems the child ought to be able
to do and what he or she actually can do, however, is the hallmark of
this kind of handicap. What children with learning disabilities have
in common is *unexpected underachievement*. Most of the time these
children function in a way which is consistent with what would be expected from their intellectual ability and their educational and family backgrounds, but give them certain types of tasks and their brains
seem to stall. As a result, their performance in school is inconsistent:
on target or even ahead of the class in some areas, but behind in others. While neurological impairments can affect any area of brain
function, the disabilities most likely to cause academic problems are
those affecting *visual perception, language processing, fine motor
skills,* and *the ability to focus attention.* Even minor handicaps in
these areas (which may pass completely unnoticed at home) can have
a devastating impact as soon as a child enters the classroom.

Many youngsters with learning disabilities also struggle with behaviors that complicate their difficulties in school. Most notorious
among these is *hyperactivity*, an extreme restlessness that affects
15–20% of children with learning disabilities. Some other problematic behaviors frequently observed in young people with learning disabilities are the following:

Short attention span: The child is easily distracted, rapidly loses interest in new activities, may jump from activity to activity, and often
leaves work or projects unfinished.

Difficulty following directions: The child may ask for repeated guidance even during simple tasks ("Where was I supposed to put it?"

"How was I supposed to do that again?"). Mistakes are made because instructions are not fully understood.

Social immaturity: The child acts younger than his or her chronological age and may prefer to play with younger children.

Difficulty with conversation: The child has trouble finding the right words, or rambles endlessly.

Inflexibility: The child is stubborn about sticking to his or her own way of doing things, even when it is not working; he or she resists suggestions and offers of help.

Poor planning and organizational skills: The child seems to have no sense of time and is often late or unprepared. Given several tasks (or a complex task with several parts), he or she has no idea where to begin, or how to break the work down into manageable segments.

Absentmindedness: The child frequently loses homework, clothing, and other possessions; forgets to do chores and assignments and/or has trouble remembering appointments and social engagements.

Clumsiness: The child appears awkward and uncoordinated; often knocks things over, spills things, or fumbles and drops objects; may have atrocious handwriting; is seen as hopeless at sports and games.

Lack of impulse control: The child touches whatever (or whomever) captures his or her interest, blurts out observations without thinking, interrupts or inappropriately changes the subject in conversation, and/or has difficulty waiting or taking turns.

These behaviors arise from the same neurological conditions that cause problems with learning. Unfortunately, when they are not understood as such they only help convince parents and teachers that the child is not making an effort to cooperate or is not paying attention. Even students come to see behaviors like these as personality defects: "I was so happy when I found out I had a learning disability," one teenager recalls. "Until then I thought I was just an airheaded klutz."

Although many children with learning disabilities are happy and well adjusted, some (as many as half according to current studies) do develop related emotional problems. These students become so frustrated trying to do things they cannot do that they give up on learning and start developing strategies to avoid it. They question their own intelligence and begin to see themselves as beyond help. Many become angry and act out; others become anxious and depressed. Either way, these children tend to become socially isolated and often suffer from loneliness as well as low self-esteem. Eventually, the secondary problems associated with a learning disability may become far more obvious—and more serious—than the handicap itself. Studies show that teens with learning disabilities are not only more likely to drop out of school, they are at increased risk for substance abuse, criminal activity, and even suicide. While most students with learning disabilities are not headed for futures this tragic, Casandra's story poignantly describes the frustration and insecurity that can follow these students into adulthood.

Parents of students with learning disabilities often find themselves attempting to cope with a bewildering array of problems. Their children appear to be bright enough, but they encounter all kinds of obstacles in school. They may be curious and eager to learn, but their restlessness and inability to stick to a subject makes it hard to explain anything to them. They have good intentions when it comes to homework and chores, but halfway through the job they forget the directions—or the objective. Many have trouble making friends. Their emotional ups and downs can pitch the entire family into turmoil. Worst of all, these children are usually miserable about their inability to meet their parents' expectations and their own cherished personal goals. Frequently they blame themselves for all these difficulties; "I'm dumb," "I'm hopeless," or "People don't like me" can become an endless, self-defeating refrain. As one mother put it: "It's the erosion of self-confidence that really kills you. There can't be much that feels worse than watching your kid give up on himself and his dreams."

This book is about helping youngsters with learning disabilities hold onto their dreams. It is also about helping their mothers and fathers negotiate the maze of challenges that so often leave parents and students alike feeling overwhelmed and helpless. The first important point is that parents are not helpless—quite the contrary. It is an established fact that the students most likely to succeed are the ones who have informed, supportive parents on their side. This factor outweighs the quality of school programming or the severity of the handicap itself in importance. Many studies have demonstrated that "quality parenting" enables children to grow into happy, independent citizens even when health at birth and educational opportunities are notably poor.

Parents do not need a Ph.D. in psychology or education to guide their children effectively. Among the aspects of parenting researchers

CASANDRA

I can remember my mother making me wear a letter from the alphabet around my neck to school. I think it was the letter *J*. I knew the letter before I left the house and tried so hard not to forget it all day. Picture a child, five years of age, walking out of her house and knowing that when she comes back through that very same door, she better know the letter.

I walked all the way to school saying the letter *J* over and over again. But do you know over the course of the day I had forgotten that letter? After school was out, I tried so hard—I mean, I looked at that letter, praying that a voice or something would give me the answer before I got home. I love my mother and I know she loves me, and all she wanted was for me to know my alphabet. But I feared her so and hated the fact I couldn't remember what she tried so hard to teach me. I remember crying and being mad at myself because I just couldn't get it. I wanted so much to yell at her: "I'm trying, damn it, I'm trying! Can't you see I'm trying! Just help me, please!"

As I got older, reading and spelling got harder and harder for me. Teachers, my family and friends all seemed to be picking on me all the time. Teachers blamed me for cutting up in class. So since everyone wanted to laugh or blame me for things, I stopped trying to read either to myself or out loud and became a clown in school and stayed to myself at home.

By the time I reached eleventh grade, I realized the damage that was done. Going to college never entered my mind, or what I wanted out of life, or what kind of job I was going to get. . . . Then I found myself feeling disappointed, not because the people that I cared about or the teachers that were supposed to teach had put me down, but because I had put my ownself down. I finally came to realize I was always going to run into people who thought I was stupid, but I knew and really believed I wasn't. I was going to graduate from high school without anyone's help, so I knew I wasn't stupid.

Therefore, why is it to this very day, now twenty-eight, I still fear reading and speaking to people I meet? I find myself only speaking to those I know won't pick on me. I'll tell you why—it's because my family and teachers have made me think that everyone I talk to is going to pick and pick on me until they can't pick anymore. In other words, every human being on earth is smarter than me. And that is wrong.

No child should ever feel like that. How in hell can someone do that to a child who is trying? Each and every child deserves the right to learn and speak their mind without someone stopping them by making them feel belittled.

Adapted from Smith, C. R. (1994). *Learning disabilities: The interaction of learner, task and setting (3rd ed.).* Boston: Allyn & Bacon.

cite as most valuable are teaching children to make the most of their strengths, encouraging them to believe they can overcome obstacles, helping them set realistic goals, and encouraging pride by involving them in responsibilities at home and in the community.

Parents of children with learning disabilities do need to learn how to work effectively with teachers and school administrators to develop an appropriate educational program—a prospect many find intimidating. Becoming an activist at the school, however, is the best way to ensure that your child's educational needs will be fully met. Because teacher training programs until recently included next to nothing about learning disabilities, you cannot assume that your child's teachers will be well informed about them or sympathetic to the special needs of children with neurological handicaps. Furthermore, many of the tried-and-true teaching methods and materials that work for typical students are useless for children with learning disabilities. Parents of successful students with learning disabilities say careful monitoring and advocacy is the only way to make sure that these children are consistently taught in a way that makes it possible for them to learn. Parents add that they often find themselves in the position of "educating the educators" about learning disabilities and the many ways children can be affected by them.

Our goal is to provide you with both the information and the encouragement you need to become an effective advocate for your child. We will examine the causes and types of learning disabilities, and discuss the ways they affect both education and social and emotional growth. We will take you, step by step, through the process of identifying learning disabilities and show you how to work with professionals to develop an individualized educational program. We will also talk about ways of addressing some of the persistent problems that can upset life at home. Let us begin, however, with the reminder that no "expert" you meet is ever going to know as much as you do about your child. More important, you are the only authority who can be depended upon to look at the whole child. Professionals are paid to concern themselves primarily with a student's problems and weaknesses; it is the *parents* who are most aware of all the ways a young person is strong and wonderful. Your most vital job is to remind your child that he or she is splendid and capable most of the time. Children who know they are mostly able—and entirely loved—do not let handicaps get in their way for long.

2

WHAT CAUSES
LEARNING DISABILITIES?

Even though students with learning disabilities are by far the largest and the fastest-growing special-needs group in the American school population, parents cannot always get clear answers to their most urgent questions when a learning problem is identified: "How did this happen?" "What went wrong?" "Can children outgrow learning disabilities?" "Is there a cure?"

These questions can be difficult to answer, because multiple factors contribute to learning disabilities. In recent years, the relative importance of these causes has become a matter of increasing research and debate. In some of the newest studies, investigators have used sophisticated imaging techniques such as positron emission tomography (PET) and magnetic resonance imaging (MRI) to watch living brains at work, and they have compared structures and activity levels in the brains of normal subjects and subjects with learning problems. In other areas of research, scientists have autopsied the brains of deceased persons with learning disabilities looking for anatomical differences, and geneticists have been searching for (and finding) evidence that some kinds of learning disability are inherited.

But while this research is producing more and more valuable information about the intricate structures and complex workings of the human brain, it is not always easy to apply this information to an individual. In addition, irregularities in brain function tell only part of the story. Children's intellectual development is also heavily influenced by their family, school, and community environment. While learning disabilities are assumed to have a biological basis, it is often the child's environment that determines the severity of the disability's impact. Science has not yet provided much in the way of medical treatments, but long experience has shown that modifying the environment can make a remarkable difference in a child's educational progress. This means that even though learning disabilities are regarded as permanent conditions, they can be improved dramatically by making changes at home and in the child's educational program.

The biological factors contributing to learning disabilities can be divided into four general categories: *brain injury, errors in brain development, neurochemical imbalances,* and *heredity.* In this chapter we will review each of these separately, and discuss how a variety of environmental factors also influence learning and development. Since there are no definitive neurological tests for learning disabilities, determining the cause of a given student's learning problems is still largely a matter of informed guesswork. When a child's home and school situations are examined and a detailed history is taken, one or more factors discussed in this chapter often stand out. It must also be admitted, however, that sometimes the only honest answer to the question "Why does my child have a learning disability?" is "We don't know for sure." We trust that ongoing research in this rapidly developing field will eventually provide us with new ways of evaluating these disabilities and pinpointing the source of individual learning problems.

BRAIN INJURY

For many years it was assumed that all students with learning disabilities had experienced some kind of brain damage. Today we know that most children with learning disabilities have *no* history of brain injury. Even when they do, it is not always certain that this is the source of their academic difficulties. Research has shown, for example, that head injuries are almost as common among typical achievers as they are among children having trouble in school. One investigator estimates that as many as 20 percent of all children suffer a serious insult to the brain by age six, yet most of these children do not develop learning problems.

Efforts to link a child's learning disabilities to brain damage caused by birth complications have also failed to find a conclusive connection. These factors are associated with some cases of learning disabilities, but they can also be found in the histories of typical and high achievers. A study of seven- to fifteen-year-olds, for example, found that 23 percent of the students reading a year or two behind grade level had a history of birth difficulties. A similar background, though, was found for 19 percent of the students reading a year or more *ahead* of grade level—hardly a convincing correlation!

There is no doubt, however, that some children's learning disabilities do arise from injuries to the brain. Among the injury types associated with learning disabilities are accidents, brain hemorrhages and tumors, illnesses such as encephalitis and meningitis, untreated glandular disorders in infancy, and infant hypoglycemia. Malnutrition and exposure to toxic chemicals (such as lead or pesticides) have also been shown to cause brain damage leading to learning problems. Children who receive radiation and chemotherapy treatments for cancer sometimes develop learning disabilities, especially if radiation has been applied to the skull. Events that cause the brain to be deprived of oxygen can result in irreversible brain damage in a relatively short time; incidents involving choking, suffocation, drowning, smoke inhalation, carbon monoxide poisoning, and some birth complications fall in this category.

Brain injuries can also occur before birth. It is well known that when certain illnesses occur during pregnancy—diabetes, kidney disease, and measles among them—brain damage to the fetus is sometimes the sad result. Prenatal exposure to drugs (alcohol, nicotine, and some prescription medications as well as "street" drugs) has been clearly associated with a variety of learning difficulties, including cognitive delays, attention deficits, hyperactivity, and memory problems. As we will discuss in the next section, the developing nervous system of a fetus is so fragile that even relatively minor insults can have significant lasting effects. The nervous systems of premature infants are also vulnerable to injury, and a significantly higher incidence of prematurity is found among children who have academic and behavioral problems.

As Teddy's story demonstrates, the effects of brain injury can be sudden and dramatic, but just as often they are subtle and delayed. Sometimes children recover from an injury well enough to handle challenges at their current developmental or educational levels, but deficits become apparent when life becomes more complex and demanding. For this reason, significant problems in school at any point following a brain injury need prompt evaluation. In general, the ear-

TEDDY

Teddy was adored by his parents and four older sisters, and it was not hard to see why. At two years old, he was a handsome, affectionate child who responded to all the attention given him with hugs, smiles, and laughter. He was tall for his age and obviously bright: he had learned to talk early, spoke in clear three- and four-word sentences, and already recognized some letters of the alphabet. Teddy loved to watch *Sesame Street* and to look at picture books, and he also loved the playground. He was so graceful on the slide and jungle gym that his father boasted Teddy was certainly slated for athletic stardom.

Teddy's life changed, however, as a result of a routine DPT immunization. The evening that he received his injection, Teddy developed a high fever, had seizures, and was rushed to the local emergency room. He was hospitalized, but it was several days before the fever and seizures abated. By the end of the week it was clear that Teddy's severe DPT reaction had caused brain damage: the little boy could walk only with assistance, and he couldn't speak at all.

Over the next six months Teddy's ability to walk and talk returned, but he wasn't the same child. Instead of sitting quietly absorbed with crayons or a picture book, he became a human tornado. His coordination was poor, and he tried to stomp through things rather than move around them. He was impulsive and easily frustrated. He could not be taken to the supermarket without climbing and grabbing things off the shelves. When his parents tried to restrain him he would kick, bite, and throw tantrums. Even worse, Teddy continued to have seizures, which required frequent trials with different doses of medication.

Teddy's "out of control" behavior caused him to be dismissed by several nursery schools. Teachers complained that he knocked down other children's block towers, spoke out during story time, and splattered paint everywhere. He grabbed other children's toys and helped himself from other children's lunches. The teachers agreed that Teddy was bright enough, but they cautioned that he would have trouble in kindergarten if he could not control himself and learn to stick with tasks. Unfortunately, the teachers' predictions proved correct. Teddy's first years in school were a disaster; he couldn't attend to his lessons for long, and he was the last in his class to master basic skills. By the end of the second grade, it

lier a child receives support following a brain injury, the better the chances are that he or she will recover—or learn to compensate for—skills that have been lost.

Brain injuries, of course, can cause multiple problems, and chil-

was obvious that reading and writing were both going to be very difficult for him. Teddy's skills always continued to develop, but his progress was so slow that the gap between him and the typical students in his class got wider every year. By the time he finished sixth grade, Teddy was reading and writing like a fourth grader. His seizures were largely under control and he had stopped having temper tantrums, but he remained an active, angry boy who was unpopular with other students and teachers alike.

During junior high school, continued low achievement and social isolation ate away at Teddy's feelings of self-worth. He became so angry and depressed that his parents became truly alarmed. After lengthy discussions, they decided to try placing Teddy in a private boarding school for students with learning disabilities. Teddy left home at the beginning of ninth grade.

Teddy's parents reported that by their first Parents' Day visit, they could see a change in their son. Teddy seemed heartened by the discovery that he was not the only student of his kind. He had made some friends, and he played on the school's soccer team. Teddy's teachers helped him complete tasks by allowing him to work in short sessions that were spread throughout the day. The school stressed learning through doing whenever possible, and Teddy found many of the projects he was assigned enjoyable and interesting. He had discovered that he could be a good student if he was allowed to do things his own way. For the first time since he was two, Teddy was thinking of himself as a success.

In twelfth grade, Teddy passed all of his state competency tests and declared he wanted to go on to college. Initially his parents panicked, afraid that demands at the college level would resurrect old patterns of frustration and failure. Several sessions with the school's guidance counselor, however, produced an ideal solution: following graduation, Teddy enrolled in a two-year culinary arts institute. He excelled in this training, earned an associate's degree, and rapidly found a job as a pastry chef in an exclusive resort. He recently became engaged to a vivacious young woman employed in resort management. Teddy's fiancé does all the driving because of his seizure disorder; Teddy does all the cooking, which his wife-to-be declares is a more than acceptable trade. Teddy is also designing the cake for his wedding, planned for June.

dren who develop seizure disorders, cerebral palsy, or other physical disabilities as a result of brain damage often have learning disabilities as well. It is important to keep this in mind when seeking services for a child following a brain injury, since subtle handicaps (such as learning disabilities) can be overlooked when there are more obvious or urgent physical challenges to overcome. Appropriate educational programming for a child with brain injuries often involves coordinating several different kinds of support: for example, a child may need physical and speech therapy as well as special education programming. Frequent monitoring may be needed to ensure that all of the necessary elements are being provided and kept in reasonable balance.

ERRORS IN BRAIN DEVELOPMENT

Development of the human brain begins at conception and continues through young adulthood. In the nine months before birth, all of the basic structures of the brain are formed. The nervous system of a fetus grows in stages, with different brain regions forming at different times throughout the pregnancy. A particularly critical developmental period is the fifth to seventh months of gestation, when cells move into their proper positions in the cerebral cortex. The cortex, a multilayered structure that forms the brain's outer shell, is involved in virtually all aspects of conscious activity. Proper functioning of the cerebral cortex is essential for higher-level thinking and learning.

During infancy and childhood, regions of the brain become increasingly specialized. New connections between parts of the brain also form, so that these specialized areas can "cooperate" during higher levels of thinking. This ongoing process of brain maturation explains why children gradually become able to do things they could not do before. Babies learn to walk and talk, for example, not only because eager parents encourage them to do so, but because the necessary neural connections are made between one and two years of age. Within a few years, the brain develops to a point where a child can take on remarkably sophisticated challenges. The task of reading aloud, for example, involves the coordinated activity of fourteen areas of the cerebral cortex, including those concerned with vision, language processing, listening, and speech.

If this ongoing process of neural "wiring" is disturbed at any point, parts of the brain may not develop normally. Experts believe that developmental errors of this kind are responsible for many learning disabilities. Support for this belief comes both from anatomical studies (which have found a variety of structural abnormalities in the brains of individuals with learning disabilities) and from research demonstrating that electrical and metabolic activity in the brains of students with learning problems is often different from that of normal learners.

The type of problems produced by errors in brain development depend in part on which regions of the brain have been affected. It is important to understand, however, that since learning and other complex behaviors depend on the activation of "circuits" involving several brain areas, impairment in one brain region can affect growth and performance elsewhere in the system. For this reason, it is unusual for a student with learning disabilities to have a single, isolated weakness; patterns of related problems are far more common. Scientists using imaging technology to study activity in the cerebral cortex have identified three patterns that occur particularly often in individuals who have academic difficulties:

1. *Left hemisphere is underactive/right hemisphere is overactive.* The left cerebral hemisphere generally specializes in language functions, and youngsters displaying this pattern have trouble with various aspects of language processing (reading, writing, and sometimes speech). Difficulties with language are also associated with poor comprehension and memory for verbal material. In addition, these students often have difficulty with tasks involving logic and analysis: they take a "global" approach to learning and do not easily understand that specific sequences of activities or events are necessary to arrive at a final solution or product. Overactivity in the right cerebral hemisphere can produce delays in learning to read, as the right side of the brain is poorly adapted to the task of decoding words by breaking them into individual sounds and syllables.

2. *Right hemisphere is underactive/left hemisphere is overactive.* The right side of the brain usually organizes and processes nonverbal information. Individuals with deficiencies in the right cerebral cortex can have problems with time sense, body awareness, spatial orientation, visual perception, and visual memory. An overfunctioning left cerebral hemisphere usually results in an excessively analytical approach to problem solving. Students displaying this pattern handle details well but "can't see the forest for the trees"; they may become so bogged down in trivia that they miss the main point of a lesson. Such students are at risk for problems with many higher-level academic tasks, including organizing research projects, writing coherent papers, and advanced math reasoning.

3. *Underactivity in the frontal lobes.* The frontal lobes of the cerebral cortex govern motor behavior, and they also include regions involved in planning and judgment, focusing attention, organizing

and evaluating information, and moderating emotions. When the frontal regions of the brain are not functioning efficiently, children typically have problems with muscle coordination, articulation, impulse control, planning and organization, and maintaining attention. Problems of this kind affect children's readiness for classroom instruction, and they create an overall impression of immaturity even when the children are capable of functioning at a high level intellectually.

Individuals with errors in their cortical "wiring" must develop alternate neural pathways for processing information. Because these pathways are not always as efficient as normal brain circuits would be, students with learning disabilities tend to process information more slowly than typical peers. As a result, these students need more time both to understand tasks and to complete them. While the additional time required is often only a matter of seconds, this handicap can have a significant impact on a student's ability to compete in classrooms. Information-processing delays can be devastating when students face "pressure" situations such as timed tests or math drills and spelling bees. In some cases, simply removing time constraints is enough to help a student with learning disabilities do better at school. More often, however, the need for extra time is only one part of a larger pattern of learning problems.

Not all developmental problems involve irregular anatomy. Experts believe that some individuals develop learning difficulties because parts of their brains simply mature more slowly than usual. Such children are not always ready to take on the tasks and responsibilities that are appropriate for their chronological age: they act like their peers in some respects, but in other areas their behavior and needs are more like those of younger children. In such cases of *maturational lag*, delayed regions of the brain may reach normal or near-normal levels of development eventually, but by this time victims are likely to have spent many discouraging years in classrooms where what they were being taught was out of synch with what they were ready to learn. Even after their brains mature, these students may continue to be handicapped because they missed out on acquiring skills and concepts that are the basic building blocks of a higher education. Too often, these students find their skills never quite catch up with the increasingly complex demands of the curriculum. If their programs are not modified, they fall farther and farther behind academically, and their problems compound as feelings of inadequacy sap their emotional energy and their enthusiasm for learning.

Why developmental errors and delays occur is not always clear. Events that disturb prenatal brain development are undoubtedly responsible for many abnormalities: during critical periods of brain formation, faults can be caused by only a few cells going astray. As we will explain later on in this chapter, irregular patterns of brain development can also be genetically determined. The good news is that most students with these types of disabilities respond positively to a stimulating educational environment and make steady progress given appropriate individualized instruction. It is also important to remember that children whose brains develop unevenly sometimes develop strengths and talents that are out of the ordinary. Thomas Edison and Albert Einstein are among the geniuses who had learning problems; the list of celebrities in sports, business, politics, and the arts who had serious difficulties with reading, writing, or math in school is a long one. Parents and special educators note that children with learning problems are often exceptionally creative: because traditional solutions do not always work for them, they become inventive about working out their own. Since teachers faced with a student who cannot read or write well will not necessarily get excited about that youngster's leadership qualities, entrepreneurial ability, or musical talent, parents need to be especially alert about noticing and encouraging emerging strengths in nonacademic areas.

CHEMICAL IMBALANCES

Brain cells communicate with one another by means of chemical "messengers" called neurotransmitters. Any change in the brain's delicately balanced chemical climate can interfere with these neurotransmitters and impair the brain's ability to function properly. People who are intoxicated by alcohol, for example, are experiencing a temporary alteration in brain chemistry. As any police officer can affirm, disturbances in speech, motor coordination, and problem-solving ability are the usual results.

A growing body of evidence suggests that neurochemical imbalances contribute to some learning disorders, particularly those involving difficulty with attention, distractibility, and impulsivity. This includes the syndrome now known as *attention deficit hyperactivity disorder* (ADHD). Children with ADHD are frequently accused of "not paying attention," but in fact they pay attention to *everything*. What they lack are the abilities to plan ahead, focus their attention selectively, and organize rapid responses. In addition, many children with ADHD are restless, impulsive, disorganized, overly talkative, and poorly coordinated. While their behavior may not seem seriously out of line at home or on the playground, these children are easily identified in the classroom by their inability to sit still and concentrate.

Investigators have found a variety of irregularities in the brains of people with ADHD. One is that many individuals with ADHD are deficient in a class of neurotransmitters called catecholamines. Catecholamines control several neural systems in the brain, including those that govern attention, motor behavior, and motivation. One view of the neurological basis for ADHD is that low levels of catecholamines result in underactivation of these systems. Affected individuals therefore cannot moderate their attention, levels of activity, emotional impulses, or responses to stimuli in their environments as effectively as people with normal nervous systems.

As early as the 1930s it was observed that stimulant drugs—which increase the level of catecholamines in the brain—temporarily normalized the behavior of children who were overactive and had poor impulse control. Recent controlled studies indicate that 70 to 80 percent of children with ADHD receive some benefit from stimulants such as methylphenidate (Ritalin) and pemoline (Cylert), showing improved attention span and ability to concentrate, reduced activity level, and greater availability for learning (see illustration). Use of these medications has become widespread; about three-quarters of a million students currently take stimulants to help them focus their attention in school. Some antidepressant drugs (notably imipramine) also increase the level of catecholamines in the brain, and researchers are beginning to explore their value in treating ADHD as well.

Medication has also been used to regulate brain function successfully in some cases of children who are *hypoactive*. These young people are lethargic and overly focused on details; they ponder problems at excessive length and have difficulty making decisions. In school they appear dull and unmotivated because they complete their work slowly and ask few questions. Interestingly, these students sometimes "perk up" when given sedatives. Experts theorize that sedative medications regulate overactive neurotransmitter systems that are abnormally inhibiting brain activity.

Stimulants and other medications can produce undesirable side effects, so the use of drugs to treat attention problems remains controversial. We will discuss the pros and cons of stimulant medication more thoroughly in Chapter 8. In the meantime, it is important to remember that medication is rarely a total solution to a child's problems. About a third of children with ADHD have additional learning

Effects of Ritalin on Handwriting

When taking the spelling test dated January 20, this fourth-grade girl was receiving Ritalin. While she was receiving a placebo on February 7, her writing skills rapidly deteriorated after the third word.

Source: Gadow, K. D. (1986). *Children on medication: Vol. 1. Hyperactivity, learning disabilities, and mental retardation.* San Diego: College-Hill Press.

disabilities that must be addressed, and virtually all of these children need ongoing support both at home and at school to help them develop effective learning strategies and maintain appropriate behavior. Studies have repeatedly shown that medication combined with a program of behavior modification works better than medication alone. In situations where medication is ineffective or undesirable, behavioral and educational intervention by themselves can still significantly reduce problem behavior and improve learning. Because students with ADHD often have problems with interpersonal relationships, teaching social skills is also very important. This kind of help pays off with improved peer acceptance and ability to make friends—which are as important as academic performance for school survival and healthy self-esteem.

HEREDITY

Research conducted since the mid-1980s indicates that heredity plays a far greater role in determining the development of learning disabilities than previously believed. Studies of the families of children with learning disabilities consistently find a higher than average incidence of similar learning problems among parents, siblings, and other related individuals. Children with ADHD are among those most likely to share the problem with one or more relatives, suggesting that the neurochemical imbalances which contribute to this disorder can be genetic in origin. There is also substantial evidence that some language-processing disabilities (which affect reading ability and are often grouped under the term *dyslexia*) run in families, although not all cases are as dramatic as Jimmy's (see box).

One recent study found that 60 percent of children with learning disabilities had parents and/or siblings with similar learning problems, while 25 percent could identify grandparents, aunts, and uncles who had experienced learning difficulties. A study of children with reading disabilities found that 88 percent had relatives who had experienced language-processing problems! Some of the most convincing data in support of the inheritability of learning disabilities comes from research involving twins. While fraternal twins have similar learning problems about half the time, identical twins—who share the same genetic "blueprint"—are found to have similar disabilities 70% or more of the time. Since both types of twins share the same environment, the higher incidence of similarity among identical twins is likely due to genetic factors.

A new research focus in learning disabilities, called *linkage analysis*, is attempting to locate a specific gene for learning disabilities by determining if learning problems regularly occur with some other trait whose genetic origin is already known. Because genes that lie on the same chromosome tend to be inherited as a unit, individuals with learning disabilities who share a known genetic "marker" (such as eye color or blood type) may have the gene for a learning disability on the same chromosome as that marker. While some evidence implicating specific genes has been collected, this research also suggests that there are probably many ways that learning disabilities can be inherited—for example, unusual brain anatomy, uneven patterns of brain maturation, and susceptibility to diseases that affect brain function all could be passed down genetically. Investigators also note that genetics are never likely to be the *only* cause of a learning disability. The author of some of the best-known twin studies estimates that when identical twins share reading disabilities, 40 percent of each child's deficit is due to genetic problems, 35 percent is due to shared environmental influences, and 25 percent is due to environmental factors unique to the individual or random factors that are not yet understood.

Clinicians who test for learning disabilities observe that when results are presented to parents, Mom or Dad frequently remarks, "But I can't do that either!" Parents such as these often struggled in school, but since learning disabilities were rarely identified a generation ago, they may have never suspected a neurological handicap. While some parents seem grateful that an explanation other than "stupidity" exists for their own history of learning problems, others find the suggestion that there is something wrong with both them *and* their child more than they want to take on. Parents who feel their own lives have been made harder as a result of educational failures may feel particularly disturbed about the prospect of their children facing similar obstacles. Education about learning disabilities—understanding that they are very different from mental retardation, for example, and that help is available now which did not exist years ago—often is needed to help these parents accept facts and move on to appropriate action. Encouragement is also important; helping a child with tasks which made you feel defeated in school takes a special kind of courage and motivation. When there is a family history of learning disabilities, parents need as much support as children do both from professionals and from other family members.

ENVIRONMENTAL INFLUENCES

Although learning disabilities are caused by physiological problems, the extent to which children are affected by them is often decided by their environments. Conditions at home and at school, in fact, can make the difference between a mild disability and a truly crippling handicap. In order to understand learning disabilities fully, then, it is necessary to understand how children's environments at home and at school affect their intellectual development and their potential for learning.

JIMMY

When Jimmy's mother called the clinic to refer her son for an evaluation, the first hint that Jimmy's learning difficulties might be hereditary
came over the phone. Jimmy's mother expressed her deep "flustration"
in obtaining adequate services for her son's "dilekia." From a woman
with a Ph.D. who was the director of a counseling center, such mispro-
nunciations were unexpected. The mother's worst fear was that Jimmy
had inherited "dilekia" from both sides of the family.

Jimmy's mother had two siblings, neither of whom had learned to
read until adolescence. One now writes books, but remains a terrible
speller. One child of the other sibling has been identified as learning disabled, and her younger child, a preschooler, is receiving speech and language therapy.

Jimmy's father has a master's degree in social work, a Ph.D. in philosophy, and now spends all his time back in law school. He is never
satisfied with his accomplishments and keeps trying to prove his competence in new ways. Jimmy's father was very late in learning to read and
still reads, in his words, "a word an hour." What he reads he remembers,
however, and he is an excellent student. His professors have always allowed him to use a spell-checker on exams.

Jimmy's father comes from a family of five children, and every one
has a reading disability. All but one sibling, who suffers from severe depression, have become vocationally successful. One of his brothers stut-
ters, and a sister gets stuck on very simple words when speaking. Her
conversations are punctuated by referring to objects as "thing" and elab-
orating when recounting an event by adding "or some such thing." An-

---

The Environment at Home

The home environment plays a major role in determining how well or
how poorly any child learns. An enormous body of research
has shown that a stimulating, encouraging environment at home produces adaptable, eager learners, even among children whose health
or intelligence has been compromised in some way. A long-term
study of orphans who were mentally retarded, for example, found
that the IQs of children adopted into families of normal intelligence
rose measurably, while the intelligence of those who remained insti-
tutionalized actually declined over the years. While the institutional-
ized group remained undereducated and underemployed, most of the
adopted children completed high school (and a third went on to col-

other brother is described as extremely disorganized; he gets lost in supermarkets and shopping malls and panics at the idea of traveling through a strange city.

Jimmy's mother had reason to believe that her 10-year-old son may not have been lucky enough to escape this genetic history. Take a look at his spelling and judge for yourself the outcome of his assessment.

Transcription: **In a race for survival I raised my sharp spear at the great beast. It fought back with its great trunk and just missed him by an inch and even though a spear had hit it doesn't give up yet it can tire you to fight.**

Adapted from Smith, C. R., *op. cit.*

lege). Animal studies have shown that an enriched environment not only has an impact on learning, it actually stimulates brain growth and development. Neuropsychologists are beginning to accumulate physiological evidence that human brains also respond to "mental exercise."

In addition, children who have received affectionate encouragement throughout their lives tend to have positive attitudes, both about learning and about themselves. Their "I can do it" spirit helps them rise to challenges and overcome obstacles. These children look for and find ways around disabilities, even when their handicaps are quite severe. "It's easy to recognize the kids who have really involved and supportive families," says a special education teacher. "Even

What Do Children Need to Learn and Grow?

The eminent psychologist Erik Erikson believed that children's attitudes about themselves and the world around them depend largely on how they are treated by adults as they grow up. Below is a summary of what Erikson believed children need most from their families at each stage of their development.

Basic Trust (birth to 1 year): Infants gain a sense of basic trust when interactions with adults are pleasurable and gratifying. Babies need parents who are warm, responsive, predictable, and sensitive to their needs. If infants regularly have to wait a long time for comfort or are handled harshly and insensitively, mistrust of others is promoted.

Autonomy (1 to 3 years): Confidence in ability to make choices and decisions develops as children exercise the exploratory skills of walking, running, climbing, and handling objects. Toddlers and young preschoolers need parents who allow them to choose from a variety of safe activities. If children are overly restricted, always forced to do things their parents' way, or shamed for making mistakes as they explore, self-doubt will grow instead of self-confidence.

Initiative (3 to 6 years): Preschoolers learn about themselves and their cultures through make-believe play; as they enact different roles, they start to think about what kind of people they want to become. Parents who support children's emerging sense of purpose and direction at this stage help them develop initiative, ambition, and social responsibility. If parents are overly controlling or demanding, children may become guilty and repressed.

Industry (6 years to puberty): During their school years, children develop their capacities for productive work, learn to work cooperatively with others, and discover a sense of pride in doing things well. School-aged children need parents who encourage their sense of competence and mastery by giving them responsibility and opportunities to use their skills and knowledge. Young people who lack this encouragement may develop a sense of inferiority and believe that they will never be good at anything.

Identity (adolescence): Teens integrate what they have gained from the previous stages into a lasting sense of identity; they develop an understanding of their place in society and form expectations for the future. Adolescents need respect for their emerging independence. Children who have not had their needs met at this and earlier stages are likely to be confused about who they are and where they want to go.

though they have learning disabilities, they see themselves as basically competent and successful."

In contrast, children who have been deprived of a nourishing environment in their early years face many discouraging hurdles even when they do not have disabilities. These youngsters are generally slow to acquire basic cognitive skills. They have poor social skills and tend to be poor communicators. They do not use their intellectual abilities to advantage and may show little curiosity or interest in learning. They often lack self-confidence. Deficiencies like these place children at educational risk throughout their school years. Studies have repeatedly shown that students who are emotionally and academically "ready" when they begin kindergarten remain near the top of their classes right through graduation, while youngsters who enter school with significant social and cognitive delays rarely catch up, even with special help.

Not surprisingly, socially and emotionally disadvantaged children also find it hard to marshal the resources needed to overcome neurological handicaps. Students with learning disabilities normally use their areas of strength to help compensate for areas of weakness, but students who have not had adequate levels of stimulation and support at home have far fewer areas of strength to draw upon. In addition, these students are less persistent than other children when they encounter problems. Teachers observe that they often anticipate failure, seeming to "quit before they start."

There are many aspects of a home environment that can undermine a child's capacity for learning. Children who do not get enough nourishing food or enough sleep will obviously suffer in their ability to concentrate and absorb information. So will children who are frequently ill due to poor hygiene or substandard medical care. Children raised by parents or child-care providers who speak English poorly and those who watch excessive amounts of television are likely to be delayed in their English language development; this affects their ability to express themselves and understand their teachers, and it also places them at risk for problems with reading and writing. Students whose families cannot provide them with school supplies, a predictable time to do homework, and a relatively quiet place to study have to be exceptionally motivated in order to achieve; so do children who live with little encouragement and low expectations. Any of these factors can significantly reduce a child's chances of overcoming a learning disability.

Emotional stress also compromises children's ability to learn. Not only can anxiety about money or relocation, family discord or illness be distracting in themselves, but over time they can erode a child's willingness to trust, take chances, and be open to new situations, which are important to success in school. It is a tragic fact that growing numbers of children are not really available for learning because their lives are dominated by fear: dangers in their homes or neighborhoods make it necessary for them to devote most of their mental energy to the urgent issue of personal protection. If the school itself is not safe, the academic prospects of an entire student body can be undermined.

While these problems can afflict any child, children raised in poverty encounter more than their share of environmental hazards. Such children—who are also more vulnerable to some kinds of brain injury and developmental problems due to inadequate nutrition and health care—are overrepresented in our special-education population. Since even preschool intervention is too late to remedy all the effects of long-term physical or intellectual deprivation, the best hope for many children may lie in making easy-to-obtain, quality education available to *parents* in such key areas as nutrition, infant and toddler stimulation, and family health care. Social programs designed to reduce the shocking number of children living in poverty (now nearly one in four in the United States) are also critical to improving children's learning potential. The cost of such programs needs to be evaluated in light of the gloomy prospects faced by students who begin school with cognitive deficits: they are less likely to graduate, less likely to find satisfactory employment, and more likely to end up in jail or in need of public assistance than more advantaged youngsters. When these long-term social consequences are taken into account, the failure to prevent learning problems becomes very expensive indeed.

The Environment at School

In order to make intellectual progress, children must not only be ready and able to learn, they must also have appropriate learning *opportunities*. If the educational system fails to provide these, students may never develop their full range of abilities, effectively becoming "disabled" even though there is nothing physically wrong with them. Unfortunately, many students must struggle to do their best under less than optimum conditions in our nation's schools.

Obviously, overcrowded classrooms, overworked or poorly trained teachers, and inadequate supplies of good teaching materials all compromise students' ability to learn. But so do many widely accepted practices that fail to provide for normal variations in learning style. A student whose orientation is primarily visual and exploratory, for example, needs to see and touch things in order to understand them. This student will not do well with teachers who lecture all the time, no matter how bright and interested in their subjects he or she may be. Similarly, a child whose approach to learning is basically reflective—that is, who needs time to consider all aspects of a problem thoroughly before attempting a solution—will do miserably in a classroom where students are hustled from assignment to assignment according to the dictates of a rigid curriculum. What about the Asian immigrant who does not participate in discussions because she lacks confidence in her English vocabulary, or because her notions of respect forbid her to be "forward" about volunteering information? When students such as these do poorly in school, is it correct to say the problem is exclusively theirs?

The truth is that many low achievers are victims of their schools' inability to adjust to individual and cultural differences. Despite the fact that the population in America's schools is becoming increasingly diverse, it is still standard practice in many classrooms to "teach to the middle," using methods and materials designed to reach the average white middle-income student of a generation ago. When children who do not fit the mold fail to progress, school officials sometimes find it easier to blame the students than to examine their own shortcomings. Incredibly, there are schools where the failure rate approaches 50 percent, and teachers and administrators are still talking about problem *children!*

For children with learning disabilities, rigidity in the classroom is fatal. In order to make progress, these students must be encouraged to work in their own way. If placed with a teacher who is inflexible about assignments and testing, or who uses materials and methods inappropriate for their needs, these students will fail. If they are regularly shamed or penalized for their failures ("Since you haven't finished your work, you're going to have to stay in from recess again, Jimmy; you really must try harder"), students are unlikely to remain motivated for long. Sadly, loss of interest in education and lack of self-confidence can continue to fetter these children even when they move on to more favorable settings. In this way, the wrong school environment can encourage even the most minor disabilities to blossom into major handicaps.

Parents of students with learning disabilities frequently observe that their children appear to be more "disabled" in some classes than in others. While this can be a reflection of the student's particular type of learning problem, it is also true that disabilities tend to fade

MANCELE

My disability in reading, writing, and spelling affected me in two ways. first I had no confidents in myself and the second is the fear I had inside of me.

My fear was and still is so grete [great] that if someone asked me to read, spell, or write down directions, I would break out in a sweat. The fear was divercateing [devastating] to me. About school I don't remember my early years because I don't thing I was taught anything to remember anything about school. However, from the sixth or seven grade, I new I had a problem. I was tested and put into what was called an opportunity class, they call it.

They sed that it would be a special class to help me. Most of the "opportunity" class was made up of young black men. We had the "opportunity" of running movies all day for other classes in our school. This was our opportunity for learning. The classes were taught by one teacher. He was subpose to teach us in all subjects, math sceance [science] and Enlish, Histery, etc. The movies were fun to show, however the only thing I learned was showing movies. So my seventh and eighth grade Education was a lost, too. Most of our tests in class were motobowt [multiple] chosuis [choice]. I got good marks some B, too. I became putty [pretty] good in taking tests. Even on my spelling lists I got 75% or 80% carick [correct]. I could menerize [memorize] anything for a short time, but in two weeks after I forget it all. Because I menorize it. It did not matter what order it was in or giving it to me. I learn the sound of each word, then the letters. But didn't know the words themself. I graduated from High school knowing I could not read or spell afbulb [above] third grade. When I had to write a book reported, the pain in my head would come and I would pannick. I would pick out key words in some books I knew, and picked out key sentence, then put them together for my book report. So now they say I have a learning disability. I say I wasn't taught.

Source: Smith, C. R. *ibid.*

or even disappear in classrooms where creative, flexible teachers make an effort to match tasks to their students' readiness levels and learning styles. Since typical children also flourish in these classrooms, it seems fair to say that at least part of the solution to the growing demand for special education services is to improve curriculum design and teacher training across the board. In the meantime, it is important for parents to realize that intervention for children with learning disabilities often calls less for "fixing" the child than improving the environment in which the child is being educated. The right class, the right curriculum, and the right teacher are critical for these children, and choosing them often makes the difference between frustrated failure and solid success. As Mancele's sad story indicates, schools cannot always be counted upon to program for students appropriately. Parents who thoroughly understand their own child's learning strengths and weaknesses are in the best position to evaluate the educational options available from year to year and decide which are the *real* "opportunity" classes.

Too often, the question "Why does my child have a learning disability?" translates into "Whom should I blame?" As one mother remembers, "My greatest fear was that *I* was somehow responsible. I questioned everything from the anchovy pizza I ate in the second month of pregnancy to my decision to go back to work when my son started school. Meanwhile, my husband was blaming everyone from the obstetrician who delivered our son to the psychologist who did the testing." Reactions like this are normal, but they are not particularly productive. In the end, understanding how a child came to have a learning disability is far less important than knowing how it affects the child's worldview and how to find the right kinds of help. Anger, anxiety, or guilt over "what went wrong" do nothing to help a child; instead, they usually serve only to exhaust parents' emotional energy and elevate their level of stress. Although parents always want to know why their child has a learning disability, they should not let worrying about it distract them from finding the support these students urgently need.

3

BASIC TYPES OF
LEARNING DISABILITY

Everyone has learning strengths and learning weaknesses. As adults, most of us confess our weaknesses willingly: we were idiots in math, for example, or rotten at foreign languages. We could not draw a straight line in art. We had trouble remembering the dates in history, never got the hang of book reports, had a "tin ear" for music, or tripped over our own feet in gym. We can afford to be cheerful about our shortcomings, because we managed to succeed in spite of them. Our weaknesses were either in areas which did not interfere seriously with our progress through school, or not severe enough to prevent us from achieving our most important goals. Along the way we developed some talents we feel pretty good about, and we use those strengths to define ourselves.

Children with learning disabilities, however, suffer an unlucky combination: not only are their weaknesses more pronounced than usual, but they also lie in those areas most likely to interfere with the acquisition of basic skills in reading, writing, or mathematics. As a result, their progress in school is repeatedly blocked. These children are often bright, creative, and even gifted in other spheres, but since they are achieving poorly in the areas most valued by our society, their talents may be judged unimportant or irrelevant. Some of these students come to feel defined by their failures. They do not understand *why* they can't do what other kids seem to find easy; they just see themselves as stupid or generally defective.

In fact, children with learning disabilities are generally found to be struggling in one or more of four basic areas that prevent smooth processing of information: *attention, visual perception, language processing,* or *muscle coordination.* Even minor weaknesses in these areas can create formidable obstacles to learning and communication in traditional classrooms.

In order to overcome learning disabilities, it is vitally important for both parents and students to understand exactly in which of these areas deficits lie. This information is essential for evaluating a child's educational program and determining what kind of changes need to be made. It is needed to establish reasonable goals both at school and at home. Most important, this knowledge will ultimately make it possible for the child to become a confident, independent learner. In general, the more youngsters with learning disabilities know about their own patterns of strengths and weaknesses, the more likely they are to accept themselves, become advocates for themselves, and plan strategies that minimize their disabilities and make the most of their skills and talents.

Precise identification of a child's learning problems involves a comprehensive evaluation, which we will discuss in Part II. Our goal here is to introduce the four basic types of disability, and describe how each can affect a child's school performance and development. Before we do that, however, any adult concerned with children who have learning disabilities must understand the following three points.

1. *Children with learning disabilities frequently have problems in more than one area.* For example, a child's primary disability (the one causing the most trouble in school) may involve problems with language comprehension, but he may also have trouble concentrating and be somewhat delayed in his fine motor development. In cases of this kind it is necessary to understand not only each of the disabilities but also how they can complicate one another. To maximize chances for improvement, all the disabilities have to be addressed.

2. *Learning disabilities do not vanish when a child leaves school for the day.* These conditions affect the way a child perceives the world, so they influence conduct at home and social and family relationships as well as academic performance. A lot of behavior that seems careless or even willfully obstructive (such as difficulty be-

ing on time, losing possessions, or chronic failure to complete chores) may at least in part be related to a child's learning problems. Parents who understand the nature of their children's disabilities are in the best position to develop realistic expectations—and they will also spare themselves a lot of fruitless nagging and aggravation.

3. *Learning disabilities can produce emotional consequences.* The reason is no mystery. How would you feel if you faced a daily requirement to do something you could not do (read a book in Sanskrit, for example)? Day in and day out, you earnestly plug away at it without success. Would you become frustrated? Anxious? Angry? Now suppose you are the only one in a group of twenty-five who cannot accomplish this task. All your peers are moving on to intermediate Sanskrit, and you can't get off of page one. Your teachers and loved ones are becoming impatient with you. Of *course* you can do it, they insist—all you have to do is try!

Nearly every child with a learning disability has experienced this scenario, and some of them live it for years. Without the right kind of encouragement and support, these youngsters rapidly stop believing in themselves and their ability to succeed. Convinced they will fail no matter what they do, they simply stop trying. Eventually, resistance to learning may become the biggest part of a child's problems in school—far more of a handicap than the original learning disability, and far harder to overcome.

Let us begin our exploration of the different types of learning disabilities, then, with a reminder that however many problems a student may encounter in school, a parent's primary concern must always be the child's emotional well-being. If you focus on protecting your child's self-esteem, you can avoid the most "disabling" aspect of learning disabilities: the desire to give up. As one special educator puts it: "It takes a lot of courage for these children to face all the problems they have in school. The kids whose parents understand and believe in them are the ones who have it. Even when it's all uphill, those kids keep setting goals and finding ways to get where they want to go."

ATTENTION DEFICIT HYPERACTIVITY DISORDER

Children suffering from ADHD make up an estimated 3 to 5 percent of the school population, but they generate a disproportionate amount of concern. Challenging to parent and to teach, they are among the children most likely to be referred for academic assistance, disciplinary action, and mental health services. At one time it was believed that far more boys than girls were affected by ADHD, but many experts now believe that both genders are equally at risk. Because boys with the disorder are more likely to exhibit aggressive or disruptive behavior, however, they get noticed and referred for evaluation and special help more often than girls do. One authority calls girls with ADHD "the silent minority": they share the risk for developing academic and social problems, but because they do not call attention to themselves they are at additional risk for not getting the support they need. When boys have attention deficits without hyperactivity, they too are less likely to be referred for evaluation and services.

Although many symptoms of ADHD are observable from early childhood, they are most obvious in situations that call for sustained mental activity (see checklist). For this reason, many cases of ADHD go unnoticed until the child starts school—at which point problems seem to multiply on a daily basis. Teachers complain that the child interrupts, can't sit still, doesn't pay attention, doesn't finish work, or won't listen. Unable to plan or stick to a course of action, the youngster soon begins to flounder academically. Perhaps even more painful, the child is left behind socially as well. Children with ADHD have difficulty learning the rules of games and are impatient about taking turns; they often impulsively blurt out whatever is on their minds without considering the effect of their words. Peers tend to regard them as rude, pushy, and inconsiderate. When birthday party invitations go out and valentines are exchanged, the child with ADHD is left with little doubt about how his or her classmates feel. Social rejection plus academic underachievement is a good recipe for loss of self-esteem. Many of these children begin to see themselves as losers at an early age.

Unfortunately, children with ADHD also have a gift for alienating adults. Many were irritable and hard to handle even as infants; they cried often and did not calm down when cuddled or held. Their "terrible twos" were more terrible than most. They were difficult to toilet train. Because youngsters with ADHD have difficulty considering alternatives, they seem stubborn and headstrong and do not respond to ordinary means of discipline. They make scenes and embarrass Mom and Dad in public. In short, these youngsters not only exhaust parents but make parents feel rejected and inadequate. Studies show that mothers of children with ADHD experience unusual amounts of stress and feel less attached to these boys and girls than to their other

Attention Deficit Hyperactivity Disorder Checklist

Attention deficits may occur with or without hyperactivity. There are also children who are primarily hyperactive and impulsive and have fewer attention problems. According to the manual most frequently used by professionals to identify ADHD, six or more symptoms from either of the following lists suggests presence of the disorder:

Inattention:
- often fails to give close attention to details; makes careless mistakes in schoolwork or other activities
- frequently has difficulty sustaining attention in tasks or play
- often does not seem to listen when spoken to
- often does not follow through on instructions and fails to finish schoolwork and chores
- has great difficulty getting organized
- usually dislikes and avoids tasks that require sustained mental effort (such as schoolwork or homework)
- frequently loses things (such as toys, assignments, books, and pencils)
- easily distracted by irrelevant sights and sounds
- often forgetful in daily activities

Hyperactivity and impulsivity:
- often fidgets with hands and feet and squirms in seat
- often leaves seat in classroom or other situations where remaining seated is expected (such as at the dinner table)
- runs about or climbs excessively in situations in which it is inappropriate
- has great difficulty playing quietly
- is often "on the go" or acts as if "driven by a motor"
- talks excessively
- frequently blurts out answers before questions have been completed
- often has difficulty waiting turns
- often interrupts or intrudes on others (butts into conversations or games)

Adapted from *Diagnostic and Statistical Manual of Mental Disorders*, Fourth Edition (1994). Washington DC. American Psychiatric Association.

children. If parents blame themselves or each other for the child's problems ("You should stop acting like such a pushover and discipline him more!" "Well, maybe he'd settle down if you spent more time with him!"), stress factors multiply. Since siblings also experience negative feelings about children with ADHD, youngsters with this disorder sometimes find themselves coming home to atmospheres not much more welcoming than the ones they left in school.

Not surprisingly, if their problems are not recognized and appropriately addressed, these children often grow into angry teenagers. Studies find disproportionately high numbers of young men with ADHD among juvenile offenders, and research indicates that teens with ADHD are also more likely to indulge in thrillseeking behavior and to abuse drugs and alcohol than their typical peers. Students with ADHD are also at risk for mental health complications such as anxiety and depression. Conduct problems, low self-esteem, and poor academic performance all reduce the chances that these students will finish school, pursue higher education, and find satisfactory employment.

As we discussed in the last chapter, problems with attention, impulse control, and hyperactivity can arise from abnormally low levels of activity in the frontal regions of the brain. Neurological indicators show that these youngsters must put enormous effort into processing information: their brain waves representing attention are lower than normal, they are slower to recognize and react to stimuli than typical children, and their ability to concentrate declines unusually quickly during mental tasks. Deficits of this kind do not impair intellectual ability (ADHD can be found among gifted children as well as among children of average and below average intelligence), but they make it difficult for youngsters to sustain attention long enough to complete academic tasks. As a result, children with ADHD often fall behind in school, and if intervention is delayed, they may fail to build the solid academic foundation they need to succeed at higher grade levels.

Parents of "itchy" underachievers must be very cautious about jumping to the conclusion, however, that ADHD is to blame. There are many other causes of chronic inattentiveness in the classroom. For example, children who suffer from frequent illnesses or allergies sometimes have trouble focusing their attention, either because of their health conditions or because of side effects from their medications. Inattention can also be a sign of undetected problems with hearing or vision: if children cannot see or hear well, they may not even be fully aware there is something they are supposed to pay attention *to*. Students who are not eating enough are often restless and inattentive; this applies to teens on crash diets as well as children who have empty cupboards at home. Young people living with high levels of stress—such as due to a parent's substance abuse or a sibling's serious illness—also find it hard to concentrate: their situations give them far more urgent things to think about than math facts or spelling words.

Inappropriate educational placement can also produce inattentive behavior. An intellectually brilliant student "stuck" with a curriculum geared to average peers may stop paying attention and start clowning around out of sheer boredom. Similarly, students who are immature or otherwise behind in their intellectual development may become bored and inattentive because they don't fully understand what is going on. Sometimes students have trouble maintaining attention because their learning styles are poorly matched with the way information is being presented to them. A child who is easily distracted, for example, will find it almost impossible to concentrate in a room where the teacher has decorated every square inch of wall space with maps, charts, posters, and other "helpful" visual aids. In contrast, students whose preferred learning style is interactive are likely to find their attention wandering during lectures or long periods of reading. Children who learn best through listening can also find it hard to maintain their focus while reading unless they read aloud—which, of course, is not permitted in most classrooms. These are only a few of many cognitive "incompatibilities" that can produce problems with concentration.

All the youngsters mentioned in the two preceding paragraphs need help in order to do their best academically, but they probably do not have attention deficit hyperactivity disorder. Parents should never accept a diagnosis of ADHD or consider the use of medication until they are sure that their children are being given appropriate work in school, and that the other causes of attention problems have been explored and ruled out. To be sure of a diagnosis of ADHD, a thorough assessment is necessary. The American Psychiatric Association recommends that all of the following conditions be met before a diagnosis of ADHD can be confirmed:

- Many symptoms of the disorder are present

- The symptoms are severe enough to impair academic and/or social functioning

- The symptoms are inconsistent with the child's developmental level

- The symptoms have persisted six months or more

- The symptoms were present before seven years of age

- The symptoms are observed both at school and at home

• There is no evidence of a health condition or mental illness that could cause similar problems

The majority of children with ADHD do not need special education services. Unless their problems are very severe, these students can function successfully in regular classrooms with the help of aware teachers, good classroom management techniques, and sometimes medication. About a third of them, however, have additional learning disabilities. Since ADHD makes remediating the disabilities harder, these children usually do need special education intervention.

Research indicates that what youngsters with ADHD usually need most is extra time and guidance to *master* information: once they have learned something, students with ADHD remember and use it as well as anyone else. Special services for children with ADHD therefore usually involve reinforcing lessons taught in the classroom and practicing new skills. These students can also be taught to monitor their own attention, and to bring themselves back "on task" when their minds start to wander. It is very important to teach these youngsters good study habits and memory strategies such as rhymes, mnemonic tricks, and visualization. Unlike other students, children with learning problems almost never think of tactics like these on their own.

Parent support and education is another key ingredient in helping the child with ADHD succeed. Many mothers state that both their sanity and their own self-esteem have been saved by support groups and newsletters designed for parents of children with ADHD. Family counseling is also often helpful: therapy may be of critical importance if a child appears to be depressed or angry, or if a lot of negativity has built up inside a family. Parenting classes and publications can help parents learn how to use positive reinforcement to reward desirable behavior, how to strategically ignore unwelcome behavior, and how to develop appropriate and effective methods of discipline. Rest and recreation for Mom and Dad are also important! Caring for children with ADHD is a demanding and often exhausting job; most parents find they can handle it better if they take good care of themselves and give themselves a break now and then.

Children with ADHD often show significant improvement by the time they reach their teens. They tend to remain energetic people, but they are no longer "out of control." If taught appropriate learning strategies and social skills, they can do well in school and on the job. Some individuals who have used medication are able to discontinue it. About 50 percent of those who benefit from medication as children, however, continue to need it in order to do their best as adults. "Hey, I figure I'm no worse off than the guy who needs glasses," says a college senior who takes Ritalin every day. "Nobody likes taking medication, but without it I wouldn't have gotten through fourth grade, let alone through high school and four years of college."

Early identification and intervention are critical for children with ADHD. The earlier the problem is recognized, the less likely it is that antisocial behavior or emotional problems will develop. It is also less likely that parents will blame themselves for the child's difficult behavior. As one mother remembers:

> For seven years it seemed like everybody was looking to me to control this kid. My husband, my mom, my friends all seemed to think I should be able to manage him, because I was the mother. People made "helpful" suggestions hinting at where they thought I was going wrong: "Do you feed him a lot of processed food? Does he get enough sleep? Maybe if you weren't working and could spend more time with him." I felt like wearing a sign: "I'm a good mother! I breast-fed him! I read to him every day!" But the bottom line was I did feel responsible. Scott was repeating first grade when we learned he had ADHD. The first thing I thought when they told me was, "Thank God! It's not all my fault!" ADHD isn't the easiest thing to live with, but I find I can deal with it a lot more effectively since I've educated myself about it and let myself off the hook.

VISUAL PERCEPTION DISABILITIES

Students with visual perception disabilities have trouble making sense out of what they see. The problem is not with their eyesight, but with the way their brains process visual information. These children have difficulty recognizing, organizing, interpreting, and/or remembering visual images. As a result, they have trouble understanding the whole spectrum of written and pictorial symbols—not only letters and words, but also numbers and math symbols, diagrams, maps, charts, and graphs.

Because they are often very subtle, visual perception disabilities are rarely suspected until a child starts having problems in school. Even then, the source of the trouble can seem baffling. As one mother remembers:

> All through nursery school, Seth's teachers told me he was extraordinarily bright. That was obvious at home, too. Seth learned to talk

early, and by five he had a near adult vocabulary. He was relentlessly curious and loved being read to. He became a walking encyclopedia on all his enthusiasms: birds, dinosaurs, Greek mythology. He couldn't wait to start school. He was so excited about learning to read for himself!

Seth loved kindergarten, but his attitude toward school changed completely in first grade. He started complaining about the work, the teacher, and the other children. By the end of October he was saying he hated school and didn't want to go anymore. Alarmed, I made an appointment with his teacher to see what was going on. She said Seth got along well with the other students, but he was falling behind in every subject. He couldn't keep up with even the *slowest* group in reading. I was stunned! Were we talking about the same kid? All through this conference I kept having the feeling some mistake had been made, and the teacher thought I was some other child's mother. When she suggested that I work with Seth at home to help him catch up, I agreed eagerly. I figured this problem had to be the teacher's fault. I could straighten Seth out; all he needed was a little extra encouragement and attention.

The teacher gave me flash cards for thirty sight words she wanted Seth to learn so he could get started in the first-grade reading primer. I chose three to start with—I think they were *boy*, *the*, and *cat*. We drilled those words for a week. Relaxed atmosphere, lots of encouragement, lots of praise. At the end of the week, Seth couldn't recognize a single word. He didn't recognize any at the end of the second week either, and the third week he refused to play this game anymore. He also started saying he didn't want me to read to him any more. It seemed like he didn't want to have anything to do with books or print at all.

By Thanksgiving Seth had made almost no headway in either reading or arithmetic, and he started complaining of stomach aches: almost every morning he cried and begged to be allowed to stay home from school. We made several visits to our pediatrician, but tests found nothing wrong. Seth's deteriorating emotional state worried me even more than his lack of academic progress—three months of first grade had turned my happy, outgoing six-year-old into a basket case! Finally, because I didn't know what else to do, I asked the school to test Seth for anything they could think of that might be contributing to all these problems.

By the end of the semester we had an explanation: Seth had a gifted IQ and a learning disability. His main problem was visual memory; he understood things just fine when he was looking at them, but he couldn't seem to hold onto any kind of mental picture. Poor Seth!

Visual Perception Disability Checklist

It is normal for children to display a few of the symptoms on this list. A learning disability may be responsible if many of these behaviors are present, and if they persist beyond the age where such errors are typical.

Writing:
- dislikes and avoids writing
- delays in learning to write
- papers are messy and incomplete; many cross-outs and erasures
- difficulty remembering shapes of letters and numbers
- frequent letter and number reversals
- uneven spacing between letters and words
- omits letters from words and words from sentences
- inaccurate copying
- poor spelling (spells phonetically)
- cannot spot errors in own work
- difficulty preparing outlines and organizing written work

Reading:
- confuses similar-looking letters (*b* and *d, p* and *q*)
- difficulty recognizing and remembering "sight" words (but can sound words out phonetically)
- frequently loses place when reading
- confuses similar-looking words (*bread* and *beard*)
- reverses words (reads *was* for *saw*)
- has trouble finding letters in words or words in sentences

Practically the whole first-grade curriculum involved memorizing visual images—letters, words, and numbers. No wonder he wasn't going anywhere!

While it is unusual for a learning disability to be identified this early, visual perception handicaps do start causing trouble in the initial grades of elementary school, where they interfere with progress in almost every subject. To understand why, let's look at the types of information processing this category includes. Visual perception skills include the ability to recognize images we have seen before and attach meaning to them (the way a preschooler will recognize a McDonald's sign and announce he is hungry), to discriminate among similar images (such as the letters *b* and *d*, or the words *skate* and

- poor memory for printed words (also number sequences, diagrams, illustrations, and so on)
- poor comprehension of main ideas and themes
- difficulty with higher-level math concepts

Math:
- poor alignment of problems results in computation errors
- difficulty memorizing math facts, multiplication tables, formulas, and equations
- trouble interpreting graphs, charts, and diagrams

Related problems:
- confuses left and right
- difficulty estimating time, being on time
- poor sense of direction; slow to learn his or her way around a new place
- difficulty judging speed and distance (interferes with many games; can be a problem when driving a car)
- has trouble "getting to the point"; becomes bogged down in details
- does not pick up on other people's moods and feelings (results in often saying the wrong things at the wrong time)
- poor planning and organizational skills
- often loses things; cannot spot objects "in plain sight"
- distaste for puzzles, mazes, or other activities with a strong visual element
- difficulty perceiving strategies for being successful in games (may not understand the goal)

stake), to separate significant figures from background details (identify the vowels in a word, for instance), and to recognize the same symbol in different forms (understanding that an *A* is an *A*, even when it appears in different sizes, colors, or typefaces). Recognizing sequences is another important visual perception skill: people with visual sequencing problems may see no difference between the words *was* and *saw* and have trouble copying even a short series of letters or numbers correctly. Not surprisingly, students with this kind of handicap are usually slow to learn their letters and numbers. Their workbooks and papers are full of reversals, omissions, and other errors that are often blamed on carelessness (see illustration).

In addition, students with visual perception weaknesses often experience difficulty with visual memory and visualization. They are often painfully slow beginning readers because they do not recognize words easily on sight and must "sound out" as they go along. They have difficulty remembering spelling rules and irregular words and usually spell phonetically (see illustration). Routine tasks like copying from the blackboard can be a nightmare: by the time youngsters look from the board to their papers, they lose significant parts of the image, or even lose the image completely. Students with visual memory weaknesses also find it nearly impossible to proofread or check their own work, because they simply cannot remember what the correct form is supposed to look like when they are looking at mistakes. Youngsters who lack the ability to visualize find it hard to picture things in their minds or to imagine solutions to problems. They become lost in the middle of projects because they cannot visualize what the end result is supposed to look like. These students tend to be concrete thinkers, and they often have trouble reasoning beyond the information that is right in front of them. A child may insist that a dime is worth less than two nickels, for example, because there is only one dime and, furthermore, it is smaller!

Some students with visual perception disabilities also have problems with spatial relationships. It is hard for them to deal with concepts of size, shape, and distance or to understand how parts fit together to form a whole. In general, students with this type of deficit have trouble making sense of maps, charts and diagrams; they are likely to have particular problems with higher levels of math, such as geometry. These children often have a hard time lining up columns of figures neatly and spacing words and letters evenly when they write. Spatial weaknesses also show up in social behavior. Teachers observe that students with this type of disability are always "in your face," talking from only a few inches away. These children may also be left out of games on the playground because their inability to estimate speed and distance accurately makes them inept at pretty much anything involving a ball.

Visual perception disabilities are usually caused by underfunctioning areas in the right side of the cerebral cortex, and students with this kind of handicap may display other "right-brain" deficits. They may have trouble, for example, distinguishing important issues from trivial details. Listening to one of these kids describe a movie often involves sitting through a rambling monologue in which every scene is recounted, but the point of the plot is never made clear. Ask them what happened at school today, and they are likely to tell you about morning announcements, the spelling quiz, and what they ate for lunch before mentioning the fire that destroyed half the west wing.

Cursive Copying and Mathematical Calculation of an Eight-Year-Old Boy with Average Intelligence Who Has Visual Perception Disabilities

Source: Smith, C. R. op cit.

Such students also get bogged down in details in the classroom. They frequently need extra help learning to isolate the main themes of their lessons and prepare outlines that will help them get to the point in written and oral presentations.

Youngsters with deficits in the right cerebral cortex are notably poor at estimating the passage of time accurately; parents complain that these kids are never ready to go anywhere, even when they have been warned that "we're leaving in five minutes." They may in addition have a poor sense of direction and problems distinguishing right from left—difficulties that often persist into adulthood. These children

Phonetic Spelling from a Bright Thirteen-Year-Old Boy with Visual Perception Disabilities

Known Words	Unknown Words
apstract	destuted
misconduct	rumedeul (remedial)
optumistic	insinuate
sublime	cunedic (kinetic)
verify	orthadocs
gushur (geyser)	caor e caos
garintey (guarantee)	oncore
norishing	ismis (isthmus)
pursowt (pursuit)	busum
cutasturfey (catastrophe)	shampane

Source: Smith, C. R. *ibid.*

may seem oblivious to their appearance and their physical surroundings (told to "clean up that mess," they may reply, "What mess?"). Some also have trouble reading facial expressions and body language; as a result, they seem out of touch with what others are thinking and feeling. "In general, these kids often strike the observer as rather self-absorbed and out of it," says a special education teacher. "They are usually the last to catch on to a fad or a fashion trend at school: by the time they catch on that stripes are in, everybody else has moved on to polka dots. This doesn't hurt their grades, but can really cost them socially. What you have to do is *teach* these kids social awareness—how to pay attention to what the other kids wear, what they like to do. Don't assume they'll pick up on that stuff by themselves. They don't."

The kind of academic support needed by students with visual perception disabilities varies, depending on the severity of their handicaps. Most of these students learn to read best with their ears—they need reading instruction solidly based on phonics, and if this is not available in the classroom, special education programming must provide it. Children with visual memory deficits need to be provided with ready access to materials they cannot memorize, such as multiplication tables, math formulas, and maps. Other than that, what many of these students seem to need most is extra time. Although these children's brains process visual information unusually slowly, many can handle visual tasks competently if allowed to work at their own pace. Some children, however, cannot perform tasks involving visual perception, no matter how hard they try; it is simply too hard for them to assemble visual elements into a meaningful whole. Intervention is important in either case: special education programming can provide both for extra time and for alternative methods of teaching and evaluation when they are necessary.

These students also benefit hugely from supportive technology. "I can't believe the difference a computer has made in my life," says a ninth grader. "It points all my letters in the right direction, straightens up my margins—even corrects my spelling. I still make mistakes, but when I correct them I don't have to copy over the whole assignment. I used to hate writing; it was so hard to get everything looking right on the paper that I just wanted to make everything short and get it over with. Now I'm getting my highest grades in English and writing stories and poems on my own time."

Students with visual perception disabilities usually need the most support in elementary school, when the demand to master systems of visual symbols is greatest. They often need less help as they get older and start to use different areas of strength to compensate for their visual processing weaknesses. Quite often they blossom in high school, where their performance is sometimes spectacular. Studies find that so-called left-brain skills involving language, logic, and analysis are the ones most closely associated with achievement in secondary school. Students with visual processing disabilities who have strengths in these areas generally become solid academic performers in most subjects (though upper-level math may remain a problem).

LANGUAGE PROCESSING DISABILITIES

By far the largest number of students identified as having learning disabilities are those with language processing problems. These youngsters can have trouble with any aspect of language: hearing words correctly, understanding their meaning, remembering verbal material, and communicating clearly. These children's difficulties begin with the spoken word, and they typically interfere with reading and/or writing when the child enters school. The severity of these handicaps ranges from mild to so profound that affected individuals find coping with English almost as hard as the rest of us might find learning a language like Russian or Japanese.

Parents are often aware that their children have some problems with language before they start school (see checklist). Youngsters with language processing disabilities may be slow in learning to speak, and may use shorter sentences, smaller vocabularies, and poorer grammar than their brothers and sisters did at similar ages. There may be signs that they do not always understand what is being said to them. Their responses to questions may be inappropriate, or they may not be able to follow directions reliably. Their memory for verbal instructions may also be poor, and this can be a source of constant irritation ("Didn't I already ask you twice to put those paints away? Why do I have to nag you about everything?"). Comprehension problems are likely to get worse when the language being used is complex: a child who can handle "Bring me the cake mix" with no difficulty may be completely at sea when asked, "Please unpack the grocery bag, and bring me the cake mix after you put the milk in the refrigerator." Problems may also be especially obvious when directions are called out to a child who is in another room. Many children who have trouble understanding words use visual cues to help compensate for their disabilities; they look for meaning in body language and facial expression, and sometimes they become accomplished lip-readers.

Many youngsters with language processing disabilities also talk in "mixed up" ways. Sometimes their brains have trouble sorting out sequences in the sounds they hear, so they mispronounce words—saying "pisketti" for *spaghetti*, or "efelent" for *elephant* long beyond the age where such mistakes are normal. These children also are weak in grammatical awareness and have problems with word sequencing: for example, they may not understand that there is a difference between the phrases *blocking a punch* and *punching a block*. It is common for these youngsters to confuse words that sound alike: they may say that an answer is "oblivious" when *obvious* is what they mean, or state that their sick cat had to be rushed to the "vegetarian." Errors like these—which are likely to get worse under the pressure of speaking before groups or authority figures—leave these students painfully open to ridicule, and some sensitive young people will go to almost any lengths to avoid talking in front of others.

There are also children who understand and use words correctly, but experience great difficulty producing the words they want from their memories. Ask them to single out the picture of the horse and these youngsters will do it without hesitation, but show them the picture and ask them to name the animal and their minds go blank. Word-finding problems frustrate some students into silence, but others launch barrages of language in an effort to find the word they are looking for. These are the kids who jabber, "Hey, you know who I saw in school, it was, you know, the guy with the hat, he wears that shirt with his name on it, he's tall and he has that thing, it's long and skinny and he sticks it in the engine . . ." Finally you gather enough clues to guess: "You mean Joe from the gas station?" and the child replies with relief, "Yeah, him." Youngsters with naming difficulties also use verbal stalling mechanisms to give themselves extra time to find words; their sentences are often punctuated with annoying pauses. "Sally lost her, um, you know, thing . . ." is a typical communication from a child with a disability of this kind.

In school, many youngsters with language processing disabilities continue to have trouble understanding and following directions, a problem that is often blamed on inattention, laziness, or disobedience ("How many times have I told you to line up alphabetically by last name, Johnny? What does it take to get through to you? Maybe if you stay in for recess today, you'll remember"). Efforts to use visual skills to improve understanding are also frequently misunderstood ("Keep your eyes on your own paper, Johnny! It's cheating to look at Susie's work!"). Problematic speech patterns may not be considered a handicap in the classroom, where students are usually expected to be quiet, but the difficulties these youngsters have learning to read and write eventually do get attention. The problems students experience with these skills reflect the problems they have processing spoken language. Some examples are as follows:

- Students with sound processing weaknesses have trouble learning to associate letters with sounds, and they find it hard to break

Language Processing Disability Checklist

It is normal for children to display a few behaviors on this list. A persistent pattern of many of these symptoms, however, may indicate a learning disability.

Speech and language comprehension:
- delays in learning to speak
- does not modulate tone of voice appropriately; speaks in monotone, or too loud
- has problems naming objects or people
- uses vague, imprecise language; has a small vocabulary
- speech is slow or halting; uses verbal "stalling" mechanisms ("uh," "um," "you know")
- uses poor grammar
- frequently mispronounces words
- confuses words with similar sounds (such as frustrate and fluctuate; may produce hybrids such as flustrate)
- often uses hand gestures and body language to help convey message
- avoids talking (especially in front of strangers, authority figures, or groups)
- insensitive to rhymes
- little interest in books or stories
- does not respond appropriately to questions (replies "Monday" when asked "Where do you go to school?")
- frequently does not understand or remember instructions

Reading:
- significant delays in learning to read
- difficulty naming letters
- problems associating letters with sounds, discriminating between sounds in words, blending sounds into words
- difficulty analyzing sound sequences; frequent sequencing errors (such as reading snug for sung)
- guesses at unfamiliar words rather than using word analysis skills
- reads very slowly; oral reading deteriorates within a few sentences (due to declining ability to retrieve sounds rapidly from memory)
- comprehension for what has been read is consistently poor, or deteriorates when sentences become longer and more complex

- poor retention of new vocabulary words
- dislikes and avoids reading

Writing:
- written assignments are short or incomplete; often characterized by brief sentences, limited vocabulary
- problems with grammar persist
- bizarre spelling errors (not phonetic); student may be unable to decipher own spelling
- ideas in written assignments are poorly organized, not logically presented
- little theme development; students more likely to write bare lists of points or events than provide details or develop ideas, characters, or plot
- on tests, consistently does better with multiple-choice questions than essays or filling in blanks

Math:
- slow response during math fact drills due to problems with number retrieval
- difficulty with word problems due to poor language comprehension
- problems with higher level math due to difficulties with analysis and logical reasoning

Related problems:
- "garbles" telephone messages; misunderstands what is heard on radio or TV
- difficulty with verbal reasoning; may understand all the words in the proverb "A rolling stone gathers no moss" but be unable to explain what it means; may find it hard to draw logical conclusions
- problems understanding puns and jokes; may not detect teasing
- difficulty making comparisons and classifying objects or ideas
- difficulty remembering information or producing facts or ideas on demand
- difficulty presenting a story or directions in logical order
- types of problems encountered learning English are likely to be repeated when studying a foreign language
- difficulty joining or maintaining conversations

down words into sequences of sound units. Even if they learn in time to tell you what a *t* sounds like, they may still be unable to tell you if that sound occurs at the beginning or end of the word *cast*— or even if it appears in the word at all. These students have trouble mastering the process of "sounding out" words, and they make bizarre spelling errors that reflect the scrambled way their brains interpret what they hear (see illustration).

• Students with comprehension problems may learn to decode words satisfactorily, but the words they read make no more sense to them than the words they hear. These children may have difficulty associating individual words with their correct meanings, or have such problems with the rules or structure of language that combinations of words confuse them. Most often, these students can manage language in small chunks, but they become overwhelmed when the material they are expected to handle gets longer and more complex. Such youngsters typically have small vocabularies, have trouble mastering the basics of grammar, and frequently use inappropriate words when writing. Memory for what has been read (but not really understood) is also likely to be poor.

• Students who have trouble finding words to express themselves in speech do no better with pencil and paper. Producing the words they need to describe what they know can be a problem even when students' vocabularies are vast and their knowledge of the subject at hand is comprehensive. Even if these students read well, they may find their difficulty speaking and writing a severe handicap in classes where student efforts are judged primarily by discussions and papers. (Not surprisingly, these young people much prefer tests with multiple-choice questions.)

Like all students with learning disabilities, children with language deficits tend to process information more slowly than usual. Their problems are likely to be magnified in the classroom, where prompt answers are usually demanded. Many times these students will know an answer to a question, but hesitate when called upon because they need time to find and arrange the words necessary to frame a coherent reply. Not hearing an immediate answer, however, the teacher is likely to assume our student has not done his homework and move on to another child. These children are among those most likely to be accused of low motivation. Too often, this accusation becomes reality as

---

Spelling Patterns of a Gifted Seventh-Grade Boy with Language Processing Disabilities

Known words		Unknown words	
friendship (handwritten)	friendship	*badge* (handwritten)	badge
remember (handwritten)	remember	*democte* (handwritten)	democrat
important (handwritten)	important	*gation* (handwritten)	quotation
comb (handwritten)	comb	*sourse* (handwritten)	source
unless (handwritten)	unless	*jusus* (handwritten)	justice
flower (handwritten)	flower	*onhibel* (handwritten)	honorable
whole (handwritten)	whole	*haytion* (handwritten)	hasten

He remembers "known" words by how they look but has difficulty approximating phonetically the spellings of "unknown" words that he has not yet learned to read.

Source: Smith, C. R. *ibid.*

---

mounting school problems eat away at these youngsters' self-esteem and natural zest for learning.

In addition to creating problems with reading and writing, language processing disabilities also have an impact on how students think. Much of our ability to remember and organize information depends on our skill at naming and describing things, and we need language to do this. For example, our new neighbor may start out as no more than a vague visual impression, but over time we use words to build a "file" on him in our minds: His name is Bob, he has an attractive wife and two small children, he drives a red truck, he works for the phone company, he likes to barbecue in his backyard, and so on. We may make associations with other "files" we have created in the past—perhaps our neighbor has an accent that reminds us of television actor Andy Griffith, and his enthusiasm for baseball makes us think he might like to meet another neighbor who is also a fan. The bigger our file gets, the better we can say we "know" our neighbor, and the more certain we would be of recognizing him if we saw him in an unexpected place. So it is with everything we learn. We use words to nail down information and store it in a way that makes it easy for us to use it later.

Research shows that the greater command students have of language, the better they are at remembering information, organizing their ideas, making associations between facts and concepts, and handling abstractions. Students with language disabilities often find themselves struggling in all of these areas. One teacher observes: "These kids' minds are like drawers stuffed full of file folders with no labels. There may be a lot of information there, but it's so disorganized that it isn't much use to them." When language processing handicaps are mild, poor memory and lack of organization may actually be the most obvious aspects of the disability.

Social development is also influenced by language disabilities. Children who have trouble understanding words or who make mistakes when they speak are sometimes so fearful of exposing their weaknesses that they become quiet, shy, and withdrawn. There are also youngsters who go to the opposite extreme, dealing with their inability to understand others' input by bullying and insisting that everyone do things their way! Neither of these children are likely to find it easy to make friends. Children with language processing disabilities can often be found at the fringes of groups, "going along with the crowd." Some prefer to spend their time with younger children, whose simpler language is easier for them to understand. Parents note that these children are often most comfortable sharing activities with one or two friends: their capacity to understand what it being said rapidly breaks down as the size of a group grows. They may also be happiest in structured situations where the rules are clearly understood ahead of time, so they will not be embarrassed by instructions that may be hard for them to follow.

Many areas of the brain must work together to process language successfully, and disabilities can result from breakdowns at several different points in the system. Difficulty with usage and comprehension is generally linked to underfunctioning areas in the left cerebral cortex. Students with severe comprehension problems sometimes show evidence of other "left-brain" weaknesses, such as difficulty with arranging facts or ideas in logical sequences. Research exploring the basis of sound processing problems (which produce the most severe reading disabilities) has recently focused on some other brain structures, notably the thalamus and the prefrontal cortex. The thalamus routes information from the ears, eyes, and other sensory organs to different areas of the cerebral cortex, rather like a telephone switchboard. The prefrontal cortex has only recently been associated with reading disabilities, and the role it plays in speech/sound processing is still under investigation.

In other areas of research, geneticists have been busy attempting to determine why language processing disorders so often run in families. One day it may be possible to test for a "dyslexia gene" and identify some of the children who will need extra help long before they enter school. For the time being, however, the best hope for children with language processing disabilities is early recognition and intervention.

Special education support is essential. Many children with language processing disabilities cannot learn to read and write by conventional methods; to master these skills, they need special materials and teachers experienced in working with language problems. Progress in reading can be slow for these children, and alternate means of getting information (such as books recorded on tape) may also have to be provided in order to help them keep up with the curriculum. Because students often need assistance breaking instructional materials into small chunks of language they can manage, it is sometimes necessary to rewrite their basic texts in simpler English, and extra time is usually needed to complete tests and assignments. If students read and write very poorly, they may need to have test questions read to them and be permitted to answer orally. Many students with language disorders also need to be taught specific strategies for organizing and remembering written and verbal material.

In addition, teachers may need to be informed of the importance of speaking to these students slowly and clearly, and to be made aware of how difficult it is for these children to process words if there is other "sound confusion." Telling students that there will be a math test on Tuesday just as the bell rings amid a general shuffling of papers and scraping of chairs, for example, puts the child with a language disability at a disadvantage. So would "burying" that information in a long list of other announcements. Parents find that simple language is often the key to improving kids' memories at home, too: "Please take out the garbage tonight," clearly articulated face-to-face, is far more likely to get results than "Honey, don't forget I want you to take out the trash after you walk the dog and do your spelling homework" tossed over your shoulder as you leave the room.

Given appropriate support, students with language processing disabilities can become successful academically. Young people whose disabilities are very severe, however, may never progress much beyond "survival level" in reading and writing. It is very important for these students to find alternative ways to learn and to communicate so that they can develop their other strengths and talents. If they remain motivated, difficulty with reading and writing will not stop them from meeting their goals. Many virtual nonreaders not only have made it to college but have been outstanding achievers there (special education support is available at many fine colleges and universities). They have made it in nearly every kind of business and profession. As Jason's story demonstrates, energetic and intelligent nonreaders can also become successful operating their own businesses—one method of guaranteeing yourself the flexibility to do things your own way! These students sometimes deliver exceptional performance in career areas where language skills are relatively unimportant: medical technology, architecture, photography, carpentry, engineering, mechanics, television production, fine arts, and computer programming, just to mention a few. Most parents' greatest fear—that lack of reading ability will make it impossible for children to complete their educations and become independent and self-supporting—is therefore without real foundation. These children, however, do need an extra measure of understanding and encouragement in order to maintain their self-confidence and some enthusiasm for education. It is very important for them to get plenty of opportunities to do the things they do well in order to balance the uphill struggle they face with paperwork in school.

A tremendous amount of technological support has become available for individuals with language handicaps in recent years. For example, some computers can scan printed materials and "read" them aloud. Students can also "write" by dictating into voice-activated word processors. Software designers are developing new applications at such a rate that almost any discussion of what is available would be outdated within months. Parents may wish to consult local parent networks, retailers, and special educators about computer options. If it is determined that a computer is essential to a child's progress in school, the machine and the programs will be provided by the school district. Parents should understand, however, that even the most sophisticated technology will not eliminate the need for competent instruction. Kids can get by without computers, but they cannot succeed without qualified, experienced teachers; locating those teachers should be a parent's primary concern.

Although language processing disabilities are permanent handi-caps, children occasionally do have late developmental spurts which bring marked improvement. The brain continues to form new con-nections into early adulthood, and there are cases where the "cir-cuits" necessary for reading have finally become complete in adolescence or even later. The motto for teaching reading skills, then, is "Never give up." It is necessary to leave educational doors open as long as possible so that late bloomers have the opportunity to reach their full potential.

FINE MOTOR DISABILITIES

To get an idea of what it feels like to have a fine motor disability, try positioning a mirror and a plain piece of paper on a table in such a way that you can see the paper in the mirror. Now try writing your name on the paper while looking only at the mirror image. Do you find it difficult? Confused by the mirror image, your brain has "for-gotten" how to guide your hand. If you found writing your name hard, try imagining that the teacher just handed you twenty-five new vocabulary words to copy!

Individuals with fine motor handicaps cannot fully control groups of small muscles in their hands. This disability has no impact on in-tellectual capacity, but it interferes with school performance because it impairs the ability to communicate in writing. Children with this type of disability cannot write neatly, no matter how hard they try. Their letters are poorly formed, and their sentences stray from the lines. Their handwriting may be so illegible that it is impossible even to guess whether words are spelled correctly. It takes intense con-centration for these students to produce even marginally acceptable written work; when they are striving for legibility, they work slowly and have little energy left over for considerations of content or style. Not surprisingly, many of these students hate to write, and so they avoid it as much as possible. Because short, sloppy papers seldom impress teachers, these children don't collect many gold stars. In classes where student efforts are judged primarily by written work, it is often assumed that these students are slow-witted, lazy, or both.

Students with fine motor handicaps experience difficulty with a surprising variety of tasks in school. Anything involving drawing or writing is a trial, from copying diagrams from the blackboard to tak-ing lecture notes. Mistakes are made in computation because num-bers are illegible or not aligned properly. In science lab, these students mangle dissections and splatter acid on their clothes. Efforts

JASON

Jason, an engineering college graduate who owns his own heating repair business, explains how his naming difficulties have affected his life. Jason always did well at remembering concepts but could never remember names, places, dates, baseball batting averages, and so forth. Consequently, he came to believe that he could contribute little to conversations. He says that today he enters conversations "from the perimeter," waiting for people to get beyond the exchange of facts to the idea level.

A six-foot-tall, brawny, handsome fellow, Jason's reticence began in elementary school when classmates in the lunchroom would outargue him with more accurate facts, no matter what the topic of conversation. He soon learned to retreat socially. An exceptional tennis player, Jason never calls the score because he fears making verbal errors. When he returned to his tenth-year high school reunion, no one remembered him.

Jason's reading and spelling difficulties have continued into adulthood. He has read one novel in his entire life and never reads the newspaper. TV is his source of information. When writing, Jason can only catch his misspellings after he finishes each word and inspects whether it "looks right." Number reversals occur continually on his order sheets, but he catches these when the sums don't make sense and the order numbers don't match those in the catalogue. Jason has learned to check and double check any written work.

Jason is a sympathetic, pleasant fellow for whom finding business partners is easy. He has always sought partners who could be the upfront salespeople, good at making small talk. Jason, on the other hand, is the mechanical genius on whose skills everyone relies, and without whom there could be no business. He describes himself as an accommodating, honest, dependable person who is always on time and always helping others out. "Since I can't teach people anything new besides engineering, I've become the nice guy. When I was sixteen, I was the first person to get my license, and so I drove everyone around. What else can I do? I want to be liked."

Adapted from Smith, C. R. *ibid.*

in art—like their handwriting—look embarrassingly immature. These youngsters are also embarrassed by their clumsiness in nonacademic settings: they spill their milk at lunch, fumble the ball in gym class, and knock other students' books and backpacks to the floor. While other kids can hide their weaknesses, fine motor problems are always on display, with predictable consequences to social acceptance and self-esteem. The anger these children feel about their inability to "do it right" can be intense and is often directed at themselves. Anger is plainly evident in Nathan's coloring, and his mother's

---

Fine Motor Disability Checklist

It is not unusual for young children to display many behaviors on this list. If symptoms persist into the school years, however, a disability may be responsible.

At home:
- appears awkward and clumsy; often drops things, spills things, knocks things over
- has difficulty picking up and using small objects such as puzzle pieces or Legos
- has trouble with buttons, hooks, and zippers when dressing; finds it very difficult to tie shoes
- unsuccessful in games and activities that involve hand skills (cat's cradle, piano lessons, basketball)
- poor coloring ability; cannot keep within lines
- art work looks immature for age (drawings from imagination are usually better than efforts at copying designs)
- difficulty using scissors
- awkward pencil grip (may hold pencil too loosely or too tightly)
- delays in learning to write; writing is large and immature, letters and numbers are poorly formed
- may be delayed in learning to speak or have articulation problems

At school:
- poor handwriting (sloppy, illegible, poor spacing, inconsistent letter size, no consistent style, strays from lines on paper)
- papers are messy (torn and crumpled with many cross-outs, smudges, and incomplete erasures)
- marked slowness, exceptional effort, and frustration noted during writing tasks
- dislike and avoidance of writing or drawing
- written efforts are short and often incomplete
- content/style of written assignments is poor (primary focus is on achieving legibility)
- computation errors are common due to illegible, crowded, and poorly aligned numerals
- in severe cases, difficulty learning keyboard skills

Nathan's Coloring

When Nathan Colors

When Nathan colors, his crayon
becomes a weapon against the white paper.
It is his mission to color in every bit of
available background.
His coloring brain comes from his toes
and grips his entire body driving its power
down into his he-man fingers.
He sucks in drool as his concentration grows.

When Nathan colors, his crayons
make a popping sound as weapon after weapon
is broken by the paper enemy.
On December 26th, Nathan's coloring can
is filled with new, smooth shiny soldiers.
By January, his army is broken into small
midget fighters.
His mother watches as he pushes 1/4" nubs
into the paper with his he-man thumb ends.

When Nathan colors, his world is
lost in the mission of wiping out white.
This is no calming, passive playtime
like it might be for other children.
Coloring is exhausting and sometimes,
it must be followed by a snack break
or, on rainy days,
a doze on the couch.

Source: Debra Morse-Little

touching observations record how exhausting trying to manage your own hands can be.

Brain areas controlling hand and mouth movements lie relatively close together in the cerebral cortex, and children who have trouble with hand coordination sometimes have articulation problems as well. These young people are doubly frustrated in their efforts to communicate, and at double the risk for being underestimated intellectually. Students with fine motor disabilities, however, often find their large motor systems are completely unaffected. Activities like dancing, running, throwing, and jumping are usually not a problem, and these youngsters may even be talented athletes in events that do not require hand skills.

Students sometimes do show improvement in motor skills over time, although they may be well advanced in school before significant progress is noted. Support for children with fine motor disabilities is usually directed at improving handwriting (guidance and practice can make a difference). There are some students who have such difficulty with written expression, however, that they must be provided with alternate means of recording information and expressing themselves. Students can be allowed to dictate reports or give them orally; they can tape-record homework assignments and be provided with copies of notes from teachers or other students. Typing is a real survival skill for these young people, and word processors can be a blessing—especially for students attempting to cope with the increased communication demands of secondary school.

Overcoming negative feelings that have become attached to writing is another matter. Sometimes this can be even harder than mastering the physical process of getting words down on paper. Unfortunately, students who have decided that they "hate to write" limit their own opportunities. They may avoid whole areas of study that might otherwise be rewarding for them because writing will be expected. Sometimes they feel that they are not qualified to pursue certain career choices or to succeed in college. In this way, a distaste for writing—which is epidemic among youngsters with attention, visual perception, and language problems, as well as students with fine motor disabilities—easily becomes a handicap in itself. Like the other secondary handicaps that evolve from learning disabilities, it may survive long after the original disability has been addressed.

Parents can do a great deal to help students with learning disabilities sidestep the "hate to write" pitfall. One of the best strategies is to encourage children to talk: young people who are used to expressing themselves orally develop many skills essential for good writing. They learn to organize their thoughts and present them in a clear, coherent manner; over time, they develop an "ear" for words and learn to use language with confidence and style. As their manual or keyboard skills progress, students transfer those strengths to paper almost automatically. Reading to children encourages an appreciation for language and also helps children develop their vocabularies and expand their imaginations. In addition, time spent sharing a story or talking over the events of the day with Mom or Dad can strengthen the emotional bonds between parent and child, fortifying the child's defenses against stress in the outside world. This is worth remembering when children with learning disabilities are feeling overwhelmed by academic demands. A half hour on the couch with a favorite book, or a trip out for some ice cream and conversation after dinner, will often do youngsters with any kind of learning disability far more good than the same amount of time spent on practicing cursive writing, multiplication tables, or spelling.

It is important to keep in mind that all types of learning disabilities can vary tremendously in severity. While some have a fairly global impact on school achievement, many handicaps are so subtle and specific that they interfere with only a very narrow range of activities. It is also important to remember that learning disabilities frequently overlap and occur in almost endless combinations: a student with a language processing disability (comprehension) complicated by ADHD will appear to have little in common with a student who has a language processing disability (word retrieval) complicated by fine motor deficits. In fact, each student with learning disabilities is virtually unique—a reality that can make identification and intervention a challenge.

Still, it is possible to make some general comments about the long-term effects of the different types of learning disabilities. First, all learning disabilities are permanent handicaps; while they may show considerable improvement over time, they cannot be entirely outgrown or "cured." They have a discouraging way of presenting themselves in different forms as a student progresses through school. For example, we may heave a sigh of relief that Susie has finally learned to read, only to notice that her spelling is pretty awful. When the spelling improves, Susie's eighth-grade English teacher may express despair over her incoherent book reports. And no sooner will Susie learn to write a decent paper than she will be expected to do it in Spanish—and to memorize the periodic table and a long list of dates for American history. Students with learning disabilities thus usually need some kind of support throughout their school years, although the level and type of help required may change.

During elementary school, support usually focuses on providing the extra time and instruction needed to master the basic skills of reading, writing, and mathematics. Students with mild language problems or uncomplicated visual perception or fine motor disabilities can usually be expected to attain passable basic skill levels during this time. Research shows, for example, that the visual perception skills of a ten-year-old are good enough to handle most of life's challenges. If children with visual perception disabilities can reach this skill level, their handicaps are likely to amount to not much more than a moderate annoyance in secondary school and after graduation. If they have been able to maintain their motivation and self-confidence, these students rapidly learn to compensate for what is left of their handicaps, and the help they need in secondary school is often minimal.

Students with more extensive language processing handicaps, severe ADHD, or multiple disabilities are less likely to reach satisfactory basic skills levels in elementary school. While efforts to teach basic skills may continue, support strategies in secondary school usually shift to teaching compensatory skills and providing students with alternate means of communicating and keeping up with the curriculum. It is of critical importance that students who have difficulty learning to read and/or write be helped to develop other strengths and talents to the fullest extent possible, and that they be encouraged to let these areas of ability guide their postsecondary school planning. Persistent advocacy may be needed to make sure that these students do not become "opportunity impaired" as a result of their basic skills deficits.

Severe language and attention problems are also more likely to have an impact on the lives of adults than other disabilities. Individuals with visual perception or fine motor disabilities will face some lifelong reminders of their handicaps (for example, they may continue to drop things, misplace their possessions, turn right when they are told to turn left, and have atrocious handwriting), but these problems will not isolate them socially or interfere substantially with their ability to produce on the job. In contrast, difficulties with comprehension, speaking, and maintaining concentration can present enduring obstacles to social and vocational growth, even when an individual's life has been arranged so that reading and writing are not major issues.

Even those most profoundly affected by learning disabilities, however, can look forward to productive and fulfilling lives if they feel loved and accepted in spite of their handicaps, and if they are encouraged to make the most of their positive qualities and invest time in activities they enjoy. This may require parents to adjust their expectations. As a mother who is herself a successful attorney recalls:

Initially I was bitterly disappointed that my son was not going to college, although after all the frustrating years he spent floundering in school, I had no trouble understanding his choice. Even I could see that his comprehension for verbal material is so poor that college was not a realistic option. Andy loves cars and he found steady work at a body shop, where he's learning on the job. He plays regularly in a softball league, and through that activity he has made a lot of friends. He also has found immense satisfaction volunteering as a "big brother" to an eleven-year-old boy with Down's syndrome; they do all kinds of things together—camping, ball games, trips to the zoo. Is this the life I would have chosen for Andy? No. But my plan would have made him miserable, and today he is so happy that I can't help but be grateful for the way things have worked out.

Part II

HOW ARE LEARNING DISABILITIES IDENTIFIED?

4

WARNING SIGNS AT HOME
AND AT SCHOOL

Because learning disabilities are defined as handicaps that interfere with the mastery of basic academic skills, they cannot be formally identified until a child starts experiencing problems in school. Not only must the child be having academic problems, but federal law states that there must be "a severe discrepancy" between a student's intellectual ability and his or her academic achievement before the presence of a learning disability can be confirmed. While the law does not specify how severe the gap between intelligence and performance has to be, most schools will not suggest evaluation for learning disabilities unless a child is more than a year behind his or her grade level in reading, writing, or mathematics.

This kind of policy makes sense from the school's point of view. Identifying learning disabilities involves hours of observation, interviews, and one-on-one assessment; it is a time-consuming, labor-intensive, and therefore costly process. School districts with limited resources—in other words, most school districts today—do not wish to waste time and money evaluating students who are unlikely to qualify for special education services. Therefore, when a student starts to fall behind, schools often recommend a "wait and see" approach, trying traditional means of "extra help" for a year or two before deciding on further action.

What this practice means in reality, however, is that children with learning disabilities often have to flounder for years before an intensive effort is made to find out how best to help them. Unfortunately, the longer a learning disability remains unrecognized, the more likely it is that a student's problems will begin to compound. Frustration and embarrassment about poor performance start to eat away at the child's motivation and self-confidence. Expectations are reduced and enthusiasm for education is lost.

It is therefore critically important that parents who develop concerns about their children's progress in school act promptly to investigate. Fortunately, parents need not wait for school personnel to recommend evaluations for learning disabilities: school districts are required to provide assessments when *parents* request them as well. (As taxpayers, parents of children enrolled in private or parochial schools are also entitled to evaluations without charge from their public school districts.) You can also arrange to have a child's learning problems assessed privately. In the next chapter we will discuss how to obtain an evaluation, and what it should include.

Our purpose here is to discuss the earliest warning signs of learning disabilities so that you will know when an evaluation is necessary. Some problems in the six areas described below will be observable well before a child starts school, while others become more obvious after the child enters the classroom. Sometimes these behaviors can indicate a problem other than a learning disability. All should be regarded as a signal that something is wrong, however—and if there are problems in several of the areas discussed here, an evaluation for learning disabilities should not be delayed.

DEVELOPMENTAL DELAYS

As we discussed in Chapter 2, learning disabilities can be caused by uneven brain development. When this is the case, a child is almost always going to be delayed in reaching some developmental milestones. Parents may note that a baby understands words or talks significantly later than other children of the same age, for example, or is very late to roll over, stand, and walk. It may be observed that a preschool child has an unusual amount of difficulty understanding directions, pronouncing words, doing puzzles, handling tableware, recognizing shapes and letters, or counting. During physical examinations, the child's pediatrician may also note subtle signs of a delay in neurological development, such as poor coordination. Children with learning disabilities are typically delayed only in some areas; in others their development will be normal or even advanced. (Delay in all areas of development is generally a sign of a more serious handicap.)

It is important to remember that a delay does not always indicate a disability. Children do not develop according to rigid timetables, and in most areas of development there is a wide range of behaviors that are normal. Most children start talking somewhere between the ages of one and two, for example, and a small percentage of normal youngsters begin to talk even later. Development can also be affected by outside factors. Children who are parked in front of television sets for hours each day, placed in substandard day care situations, or raised by caretakers who do not speak English are all likely to be delayed in their language development, yet they are not disabled. Similarly, youngsters who do not have access to play materials like construction toys, crayons, puzzles, and scissors may be late developing fine motor skills and eye-hand coordination, but they will catch up given the opportunity. If there are no environmental concerns of this kind, however, significant delays may signal irregularities in the brain. At the end of this book there is an Appendix including charts that describe milestones in the development of language and perceptual-motor skills. In general, the longer a youngster is delayed in reaching these stages of development, the more a parent needs to be concerned.

Parents need to be especially alert to developmental delays as a child approaches school age. Research demonstrates that children who begin school with developmental delays often progress at a slower than usual rate; as a result, the gap between them and their average peers grows every year. Studies that have tracked such students over lengthy periods find that they tend to remain low achievers throughout their school years, and they have a much higher than usual rate of retention and failure to complete school. It is therefore important to address developmental delays before children begin kindergarten, through enriched preschool programming. Federal law requires public school districts to provide such programming without charge to children who have been identified as developmentally delayed after the age of three (in some states, services are also available for infants and younger children). The special education department of your local school district will also offer a screening program to help identify children in need of these services.

What skills are most important for a successful start in school? The checklist on pages 72–73 lists some basic indicators of school readiness. Children who are not comfortable with a majority of these skills at the age of four and a half years will almost certainly benefit from a year of preschool programming before starting kindergarten. Even when children do have these skills, it may be unwise to start them in school before the age of five (for girls) or five and a half (for boys, who mature later than girls do). Many of today's kindergarten classes present information at a very rapid pace, and children who begin school at younger ages often have problems keeping up even when they do not have delays or disabilities. Research suggests that starting a child in school at age four is advisable only when children have mastered most of the skills on the checklist *and* flexible, individualized kindergarten and first-grade programming is available.

If delays persist beyond school entry, parents should not hesitate to request early intervention. The first step is to help the child's teacher identify the skills that are delayed. Arrange to talk to the teacher at the earliest opportunity—before the beginning of school, if possible. Describe your concerns, and ask what can be done to help your child catch up in problem areas. Basically, the teacher has three options:

1. *Intensify readiness instruction.* The teacher can arrange to provide extra help in areas where the child is behind. The additional instruction may be provided by a teacher, a classroom aide, a parent volunteer, or a student tutor.

2. *Try different instructional methods and materials.* The teacher can see if the student responds to activities or materials different from those being used by the rest of the class. A student who has been unsuccessful learning to recognize letters and numbers in a workbook, for example, might succeed when asked to cut these figures out and paste them on sheets of paper.

3. *Reduce the academic load.* If the child appears overwhelmed by demands to absorb too much too soon, the teacher can slow the rate of instruction and focus on the skills that are most important for success in first grade (usually prereading, counting, and writing skills). This kind of intervention gives students room to build a solid academic foundation at their own pace.

If necessary, these strategies can be continued in first grade. If the student has not responded to these methods by the middle of the first-grade year, however, an evaluation for learning disabilities is in order. Any discussion of retention should take place with the results from an evaluation on the table. A child who has information processing problems will usually not benefit from repeating lessons that did not work before. Individualized programming addressing the specific disabilities is needed while the child moves on with class-mates to the next grade.

INCONSISTENT PERFORMANCE

One of the most confounding (and sometimes maddening) aspects of living with children who have learning disabilities is that their be-havior is erratic. They are competent—even exceptionally able—sometimes, but other times they appear totally lost. Memory is an area where inconsistency is often most obvious; children with learn-ing disabilities typically remember some kinds of information much better than others. (Research indicates that it is *entering* information into memory that is the problem; once information has been entered, most children with learning disabilities can recall and use it as well as anyone else.) This is easy enough to understand once you know your child has a learning disability, but before then parents go crazy trying to figure out how a kid can remember all the lyrics to every popular song he ever heard on the radio but not where he left his new jacket, or how a student who remembered to do a homework assign-ment (and spent three hours on it) can then forget to hand the paper in!

Inconsistency can show up in any aspect of a child's activities. A child with learning disabilities may be able to draw well but not write clearly, for example, or he might be terrific at running, jumping, and climbing but unable to bounce a ball. A child who teaches herself to read before starting school may have problems counting up four forks or spoons, or she might speak brilliantly but find it impossible to put words on paper. Discrepancies of this kind puzzle parents and sometimes convince them that children are being inattentive or un-cooperative. This type of behavior is typical of uneven brain develop-ment, however.

When a child with learning disabilities starts school, the baffling pattern of erratic performance continues. While many typical chil-dren are better in math than in language skills (or vice versa), the child with learning disabilities may be good in math on Tuesday and be unable to comprehend math at all on Thursday (this is quite likely if the child has a language processing handicap and the teacher has just introduced word problems). These children may love history one week and hate it the next because a paper has been assigned, or find that their best subject in third grade becomes their worst nightmare in fourth because there is more material to memorize. Performance

Is Your Child Ready for School?

If your child can do many of the tasks on this checklist *before* beginning kindergarten, he or she is well on the way toward school success. The remaining skills will need to be developed during the kindergarten year in order to promote success in first grade.

- Sings the alphabet song
- Recognizes and names alphabet letters
- Identifies words that rhyme; adds a rhyming word where appropriate in a story
- Identifies whether dictated words begin with the same or different sounds
- Claps to the number of syllables heard in a word
- Recognizes and names common colors, objects, and body parts
- Tells full name, age, address, telephone number, and birthday
- Comprehends age-appropriate vocabulary and stories
- Recites familiar nursery rhymes
- Completes sequences (e.g., breakfast, lunch, _____; yesterday, today, _____)
- Completes analogies (e.g., in daytime it is light, at night it is _____; birds fly, fish _____)
- Can respond to various question forms, such as how many ("How many eyes do you have?"), which ("Which is slower [longer, more]?"), where ("Where do people buy gas?"), whom ("Whom do you go to when you are sick?"), what ("What do you do when you are hungry?" "What is a house made of?"), why ("Why do we have stoves?"), what if ("What happens if your ice cream gets hot?")
- Expresses opposite relationships ("How are a spoon and a glass different?")
- Tells simple stories that contain several characters interacting

may be inconsistent even within a given assignment or activity. A student may read a word correctly in the title of a chapter but fail to recognize the same word in the first paragraph—or she might write beautifully for two lines, after which handwriting deteriorates into illegibility. Sometimes parents blame teachers for these problems, while teachers (who may be equally bewildered by erratic behavior) start using phrases like "lacks motivation" and "needs to try harder." All sorts of incentives, punishments, and rewards may be employed to make performance more consistent. Since they do not address the

- Follows two- and three-step simple directions, such as "Put on your boots, get your jacket, and get in the car"
- Succeeds at simple concentration-type games requiring matching pictures from memory
- Recognizes name in writing
- Prints his or her name
- Recognizes some common signs or labels by their shapes (McDonald's, Coca-Cola)
- Sorts and names objects by category: food, clothing, animals
- Recites and recognizes numbers up to ten
- Counts groups of objects, to ten or more
- Matches equal sets of objects, such as three triangles being the same amount as three circles
- Points to positions in a series; beginning, middle, end; first, second, last
- Recognizes and names common shapes such as circles, squares, and triangles
- Copies designs: circle, cross, square, X, triangle
- Copies letters and simple words
- Draws recognizable house, person, tree
- Cuts out picture fairly close to edge
- Dresses self fairly independently
- Ties shoes
- Uses fork and spoon appropriately; cuts soft food with knife
- Usually finishes age-appropriate activities (such as a puzzle, listening to a short story, making an object out of clay) rather than abandoning activities in the middle
- Develops friendships and plays cooperatively with other children

underlying cause of the problem, these strategies are rarely successful for long.

It is sometimes noted that children with learning disabilities work better at home than at school. This is likely to be the case with children who need extra time to process information (Mom and Dad don't usually ring a bell and force a child to move on to a new activity) or who benefit from one-on-one instruction. If children are consistently having trouble completing class work or tests in the time allotted, frequently need instructions to be rephrased or repeated, or

Children with Learning Difficulties Often Have Problems with Memory

NANCY Reprinted by permission of United Feature Syndicate Inc.

often have difficulty explaining what they know to you, these are also clues that a learning disability may exist, and that it is time to ask for an evaluation.

LOSS OF INTEREST IN LEARNING

Most small children, including those with learning disabilities, love to learn (of course, they think of it as exploring rather than learning). It is wonderful to watch the determined optimism of babies who are learning to climb stairs or to walk: repeated failure hardly discourages them at all. Some of us can't resist spoiling our toddlers with too many toys, because we love that gleam that they get in their eyes when they have the chance to discover something new. How many of us have at some point fallen into bed exhausted from trying to answer questions for a child with a serious case of the "whys"? (One father we know remembers that once his five-year-old son—a very bright lad who was later discovered to have learning disabilities—was in bed and half asleep when he asked his hundredth question of the day: Why did America fight World War II?) While it can be hard to keep up with children's relentless curiosity, most parents find this open delight in learning one of the most appealing aspects of childhood.

Similarly, there is nothing much sadder than watching the erosion of enthusiasm for learning that can take place after a child with learning disabilities starts school. Some parents recall that this process occurred almost overnight—that their children went from being happy, eager-to-tackle-anything preschoolers to declaring "I hate school and everything connected with it" in a matter of weeks. Other students gradually become disenchanted with subjects that once interested them. For example, a student who has difficulties with reading comprehension may enjoy science in elementary school (when the curriculum includes many hands-on activities) but start to lose interest in secondary school when science reading requirements increase. It is very common for students with learning disabilities to develop a distaste for subjects that demand research and writing, which are problem areas for most students with information processing handicaps. Students with relatively mild disabilities who are successful in elementary school may become discouraged and disinterested in secondary school, when they are faced with the challenge of organizing and remembering larger amounts of information.

If students' learning disabilities are not identified and appropriate help provided, disinterest in learning usually progresses to outright avoidance. Children start developing strategies to spare themselves the frustration of trying to accomplish tasks that are painfully difficult or impossible for them. These kids become expert procrastinators; it takes them forever to get around to doing their homework. Often they rush through it, leave it unfinished, or claim that "I did the homework in school." Some children complain chronically of fatigue, stomach aches, or other afflictions and beg to be allowed to abandon schoolwork or stay home from school entirely—and they are not necessarily faking it, since discomforts related to stress can be very real. If the situation is allowed to deteriorate into junior high and high school, teens may start cutting classes, become truant, or even drop out of school entirely.

There are causes other than learning disabilities for a loss of interest in learning. Family problems, health concerns, an ineffective teacher, or a poor match between student and curriculum can all affect enthusiasm for education. And of course around puberty, the whole school population has a hard time keeping its mind on learning, as any middle school teacher knows. In general, however, an unexpected loss of interest in learning—whether sudden or gradual—is a sign that *some* kind of intervention is needed. A "wait and see" approach can have serious consequences here: once a student has stopped enjoying learning and started to avoid it, it can be very difficult to restore motivation.

Listed below are a few common early signs that a student's interest in learning is declining:

General complaints about school. Sometimes a student in academic trouble will issue a barrage of complaints that appear to have nothing to do with learning: the teacher is unfair, the other students stuck up, the playground too crowded, the cafeteria food disgusting. When children repeatedly claim to hate school, parents would be wise to check with teachers about how things are going academically.

Persistent complaints that work is too hard. Children with learning disabilities frequently feel "over their heads" in some classes or subjects. This kind of complaint needs to be investigated promptly, as students who cannot do the work assigned to them rapidly lose confidence in themselves and quit trying.

Complaints of boredom. Children having trouble understanding schoolwork are as likely to complain that the work is "dumb" or boring as to say it is difficult or hard to understand. (Persistent complaints of boredom may also indicate that students are not being given work appropriate for their intellectual levels; this is a frequent problem for students with superior intelligence.)

Refusal to talk about school. When young children who previously bubbled over with reports on their school day start giving you one-word answers ("What happened in school today?" "Nothing." "How was the spelling test?" "Okay.") it's a good idea to find out what undermined their enthusiasm. This sort of response is, of course, more or less normal for adolescents.

Loss of pride in schoolwork. Children with learning problems often become ashamed of their written work, which tends to be messy, incomplete, and liberally overwritten with the teacher's red pencil. Parents should be concerned if students stop showing them schoolwork or stop bringing it home.

UNEXPECTED UNDERACHIEVEMENT

The definitive characteristic of a learning disability is unexpected underachievement—the student is simply not doing as well in school as expected, given that student's intelligence, health, and opportunities. Taken by itself, however, underachievement is not a particularly strong indicator. As Alexander's story demonstrates, a great many factors can influence school performance. Most students who are having trouble working up to potential do *not* have learning disabilities; like Alexander, though, they may be in need of some form of help in order to do better.

Parents need to be particularly concerned whenever children have a hard time learning to read, write, perform elementary calculations, or sustain attention long enough to absorb an average lesson. Research suggests that the longer children struggle in these basic areas without appropriate help, the poorer their chances of catching up with typical peers, regardless of the source of the problem. It is therefore important for parents to monitor basic skills development carefully throughout elementary school. Support should be requested as soon as children fall behind in any basic subject, and if traditional means of providing extra help do not bring prompt improvement, requesting a learning-disabilities evaluation is a reasonable next step.

There are times when parents need to be concerned, even when youngsters are achieving at average levels. The expected achievement level for children who have superior intelligence is better than average: a nine-year-old fourth grader with an intelligence in the top 2 or 3 percent of her age group ought to be able to read fifth- and sixth-grade books, for example. Average school performance merits investigation when a child speaks, draws, or understands concepts exceptionally well or is doing very advanced work in other academic areas. Average academic work should also be investigated when it is accompanied by marked slowness or extraordinary effort—particularly if other warning signs discussed in this chapter are present.

Parents should also be concerned about unexpected *drops* in achievement. Learning disabilities often assert themselves at fairly predictable "stress points" in the educational process. Children with mild information processing problems may learn to read satisfactorily, for example, but develop academic difficulties around fourth grade when demands on reading comprehension typically increase dramatically. The need to organize schedules and larger amounts of information in junior high and new expectations concerning writing, research, and ability to work independently in high school may also cause students with learning problems to stumble. Typical students frequently experience temporary setbacks at these educational junctions, but if a child does not "bounce back" within one school year, parents should investigate without further delay.

PERSISTENT BEHAVIOR OR EMOTIONAL PROBLEMS

Children with learning disabilities have been observed to have a wide variety of behavioral problems. In some cases, these will be evident early. Children with attention deficit hyperactivity disorder, for example, are often cranky and irritable even as infants and they are no-

ALEXANDER

Alexander's mother and school psychologist referred him to a university clinic for evaluation. Because the ten-year-old fourth-grader had persistent written language difficulties, they wondered if it would be appropriate to identify him as "learning disabled."

Alexander's background revealed a great deal of turmoil. He had moved seventeen times and attended four different schools. His parents divorced when he was three years old. His mother had recently remarried, and Alexander was having trouble accepting a new authority figure in the house. To complicate family matters, it was apparent that Alexander's biological father disliked and avoided Alexander, while showering affection on his younger sister. Alexander claimed to have no close friends among his peers. He appeared to be a rather lonely and isolated little boy.

Testing showed that Alexander was an incredibly gifted child. His vocabulary and reasoning ability were equal to those of most adults. He scored at high school level in all areas of achievement with the exception of written expression, where his achievement was average for his age and grade. Alexander's spelling, sentence structure, and punctuation were perfect, but he took an unduly long time getting words down on paper. He also developed his ideas in such a detail-oriented way that it was impossible to guess the main thought he was trying to convey. In conversation as well, Alexander included many unnecessary details and had trouble getting to the point.

The evaluation revealed a captivating youngster struggling with many personal issues. Alexander's writing difficulties were found to be primarily due to very poor motor planning. He could not write a word without actually thinking about telling his hand how to move. It was also difficult for him to touch his thumb to each successive finger, figure out how to skip, or walk through a doorway without bumping into the frame. His mother reported that Alexander often dropped tableware when setting the table, and that getting a coin into a vending machine slot was very difficult for him. Given a little extra time to think, however, Alexander could perform these tasks successfully.

toriously difficult to live with as preschoolers (studies show that the stress experienced by parents of children with ADHD peaks when the children are between three and six years old). The problems youngsters with visual perception and language processing disabilities have understanding and remembering information can also create

Alexander's overly analytical personal style complicated his writing difficulties. The boy typically became so concerned with keeping track of minor points and details that he forgot his main ideas. When he was shown how to plan and outline, instructed to begin each paragraph with a topic sentence, and encouraged to dictate or tape-record his assignments rather than write them out, however, Alexander quickly began to produce work that was very superior for his age and grade.

Alexander's school psychologist and his parents thought he should be identified as "learning disabled." Without this label, they feared they would be unable to convince the boy's classroom teachers to give him extra time to do written work or allow him to tape-record his assignments. Alexander objected, however, adding that he would feel dumb going to a special teacher for help that could so easily be provided in his classroom. He pointed out that he could tape most of his assignments at home and transcribe them before handing them in.

Alexander was right. The child who is truly "learning disabled" requires a quality or intensity of instruction that cannot be provided in an ordinary classroom. Although Alexander had some significant weaknesses, simple adjustments in his educational program were all that would be needed to promote success. In their report, the evaluation team recommended that these minor modifications be made in Alexander's program. They also suggested weekly counseling for emotional issues, and they strongly encouraged Alexander's parents to seek out and involve their son in programs for gifted children. In addition, the team explained Alexander's weaknesses to him and described how he could work around them.

Fortunately, Alexander's school proved cooperative, and his teachers implemented the evaluation's recommendations. If they had not, however, assigning Alexander a "handicapped" label might have been the only way to get support for him. This is how rigid educational systems can *create* disabilities instead of minimizing them. There are always fewer "disabled" students in classrooms where teachers are flexible and skilled at individualizing instruction.

Adapted from Smith, C. R. *op cit.*

an impression that these youngsters are rude or disobedient. These behaviors have far more to do with neurology, however, than any conscious choices made by the child.

When children with learning disabilities start school, behavior problems start multiplying. As Joe's story poignantly illustrates, frus-

JOE

I always would end up in the boneheaded reading section. . . . All of my friends were over on the other side, and I was over with those "others." I hated being over with the other kids. They were the ones the "cool" kids picked on. It was a pain to be with them. I was really scared about something rubbing off on me. And I am sure now that they felt the same about me. . . .

It was funny, I always knew I have a problem learning like everybody else, but I always knew I wasn't dumb. I was scared all the time of being thought dumb, but in my heart I knew I wasn't. I hated being set apart. It made everything so tense for me.

So, like a lot of learning-disabled kids I was beginning my career of sticking out, being different. I was noisy, not because I wanted the negative attention it got me, but because I needed and wanted acceptance from my peers and couldn't figure out how to be one of them.

I felt different enough from my classmates that stress began piling upon stress. Soon I couldn't trust anything. If a teacher were to ask me what county I lived in, I could be thinking "Gallatin County" and out would pop "America." This would happen often. The classroom would be disrupted and the teacher would be mad. I didn't want to be a smart Alec, but the teacher thought I did and my classmates thought I did. If the principal became involved he thought I did, and heck, even my parents began to think I did. . . .

There were times I would do or say something and my friends would look at me like I was from another planet. It would mostly happen to me when I would come upon a group of my friends somewhere and try to join the conversation. I would listen in a group and then give the group my ideas. When I did that, the conversation would die and they would all look at me.

tration and anxiety over schoolwork combined with painful lack of success in social relationships can have a powerful impact on a student's emotional state. How children react to this stress depends on precise circumstances and the child's temperament. While some are able to bounce back from academic disappointment, others become angry, hostile, withdrawn, or depressed. Emotional upheaval is not always obvious at school, but it is usually apparent at home. One mother remembers: "When my daughter began school, it seemed like she developed a split personality. She tried very hard to be a good girl

I'd die a thousand deaths. . . .

I thought people were starting to laugh at me and maybe even call me dumb, stupid, or retarded. I was never sure, but to me it felt that way, and I started to react to these feelings. What I started to do was go totally nuts every time the word *dumb* or a synonym of it was associated with me. I beat up people for even thinking I was dumb.

A close friend took me aside one day and talked to me about how many people were scared of me and asked if that was what I wanted. The answer was easy: "No, I don't want anyone scared of me." So I came up with another answer, and that was the one I stayed with for a long time. I just went quiet, and just didn't join things as much. . . .

I hated that part of me that I couldn't seem to control . . .

I was totally lost. I was going farther and farther down a road I didn't like, and I was getting into more and more trouble. I was starting to get caught skipping classes, and my parents weren't happy with me. I was feeling angrier and I wasn't having much luck expressing it. I would be in class, trying to listen to the teacher and not be a nuisance, and something—anything—would happen and I'd get mad. I would be in the hall walking just after class, and rage would just start welling up in me. I would reach over and smack a locker and bust up my knuckles.

The people around me would look at me like I was a totally freaked-out person. The sad fact was that I was feeling freaked out. . . . I was pulling farther away from everybody around me, and I wasn't talking to people anymore. Not talking was driving me crazy, but I was scared to open up.

There were people who were reaching out to me and trying to help me, but I'd just blow them off as fast as I could.

Adapted from *Cookie and I*. Reprinted with permission of Joseph Lair.

in the classroom and got glowing behavior reports from her teachers. Then she came home and kicked furniture and yelled at everybody in the family for the rest of the day."

Behavior problems in the classroom or a change of mood at home can be the first signs of a learning problem. Sadly, they are not always recognized as such; instead, they may be perceived as defects in the child's character or personality. The unfortunate outcome is that adults—teachers and parents alike—may see academic problems as resulting from undesirable behavior, instead of the other way around.

Young people with learning disabilities are forever being accused of being stubborn, insensitive, lazy, irresponsible, careless, and uncooperative. Their low achievement is blamed on indifference to their parents' and their teachers' wishes and unwillingness to apply themselves. Such misperceptions can have disastrous consequences: not only do conflicts with adults over these issues add to a child's stress level, but in the absence of any other explanation students all too quickly come to accept these negative views of themselves as correct. Since youngsters who have decided that they are "no good" generally find it easier to conform to negative expectations than to rise above them, a vicious downward spiral can thus be created.

To avoid this kind of self-perpetuating defeat, parents need to recognize behavior problems as what they usually are—cries for help. Persistent misbehavior generally indicates that children's needs are out of synch with their environments in some important respect (a learning disability is only one of many possibilities). Emotional problems such as excessive fear or anger also suggest that a child is under some kind of stress and that intervention is needed. It is seldom wise to delay addressing emotional or behavioral issues in the hope that the child is "going through a phase" and will outgrow them. Problems in the areas described below seldom resolve themselves, and most often get worse with time. Children who have developed behavior or emotional problems may need a program that combines professional counseling with intervention at school.

Persistent problems in the areas listed below, combined with underachievement, should be addressed by a psychological *and* an educational evaluation:

Excessive anger or hostility. This may be expressed verbally (sarcasm, cursing and name calling) or physically (destroying property, bullying, fighting, tantrums, and rages).

Excessive anxiety. Fears may not appear connected with school: a child might develop excessive anxiety about strangers or separation from parents, for example.

Depression. Symptoms may include isolation, feelings of sadness or pessimism about the future, loss of interest in activities once enjoyed, changes in weight or appetite, changes in sleep patterns, feelings of guilt or worthlessness, fatigue or loss of energy, restlessness or irritability, and inability to concentrate or make decisions. The National Mental Health Association recommends seeking professional help if five or more of these symptoms persist for longer than two weeks.

Escapist behavior. This may include excessive fantasizing and day-dreaming, or obsessive involvement with television or video and adventure games; it can later include drug and alcohol abuse and promiscuous sexual activity.

Thrill-seeking behavior. Such children enjoy placing themselves in danger and "living on the edge." They may be attracted to heights, speed, violence, or illegal activity.

Antisocial/oppositional behavior. This is a willful refusal to obey rules or comply with authority (which is not to be confused with *inability* to comply or to understand what authorities want). It typically involves repeated conflicts with adults and truancy; it may also include substance abuse and such criminal activities as setting fires, theft, and vandalism.

DECLINING CONFIDENCE AND SELF-ESTEEM

Loss of confidence and self-esteem is perhaps the most common "side effect" of a learning disability. All too often, children blame the problems associated with these handicaps (low achievement in school, failure to live up to parental expectations, lack of acceptance by peers) on themselves. They assume that they are stupid because they do not do well in school, and that they are unlikable because they do not have hordes of friends. It can be heartbreaking to hear how mercilessly these kids regard themselves. One mother remembers her first-grader concluding: "Mommy, even the dumb kids in the class can do this stuff, so I must be *dumber* than dumb, whatever that is." Even after learning problems have been identified, youngsters may continue to berate themselves for needing extra help and being "different." There is probably no society that values conformity as much as a classroom. Children all too easily define being different as being a misfit and a loser.

If these negative self-impressions are not addressed, a child's emotional well-being is likely to be affected, as described in the preceding section. Low self-esteem also rapidly undermines academic motivation. Youngsters with learning disabilities are exceedingly vulnerable to a condition known as *learned helplessness.* This term was coined by well-known psychologist Martin Seligman. In studies with animals, Seligman demonstrated that when experience teaches a creature that its efforts have little impact on its circumstances, the creature becomes passive and stops trying to influence events. In one experiment, dogs were trained to avoid an uncomfortable electric shock by jumping over a barrier. Most learned to escape the shock promptly, but dogs who had previously been given shocks they could not escape proved unable to learn this task. Convinced that they were helpless, these animals made little effort to save themselves even when provided with the opportunity.

Studies examining student attitudes reveal that the same phenomenon applies in the classroom. Long-term low achievers tend to see themselves as unable to learn; they anticipate failure and are far less persistent than students who believe there is a relationship between hard work and success. Once a student stops trying, of course, continued failure is pretty much guaranteed. Belief in one's ability to succeed is therefore essential for any kind of achievement. One study of students with learning disabilities determined that self-concept and motivation were far more powerful predictors of academic progress than intelligence!

Parents need to be concerned, then, when they hear negative self-talk: "I'm dumb," "I'm hopeless," "Nobody likes me," "I can't do anything right," and so on. Alarms should also go off if a child makes frequent use of "I can't," whether in regard to his or her ability to add, dance, play sports, or talk to the opposite sex. (One wise teacher we know encourages students who say "I can't" to add "yet" to the end of the sentence.) If students seem to have become discouraged about schoolwork, it is important to draw teachers' attention to the problem as early as possible, and to see what can be done about restructuring tasks so that students can start experiencing success. In the long run, showing students what kind of effort produces results ("See? You practiced with the new method, and you went up to a B in spelling!") is a far more effective motivator than external incentives and rewards ("Okay, five dollars if you bring your spelling grade up to a B, and for an A you get ten"). Once students start achieving, success becomes its own reward, and external inducements may be unnecessary.

It is also important to remember that parental attitudes have a major impact on children's self-esteem. Unfortunately, some parents of children with learning disabilities promote helplessness by having low expectations. Studies show that such parents tend to regard failures as indicative of their youngsters' true ability, while they view success as resulting from factors beyond the child's control. If a child comes home with an A on a test, for example, these parents might say, "Well, you made some lucky guesses" or "I guess the teacher was in a good mood." Children exposed to this attitude see little relationship between personal effort and achievement. Working hard to solve problems therefore makes no sense to them.

Positive parents, on the other hand, view their children as essentially capable and competent—even when they are having problems in school. When problems occur, these parents look for causes that do not involve questioning the child's basic ability. Presented with an F, they may say, "Well, you did not get a good night's sleep before that exam" or "You can do better next time if you put more time and effort into studying." Children exposed to this outlook understand that there are things they can do to influence events and bring about positive change. These children can usually be counted on to apply themselves to problems, and they derive personal satisfaction from overcoming them.

It is therefore extremely important for parents of children with learning problems to maintain a positive and encouraging attitude. Your most important job as a parent is to convey to your children that they can succeed; helping them find the means to do so comes second. The fact is, the most skillful teaching in the world will not do much for a child who lacks the will to try. "Self-confidence is the magic ingredient that we can't always provide," one teacher says; "The kids who have it usually learn it at home—and they always rise to the top."

There is one final warning signal that should not be ignored: parental instinct. Very often, when students with learning disabilities are identified, we hear parents (most often a child's mother) say, "I *knew* something was wrong; I was sure there was more to it than immaturity" (or "getting used to the new teacher," "the new book," "paying more attention," or "trying harder"). Parents frequently allow themselves to be talked out of these gut feelings, however, by professionals who are supposed to know more about child development or education. Our natural, human desire to believe our children are perfect (or at least normal) sometimes contributes to this process. When a teacher says a student who is falling behind may outgrow the difficulty, or that there's nothing wrong that can't be overcome with a little extra effort, who wouldn't prefer to believe that rather than accept the possibility that the child may have a handicap or other serious problem?

Our experience, however, is that "gut instinct" is trustworthy. Your knowledge of your child, your sense of your child's happiness and well-being, and your feelings about what the child ought to be able to do are as valuable as any of the other types of information discussed in this chapter. What this means in practical terms is that if the school's explanations for your child's lack of progress don't make sense to you—or if you lack confidence in the solutions being proposed—you should trust your judgment and keep looking for other answers. To do so, you may have to learn to be assertive with professionals who think you are overreacting, overprotective, overly emotional, or overinvolved. We find that the best way to counter those opinions is to become well-informed and to be persistent; this is a virtually irresistible combination.

It also helps to remember that the law is on your side. If your child is falling behind in school and you believe that he or she needs an evaluation for developmental delays or learning disabilities, you are entitled to ask for one without charge from your public school district. If your gut is telling you that your son or daughter has special needs, there is therefore no reason to hesitate about getting professional help to identify the problem. Prompt investigation is in the best interest of your child. Whether or not a learning disability is identified, an evaluation will provide valuable information about how your child learns, and it will suggest ways to improve both comfort in school and school performance.

5

THE LEARNING DISABILITIES
EVALUATION

In order to determine that a learning disability exists, it is necessary to show that a child's learning problems are consistent with the description set forth in the Individuals with Disabilities Education Act (IDEA), a large package of federal legislation enacted by Congress to protect the rights of students with all types of disabilities and their families. IDEA defines learning disabilities as follows:

"Specific learning disability" means a disorder in one or more of the basic psychological processes involved in understanding or in using language, spoken or written, which may manifest itself in an imperfect ability to listen, think, speak, read, write, spell, or to do mathematical calculations. The term includes such conditions as perceptual handicaps, brain injury, minimal brain dysfunction, dyslexia, and developmental aphasia. The term does not include children who have learning problems which are primarily the result of visual, hearing or motor handicaps, of mental retardation, of emotional disturbance, or of environmental, cultural or economic disadvantage.

Federal law also specifies the criteria that must be used to identify learning disabilities. States may write their own guidelines, but they can be no narrower, or more exclusive, than these criteria:

A team may determine that a child has a specific learning disability if:
   (1) The child does not achieve commensurate with his or her age

and ability levels in one or more of the areas listed in paragraph (2) of this section, when provided with learning experiences appropriate for the child's age and ability levels; and

(2) The team finds that a child has a severe discrepancy between achievement and intellectual ability in one or more of the following areas:

Oral expression
Listening comprehension
Written expression
Basic reading skill
Reading comprehension
Mathematics calculation
Mathematics reasoning

The team may *not* identify a child as having a specific learning disability if the severe discrepancy between ability and achievement is primarily the result of

(1) A visual, hearing or motor handicap;
(2) Mental retardation;
(3) Emotional disturbance; or
(4) Environmental, cultural or economic disadvantage.

[Note: IDEA recognizes ten different types of disability. Students with disabilities in the first three areas mentioned above may qualify for special education services under guidelines described elsewhere in the act.]

In other words, an evaluation for learning disabilities must not only prove that there is a significant gap between a child's potential to learn and his or her actual performance in one or more key academic areas, it must also determine that the child has had adequate learning opportunities and investigate and rule out a variety of other possible causes of underachievement. No one test—and no one individual—can possibly be expected to provide all the information and expertise needed to make these judgments. The law therefore requires public school districts to use multidisciplinary teams of professionals in the identification process. Teams are also required to use a variety of assessment methods when investigating learning disabilities.

Members of assessment teams have a wide range of tools and techniques available to them for gathering information. The goal is to use as many methods as needed to develop a well-rounded view of the student. A comprehensive evaluation goes far beyond pinpointing a child's learning weaknesses; it should also identify the student's strengths and determine how his or her performance is affected by different teaching approaches and environments. While the selection of evaluation methods will vary according to the nature of a student's problems, a thorough comprehensive learning disabilities evaluation ought to include the following:

• A review of school records and an examination of the student's work

• Preparation of a medical and social history covering major aspects of the student's growth and development

• Observation of the student in the classroom (in some cases, it might also be desirable to observe the child at home)

• Interviews with the student and important individuals in the student's life (parents, teachers, others who spend significant amounts of time with the child)

• Tests and other assessment measures to establish learning potential, academic achievement levels, and information-processing abilities

• An examination of the curriculum and a review of the teaching methods and materials that have been used with the child so far

This work is usually done by learning specialists, psychologists, and social workers employed by the school system. When you consider that evaluating a child for learning disabilities can occupy four or more professionals and is typically spread out over several weeks, it becomes easier to understand why school districts are reluctant to undertake assessments without clear cause. It has been estimated, in fact, that as much as 40 percent of the cost of educating students with learning disabilities is related to the painstaking procedures that must be followed both to identify them and to monitor their progress.

If a comprehensive, multidisciplinary approach to evaluation is not taken, however, students' learning problems may be misunderstood. Consider the students whose stories appear in this chapter. Maria and Jessica were both incorrectly identified until home visits and interviews with their parents placed their learning difficulties in a broader context. Rachel's baffling writing habits would never have been explained by testing (oddly, adults often forget to *ask* students why they do what they do; this step yielded key information in Rachel's case). In contrast, Casey's ability to compensate for his disability on tests masked visual memory problems that were actually quite severe. One special educator compares investigating learning problems to the way a detective solves mysteries. "Detectives have to gather evidence from as many sources as possible," she explains. "Otherwise they might end up arresting the wrong guy. We also have to gather evidence from as many sources as possible in order to avoid drawing the wrong conclusions about a student's lack of progress in school."

The most important factors affecting the quality of a learning disabilities evaluation, then, are as follows:

- The experience and skill of the members of the evaluation team

- The variety and relevance of approaches they employ

- The quality of the specific tests and other assessment tools they select

An evaluation's outcome can also be influenced by the way different localities interpret federal law. As we have explained, "a severe discrepancy" between achievement and intellectual potential must be shown to exist before a learning disability can be identified. Each state is left to define for itself, however, what "severe discrepancy" means. Some states do so in a way that seems intended to include the greatest numbers of students with learning problems, while others seem determined to provide special education services to only the most severely affected. This helps explain why more than 9 percent of the students in Massachusetts have been identified as having learning disabilities while fewer than half as many (4.5 percent) have been similarly identified in the neighboring state of Vermont. Alaska has determined that 7.5 percent of its students have learning disabilities, while Georgia has identified fewer than 3 percent (currently the lowest rate in the nation).

Authorities have pointed out that policies concerning the identification of students in need of special education services sometimes seem to be motivated by economic concerns at least as much as by concerns for student welfare. It costs more to educate students with learning disabilities, and while federal reimbursements offset a small portion of the increased expense, restricting the number of students who get special education help can be viewed as a cost-containment measure. It has been argued that a student's chances of getting help for a learning disability are greater in relatively "wealthy" states (like Massachusetts) than in states where the average family income is lower and school districts have fewer resources. Whether or not this is true, local special education policies can have a major impact on determining who becomes eligible for services.

Given all these considerations, what can a parent do to ensure that an evaluation for learning disabilities is thorough and fair? Taking the following steps will help you gain the most useful information from the assessment process.

1. BECOME INFORMED ABOUT FEDERAL AND LOCAL REGULATIONS

Information about eligibility for special education services is available from your public school district. The publication you receive should include a summary of the legal rights of students with disabilities and their families, and it should also explain what formulas or guidelines are used in your state to establish that a learning disability exists. Must students be functioning one or more years below grade level in some subject to qualify for special education services? Or does the state use a "discrepancy formula" that compares achievement with intelligence test scores? The figure on page 94 explains the use of standard deviations to determine discrepancy; a majority of states use some variation of this formula. While all equations for establishing learning disability are arbitrary, imperfect, and to some degree unfair, these are nevertheless the rules you are going to have to work with, so make sure you understand them.

2. INVESTIGATE THE INVESTIGATORS

When seeking an assessment for learning disabilities, you have two choices: ask for a free evaluation from your school district (this request should be made in writing, and directed to the special education department or to the principal of your child's school) or pay for an independent assessment. Either way, find out exactly who your child will see over the course of the evaluation. What are their qualifications and areas of expertise? Do they have specific experience in the suspected area of disability? Are team members sensitive to cultural issues that you feel are important, and to social or emotional issues that could be affecting your child's performance? Who will coordinate the activities of different team members, keep track of test results, and make final recommendations? Whom should you contact if you have questions?

If you are seeking a free evaluation from your public school dis-

JESSICA

Jessica was brought to a university psychoeducational teaching clinic by her mother, who refused to accept the results of a school assessment that had determined Jessica was mentally retarded. The seven-year-old had made almost no progress in first grade, and she had performed in the retarded range on a standard IQ test. In addition, the psychologist who had administered the test indicated that Jessica's responses seemed random on many tasks. It was as if she did not even understand what she was expected to do.

Jessica's mother told the clinic staff that the child's father had died five months ago. He had battled cancer for five years, and during that time the family's activities had revolved around his needs. The family was supported by public assistance. There was barely enough income to cover the most basic necessities; there was no money for "extras" for Jessica or her two younger brothers. None of the children had received regular dental and medical care or attended preschool programs.

A visit to Jessica's home found it barren of books, children's games, or toys. Jessica's brothers were amusing themselves by throwing themselves at a wall and seeing who rebounded farthest. Jessica's mother confirmed that the children had never owned blocks, puzzles, picture books, or crayons. It seemed possible that Jessica's poor performance on the IQ test was at least partially because she was unfamiliar with the types of tasks the test asked her to perform.

Clinic staff decided to administer another intelligence test. Before doing so, they spent some time playing with Jessica, using "games" that were similar to the tasks on the test: for example, the girl was encouraged to point out similarities between objects, copy designs, and create sequences from pictured events. Before taking the test, Jessica was reminded to approach the questions in the same way she had when playing. This time she scored well within the normal range. The first test had tapped Jessica's relatively empty cultural experience, not her cognitive abilities.

The clinic began to look for other explanations for Jessica's poor performance in school. Eventually she was found to have language processing disabilities that required special services from the speech pathologist and a learning disabilities specialist. When these were provided, her schoolwork began to improve. Clinic staff also helped Jessica's mother find free preschool programs for her two boys and guided her to a parenting workshop where she could learn more about her children's needs and develop her own parenting skills.

Adapted from Smith, C. R. *op. cit.*

trict, you may not have much choice about who is assigned to your child's evaluation team. Experienced parents note, however, that it can pay to "ask around" among parents of students who have learning disabilities to see if any school district personnel are known to be particularly sensitive and skilled with evaluations. A psychologist at a different school may have a good reputation for working with children from particular minority groups, for example, or there may be one special education teacher who has a great deal of experience sorting out reading problems. If this is the case, you can request that this professional be assigned to your child's evaluation. Your school district's special education department should be able to direct you to support organizations for parents of students with disabilities in your area; these organizations are an excellent place to start when looking for information about evaluations.

Is a private evaluation likely to be better than those done by the public school district? Not necessarily. Federal guidelines concerning evaluations apply only to agencies receiving public funds. Private agencies and practitioners can (and sometimes do) get away with "quickie" evaluations that could overlook significant factors contributing to a student's academic problems. If the evaluation is thorough, it is probably also going to be expensive; fees for private assessments can run into the hundreds or even thousands of dollars, depending on how many specialists are involved. (Health insurance may cover part of these costs, and some agencies do offer sliding fees based on income.) In addition, school district policies on outside evaluations vary: the district may accept a private assessment in place of its own, or it may insist on doing its own evaluation as well before providing services. For all of these reasons, most parents prefer to start with a school district evaluation, reserving the right to follow up with a private evaluation if they disagree with the school district's findings.

A private evaluation, however, does give you more control of the assessment process. Not only can you select the professionals who will be involved, but you can also choose whether or not to share the information they obtain with your school district. Beginning with a private evaluation might make sense if you have reason to lack confidence in your school district's special education department, or if you are considering seeking private help for the child rather than obtaining special education services in school. Professionals who conduct evaluations can be found in private practice, as well as connected with colleges and universities, hospitals, and mental health

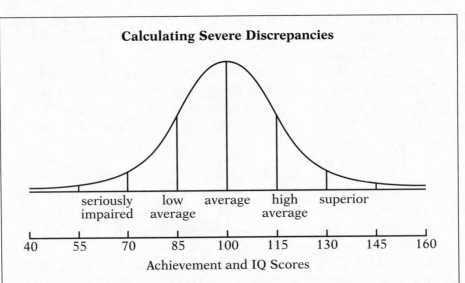

Calculating Severe Discrepancies

seriously impaired   low average   average   high average   superior

40   55   70   85   100   115   130   145   160

Achievement and IQ Scores

Each section of the chart represents one *standard deviation*. Most school districts state that a student's ability (as judged by an IQ test) and achievement (as judged by an achievement test) must be 1½ to 2 standard deviations apart (1½ to 2 sections apart on the chart) in order to determine that a learning disability exists. For example:

Jim has an IQ of 100 and a reading score of 70. These scores are two standard deviations apart—enough to identify a learning disability in most states.

Jennifer has an IQ of 100 and a math score of 85. Although she is behind, one standard deviation is considered within the normal range. She will need extra help in the classroom but will probably not be identified as "learning disabled."

Darryl has an IQ of 130. His writing score is 105. Even though his achievement is average, it does not reflect his very superior intelligence. Darryl's discrepancy of 1½ standard deviations will identify a learning disability in some states.

Alana's IQ of 70 is considered retarded. Her reading comprehension score is 40, which suggests that she also has a specific learning disability. While not all states will recognize a mentally retarded student as "learning disabled" also, it should be recognized that Alana will need unusually intense instruction in reading comprehension in addition to other special education services.

clinics. Your school district's department of special education can provide you with a list of people in your community who do this sort of work (they are required to provide this information to parents seeking second opinions). Parent support groups are also a good source of information about independent evaluations.

3. ASK ABOUT TESTS

Federal law provides very clear guidelines in the matter of testing for learning disabilities. Tests must be conducted on a one-to-one basis (previously taken group tests are not acceptable for assessment purposes), and given in the student's native language. The team is also required to use tests that are free of "cultural bias," meaning they must not put children from racial or culturally underrepresented groups at a disadvantage (this is much easier said than done, as we will see below). Within these guidelines, however, evaluation teams have a vast array of different test instruments to choose from.

It is important to understand that every test comes with its own set of strengths and weaknesses—there is no one test or set of tests that works well for all students in all situations. Tests must therefore be selected with care, on a case-by-case basis. The team coordinator ought to be able to answer these questions about the testing proposed for your child:

Which tests do you plan to use, and what are they intended to measure? At the very least, the evaluation team will have to administer a test to estimate learning potential (usually an intelligence test) and one or more tests to establish achievement levels in reading, writing, and/or mathematics. These are needed to establish that a discrepancy between performance and intellectual ability exists. The team should then follow up with measures designed to determine which types of information processing give the student the most trouble in areas of weakness. Are the student's math problems, for example, due to difficulties with verbal logic and sequencing, distorted perception, sloppy handwriting, or a faulty memory? In a careful evaluation, a variety of methods will be used to assess a student's abilities. Paper-and-pencil tests alone, for example, would not identify problems a student might have producing or understanding speech.

In our Appendix you will find a series of charts describing some assessment measures frequently used in evaluations for learning disabilities. If the evaluation team proposes tests other than those on the list (there are literally hundreds of tests to choose from, and we could not describe them all), ask how the test works and what sort of information it is expected to provide.

Why have these particular tests been selected? What makes them the best choices for this child, and for this child's particular type of learning problem? "We always use these tests" or "These are the tests our people are trained to use" are not satisfactory answers to this question. The evaluation team should be able to explain why the tests' content or design is appropriate for your child's age, experience, background, and/or learning patterns. In addition, the team should select tests that have proven *reliable* and *valid* (meaning that the test scores consistently from one administration to the next, and it has been demonstrated that the test actually measures what its authors say it will measure).

Will my child's learning problems interfere with taking any of the tests? A written test would put a student with weak handwriting skills at a disadvantage in all areas being tested, for example, and the results of such a test could not be considered fair or valid. Similarly, a heavily verbal intelligence test would not reflect the true thinking power of a child who has language processing problems.

Are test contents appropriate for my child's linguistic and cultural background? The contents of standardized tests tend to be keyed to the majority culture. Students from other cultures may be at a disadvantage when taking these tests, as Maria's story shows. Many experts feel that overdependence on culturally biased standardized tests is largely responsible for the fact that children from racial and cultural minority groups are over-represented in the special education population. Since there are few reliable tests keyed to minority cultures, the use of alternative information-gathering methods is very important when evaluating minority students. It is important that the team include professionals who are familiar with such alternative techniques, and with the culture of the child being evaluated.

If English is not the student's first language, or if a language other than English is spoken at home, testing should be conducted in the language in which the student is most fluent. State education departments often maintain lists of professionals who are qualified to test in languages other than English and can supply this information to local school districts.

If a test compares my child's work with that of a larger group of students, what does the larger group look like? Many tests rate a child's performance according to how it compares with that of children in a larger group. For many standardized tests, though, the comparison group is composed primarily of middle-income white students. If the

MARIA

Five-year-old Maria had failed her kindergarten screening test and been referred for additional testing. A school-administered IQ test found that she performed within the retarded range. A self-contained class for retarded children was recommended. Very upset, Maria's father insisted on a second opinion.

A home visit found that Maria's mother spoke only Italian. Her father, an Italian-American, spoke Italian at home until a year ago, when he realized that Maria needed to start learning English. One year of English was not enough, however, to allow Maria to perform well on the highly verbal intelligence test she had been given. In addition, the child's mother—admitting that she was somewhat overprotective—explained that Maria had led a very sheltered existence. The child had never used scissors or a knife, played unsupervised, or helped with cooking or other chores. Maria's mother was proud of her management of the household and boasted that Maria did not have to do anything—even dress herself! Television was not allowed in the home because of fears that it would warp Maria's mind. As a result, Maria's understanding of American culture was limited; she did not have the same fund of general information as other children her age. She could identify the characters of Italian fairy tales, for example, but not George Washington, Cinderella, or Bert and Ernie.

It was obvious that the IQ test given to Maria had been culturally inappropriate. It was suggested that Maria continue with kindergarten and also be allowed to watch some quality children's television programs (such as "Mister Rogers' Neighborhood" and "Sesame Street") at home to help her develop her language skills. Her parents were urged to read to her from English-language children's books and also to involve her in out-of-home activities (trips to museums, children's theater, or the zoo) to increase her exposure to American culture. These measures brought some improvement in her English, but by the end of first grade Maria's language skills were still sufficiently delayed that language therapy was recommended. Maria is now in third grade and doing average work; her language therapy will be discontinued next year. Maria's parents continue to support her, and thanks largely to their love and encouragement she is a happy, well-adjusted, and charming little girl.

Adapted from Smith, C. R. *ibid.*

child being tested is a white, middle-income student who has had average educational opportunities, the test may provide useful information. If the child comes from a different kind of background, however, the comparison might not be fair. An "army brat" who has attended seven schools in four states and three foreign countries, for example, might have strengths very different from those tested on most standardized exams. Whenever possible, a child's performance should be compared to that of students from similar socioeconomic and educational backgrounds.

How similar are the problems in the test to problems encountered in the classroom? The most useful tests relate closely to what students have been taught. Unfortunately, students are sometimes given standardized tests that have little or nothing to do with the school's curriculum. A test might evaluate spelling by asking students to identify the correctly spelled words on a list, for example, when in the classroom students write spelling words from dictation (a task that involves very different mental skills). Many tests evaluate only a narrow range of skills that may or may not be representative of the instruction the child has received.

When the test relates poorly to the curriculum, "problems" identified by the test may simply indicate that the student has had no experience with the area being tested. To avoid this pitfall, some teams use *curriculum-based assessment* (CBA), which evaluates achievement on the basis of how well a student has mastered actual class content compared with other students in the same class or grade. Since CBA tests how well a child has learned what has actually been taught (as opposed to some testmaker's idea of what students of a certain age should know) and compares his or her performance with that of other students who have been taught the same thing, its results can be more accurate and of greater value in identifying learning disabilities than those of standardized tests. You should ask if your team plans to use CBA to any extent. (Curriculum-based assessment is also useful for keeping tabs on a child's progress in school. For more on CBA, see Chapter 8.)

Is special training needed to administer, score, or interpret any of these tests? If so, do members of the evaluation team have the required training? It is important to understand that interpreting the scores of *any* test requires experience and judgment. Those responsible for interpreting test scores should be thoroughly familiar with all the tests used and understand each test's advantages and disadvantages. In addition, examiners must have the skill and sensitivity to interpret scores in the light of each individual student's educational experience, cultural heritage, family background, emotional state, and level of motivation; conclusions based on numbers alone are seldom valid.

Where, when, and how will the tests be given? Will the child be tested at school or taken to another facility? Will most of the tests be given by the same individual, or will many different people be involved? Will the tests be scheduled over a reasonable period of time so that the child will not become tired? Children need time to become accustomed to new surroundings and new people; they cannot be expected to do their best when they are unfamiliar with the person testing them, the test environment, or if tested for four or five hours straight. Whenever possible, arrange for the student to meet the people who will conduct the evaluation and visit the test site(s) in advance. And while everyone may be anxious to know the outcome of the evaluation, it is usually best to spread testing out over a period of several weeks.

Testing is a complex and controversial subject—one on which authorities often disagree. It is worthwhile from the beginning, however, to sort out how tests are selected and used. Not only are tests an important part of the identification process, but they help guide education planning. If a child is found to have a disability, periodic retesting will also be required to evaluate academic progress. Discovering how your child reacts to different testing situations and which tests most accurately reflect his or her strengths and weaknesses therefore has long-term benefits.

4. FIND OUT WHAT OTHER KINDS OF INFORMATION WILL BE COLLECTED

Tests can never be relied upon to provide the whole picture in a learning-disabilities evaluation. Tests cannot establish, for example, whether illness or other problems have compromised a child's learning opportunities, determine whether materials or methods used by a particular teacher are contributing to a child's problems, or evaluate what role emotional issues might be playing in preventing a child from working up to his or her potential. Evaluation teams typically use interviews with students, parents, and teachers, observation of the child at work and play, and reviews of school and medical records to address these concerns. The team may also use informal methods like trial teaching (a process of systematically trying out different instructional techniques) to shed additional light on how a student thinks and approaches academic tasks.

An understanding of a child's family background and home environment is usually essential for interpreting learning patterns. For this, the team will need your cooperation; share as much information as you can about your child's growth and behavior. If you have any concerns about the child's physical, social, or emotional development, alert the team promptly. The team will also want to know if there are any current health concerns, or if there are family circumstances (such as a move, sibling conflicts, or the loss of a loved one) that might be affecting school performance. They may ask questions about your family in general: what you like to do for fun and recreation, for instance, or how you divide household responsibilities and handle discipline. They will very likely be interested in whether other family members have experienced any kind of problems in school. While such inquiries may seem nosy, the team is not trying to violate your privacy or blame you for your child's school difficulties. Remember that part of the process of investigating learning disabilities involves *ruling out* other possible causes of learning problems. Checking the home environment is standard procedure.

The team should be equally thorough about investigating the child's environment at school. Sadly, though, this is not always the case. Some evaluation teams operate under the narrow-minded assumption that since there is "something wrong" with the student, he or she should be the exclusive focus of the evaluation. As we explained earlier, however, the school's environment and educational practices can contribute significantly to learning problems. If the evaluation team does not seem aware of this, ask how they intend to determine if making the following adjustments would have an impact on your child's school performance:

Changing the setting. Does the student's performance improve in a room that is quieter, for example, or one that has fewer visual distractions? Might the child do better if he or she is seated closer to the teacher, or to the blackboard?

Changing methods of presentation. Does the student do better if given more visual cues, or if the teacher uses simpler language? Do hands-on projects hold the child's attention better than paper-and-pencil tasks?

Changing the curriculum. If a student is having trouble learning to read using the whole-language method, does adding a phonics component bring results? Has math become a struggle with memorization at the expense of understanding concepts?

Changing the task. Does the child do better if assignments are broken down into simpler components or stages? If information to be read is "previewed" by the teacher? If allowed to present information orally instead of in writing?

Changing motivational techniques. Does it help to offer the student feedback throughout a task, rather than wait until a finished assignment is handed in? Does an ungraded approach reduce anxiety and help the child focus better on the work?

Changing the time limits. Can the child do the work satisfactorily if allowed additional time?

If making these adjustments significantly improves a child's achievement, special education services may be unnecessary. Children should not be described as "learning disabled" if their needs can be accommodated by making reasonable changes in the instructional setting, task, or methods.

Of course, you will also want to find out if the team anticipates referring your child to any specialists for additional information. Does your child's eyesight, hearing, or speech need to be screened? Is physical, occupational, or speech therapy needed? Is a psychological examination recommended? If this kind of information is considered essential to the evaluation, these services will be performed at no cost to you. A team may also suggest that you consult specialists such as an audiologist, an opthalmologist, a neurologist, or an allergist at the conclusion of the evaluation. In those cases, following through on the recommendations is your responsibility, and the work is done at your expense.

5. PREPARE YOUR CHILD FOR THE EVALUATION

Do give your child as much information as you can about what is going to happen before the evaluation; failure to so only invites stress, confusion, and anxiety (all of which can affect evaluation results). The straightforward approach usually works best. Tell children that an effort is going to be made to find out why they are experiencing difficulty in school, and that some people are going to want to talk to them, engage them in some different educational activities, and give them some tests. Explain that these are *not* like tests at school—the child cannot pass or fail, because the tests are only intended to pro-

RACHEL

Rachel turned five right before entering kindergarten. At the beginning of the year she could write her name in capitals, but she sometimes reversed letters—fairly common in this age group. Rachel's teacher noted that the child's drawing ability was far beyond age expectations: it showed excellent attention to detail and appreciation of spatial relationships. Rachel was also well coordinated and had good fine motor skills.

After about two months of school, Rachel began to write her name from right to left, reversing all of the letters. When her teacher corrected her, Rachel would respond irritably, "I know." The next day she would write her name correctly on one paper and in reverse on another. The teacher was confused and began to wonder if Rachel might have a learning disability. Yet the fact that Rachel could write her name correctly— combined with her excellent drawing skills—led the teacher to believe there was nothing wrong with the girl's visual perception abilities. Rachel also knew the difference between right and left and could indicate each direction correctly. Baffled, the teacher continued to monitor the situation and to remind Rachel that she should write from left to right.

Soon Rachel began to write other words in mirror-style writing. Exasperated, the teacher finally asked the little girl why she chose to write this way. Rachel responded, "This is the way I'm *supposed* to write in Hebrew!"

A call to Rachel's parents cleared up the issue. Rachel had begun Hebrew instruction in religious school at the same time she started kindergarten. Apparently she had decided to make the English language conform to Hebrew rules (Hebrew is written from right to left). Because Rachel had excellent visual perception skills and a keen sense of direction, it made sense to her that if you were going to reverse the direction of a word, you should reverse the direction of all the letters, too!

The possibility of delaying further instruction in Hebrew until Rachel had mastered the basics of writing in English was discussed, but in the end all this bright child needed was an explanation that different languages had different rules. By January, Rachel's writing (in both English and Hebrew) was perfect.

Adapted from Smith, C. R. *ibid.*

vide information on how the child learns. Encourage the child to give adults feedback throughout the assessment process: evaluators will want to know which tasks the child finds easy or hard, and they will appreciate any information they can get on how he or she approaches and solves problems. It may help to assure the child that if any test becomes too hard or frustrating, the evaluators will stop and move on to something else.

Also tell children as much as you can about where and when different stages of the evaluation will take place, and about the professionals who will be involved. Young children may need reassurance that the adults involved in the evaluation will be friendly and kind (by all means, introduce them to the evaluation professionals in advance if you can). For all students, it is important to emphasize that the point of the whole process is to find better ways of teaching them. Avoid explanations that blame or shame the child, such as "We want to find out why you're failing" or "We're going to figure out what's wrong with you."

Older children and adolescents may want to know much more about the evaluation process. We feel it is best to be as honest and open in answering their questions as possible; in general, the better youngsters understand why something is being done, the more cooperative they tend to be. The best approach is to arrange a preevaluation meeting with the team coordinator so the child can ask questions directly. *Never* try to trick a child into participating in an evaluation, or lie about what is going to take place—even if it might be unpleasant. Doing so will not protect the child in any way, and may very well result in undermining the trust your child places in you.

6. START KEEPING RECORDS *NOW*

Learning-disabilities evaluations generate enormous amounts of paper, much of which will be passed on to you. There will be papers requesting your permission to evaluate your child, papers notifying you of appointments and explaining your rights, test results and reports from the various professionals who see the child (request copies of these if they are not given to you), and a final report with recommendations. Since every stage of identifying and educating a child with disabilities is governed by federal and state law, some of these papers are actually legal documents; they are designed not only to give you information but to protect your rights and demonstrate that the school district is operating in compliance with regulations. Special education communications therefore need to be preserved with the same care you would give any other important legal records. Some parents like to use a looseleaf notebook to collect their papers, while others prefer folders or accordion files. Patricia McGill Smith, head of the National Parent Network on Disabilities (and the parent of a child with disabilities), suggests: "If you are not a naturally organized person, just get a box and throw all the paperwork in it. Then when you really need it, it will be there."

When might you need it? Documentation will be important in the event of any kind of dispute with the school district—if you feel an evaluation has been inadequate, for example, you will have to document your concerns (this may involve collecting even more paper from outside specialists). Documentation may also be needed to enforce programming. If the special education department determines that your child is entitled to have test questions read aloud, for example, this decision is legally binding on *all* of the child's teachers— a fact that may have to be explained to the high school chemistry teacher a couple of years down the road. You will also have to document the presence of a learning disability to qualify your child for special accommodations (extension of time limits, for instance) on national tests such as college entrance examinations, and to prove that the child is entitled to services beyond high school (children with disabilities are eligible for special vocational programs, reasonable accommodations at their jobs, and educational assistance in college). If you move, you will of course need records to show that your child is entitled to services in his or her new school.

An equally important reason for keeping these records is that they will be the foundation of your own efforts to understand how your child learns. Reports and other documents are the starting point for asking questions of educators, psychologists, and specialists. They can also help with problem-solving and serve as the inspiration for new ideas. (Does the psychologist's report say that your daughter suffers from low self-esteem, while noting elsewhere that her motor skills are exceptional? Perhaps she would benefit from involvement in after-school activities in which she would be likely to excel, such as sports or a crafts program.) So even if the papers you receive sometimes seem dense, repetitive, and so riddled with jargon you're not sure that they are written in English, get in the habit of saving them. You never know which ones you're going to need.

CASEY

Casey's mother insisted he did not know his addition and subtraction facts. His second-grade teacher was surprised to hear this. Casey had been slow to learn to read and was a poor speller, but he had always done quite well in arithmetic. Even on pop quizzes he usually got at least 80 percent of the problems right.

Alerted by his mother's concerns, however, the teacher observed Casey during the next two weekly math tests. She noticed that Casey attacked the tests in an unusual manner. He answered questions out of order, starting in the middle and then jumping around until all the problems were done. As usual, his scores were in the B to B-plus range.

Intrigued, the teacher took Casey aside and asked him why he did his tests this way. Somewhat embarrassed, Casey admitted that he had not succeeded in memorizing addition and subtraction facts like the other children in the class, but he had worked out a system for timed math quizzes. "First I find the easiest problem," he explained. "Like here, it's 7 + 1, which is easy to figure out: 8. Then I know that 7 + 2 has to be one more than 8, so I look for 7 + 2 and write 9. Then I find 7 + 3 and write 10, and next I look for 7 + 4 and write 11, and I go on like that until the time runs out."

Casey had figured out that subtraction facts also followed a sequence, so he used the same method for subtraction tests. When quizzed orally on math facts, however, it was obvious he had not memorized any of them—although he could add and subtract in his head well enough to produce correct answers if he was given a little time.

Casey was obviously a bright and resourceful lad. The fact that he was not retaining math facts, however, combined with his other academic difficulties, suggested to his teacher that he might have a learning disability. Casey's mother agreed to an evaluation. As it turned out, Casey did indeed have visual perception deficits that made it hard for him to remember many kinds of information. Casey was unable to picture things in his mind, which made tasks involving rote memorization very difficult. Imagining the spelling of irregular words was also beyond him. Casey read slowly because he had to sound words out as he went along: because he did not carry images of words in his head, he did not easily recognize words that he had seen before. Although he used his superior intelligence to compensate for these problems and was passing all his subjects, Casey's evaluation suggested that with special education support he could do much better than the B's and C's he was earning.

7. GIVE YOURSELF TIME TO DEAL WITH EVALUATION RESULTS

When the evaluation has been completed, you will be invited to a meeting to discuss the team's findings. If a disability has been documented, recommendations for special education services may also be made at this time. (If a child has been found to have a disability, the law requires services to begin immediately. If specific services are not discussed at your first meeting, a second meeting on implementation should be scheduled promptly.) At your initial meeting, a member of the evaluation team should be prepared to share assessment results with you, explain your child's learning strengths and weaknesses, and describe specific disabilities if any have been identified. Any discussion of educational placement should include an explanation of all the possible options. By law, your child must be educated in "the least restrictive environment" available. As a result, most children with learning disabilities remain in regular classrooms part of the time, with varying levels of special education support. (For more on educational options, see Part III, where placement and programming are discussed in detail.)

The school district *cannot* initiate services or assign your child to a special program without your permission (unless they are willing to go to court, an action that is usually reserved for protecting children's welfare in extreme cases). Therefore, before services can begin you will be required to consent to an Individualized Education Program (IEP) that specifies educational goals for your child for the next school year, outlines the methods that will be used to reach those goals, determines school placement, and specifies accommodations and special education services to be provided. The IEP is, in fact, a legal contract: once it has been approved, the school district *must* provide all the services described (if services are to be added or changed, the IEP must be formally amended). The IEP therefore needs to be prepared and read with care. Parents sometimes complain, however, that they felt pressed to approve an IEP before they fully understood the nature of their child's disability, the types of special education programs available, or their rights with respect to special education evaluations and program planning. "At my first meeting I was handed a thick evaluation report, an even thicker handbook of rights and regulations, and a proposed IEP," one mother remembers. "It was a lot of new information, much of it legal and technical. I felt so overwhelmed and intimidated I figured I'd better just go along with the professionals. I agreed to their recommendations, hoping I could make sense of it all later."

School districts don't usually mean to confuse parents and hustle them into decisions, but professionals sometimes forget that parents are not as familiar with the law and the language of special education as they are. For your child's sake, however, it is important that you take all the time you need to understand evaluation results and recommendations. If you have already educated yourself about laws governing the identification and education of students with learning disabilities, you will be ahead of the game. It is also reasonable to ask for a copy of the evaluation report in advance so that you have a chance to review it, share it with others who are concerned about your child's welfare, and prepare questions before your initial meeting. At the meeting, do not hesitate to ask for plain-English translations of any terms or language you do not understand; if the time allotted for the meeting runs out before all your questions have been answered, then ask for another meeting. The law protects your right to think recommendations over before making a decision, to seek a second opinion, and to participate in all aspects of education planning (including the preparation of the IEP), so there is no reason to feel pressured into premature action.

You may find you also need time to cope with the emotional impact of an evaluation. Many parents say the news that their child had a disability hit them very hard—even when the handicap was comparatively mild, or when they already strongly suspected something was wrong. The weeks following identification of a learning disability can be an emotional roller-coaster ride in which any or all of the following reactions may be experienced:

Denial: "They've made a mistake! Tests aren't perfect, after all . . . They just don't realize that she's sensitive; she needs extra encouragement and understanding . . . All he needs is a little extra help . . . I'm sure he'll outgrow it if we give him time."

Anger and blame: "These so-called experts don't know what they're talking about! That teacher has always had it in for my kid . . . It's the school's fault! It's the day care provider's fault! It's the book's fault! Hey, he doesn't take after anyone on *my* side of the family."

Bargaining: "Maybe it will go away if we spend more time with her [or help him more with his homework, get her a tutor, or send him to a private school] . . . I'll quit work . . . Let's try another reading program . . . I'll take her to another specialist . . ."

Seeking Support

Receiving the news that a child has a disability can have a powerful emotional impact. Here, parents who have been through it share what helped them cope:

Seek assistance from experienced parents. There is nothing like the support of other parents who have "been there." Not only can they offer practical information, but they understand the fear, confusion, and pain that parents of children with disabilities often feel. Many communities have organizations and support groups for parents of children with different kinds of disabilities. Parents involved in these groups are eager to reach out and help.

Share your feelings with significant others in your life. Many people find it easier to share facts than feelings: for example, a mother who is used to being a source of strength for her family may feel uncomfortable about admitting that she feels helpless and lost. While the temptation to keep your pain to yourself may be great, sharing how you feel with your mate, your friends, and others who are close to you will lighten your burden. The worst kind of pain is that suffered alone.

Look for the positive. Sometimes bad news can seem so overwhelming that it overshadows everything; we forget that there is still much about our lives—and our children—that is good. The child who cannot yet read may be exceptionally sensitive to others' feelings, for example, or she may display admirable courage and perseverance. If you are not a natural optimist, focusing on the positive can take active effort. It can help to seek the company of positive people, letting them help you see the bright side.

Seek information. Many parents say that the cure for fear is knowledge— the more they knew about their children's disabilities, the less frightening they seemed. Information is available from many sources: your child's teachers, members of your child's evaluation team, parent support groups and organizations, books, magazines, and newsletters. "Make people talk to you in English," one mother advises. "Experts have

---

Guilt: "It's my fault . . . I didn't take the right kind of care of myself when I was pregnant . . . I should never have put him in day care . . . Maybe that twelve-year-old baby-sitter dropped him and never told me . . . I allowed her to eat too much junk food . . . I deserve this; God is punishing me."

a way of lapsing into unfamiliar terminology. When they start talking gobbledygook, just stop them and ask what they mean. That way, you'll learn the terminology, too."

Learn to recognize and deal with anger. It is almost impossible to avoid bitterness and anger when you are forced to let go of cherished hopes and dreams. Some parents find themselves lashing out at everyone after discovering that a child has a disability—including the child. You will have to recognize your anger and be honest about it before you can let it go. Close (and nonjudgmental) friends and professional counselors can both be very helpful with this process.

Allow others to have their feelings. For a time your family may seem emotionally "out of synch" as everyone struggles with finding his or her own way to adapt to a new reality. Try to be patient with those whose reactions are different from your own. If there are other children in the family, encourage them to talk about their feelings and fears. Their concerns may surprise you: "My five-year-old wanted to move out of his brother's room because he was afraid dyslexia was catching," one mother recalls.

Take care of yourself. When you are under stress and concerned about others, it is easy to neglect your own needs. There is no advantage, however, to burning yourself out. Try to get enough rest, eat properly, and make time for recreation (we know it's hard, but try anyway). Reaching out for support is also an important part of taking care of yourself. If you feel overwhelmed by depression, anger, or anxiety, don't hesitate to seek the help of a qualified therapist or counselor.

Take it one day at a time. If your seven-year-old has just been found to have a learning disability, you do not have to worry about college and careers today—only about the challenges of second grade (which may be plentiful). If you take on the entire uncertain future, it will deplete the strength you need to handle what's on your plate right now. "Regrets about yesterday and anxiety about tomorrow won't do anything for your child today," one mother says. "Usually, I find that the best way to handle the future is to pay attention to what's right in front of me."

Fear: "Will she be able to go to college? Will he ever be able to support himself? Will a normal person want to date my child? Who will look after her when I'm gone? Can I love him the same way I did when I thought he was 'perfect'?"

Grief and loss: "Our future has been destroyed . . . All my dreams are shattered . . . It breaks my heart to think of what might have been . . . I feel like someone died."

Though often intense and profoundly upsetting, all of these reactions are normal. As with other kinds of loss, accepting the reality of a disability can require a period of mourning, during which you may find yourself in need of extra understanding and support. In the checklist on pages 108–9 parents share advice on what helped them most as they worked through the emotional consequences of discovering that their child had disabilities. There are no "quick fixes," however; the acceptance process takes time.

Remember that all adults who are close to your child—whether it is the mother, father, or grandparents—are likely to experience some emotional reaction to the news that the child has a disability. They will not necessarily, however, all react the same way at the same time. Mom may be swamped with guilt, for example, while Dad is angrily accusing everyone in sight; meanwhile Grandma (who has never heard of learning disabilities and fears the child is retarded) is grieving deeply not only for her grandchild but for you and the heartache you are experiencing. As a result, communication can be difficult during this time—a fact that can complicate making decisions. The potential for effective teamwork is usually greatly improved when all adults who are regularly responsible for the child's care attend special education meetings, so that everyone starts out with the same information and has ample opportunity to ask questions and voice concerns. If there is continuing disagreement about what should be done for the child, getting a second professional opinion may help resolve the difficulty (see below).

8. WHEN IN DOUBT, GET A SECOND OPINION

If you disagree with the results of the assessment completed by your public school district, you have the right under federal law to obtain an Independent Educational Evaluation—that is, an evaluation by experts not employed by the school system. You can pay for this evaluation yourself, or you can ask the school district to pay for it. To receive payment from the district you may have to request a formal hearing, at which an independent hearing officer (also not employed by the school system) will rule on whether or not the district's original evaluation was adequate. Regardless of who pays for the second opinion, however, the district is obliged to consider the Independent

Educational Evaluation in determining eligibility for special education services.

The Independent Evaluation must use the same state and federal criteria to determine whether or not a disability exists, but the assessment team may use different tests and other methods in its investigations (it is important to tell professionals conducting an Independent Evaluation what tests have already been used, since repeating the same tests in a short time period can undermine the accuracy of results). If the results from the outside assessment conflict with those of the school district's evaluation, the district has two choices:

• Accept the Independent Evaluation and act on its results.

• Defend its own evaluation. This process requires one or more hearings before an independent hearing officer, who will rule on which assessment is valid.

Faced with conflicting evaluations, school districts often prefer to avoid time-consuming hearings. Either they accept the Independent Evaluation outright, or they become willing to negotiate about services. They might suggest providing certain services on a trial basis, for example, and evaluating progress after a specified period of time, after which services may be increased or decreased. It is usually best for children if parents and school officials can cooperate in this way rather than become locked into adversarial roles.

Remember that if a student's learning problems are not considered severe enough to warrant special education services, an assessment can still be used as a basis for requesting other kinds of help at school. Many types of educational assistance—providing tutoring, allowing extra time for some assignments, altering instructional methods, and making modifications in the curriculum, for example—can be negotiated informally with teachers. (The guidelines we suggest for helping children with learning disabilities at home also can be used successfully with youngsters who have other kinds of school-related problems.) Parents of children whose test scores "just miss" the criteria for learning disabilities may have to be assertive about advocating for their children's needs, however. Research suggests that these students are among the most likely to "fall between the cracks" of the public education system.

If you are convinced that your child needs special education services and the school district refuses to provide them—or if you feel strongly that the services being offered are inappropriate—you do have the right to place your views before an impartial hearing officer at a *due process hearing*. You also have the right to be represented by an attorney at this hearing; the school district is required to give you information about finding legal assistance if you need it. If you win your case, the district can be required to pay your legal costs. If the dispute is resolved in the district's favor, though, you will be responsible for your own legal expenses.

What happens if you disagree with the results of both assessments? This sometimes happens, and the law leaves the last word about special education with parents: you are free to reject the school district's recommendations in the matter of your child's education. Before doing so, however, it may be wise to do some serious soul-searching. Is your decision based on your child's needs, or could denial and wishful thinking be influencing your actions? There are some parents who are so invested in having "perfect" children that they simply cannot tolerate the idea of a disability; it's too damaging to their pride. Most special education professionals have also met parents who insist that their children *are* learning disabled because they cannot bear to accept that they are mentally retarded, emotionally disturbed, or intellectually incapable of above-average work. Sometimes such parents take their youngsters from specialist to specialist in search of someone who will tell them what they want to hear. Of course, the big losers in such situations are always the children, who get lots of attention but very little in the way of useful educational assistance.

Parents may also resist accepting the results of an evaluation because they fear their children will be stigmatized. These concerns are sometimes fueled by comments from the children, who may vigorously assert that all kids in special education programs at school are branded "dummies" and regarded as social untouchables. The sensitivity with which children with disabilities are treated by both teachers and other students in local schools certainly is an area of legitimate concern—one that we will discuss at length in future chapters. The disadvantages of being labeled as handicapped, though, must always be weighed against the hazards of failure to provide appropriate help. As one special educator puts it: "Parents often worry that placing children with learning disabilities in a special education program will identify them as 'different.' Believe me, kids with learning disabilities already *know* they are different. What they need most is to feel understood for a change, and a chance to succeed. Usually, their best shot at those things is through some kind of special education intervention."

Remember, your child's attitudes about having a learning disability will be strongly influenced by your own. If you regard special education intervention as a disaster, chances are your child will, too. If you are comfortable with intervention and view it as an opportunity for growth, however, your child will probably approach it positively. Thus one of the most important ways you can take care of your child is to do a thorough job of addressing your own worries and concerns. Never feel embarrassed about asking questions, or apologetic about wanting more information. The more information you have—and the more actively you participate in the evaluation and education planning processes—the more likely it is that your child is going to get exactly the kind of help he or she needs.

6

BECOMING AN EXPERT
ON YOUR CHILD

You don't have to become an authority on education to help a child
with learning disabilities. It *is* necessary, however, to become an "expert" on your child, and to develop an in-depth understanding of
what he or she needs in order to learn. This is not always an easy
matter. The difficulties children with learning disabilities encounter
in school are seldom traced to a single, easy-to-understand problem.
More often, they arise from clusters of overlapping problems: for example, neurological handicaps, an inflexible educational environment, poor social skills, and a variety of health and emotional
concerns may all be contributing to a youngster's struggle to keep up
in class.

Children with disabilities need multi-level support that addresses
all of their varied needs. The problem is that school personnel cannot always be relied upon to look beyond the most urgent academic
concerns. If this is the case, the support provided may be only partially helpful, or even harmful to the student's best interests. For example, one mother found that her sixth-grade daughter—a talented
artist—was being regularly removed from art class to get extra help
in reading. "I guess it made sense from the school's point of view,"
she says. "They saw art as a nonessential subject. What they didn't
understand was that, for Linda, art is the *most* essential subject. Art
class is where she gets to shine, win respect, and feel good about her-

self. What kind of sense does it make to take that away so that she can spend more time doing what she does poorly?" The mother met with the principal, and it was determined that Linda could instead get reading help during social studies, using the materials from that class to build both comprehension and writing skills.

Linda has what children with learning disabilities need most: a parent who understands her needs, monitors her educational program, and is willing to speak up for her at school. When a youngster's learning disability is first identified, however, not many parents feel ready to take on this role. Faced with a tangled web of interlocking problems (not to mention an evaluation report full of unfamiliar terms), most feel overwhelmed and unsure of what to do next. Few start out with enough confidence to march into school, evaluate the programming and the classroom environment, and make suggestions for changes! Experienced parents say they developed this confidence, though, as they became more aware of how their children perceived and interacted with the world around them. As one mother put it: "The better I understood my son, the easier it was to recognize the conditions that make it possible for him to do his best, and to avoid situations that would only frustrate him and end in failure."

How do you get started on becoming an expert on your child? Below are seven basic questions parents must ask to get a handle on what young people with learning disabilities need in order to succeed in school. The answers will come from several sources: the learning disabilities evaluation, the child's teachers, the child himself or herself, and your own observation. While some of these questions can be answered relatively quickly, others may take some patient investigation. We think you will find, however, that as you become more attuned to these issues, your confidence in your ability to make sound decisions on your child's behalf will grow. By the time you have answered these questions, you should be well on your way to becoming a powerful partner in your child's education.

1. ARE THERE PHYSICAL OR HEALTH CONCERNS WE HAVE TO ADDRESS?

Learning-disabilities evaluations sometimes raise questions about health issues that may be contributing to a student's problems in school. For example, the student may have problems with extreme fatigue, vision, or hearing that require attention. Learning disabilities can also be accompanied by physical disabilities that require ongoing therapy and/or seizure disorders requiring medication. Students who suffer from frequent illnesses, unmanaged allergies, or other chronic health conditions in addition to their learning disabilities are at a double disadvantage in the classroom. In cases such as these, stabilizing the child's physical condition is essential to achieving academic success.

A learning-disabilities evaluation will usually indicate if physical or health problems or developmental delays are suspected. If problems have been noted, it will be important to determine what therapeutic services (if any) will be provided by the school district in addition to educational services. While public school districts have the resources to provide assistance in the areas of physical and occupational therapy and can also supply devices to augment vision and hearing, these services may be offered only if a child's problems are considered severe enough to interfere significantly with performance in the classroom. If you feel your child needs these services, ask the district to consider the total or *cumulative* impact of the child's disabilities. A mild comprehension delay compounded by a slight hearing loss can add up to a very severe obstacle to learning, for example, even when neither problem would be viewed as terribly serious on its own.

It is also very important to be aware of the influence that everyday health issues have on school performance. Youngsters who skip meals, suffer from frequent colds, or don't get enough sleep rarely do their best in school. The impact of poor health habits on children who are also struggling with disabilities can be devastating. Balanced meals, healthy exercise, adequate rest, and regular medical and dental care are therefore a crucial part of treating learning disabilities successfully.

Do not expect, however, that a learning disability will be "cured" by diet, medication, or physical therapy alone. Supposed quick fixes for learning disabilities—sugarless and chemical-free diets, vitamin supplements, motion-sickness medications, eye exercises, and special reading lenses, for example—are proposed from time to time, and sometimes they are promoted aggressively (for a price!) to parents eager to help their children. So far, none of these methods have proved to be of widespread or lasting value. To date, the most effective treatment for learning disabilities remains appropriate educational programming, planned to fit the child's individual needs.

2. WHAT IS MY CHILD'S OVERALL LEARNING POTENTIAL?

Every learning-disabilities evaluation attempts to establish the child's capacity to learn, in order to determine if academic expectations are realistic. An intelligence (or IQ) test is typically used to measure intellectual potential. In general, students with high scores on IQ tests can be expected to make faster progress in school than students whose scores are lower; subscores on different parts of the test also indicate areas of intellectual strength and weakness. Some types of programming decisions are based largely on IQ test scores (for example, whether a student is eligible for programs for gifted children). A very low IQ test score can lead to identifying a child as mentally retarded. A learning disability is suspected when the IQ test suggests a child's academic performance should be much better than it actually is.

A properly administered IQ test can do a good job of measuring verbal problem-solving ability, fund of accumulated knowledge, and skill with tasks involving visual perception, numbers, and logic. Since these are the things that tend to help children get ahead in school, IQ tests are the best predictors we have of a child's ability to handle ordinary school-work. It is therefore important to go over the results of IQ tests carefully, preferably with the person who gave the test to your child. Do not settle for being given a number and a quick explanation ("Your son's IQ is 98, which is in the normal range" or "Kim's IQ is 125, which makes her a very bright little girl"); insist on seeing subtest scores (that is, scores received on different parts of the test) and ask to have the types of tasks and problems included in each of the subtests demonstrated or explained to you. Youngsters who have learning disabilities often do much better on some parts of IQ tests than others. You want to know exactly which types of task gave your child the most trouble, as well as which tasks he or she did best. Take your time over this information. The better you understand it, the more accurately you will be able to predict what kinds of activities and assignments will be hard for your child in school, and which will invite success.

Do not make the mistake, though, of thinking that IQ tests measure real intelligence. There are many aspects of intelligence that IQ tests do not address, such as creativity, "street smarts," or good judgment about people (how many of us would call a book-smart person with no common sense "intelligent"?). Nor do these tests address a child's aptitude for achievement in nonacademic areas.

In recent years many authorities have endorsed the concept of *multiple intelligences*, proposed by Harvard psychologist Howard Gardner. Gardner suggested that there are at least seven different kinds of intelligence that contribute to an individual's potential for success, and that evaluating only a few of these (as most IQ tests do) cannot produce a realistic estimate of an individual's overall ability. Gardner's seven types of intelligence are summarized on pages 120–21. If you believe your child has significant potential in any of these areas, you will want to make sure that school personnel are aware of it and are fully committed to nurturing those talents. In addition, it may be important to provide appropriate opportunities for growth (such as involvement in sports leagues, volunteer work, or music lessons) after school.

3. EXACTLY WHERE ARE THE AREAS OF DISABILITY?

Quite often, parents are offered only vague descriptions of their children's learning disabilities. You may be told that your child has "a written expression handicap," for example, or that the child is "moderately dyslexic" (which simply means that the youngster has some trouble reading). The trouble with terms like these is that they give you absolutely no idea what the student actually can and cannot do. *Why* does the child have trouble writing—is it a matter of penmanship? Difficulty retrieving words from memory? Inability to organize ideas? Problems with spelling? Is progress in reading blocked by an inability to recognize the shapes of letters and words, or problems sorting out sequences of sounds? Or is comprehension perhaps the issue (that is, the child reads words without understanding them)? Are attention deficits contributing to the problem? Are the disabilities mild or severe?

As we explained in Chapter 3, there are four types of information-processing weaknesses that can cause a learning disability: those affecting attention, visual perception, language processing, and fine motor skill. It is of vital importance that you understand the precise nature of your child's disabilities (remember, it is possible to have disabilities in more than one area). It may be obvious that the child has problems remembering verbal instructions, for example, but until you know if the problem is with sound processing, understanding vocabulary, or difficulty concentrating on what is being said (among other possibilities), it will be hard to plan effective intervention strategies.

Ideally, the learning-disabilities evaluation will explore areas of disability in some detail, but this is not always the case. To identify a learning disability, the evaluation must only establish that a student is performing less well than expected given his or her intelligence and past learning opportunities. Some evaluations determine that a child is of average or better intelligence and also significantly behind in some skill area and pretty much leave it at that. If detailed information about your child's disabilities is not provided by the evaluation, you may want to talk to your school district's special education department about additional assessment measures, or invest in having a more thorough assessment done privately.

Your child's teachers may also be able to help pinpoint areas of disability. Experienced special education teachers are particularly good at clarifying learning problems. These teachers also have a gift for explaining learning disabilities understandably, and parents find that teachers can be a rich source of practical advice for commonly encountered problems (such as how to encourage a student who hates homework or has problems getting organized). Most teachers welcome the opportunity to work with parents. As one teacher puts it, "The parents we consider troublesome are the ones who *don't* get involved with their kids—the ones we never see."

Your own observations can also be an important source of information—in fact, you probably already know more about how your child's brain works than you think you do. Think about how you communicate with your child when it's *really* important to get the point across (for example, when you have to convey safety information). Do you use fewer words or speak more slowly? Turn off the television and make the child look at your face? Use a lot of body language? Write the message down or draw a diagram? Ask the child to repeat the message back to you several times? Whatever your answer is, it shows that you have instinctively recognized something about how your child learns, and you routinely act on that information. Your child's teacher will have to use similar methods to get through to your child in the classroom.

You can learn even more about how your child thinks if you train yourself to observe him or her systematically. To do this, you have to begin by clearing your mind of assumptions about the child's behavior, which often take the form of judgments ("That girl is so absent-minded she'd lose her head if it weren't screwed on!" "He's a stubborn kid who needs a firm hand, and that's all there is to it!"). Then select one type of behavior to focus on at a time. You might start, for example, by observing what types of activity best hold your child's attention. As objectively as you can, watch your child at work

More Than One Kind of Intelligence

Most "intelligence tests" measure language ability, visual perception, and aptitude for math and logic. Psychologist Howard Gardner, however, believes that there are seven types of intelligence that contribute significantly to an individual's potential for achievement.

Linguistic Intelligence: Children who are strong in this area have large vocabularies, express themselves well, and find the use of language rewarding. They like to read, write, and tell stories; they also enjoy word games and delight in tongue-twisters, riddles, and rhymes. These youngsters also use language to organize and help them remember information. Memory prompts like "In fourteen hundred and ninety-two, Columbus sailed the ocean blue" and "Every Good Boy Does Fine" (familiar to music students) were devised by linguistic thinkers.

Logical-Mathematical Intelligence: Even as preschoolers, these children take an orderly, systematic approach to life. They love sorting and categorizing objects; they are intrigued by patterns and relationships; they set up tests and experiments to check their observations and ideas. Usually, these kids learn to compute quickly (often in their heads). They are good at games that call for logic and strategy, like "Battleship" and chess. As they grow older these children become fascinated by abstract concepts, and they ask "deep" questions like "Is time real?" They seem to bond instantly with computers.

Spatial Intelligence: Youngsters with a high level of spatial intelligence know immediately if you have changed something in a room; their keen sense of how objects relate to one another and how parts fit together to form a whole detects even subtle alterations in their environments. These kids seem to think in visual images, and often excel in art and construction activities. Some are also fascinated by machines; they may design inventions in their heads or build contraptions out of whatever is at hand. If situations become too wordy these students may slip away into daydreams.

and play for a week. At the end of the observation period, collect your observations (this is much easier if you take notes) and see how they add up. Was the child glued to the television, but restless when Dad tried to read to her? Does she stick with any type of art project but seem bored by music? Does she make mistakes when you explain directions to her but understand when you demonstrate? Taken together, these observations suggest a child who needs to use her

Musical Intelligence: Aptitude for music is often obvious when children are very young. Children with strengths in this area are sensitive to sounds in their environments and easily remember rhythms and melodies. Some of these kids are strongly motivated to play musical instruments, but others seem content to make music part of their lives by building large collections of tapes and CDs. They may claim they can't concentrate unless music is playing. (It's true; let them play the radio.)

Bodily-Kinesthetic Intelligence: Young people with strengths in this area have an unusual ability to control their bodies and express themselves through movement. They may be gifted athletes, actors, or dancers. These children *need* to move—if forced to sit still, they fiddle, tap, and squirm. They also use bodily sensations to process information, learning by manipulating objects, tracing, and touching. Free time goes to physical activities such as skating, swimming, or hiking. These kids also seem to love amusement-park rides that hurl them through space.

Interpersonal Intelligence: Children with strong interpersonal skills relate exceptionally well to other people. They make friends easily and thrive on social contact. Because they are super-aware of others' thoughts and feelings, these youngsters are often chosen to lead groups or mediate conflicts. Natural born organizers, they typically commit a great deal of time and energy to community projects and extracurricular activities, and they usually involve others in whatever enterprises they undertake.

Intrapersonal Intelligence: The expression "marching to a different drummer" aptly describes children with a high degree of intrapersonal intelligence. They have a very strong sense of who they are, and they are not particularly concerned about what others think about them. Their lives are guided by inner feelings and ideas; they value privacy and often prefer solitary pursuits to group activities. While they may not be "popular" in the conventional sense, these youngsters' self-assurance, sense of purpose, and spirituality are admired and often envied.

eyes to assist her ears. How might that affect her performance in school?

Left to themselves, children with disabilities will usually gravitate toward situations that make them feel comfortable and competent, and avoid those they find difficult and frustrating. Try observing the following behaviors, and think about the impact they might have on your child's achievement and adjustment in school:

- How does the child behave in groups of people? In what kind of groups is the child most relaxed and comfortable?

- What type of activities does the child choose given free time (assuming television is unavailable)? What kinds of toys or games does the child find frustrating or avoid?

- How does the child interact with adults? How does the child respond to guidance or criticism from authority figures?

- In what kind of settings does the child seem most happy and well-behaved? Is behavior affected by a change in environment?

Don't forget that your child is an important source of information, too. *Ask* the youngster why some homework assignments are easy and some are hard, or why certain activities are frustrating and some chores impossible. Sometimes their explanations are remarkably lucid. "After months of nagging, I finally asked my son why it took him forever to pick up his room," one mother recalls. "He said, 'It's that I don't know where to start, Mom. It looks like a big jumble, and I can't figure out what to do first.' We sat down and made a list of cleaning steps—pick up dirty clothes and put them in the hamper, put trash in the basket, and so on—and posted it on the back of his bedroom door. Referring to the list as he went along, he cleaned his room in a fraction of the time it had taken him before."

Since learning disabilities can be very subtle, it may take time and input from several sources in order to reach a thorough understanding of them. Persistence pays off, however—and there is nothing more important to planning effective educational strategies than knowing exactly how your child thinks and understands the world.

4. WHAT ARE MY CHILD'S STRENGTHS?

Every child, regardless of his or her intelligence level or degree of handicap, has areas of relative ability. Among children with learning disabilities, achievement in areas of competence usually ranges from average to outstanding. For example, a junior high school student who reads like a second grader may function at or above grade level when it comes to math calculations. A child whose language comprehension difficulties interfere with progress in many academic subjects may nevertheless demonstrate exceptional ability with computers or electronics.

A learning-disabilities evaluation identifies academic strengths as well as weaknesses, but all too often it is the weaknesses that take center stage. This is especially likely to be true if a child's disability interferes with reading. Reading skill is perceived as so essential to survival that educators (and often parents) tend to regard everything else as relatively unimportant. The unfortunate result is that students with reading problems may find that their gifts and talents have been either overlooked or devalued.

It is extremely important to identify the strengths of students with learning disabilities for several reasons. First, students with disabilities must rely on areas of strength to compensate for areas of weakness; although they do this instinctively to some degree, the learning process can be greatly simplified if everyone (especially the student) clearly understands what the areas of strength are. Second, in order to maintain their self-esteem, it is essential that students with disabilities get ample opportunity to do what they can do well. School usually gives them plenty of practice with what they do badly, and without some balance children are very likely to end up feeling like failures. Finally, students working in the way they find most comfortable are more productive, and far less likely to suffer the stress and loss of motivation experienced by youngsters struggling to perform "out of their element." The parable of *The Animal School*—reproduced on page 124—illustrates how ridiculous it is to ignore individual strengths in education. What's not so funny is that in many real classrooms teachers continue to squeeze children into standard molds, and then blame the kids if they don't fit.

The learning-disabilities assessment should give you some idea what your child's scholastic strengths are. Don't forget, however, to look beyond the academic subjects. Involvement in athletics and the arts saves the sanity of many students with disabilities. These youngsters can also be uncommonly inventive problem-solvers, and some develop outstanding communication skills, unusual sensitivity to others, and dynamic personalities. "My students have won community service awards and prizes in photography, drama, and dance," says a special education teacher. "Many have interests they have explored through jobs and volunteer work, and a few have started successful home businesses. What I'm saying is, if your student has trouble reading but made a 400 percent profit on his lemonade stand, do continue to encourage reading—but back his next business venture also."

The Animal School

Once upon a time, the animals decided they must do something heroic to meet the problems of "a new world." So they organized a school.

They adopted an activity curriculum consisting of running, climbing, swimming, and flying. To make it easier to administer the curriculum all the animals took all the subjects.

The duck was excellent in swimming, in fact better than his instructor; but he made only passing grades in flying and was very poor in running. Since he was slow in running, he had to stay after school and also drop swimming in order to practice running. This was kept up until his web feet were badly worn and he was only average in swimming. But average was acceptable in school so nobody worried about that except the duck.

The rabbit started at the top of the class in running, but had a nervous breakdown because of so much make-up work in swimming.

The squirrel was excellent in climbing until he developed frustration in the flying class where his teacher made him start from the ground up instead of from the treetop down. He also developed a "charlie horse" from over-exertion and then got C in climbing and D in running.

The eagle was a problem child and was disciplined severely. In the climbing class he beat all the others to the top of the tree, but insisted on using his own way to get there.

At the end of the year, an abnormal eel that could swim exceedingly well, and also run, climb, and fly a little, had the highest average and was valedictorian.

The prairie dogs stayed out of school and fought the tax levy because the administration would not add digging and burrowing to the curriculum. They apprenticed their children to a badger and later joined the groundhogs and gophers to start a successful private school.

Source: George H. Reavis.

5. WHAT KINDS OF ACADEMIC SUPPORT DOES MY CHILD NEED?

Learning-disabilities evaluations document a student's academic status in considerable detail. It should be clear from the assessment, for example, how your child's achievement in reading, writing, and arithmetic compares with that of other children in the same grade.

The evaluation should also indicate the specific skills within these broad areas that present problems: for example, it might indicate that a child understands math concepts but has difficulty with computation because of problems remembering math facts and formulas. What the evaluation report probably will *not* tell you, however, is how much of your child's academic problems have to do with a learning disability as opposed to such other factors as use of inefficient or inappropriate learning strategies, mismatch with the teacher's instructional style or the curriculum, or failure to master class content at earlier stages of education. In most cases, it is a *combination* of problems like these—not a learning disability alone—that is responsible for a student's falling behind in school. To be successful, educational programming for children with learning disabilities needs to address the learning disability *and* recognize these other academic concerns.

Let's look at the issue of learning strategies. Studies show that children with learning disabilities often approach learning in an inefficient and disorganized way. They do not analyze tasks or approach problems systematically. They seem unaware that there are techniques that can be used to assist memory. They do not know how to use outlines or take effective notes. Given a complex task like a report or a research paper, many of these children seem clueless as to how they might even begin. Sometimes poor learning strategies (educators call these strategies *metacognitive skills*) have as great an impact on school performance as a student's learning disability does.

Metacognitive skills can be taught, but in regular classrooms they almost never are, since most children figure these tricks out on their own. Instruction in these skills, however, can be provided through special education. The checklist on pages 126–27 presents some self-help techniques that are frequently overlooked by youngsters with learning disabilities. If your child does not make use of these strategies regularly, you may want to ask your special education department about learning strategy instruction.

Your child's personal learning style may also be contributing to his or her lack of academic progress. Research reveals that some students simply are better suited to traditional methods of education than others. For example, most school systems reward reflective learners (students who consider material thoroughly, pay attention to details, and put a lot of planning into a response). Impulsive learners (who are good at grasping a quick overview of a situation, but may react without thinking things through because they consider details unimportant) get less respect and may even be perceived as careless

Metacognitive Skills

Metacognitive skills are informal strategies that good students use to help themselves learn, store, and recall information. Most students figure these methods out on their own, becoming increasingly skillful in their use as they grow older. Students with learning disabilities, however, may not use strategies like those listed below unless they are *specifically taught* how and when to do so.

Organization and time-management skills
• Keep an assignment notebook
• Record due dates on a calendar
• Make lists of things to do
• Estimate the amount of time a project or an assignment will take
• Set deadlines (What has to be done today, tomorrow, by the end of the week?)
• Establish a work schedule
• Organize a notebook with pockets and dividers
• Develop a filing system for items that need to be saved
• Maintain a clutter-free work space

Study skills
• Read directions
• Take notes from lectures and books in your own words
• Preview text (look at introductions, headings, italics, illustrations, and summaries to become familiar with material before reading entire text)
• Highlight or underline important information
• Reorganize or regroup information (e.g., put key words or facts on index cards; create charts or lists of related facts and concepts)
• Make an outline
• Write and revise a rough draft
• Proofread work for completeness and accuracy
• Reward oneself for tasks or stages of a task completed

and unprepared. Similarly, lessons and assignments beyond primary school increasingly favor students who are good at organizing material independently, handling abstractions, making inferences, and figuring things out on their own. Concrete thinkers (who prefer explicit directions, structured tasks, and direct teaching of key facts and concepts) find the deck increasingly stacked against them as they get older. Research suggests that some children identified as "learn-

Test-taking skills
- Ask what material will be covered on the test; what format will be used (e.g., true/false, multiple choice, essay)
- Review notes and text on a regular basis (rather than cramming right before an exam)
- Set aside extra time to study the most difficult material
- Find a study partner or form a study group
- Look through the test and plan a test-taking strategy (such as leaving the most time for the essays or doing the easiest questions first)
- Determine when it pays to guess (and when it doesn't)

Memory skills
- Use verbal rehearsal (repeat "8 times 8 equals 64" until learned; repeat "I will not touch Grandma's piano" quietly or silently throughout visit)
- Invent rhymes ("Thirty days has September . . .")
- Use acronyms and mnemonic devices (e.g., "HOMES" for the five Great Lakes: Huron, Ontario, Michigan, Erie, Superior)
- Use visualization (e.g., call up a mental picture of a location, a chart or diagram, a previously made outline)
- Create associations (e.g., for state capitals: People are *tall* in Florida [Tallahassee]; they're *mad* in Wisconsin [Madison]; they're *busy* in North Dakota [Bismarck] . . .)

Problem-solving and decision-making skills
- Identify the goal to be reached or the main problem to be solved (separate main objectives from less important issues)
- Gather information using different techniques (brainstorming, asking others, library research)
- Make lists of possible courses of action or solutions
- Evaluate and eliminate options using such factors as practicality, risk involved, and time required
- Test solutions to see if they will work

ing disabled" are impulsive, concrete learners whose primary problem is that they are poorly matched with the teaching methods to which they have been exposed. When material is organized and presented to them in a way they can make use of it, these children make steady progress.

Students can also be victims of the school's curriculum. Although battles have been waged for decades in the education community over the best way to teach reading, writing, and arithmetic, the truth is that there is no program for any of these subjects that works for all students all of the time. Even among typical students, any given reading or math curriculum will work better for some than for others. Children with learning disabilities (who are less adaptable than other students) are likely to have a particularly hard time in classrooms where there is little curricular flexibility. One mother related that her son, who was considered dyslexic until third grade, learned to read almost overnight when given phonics instruction at age nine. He did not have a reading disability, but his relatively weak visual perception skills made it almost impossible for him to benefit from the school's chosen reading curriculum, which stressed whole-word recognition.

When children are poorly matched with instructional methods or the curriculum—or when they have trouble keeping up with the rate at which teachers present new information—they may not master all the class content necessary to succeed at the next academic level. You cannot expect students to succeed at fractions or algebra, for example, if they have failed to come to grips with the basics of addition and subtraction. For students with learning disabilities the problem of missed content often compounds their academic difficulties. "When the basics of punctuation and capitalization were taught in third grade, my daughter was still struggling to keep her letters on the lines," one mother recalls. "All that stuff about when to use a comma and when to use upper case went right by her. As a result, Sarah lost points for capitalization and punctuation errors on her written work for years. The problem wasn't that she couldn't understand that material; it was that she had missed the *opportunity* to learn it." This family finally hired a tutor to teach Sarah the rules of written English during the summer before she started high school, and she learned them very quickly.

In the next section of this book we will discuss how compensating for a disability, practicing basic skills, developing better learning strategies, and reviewing class content are blended into a successful educational program. Meanwhile, remember that you are a teacher's best source of information about your child's behavior and academic history. Be prepared to share your perceptions of how your child learns, and ask how the teacher or special education department plans to address such issues as an unsuitable instructional style or curriculum materials, inefficient learning strategies, and the need to catch up with information missed the first time around.

6. WHAT KIND OF SOCIAL SUPPORT DOES MY CHILD NEED?

There are several characteristics of learning disabilities that can interfere with social success, including problems with verbal communication, difficulty interpreting facial expressions or "body language," failure to understand the rules of games, and impulsive habits (such as interrupting, making irrelevant comments, or outbursts of inappropriate behavior). As a result, youngsters with learning disabilities sometimes have problems entering into and maintaining social relationships. Children with ADHD (who tend to be impulsive) and children with severe visual perception handicaps (who frequently misjudge the timing and rhythm of social interplay) have the most trouble making friends, but even children with less serious disabilities may find themselves consigned to the social sidelines. Social rejection can have an even bigger impact on children's self-esteem than academic failure. As any fourth grader will tell you, it's much more important to be popular than to be smart.

Social confidence also affects academic success. Children with good interpersonal skills relate positively to teachers as well as to peers. These students are more likely to show off their accomplishments, and when they are having problems they are more likely to ask for help. Not only do these expressive and likable youngsters get more approval and encouragement from teachers, research indicates they get more "strokes" from their parents, too. The support these students receive from adults helps them to aim high when they set goals, and to keep trying when they suffer setbacks.

Most children pick up social skills by copying the behavior of the people around them. Students with learning disabilities, however, may need to be taught these skills more directly. Some school districts offer social skills training through special education. These programs use a variety of small-group activities to teach and practice such social fundamentals as starting a conversation, responding appropriately to others, and expressing feelings. Typically these lessons are very practical and detailed. The box on page 130, for example, presents instructions for asking for help.

There is also a great deal parents can do to encourage social growth. For example, research shows that appearance can contribute significantly to popularity, so children should be encouraged to pay attention to posture, grooming, and neatness. "We teach our kids that a friendly smile and expressing interest in others can also go a long way toward winning acceptance," a special educator suggests. "The fact is, people tend to like people who they think like them." Making an effort to understand your child's temperament and behavior patterns can also help you arrange social events that bring out the best in the youngster's personality, and avoid situations that put him or her at a disadvantage. "I was a basket case after my son's seventh birthday party," one mother remembers. "Tony became so frantic and overstimulated that I don't think he enjoyed it much, either. Given his tendency to go off the wall, I don't know what made me think it would be a good idea to invite six energetic little boys for an overnight. For Tony's eighth birthday, I arranged to take him and *one* friend to an amusement park. The rides and the water slide gave them plenty of outlets for their energy, and we were all tired—but happy—at the end of the day."

6. WHAT KIND OF EMOTIONAL SUPPORT DOES MY CHILD NEED?

Children with learning disabilities sometimes face a long course of intimidating obstacles once they start school: teachers who don't un-

---

Getting Help

Body Basics
  Face the person
  Make eye contact
  Use a serious voice tone
  Have a serious facial expression
  Keep a straight body posture

Other Skill Steps
  Say the person's name
  Ask if the person has time to help you
  Explain your problem
  Ask for advice
  Listen carefully to the person's advice
  Ask questions if you do not understand
  Do the task while the person watches, if needed
  Ask for feedback if needed
  Thank the person

Source: Schumaker, J. B. (1992). *School Psychology Review, 21,* p. 389.

derstand them, books and assignments that make no sense, students who are cruel to anyone who is "different," and sometimes parents who blame or berate them for their failure to measure up to expectations. It should come as no surprise, then, that youngsters who have learning disabilities suffer from more than their share of emotional problems. Even students whose disabilities have been identified and whose families are supportive can experience greater than normal levels of frustration and stress, as the entry from Nick's journal on page 132 illustrates with heartbreaking clarity.

At the very least, these youngsters need an extra measure of encouragement and understanding from their families in order to hold on to their courage and self-esteem. Some students, however, need more. Prolonged feelings of anger, anxiety, or helplessness are often best addressed by professional counseling. Professional intervention should be sought without delay if a student has developed destructive (including self-destructive) tendencies or is exhibiting symptoms of depression. Once these patterns have developed, it is unlikely that the student will make significant academic progress until the emotional issues have been resolved.

Professional guidance may also be needed to help family members learn to deal with a child's learning and behavior problems appropriately. Parents, too, develop self-defeating patterns—establishing unrealistic expectations, being inconsistent about rules, becoming overprotective, and helping too much are a few that are very common. A skilled family counselor can help you identify these unproductive habits and suggest ways of interacting with your child that are more comfortable and bring better results. Counselors can also help you work through feelings of guilt, anger, or anxiety that may be interfering with your effectiveness as a parent. In Chapter 10 we will talk more about the family dynamics of living with a learning disability, and we will also discuss how to find a good family therapist.

Parents sometimes wonder how much to tell children about their disabilities. Will children be traumatized by discovering that they have a handicap? We feel that *not* talking to children about learning disabilities presents a far greater threat to their emotional health. Remember that children who have learning problems almost always sense that they are different in some way. The explanations they imagine for why they are different, however, are often far worse than the truth. "I couldn't do anything right, and I had such a hard time getting along with everybody, I just figured I was a bad person," says a man whose ADHD was not identified until he was an adult. "As a kid, I spent a lot of time worrying about going to hell. If someone had

NICK

Nick's mother shares the following introduction to his journal: "Nick was in the fifth grade at the time of this journal entry, in complete despair over his inability to make any sense out of the class that he was in. The teacher Nick had during the mainstreamed portion of his school day seemed certain she could handle Nick's slow work pace and misunderstanding of assignments by making him sit on a bench during recess. Nick didn't tell me about the 'benchings' at first, apparently quite sad that the year was beginning so badly."

The hardest thing I ever had to do is get a good grade on my vocabulary test. Because I have a hard time remembering things. I study and study and I can't get it. I try hard but I need *more time.* My mom has been a big help. Now I have to do a poem. I can't do it see I told you now I have to sit on the bench. I wish I could slap myself and get rid of my learning problems, but Mrs. Saunders doesn't understand. My Mom and my Dad will talk to her and my Dad has been a big help too. I've been on the bench for two weeks. This is getting me really mad. My friends understand why doesn't Mrs. Saunders understand. I hope I pass fifth grade. I'm really scared. Somebody help me. Alls Mrs. Saunders does is putting people on the bench. She yells at everybody . . . I'm not having much fun this year. I hate myself. Life isn't fair. I'm not happy. But when I'm around my Dad he makes me feel really good. I love him very much . . . I feel like I'm in jail and I will never get out. I want to tell her what I feel like but she will yell at me. I'm to get my guts up and tell her. I'm really sad with a capital S. . . . . I'm at the library now. Maybe I will talk to Mrs. Saunders.

Source: Rita Ter Sarkissoff.

told me I had a different kind of brain back then, I would have been grateful."

"It's *very* important to get across to these kids that they aren't dumb," a special educator says. "Usually stupidity is the only explanation they can think of for their problems in the classroom. In addition, they need to understand that there is more than one way to solve problems, and that success comes from finding the right approach—not from 'just trying harder,' as they have so often been urged to do." Experienced parents add that students who understand their handicaps (and how to get around them) are far more motivated and more likely to set challenging goals for themselves than students who are confused about their disabilities or ashamed of them. "It was a sad day for me when my fourth-grade son asked if he'd outgrow his disability and I had to tell him that he wouldn't," a mother remembers, "but he took the news very matter-of-factly. He said 'Well Mom, if I can't outgrow it, I'll have to outlearn it, won't I?'" This student (now on the dean's list at a select college) participated in all special education meetings about his program from the fifth grade on. "In high school, I used to explain to my teachers how they should explain things to me," he says. "Most of the time they appreciated the help."

This youngster found that self-confidence came from learning to deal with a handicap—not from hiding it, or pretending he didn't have one. When asked how he developed such a positive attitude, he explained it this way:

> Well, for one thing, I always knew my parents were on my side. I remember one time in elementary school, a teacher refused to put me in the advanced reading group because my writing skills were still pretty bad and the advanced students had to write book reports. My mother was in that classroom the next day, with my reading scores in one hand and a copy of state laws applying to learning disabilities in the other. They had a polite discussion, and I was put in the advanced reading group. I gave my book reports orally.
>
> But most of the time, my folks acted like having a learning disability was no big deal. It was something that had to be dealt with, but not something to get upset about, you know? So I guess I just grew up thinking I was basically okay.

Students with learning disabilities *are* basically okay. If school problems begin to seem overwhelming, it is important to get back in touch with that fact. Take a deep breath, take the child out, and do something fun. On any given day, the most valuable thing you can do as a parent "expert" is to enjoy and appreciate your child as a unique human being. For most children, self-esteem depends largely on how they feel about the person they see reflected in their parents' eyes.

Part III

AN APPROPRIATE EDUCATION

7

BECOMING AN
EDUCATION ACTIVIST

For many parents, identification of a learning disability is accompanied by some element of relief—at last, the cause of all those puzzling problems at school has been discovered! While no one may be thrilled about the idea of special education, at least it is good to know there are specialists who understand learning disabilities and know how to deal with them. Once these experts take over, surely the student will start making progress, and all will be well.

Sometimes things actually work out that way. Other times, however, families find themselves facing scenarios like this one:

◆ Nine-year-old Susie has recently been found to have language processing disabilities that are compromising her efforts in reading. While she does average work in math and most other subjects, she reads at a second-grade level. It is expected that Susie's reading will improve with one hour of special education instruction per day. It is therefore recommended that Susie remain in her regular fourth-grade classroom but go to the school's "resource room" for an hour each afternoon to work on reading skills with a special education teacher.

This type of arrangement (which is common for students with learning disabilities, and is consistent with the legal mandate that such students be educated in "the least restrictive environment") seems satisfactory all around. Susie's parents are glad that she is finally going to get the specialized help she needs. Susie is pleased that she will be able to stay with her fourth-grade friends most of the time. School administrators are happy because this system makes efficient use of the special education teacher: working with small groups an hour at a time, one learning specialist can serve twenty or more students in a day. Since Susie's school has identified relatively few students with disabilities, they are getting by with "half a teacher" (one special education teacher serves two schools, one in the morning and one in the afternoon).

Within two months, however, it is obvious that Susie's program is not working. Not only is Susie showing no signs of improvement, but her performance is actually slipping in some areas. She is failing social studies, and her marks in math and science have also dropped. She has a shocking amount of homework—two or three hours worth every night—and Susie's parents now spend most weekday evenings at the kitchen table helping their daughter through her assignments. These sessions are often punctuated by tantrums and tears, as Susie insists she can't do what is expected of her. The level of academic anxiety the little girl is suffering is worse than anything she has experienced before. To make matters even more painful, Susie's workload leaves her little time or energy left over for recreation. Her friends have stopped including her in after-school activities because she always has "too much homework to do."

What went wrong? Susie's father suspects Susie's teachers are incompetent, while Mom worries that Susie's handicap may be much more severe than originally supposed. The truth, however, is that Susie is a victim of increased curricular demands and poor coordination between her special and regular education programs. Let's take a look at what's actually going on at Susie's elementary school:

◆ Susie is pulled out of her regular classroom for reading help between one and two o'clock in the afternoon. During this period her classmates are scheduled for lessons in social studies (Monday, Wednesday, and Friday) and science (Tuesday and Thursday). Although it would make more sense to pull Susie out in the morning during the fourth-grade reading period, this is not possible because the special education teacher does not arrive at Susie's school until after lunch. Susie therefore spends most of her mornings involved in reading activities that are completely inappropriate for her. She misses science and social studies entirely. Math—previously Susie's best subject—is taught in the mornings, but this year math is not making much sense to Susie. Word problems have been introduced, and Susie cannot understand the problems well enough to figure out which of her math skills to apply.

Mr. Jones, Susie's classroom teacher, is a solid, experienced instructor. He has never received any training in learning disabilities, however, either at the college he attended twenty years ago or since that time. As a result, Mr. Jones knows next to nothing about these handicaps and how students are affected by them. He has been told that Susie has a learning disability but was given no additional information (the results of Susie's evaluation are locked up with other "confidential" files). In any case, Mr. Jones' view is that dealing with Susie's learning disability is the special education teacher's job. He is aware that Susie is doing poorly, but so are ten other students in his class of twenty-nine. Mr. Jones does not lack for things to do, and he is grateful that somebody else is looking after Susie's problems.

No one has told Mr. Jones he has to do anything special for Susie, so he assumes she is responsible for the same work as the other fourth graders. Since Susie misses social studies and science, Mr. Jones sends the classwork in those two subjects home for her to do, in addition to her regular assignments. The science and history texts and worksheets Susie is given are much longer and more complicated than anything she received last year (in most schools, demands on reading comprehension increase dramatically in fourth and fifth grades). In addition, Susie is trying to complete this work without benefit of the instruction and activities—discussions, films, experiments, and the like—that other fourth-graders received in class. In effect, Susie must do more work (special instruction in reading has been tacked on to her regular fourth-grade curriculum) with less help than any of her classmates. No wonder she is complaining!

What about the special education teacher? Isn't she supposed to coordinate with Susie's classroom teacher and keep an eye on Susie's program? Technically she is, but let's look at this teacher's day. Ms. Smith has been assigned twenty-five students in the first through sixth grades this year. The law requires her to implement an individualized program for each one of them. Every minute of her time is devoted to direct instruction except for lunch, which she spends commuting from one school to another. Ms. Smith is a competent and caring teacher; she would like to meet with each of her students' classroom teachers (between the two schools, there are more than fifteen of them) and tell them more about her students and their learning disabilities. But when is she to do so? She has no free period. She is not even invited to the regular teachers' staff meetings (she attends special education staff meetings at the school district's central offices). Ms. Smith makes an effort to intervene when she becomes aware that one of her students is having a problem in the classroom, but she rarely has time to do more.

Since Susie is new to her as a student, Ms. Smith has spent several weeks investigating which reading materials are likely to help the youngster best. This exploratory process is important to the success of the program, but meanwhile Susie does not appear to have made much progress. Because she sees Ms. Smith as a reading teacher who has nothing to do with Mr. Jones, Susie has said nothing about her problems with homework or the classroom. And because Susie's parents think their daughter's difficulties are primarily due to her learning disabilities, they have not contacted anyone at school about their concerns; they are simply trying to help Susie keep up as best they can. As a result, Ms. Smith does not know that Susie's overall program is impossibly unfair. Unless someone—the classroom teacher, Susie, or Susie's parents—approaches her, Ms. Smith will probably remain ignorant of the problem until the failing grades on Susie's report card alert her (assuming someone shows her the report card).

Can coordination and communication among professionals really be this bad? Unfortunately, they can. At nearly every gathering of parents of students with learning disabilities, educational nightmares like Susie's are shared. There are tales of students who can't spell being humiliated by being required to participate in spelling bees, students who can't read being assigned college-level texts, and students who can't write being given zeros for sloppy or incomplete written work. Parents often report that they did not learn of the problems their children faced in school until months or even years after the fact. "When he was in high school, my son told me that his sixth-grade teacher made him sit in a kindergarten chair because his writing looked like kindergarten work," one mother remembers. "When I asked Sean why he never said anything about it then, he told me he was too ashamed—then added that he was doing so badly that year, he halfway figured he deserved the punishment."

To understand why problems like this occur, it is necessary to know something of the evolution of special education programming. First, we must recognize how new this field is. It was not until the mid-1970s that states were required by the federal government to educate children with disabilities. Before that, public schools could—and sometimes did—turn students with disabilities away, claiming they had neither the facilities nor the staff to cope with their special needs. In 1975 Congress passed Public Law 94-142, The Edu-

PARENTS SHARE . . .

My daughter loves science, and she did exceptionally well in her junior high science classes in spite of her dyslexia. Yet at the end of eighth grade her teacher did not recommend her for the high school honors science class. When I asked why, the teacher said he had no doubt Karen could handle the concepts, but felt Karen's slow work rate would put her at an overwhelming disadvantage in the advanced class. I argued that Karen's placement should be determined by her *abilities*—not her *disabilities*—and added that placing her below her intellectual level would undermine her motivation. I offered to meet with the honors science teacher and explain the adaptations Karen would need in order to succeed. That's what did it. A lot of teachers don't know much about learning disabilities and people are afraid of what they don't understand. Once the honors teacher understood that working with Karen wouldn't destroy his whole curriculum, he welcomed her in.

cation of All Handicapped Children Act. (PL 94-142 has since been amended several times, and in 1990 it was renamed the Individuals with Disabilities Education Act, or IDEA.) This legislation required each state to provide a "free appropriate public education" to school-aged children with any of ten different handicapping conditions, including students with "specific learning disabilities."* The law further stated that these students were to be provided with individualized education programs designed to meet their unique needs.

Federal law determined that special education instruction could be provided in a variety of settings (including regular classrooms, special classrooms, special schools, the student's home, and hospitals or other institutions), but it added that an effort should be made to educate students in the *least restrictive environment*. To the maximum extent possible, children with disabilities were to be educated at their home schools with nondisabled peers. Placement in regular classrooms with appropriate supports and accommodations was

---

*For the federal definition of specific learning disabilities, see Chapter 5. The other disabilities recognized by IDEA are mental retardation; hearing impairments including deafness, speech, or language impairments; visual impairments including blindness; serious emotional disturbance; orthopedic impairments; autism; traumatic brain injury; and "other health impairments."

Is Private School the Answer?

Parents who are frustrated with their public school experience sometimes wonder if their children would fare better in private institutions. Are youngsters with disabilities likely to do better in private school? The answer is . . . maybe and maybe not.

Children who have mild information-processing problems may do better in private school if that school provides smaller classes, more individual attention, more elastic time constraints, and more flexibility in both curriculum and instructional style than the public school. If a student needs specialized instruction to master basic reading, math, or writing skills, however, these advantages alone will not produce improvement—the child must also have the assistance of a learning-disabilities specialist. Parents should also be aware that teachers in private and parochial schools are not necessarily any better informed about learning disabilities than teachers in public schools. It is still necessary to work with them closely to make sure that materials, assignments, and activities are consistently appropriate and meet the child's needs.

At the other end of the spectrum, students whose disabilities and/or attention problems are so severe that it is very difficult for them to function in a traditional classroom may benefit from attending a private school exclusively for children with learning disabilities. These schools are staffed primarily by learning specialists, and they offer a range of opportunities and services that is beyond the scope of most public institutions. A major disadvantage is that day schools of this type do not exist in most communities; many are boarding schools whose tuition can rival the cost of some colleges. Students also have mixed feelings about "special" schools. Some are happy and relieved to discover there are other students like themselves (and teachers who can teach them), but others see placement in such schools as a mark of inadequacy and failure. Students who have positive attitudes are generally most successful in this setting.

Many parents straddle the public/private issue by supplementing a public school education with private tutoring. This approach can work well if tutors are chosen with care, and if work is scheduled in a way that avoids overloading the student. It is also important to coordinate the activities of teachers and tutors in order to avoid unnecessary confusion (for example, if a student's teacher is working with one type of reading program and the tutor is using a system that is completely different, the child may end up becoming even more perplexed). Parent support groups are often a good source of information about tutors for students with different kinds of learning problems.

preferable to placement in separate special education classes. According to the law, removal from the regular education environment is acceptable only "when the nature or the severity of the disability is such that education in regular classes with the use of supplementary aids and services cannot be achieved satisfactorily."

The law's emphasis on the least restrictive environment resulted in part from aggressive advocacy on the part of groups representing parents of children with disabilities. These parents were all too familiar with educators' tendency to segregate special-needs students, placing them out of sight and out of mind of the typical school population. Parents felt that this practice unnecessarily stigmatized their children, robbed them of social support, and resulted in lowered expectations and a second-rate education. "Mainstreaming" children with special needs—that is, including them in regular education activities for part of the school day—was advanced as an important way of improving their opportunities.

Following this legislation, children with learning disabilities rapidly emerged as America's single largest special-needs group. (Nationally, students with learning disabilities now comprise about 50 percent of the total special education population.) This generated a tremendous demand for teachers specializing in learning disabilities, and an explosion of university programs designed to prepare such teachers. Still, many schools found themselves identifying students with disabilities at a much faster rate than they could find specialists to work with them. Combined with the budget constraints chronically faced by many school districts, this shortage forced the development of programs that enabled available learning specialists to serve the greatest possible numbers of students. So-called pullout programs (which placed students with disabilities in typical classrooms but removed them for small-group instruction with a special education teacher for an hour or two a day) made efficient use of the learning specialists' time and also fulfilled the least-restrictive-environment mandate. At the moment, most students with learning disabilities are educated in some variation of this model.

But what about the regular classroom teachers? When IDEA was passed, very few of these teachers had any special education training. (Today most teacher education programs offer some information about learning disabilities, but it is often minimal.) Nevertheless, students with disabilities were placed in their classes on a regular basis. While some school systems made efforts to provide in-service training on learning disabilities to teachers, others simply assigned the students and expected teachers to cope as best they could—a practice

PARENTS SHARE . . .

My son is talented in art and loved drama. Those were two of the main things that kept him interested in school. One year I had to go toe-to-toe with the high school principal, who said Randy couldn't work on the school play because he was close to failing math that term. The principal came around when I pointed out Randy had started to fail when the math class switched from a geometry unit to an algebra unit. Randy does OK in geometry because it has a strong visual element, but he has problems with sequencing and memorization, so algebra is very hard for him. I suggested the teacher try to make algebra concepts more visual and concrete—and sure enough, when she did that Randy began to improve. Meanwhile, he designed a fantastic multi-level set for the play on his computer. . . . Today he's a computer animator considering an offer from Disney.

critics refer to as "dump and hope" (that is, dump the children in the classroom without support and hope it will work out somehow). Often workshops on disabilities were offered to teachers, but they were optional. Understandably, many regular classroom teachers were uncertain about their responsibility toward students with learning disabilities. Were they responsible for basic skills instruction, or was the special education teacher? Were they expected to provide different materials or use different instructional methods for students with special needs? Were they supposed to modify the curriculum or grading practices for these children? Was giving "special treatment" to students with disabilities fair to typical children in the class?

The confusion created by a lack of clear guidelines was compounded by the diverse yet highly specific needs of students with learning disabilities—as well as the fact that many students with information-processing problems did not appear to be handicapped at all. Since most children with learning disabilities spent more than half their time with teachers who were not quite sure what these students needed or who was supposed to provide it, it's no surprise that the quality of learning-disabilities programming varied tremendously from school to school, and even from classroom to classroom.

Today it is well understood that teacher education and support are the keys to successfully including students with disabilities in typical classrooms. Yet this training and support is provided so inconsis-

tently that in 1993 Albert Shanker (representing the American Feder-
ation of Teachers) called for a moratorium on "inclusion" policies,
stating that "unwise and unrestrained inclusion is creating unbear-
able conditions in classrooms across the country." Other organizations support the principle of inclusion, but they urge more care in
the way these policies are implemented. The National Education Association, for example, states that in order for inclusion to work, it
must be accompanied by the following:

- A full range of educational placements and services for students
  (so that students will not be placed inappropriately for lack of viable alternatives)

- Professional development for staff

- Adequate time for teachers to plan and collaborate with one another

- Class sizes responsive to student needs

- Appropriate staff and technical assistance

Many groups representing families of students with disabilities
heartily support these goals, and some are working actively with
school districts to develop new policies and improve local programs.
Yet even when there is administrative support for reform, lack of adequate funding may still block appropriate staff development, new
services, and reductions in class size. As a result, regular and special
educators alike continue to struggle to do their jobs under difficult
conditions, and the quality of programming available to children
with learning disabilities remains extremely variable.

The collective wisdom of knowledgeable parents, therefore, is that
children with learning disabilities need advocates to be sure that the
education they receive is consistently appropriate and effective.
Without active oversight, these students are too likely to end up overwhelmed and underassisted. Many parents state that they stepped
into the advocate role because there was no one else to perform it; in
other words, they became education activists by default. "I knew
nothing about education when I started out," one mother says. "I
only knew that what my son was getting in school wasn't helping
him. What I found was that there was almost no communication between the regular teachers and the special education staff at his
school. I became sort of an unofficial go-between—explaining learning disabilities to the classroom teacher, and explaining the fifth-
grade curriculum to the special ed teacher. I did the same in sixth

A Word About Being Fair . . .

"It's not fair to expect all the other kids to write out their book reports but allow Jane to give hers orally. She should do the same work as the others."

"Why should Johnny be allowed to use a calculator on tests when the other kids can't? It gives him an unfair advantage."

"If I take off points for every one else's spelling errors, I should do the same for Sue. Otherwise, I'm not being fair."

Classroom teachers sometimes resist modifying assignments, materials, or grading practices to accommodate students with learning disabilities on the grounds that making these adjustments is not fair to other students in the class. Fairness, these teachers insist, means that everyone should be treated the same.

Yet these teachers would never demand that a student with a broken leg be deprived of his crutches and made to participate in gym. Nor would they suggest that hearing-impaired students attend class without their hearing aids, or that blind students make do with regular books instead of texts in Braille. Perhaps it is necessary to give some additional thought to what fairness really means.

First, most of us would agree that being fair means you don't ask anybody to do the impossible. If you would not expect second graders to do

grade, and again in seventh. On the way I learned a lot about education, and also about cutting through red tape and handling bureaucracies." Not only do parents like this secure better educations for their children, but they are sometimes instrumental in creating new programs and services where none existed before. Parent-professional groups such as the Learning Disabilities Association of America (LDA) and Children and Adults with Attention Deficit Disorder (CHADD) both provide information and support to families and work energetically for legislation that supports students with learning disabilities and protects their rights on local, state, and national levels. (For the addresses of these and other advocacy groups, see the Appendix.)

Exactly what does a parent need to do to provide students with adequate support and prevent problems? Experienced mothers and fa-

calculus problems or a child with severe cerebral palsy to do broad jumps, you should not expect a child with fourth-grade reading skills to read tenth-grade books without help. Nor should you expect kids who are slow in processing information to perform satisfactorily on timed tests, or ask children with attention deficit hyperactivity disorder to sit at their desks for three hours without a break.

Second, being fair means you don't punish children for having handicaps. If the homework that takes most students forty minutes to do takes a student with learning disabilities three hours—leaving little time left over for recreation—*that* is not fair. Such situations make it much harder for the student with disabilities to learn and deprive that student of opportunities for normal social and emotional growth.

Third, being fair means you do not deprive children with disabilities of the means of doing what typical children can do on their own. If you do not object to giving a wheelchair to a student with a spinal cord injury, you should not object to providing the student who cannot memorize with a calculator, or allowing the student who has writing problems to demonstrate knowledge by dictating some assignments. These modifications equalize students' opportunities; they do not give students with disabilities "advantages."

In short, treating students equally means sometimes you have to treat them differently. Fairness means giving children equal access to a quality education—not insisting that everybody must do everything exactly the same way.

thers advise that there are three basic areas where parental involvement and advocacy make a big difference.

1. PREPARING INDIVIDUALIZED EDUCATION PROGRAMS

According to federal law, identification of a learning disability must be immediately followed by the preparation of an Individualized Education Program (IEP) for the student. An IEP document spells out educational goals, specifies all the services, supports, and accommodations to be made available, and identifies the type of classes to which the child will be assigned. The IEP is reviewed and updated at least once a year. Parental consent is required for first-time assignment of special education services and for changes in placement. Once a student has been assigned to special education, school districts can make other changes in the student's program without parental consent, but they may do so only after making a reasonable attempt to obtain parent input and approval. (School districts are allowed a certain amount of leeway to act on behalf of students whose parents choose not to participate in the IEP process. IEP committees include parent-advocates to assist parents and represent the rights of students whose own parents are not present.)

As we mentioned in Chapter 5, the IEP is in effect a contract: the school district is legally obliged to provide the assistance and services described in this document. The fact that specified services or equipment do not presently exist cannot be used as an excuse for failure to provide them (in other words, if a student's IEP states that he is to have access to a computer in the classroom and there are no computers there now, the school must get one). In addition, the IEP serves several other important functions:

- IEP meetings provide an opportunity for parents and educators to share their perceptions of the child's needs, resolve conflicts, discuss options, prioritize goals, and make decisions about the child's educational program. IEP meetings are required following the initial identification of a learning disability and once a year thereafter. Parents may also request a meeting to review or revise an IEP if a student is not making satisfactory progress, or if new concerns have arisen.

- The IEP serves as a management tool. It is used by school districts to ensure that children with disabilities receive educations and services that are in compliance with federal and state guidelines. Monitors from government agencies may review IEPs to make sure schools are fulfilling their obligations under the law.

- The IEP serves as a device for tracking and evaluating a student's progress from year to year. An IEP is not a "performance contract"—that is, schools and teachers cannot be held legally responsible if a student does not meet IEP objectives. Failure to make progress toward the goals specified on an IEP, however, strongly suggests that modifications need to be made in a student's program.

In the next chapter, we will discuss some of the most important questions that have to be resolved when preparing an IEP. Our purpose here is to emphasize the importance of participating fully in IEP meetings. Federal law requires public agencies to notify parents of the time and place of these meetings well in advance. If you are un-

---

PARENTS SHARE . . .

I had to fight just to get my son *tested*. The school kept saying, "He's so bright, and he's not failing, so he can't have a learning disability." I *knew* he was bright—that's why I couldn't understand why some kinds of school work were such a struggle for him. Finally I insisted on an evaluation. It showed he had both a learning disability and a gifted IQ. . . . So many people think "smart" and "LD" can't go together—even teachers, who you'd think would know better. Adam was actually relieved to find out he had a learning disability. He'd been knocking himself out to get C's—which was OK with the school, but not OK with Adam. After his program was modified, he made the honor roll. He got one of those "My child is an honor student" bumper stickers—you should have seen the grin on his face when we put it on the car!

---

able to attend a scheduled IEP meeting, it is reasonable to ask for the meeting to be rescheduled at a more convenient time. If it is impossible for you to attend a child's IEP meeting in person, then the school district should make an effort to secure your participation through other means, such as individual or conference telephone calls. The school district is also required to provide interpreters if parents are hearing-impaired or speak languages other than English. Despite these provisions to protect parents' rights, a surprisingly high number of parents never take part in preparing Individualized Education Programs. "I think many parents just don't realize what an important document the IEP is," one special educator says. "If it were my child, I'd take a day off from work—even a day without pay—to make sure her needs were being addressed properly."

2. MONITORING STUDENT PROGRESS

As Susie's story demonstrated, preparation of an appropriate IEP does not guarantee that a student's program will go smoothly. There are many things that can interfere with the implementation of an IEP, including unrealistic or badly stated goals, poor staff communication, large class size, scheduling problems, and shortages of space, materials, and support personnel. Student resistance can also be a problem, particularly among youngsters who experienced long periods of failure or frustration before their disabilities were identified.

These young people often lack faith in themselves, and many have developed behaviors that contribute to their academic problems. Daydreaming, procrastination, misbehaving to get attention, and manipulating others into reducing expectations or feeling sorry for them are a sampling of the counterproductive coping strategies often used by children with learning difficulties at school and at home.

Because so many of them have become discouraged, it is important for students with learning disabilities to start experiencing success as soon as possible. Once these students realize they are moving forward, their motivation and level of commitment to academic tasks usually improve. To maintain their enthusiasm, these youngsters need to be able to see themselves making progress on a regular basis. Many are very sensitive to setbacks; even short periods of frustration can be enough to cause these students to give up and revert to undesirable patterns of behavior.

For this reason, wise parents do not wait for report cards or for legally required annual reviews to see how their children are doing in school. Instead, they monitor student progress much more closely—often on a weekly or even daily basis. When they see problems (either with academic progress or emotional well-being), these parents contact the school and seek intervention promptly. This proactive stance protects children from experiencing damaging lengthy periods of defeat, and often leads to important adjustments in student programs.

In order to monitor a student's progress effectively, it is essential to develop cooperative relationships with the child's teachers—and sometimes with school administrators as well. This is a prospect some parents find intimidating, since there is something about meeting a teacher (or, heaven help us, a principal) that makes almost everyone feel like a student again. If we were successful as students, this is usually not a big obstacle to communication. Parents who did not do particularly well in school, however, may find themselves feeling frightened and powerless the moment they set foot on school property. Parents who felt they were treated unfairly in school (this group includes many parents who themselves have information-processing problems) may also feel hostile toward teachers and other education authorities. Such parents may have trouble dealing with teachers effectively because of a lack of assertiveness or a chip-on-the-shoulder attitude.

In Chapter 9 we will talk more about establishing relationships with your child's teachers and developing methods for monitoring student progress. It helps to begin, though, with a realistic idea of what you can expect from these important people in your child's life.

The guidelines for parent-teacher partnerships on pages 152–54 will help you identify what you can expect from a regular classroom teacher. These guidelines can also be used to evaluate how effectively teachers work with students who have learning problems.

3. PROVIDING APPROPRIATE SUPPORT AT HOME

The key word here is *appropriate*. Susie's devoted parents thought they were supporting their daughter by committing themselves night after night to helping her through her homework. The truth is, however, that they might have been doing her more harm than good. Quite possibly, their assistance made Susie feel dependent on them and reinforced her certainty that she could not succeed on her own. By doggedly enforcing unrealistic academic demands (no fourth-grader should be doing three hours of homework a night!) these parents also endangered their personal relationship with their child. Rather than experiencing what Mom and Dad were doing as supportive, Susie perceived them as unsympathetic slave drivers!

Does this mean parents should not help students who have learning disabilities with their schoolwork? Of course not; these youngsters need help with assignments on a fairly regular basis. Parents do need to learn to distinguish, though, between the kinds of help that sabotage self-esteem and the types that build self-confidence, independence, and good study habits. For example, Susie would have been far better off if her parents met with her teachers about reducing her unreasonable homework load and structuring her assignments so that Susie could do more of the work on her own. Susie's parents could contribute to her success by helping her break tasks down and set realistic deadlines, by establishing a structured time and place for doing homework, and by offering praise or agreed-upon rewards as segments of work were completed. In addition, they might agree to read certain texts to Susie (the science and social studies materials that are beyond her reading level, for example), and get the teacher's consent to allow Susie to dictate certain assignments to them so that the amount of writing she has to do does not become overwhelming. This kind of support lets Susie sidestep her disabilities while leaving her responsible for the actual work of learning and remembering information, interpreting concepts, and answering questions. Susie's life at home is likely to be a lot more peaceful, and when she succeeds, she will know she has done so on her own intellectual merits.

Guidelines for Parent-Teacher Partnerships

Regular classroom teachers are not trained in special education, and they should not be expected to function as special education teachers. Teachers can be expected to respect students' basic human rights, however, and to make reasonable accommodations for a disability (for discussion of accommodations, see Chapter 8). The guidelines below outline what parents of children with learning disabilities should expect from any teacher (basic), what a good teacher will provide (better), and behavior that identifies the truly exceptional teacher (best).

BASIC	BETTER	BEST
1. Children will not be criticized, shamed, scolded, humiliated, or made to feel embarrassed or guilty about their learning disabilities. The teacher will not tell them they are lazy, stupid, stubborn, or worthless.	Students will be encouraged to work around their learning problems while facing them honestly. Teachers will be sensitive to the social and emotional issues associated with learning disabilities and protect special needs students from children who tease or try to make them feel inferior.	Teachers will help the class reach a better understanding of learning disabilities. Activities will be designed so that special-needs students can make real contributions.
2. Children will never be asked to do work they are totally incapable of doing.	Children will be asked to do as much of the regular classwork as possible. When necessary, they will be given smaller amounts of the regular work or alternate assignments.	The teacher will work with special education staff to see that class materials are consistently adapted to students' ability levels and learning styles, or that special materials are provided that teach the same concepts at levels students can handle.
3. In reading, writing, and math, children will be given instruction appropriate to their level of skill. (No child reading at a second-grade level will be asked to work independently from a fifth-grade reading book, for example.)	In addition to understanding students' weaknesses, teachers will nurture strengths. (For instance, a child with poor writing but good drawing skills might be asked to illustrate a story written by another student for the school literary magazine.)	Teachers will maximize opportunities to individualize instruction. Options like cross-age grouping, peer and volunteer tutors, and creative use of computers will be used to help reinforce learning.

BASIC	BETTER	BEST
4. Children will participate in subjects such as science, social studies, health, music, art, and physical education to the greatest extent possible. Either students' work will be adjusted so that they can do it alone, or assistance will be provided as needed.	Teachers will vary their presentation methods to accommodate students with disabilities (for example, overhead projectors will be used to assist children who need visual reinforcement; hands-on materials will be provided to assist concrete learners).	Children will be taught organization, good study skills, and appropriate educational strategies so they can succeed in these subjects.
5. Students will be tested fairly. Disabilities will not be permitted to interfere with demonstrating knowledge. (The knowledge of a student with handwriting problems, for example, would not be judged on the basis of handwritten essays.)	Teachers will be flexible about time limits imposed for tests and test settings (quiet rooms will be made available for distractible students, for example).	Teachers will use a variety of evaluation methods to accommodate different learning styles (students might be given a choice between writing a final paper and taking a short-answer test, for example).
6. Children will not be prevented from taking part in enrichment activities as punishment for poor performance in school work. Art, music, physical education, recess, or field trips will not be withheld on the grounds that work was not finished or that the student failed a particular assignment. (Of course, those activities might be withheld for bad behavior.)	Field trips, special projects, drama, art, music, and sports will be regarded as worthwhile elements of the student's program. Achievement in these areas will be recognized and valued.	Teachers will help children discover outlets for their talents and energy and actively encourage participation in extracurricular activities.
7. The child will not be allowed to disrupt the class. The teacher will not tolerate temper tantrums, lack of respect, rudeness, foul language, physical injury, or damage to property.	Behavior problems will be avoided by good classroom management. The teacher will encourage children to express anger and frustration in ways that do no harm to themselves, to others, or to property. Children will be recognized and rewarded for their successes so they will learn to find satisfaction in good behavior.	The teacher will plan activities that enable students to succeed in order to help them improve their self-concepts and build self-esteem.

continued

BASIC	BETTER	BEST
8. The teacher will cooperate with parents and provide information about children's progress as needed.	The teacher will take the lead in seeing that the school and the home are working together in the best interest of the child. Teachers will suggest ways parents can help support the child academically and will remain flexible and open to suggestions from parents and other professionals.	The teacher will also attempt to coordinate instructional planning with psychologists, social workers, special education teachers, therapists, and others concerned with the child's welfare.

Adapted from Stevens, Suzanne H. (1980). *The learning disabled child: Ways that parents can help*. Winston-Salem, NC: John F. Blair.

Even more important than providing academic assistance are the jobs of providing emotional support to children with information-processing handicaps and making sure that these children feel they are valued and functioning members of a family. Many studies show that a sense of self-worth and belonging are more critical to a child's future success than academic skills. For this reason, the following types of activities may be just as valuable to your child as homework:

- Taking a fair share of household responsibilities

- Enjoying hobbies and recreational activities (such as sports, collecting, music, or arts and crafts)

- Participation in group activities (such as Scouts or 4-H Clubs)

- Involvement in community service projects (cleaning up the environment, help for the homeless, volunteering in political campaigns, and so on)

- Taking part in religious observances and traditions

- Enjoying travel and family outings

Try to avoid making participation in these activities or sharing in family fun conditional on success in school. All children need to believe that they belong and have value independent of their ability to perform academically. This is especially important for students with learning disabilities, whose progress in school is so often slow or erratic. "Becoming over-focused on school performance is a trap that catches many parents of students with learning disabilities," says one special education teacher. "So many try to take on the job of trying to teach their kids what they have been unable to learn in school. What this can mean, though, is that the kids never get a break. What children usually need most when they get home is love, acceptance, and a reduction of stress. These are gifts parents are uniquely equipped to provide."

In the following two chapters we will discuss constructive things parents can do to support students academically. In Part IV we will talk more about emotional support, and we will also look at how different parenting styles affect children's progress in school. In the meantime, if your instincts are telling you that your student has struggled enough for one day, trust your gut and arrange something fun. In the end, your understanding and encouragement ("You're a hard worker, and I'm so proud of you for sticking with that difficult stuff!") will do your child as much good as finishing those last three vocabulary words or math problems.

Once they become involved at school, many parents find themselves expanding their interests and activism beyond their children's immediate needs. Some volunteer in classrooms and become active

---

PARENTS SHARE . . .

My daughter's weakness is auditory processing—she needs extra time to understand what she hears. There was one third-grade teacher—if Jenny didn't respond to directions right *away,* this woman got right in her face and started yelling. This only confused Jenny even more. When she's bombarded with a lot of noise, she shuts down—like a soldier with shell shock. I learned it was very important to meet with teachers who were screamers early on. I would explain that Jenny needed extra time to process verbal instructions. I told them she did well with visual material, and suggested ways they could give her information that would help her succeed. Then I would talk about Jenny's response to loud voices, so that even if they didn't help her, at least they wouldn't shout at her. Fortunately, we didn't run into too many teachers like that—but wouldn't you know, Jenny's very first job supervisor was a screamer. Jenny did a good job handling that situation herself, though. She met with him and asked if he'd give her job assignments in writing . . .

in parent-teacher organizations, while others serve on administrative committees that oversee the educations of students with disabilities or plan new programs and services. When one mother found there were so few computers at her son's elementary school that he had problems getting access to one on a regular basis, she teamed up with another parent to write a series of grant applications that eventually provided the school with forty personal computers! Working with organizations like the Learning Disabilities Association of America, parents have also been instrumental in shaping state and national policies concerning the rights of students with disabilities and their families. In fact, without parent activists, it is unlikely that students with learning disabilities would have many of the protections and services to which they are now legally entitled.

There is still, however, a great deal of work to be done. In too many schools, a lack of awareness of the needs of students with disabilities, inadequate support for teachers, inflexible scheduling and curriculum requirements, shortages of appropriate equipment and materials, and the absence of a clear special education philosophy continue to impede quality programming. These issues need to be addressed on a school-by-school basis. The schools at which these issues are resolved successfully will almost certainly be those where parents have become actively involved, both in asking for change and in working to bring change about.

8

DEVELOPING AN EFFECTIVE EDUCATIONAL PROGRAM

Once a learning disability has been identified, federal law requires that an Individualized Education Program (IEP) be developed within thirty school days. The law also requires school districts to make an effort to include parents in the program-planning process.* There-fore, soon after eligibility for special education services has been de-termined you will receive a written invitation to participate in an IEP meeting. The purpose of this meeting is to present professional views of your child's learning problems, inform you of available educa-tional options, and secure your ideas about what your child needs. At the IEP meeting the school district will be represented by a commit-tee that includes one or more representatives of the department of special education, at least one of your child's teachers, and (if identi-fication is to be discussed) one or more members of the evaluation team. You are entitled to bring to the meeting anyone you would like to have present to support you or your child (friends, family mem-bers, or outside professionals).

---

*Federal regulations apply only to institutions receiving public funds. Private and parochial schools do not necessarily observe these procedures. Parents should be aware, however, that special-needs students enrolled in private and parochial schools are entitled to many free services from their public school districts, including speech therapy, physical and occupational therapy, and special education. For additional in-formation, contact your school district's department of special education.

Among the decisions to be made at an IEP meeting are the following:

- What special services does the student need, and who shall provide them?

- In what kind of class (or classes) will the child be educated?

- What kinds of special accommodations or modifications in the child's program will be allowed?

- What (if any) special equipment or technical support will be provided?

- What specific academic and behavioral goals will be established for the coming year?

- What (if any) special teaching programs will be used?

The outcome of these decisions is summarized in writing in an IEP document. This document must also include a statement of the duration of specific services (the number of hours per day, and days per week), a summary of the student's present achievement levels, and information on how progress toward specified goals is to be evaluated. Once the IEP document is complete, federal law requires that the described program be implemented without delay. The IEP must be reviewed and (if necessary) revised at least once a year.

Experienced parents note that it pays to go into IEP meetings prepared. "Don't count on the school district doing a thorough job of going over your rights or explaining how the special education system works," one mother cautions. "There usually isn't time. Our district schedules thirty to forty-five minutes for an IEP meeting—barely enough to discuss specific recommendations for the child." Unprepared parents also risk feeling outranked by professionals at IEP meetings; many say that, as beginners, they found themselves agreeing to recommendations without fully understanding the implications of their decisions. While programs can, of course, be changed if they prove ineffective or inappropriate, it is obviously better if a student can be put solidly on the road to success from the beginning.

What do you need to know to plan an effective educational program? The first step is to determine exactly what types of help the child needs. Although IEPs must be highly individualized to meet the combinations of needs unique to each student, nearly all programs for children with learning disabilities must include four basic components in order to be successful. One of a parent's most important responsibilities is to make sure that the school district covers all four of these bases, listed below.

1. THE PROGRAM MUST TEACH AND REINFORCE BASIC SKILLS

Students with learning disabilities usually need both individualized instruction and a lot of extra practice in order to master basic skills (reading, writing, and/or performing arithmetic calculations); specialized texts and teaching materials may also be required. The child's program should provide both teaching that is appropriate for the student's basic skills level and adequate opportunities to practice new skills as they develop. Usually, this kind of instruction needs to be delivered one-to-one or in a small group setting. Basic skills instruction may require a substantial commitment of time in the early stages of a special education program. As students progress, time allocated for this work typically decreases.

Most students with learning disabilities benefit from a "back to basics" approach to skills development, especially for reading. Research indicates that nearly all these students need a thorough grounding in phonics (that is, learning to decode words by sounding them out) in order to read successfully. No matter what instructional methods and materials are being used, progress in basic skills needs to be closely monitored to make sure that the programs are consistently effective. If a student does not start showing improvement within three months of starting a new reading or other basic skills curriculum, then the program should probably be reevaluated.

Basic skills instruction must also be governed by realistic expectations. Not all children with learning disabilities can reach average levels in reading, writing, and arithmetic, even with years of remedial help. For a student with severe language processing disabilities, basic literacy (often defined as reading at a third- or fourth-grade level) might be the highest attainable goal. Many students with learning disabilities will never be good spellers, and higher mathematics will always remain a mystery for some. In cases such as these, it is very important to teach students *compensatory skills*—ways of getting around what remains of their handicaps—so they can go on to achieve their personal goals. "There is a big difference between being illiterate and being uneducated," a special education teacher explains. "Even a person who can't read or write at all can become educated if he knows other ways to get and give information. Part of the school system's job is to teach the student with disabilities exactly what those other ways are."

2. THE PROGRAM MUST ENABLE THE STUDENT TO KEEP UP WITH CLASS CONTENT

Students with learning disabilities often have trouble keeping on top of subjects like health, science, and social studies, either because material is presented in a way that is inaccessible to them (for example, texts are beyond their reading capabilities, or lectures and demonstrations are too fast-paced for them to follow) or because getting special help removes them from the classroom for substantial periods of time. To prevent this problem, it may be necessary to modify academic tasks for students with information-processing weaknesses to some extent. For example, if a student has trouble keeping up with assigned reading, material can be read to the child, a simpler book can be substituted, or—if text is not essential to understanding a subject—it can be reduced or eliminated. Students who have trouble writing can be provided with copies of lecture notes, allowed to take some tests orally, and permitted to dictate long reports. It is also possible (and a good idea) to restructure some assignments so that students can work from a position of strength. Instead of writing a report on a South American country, for instance, a student might be asked to build a relief map of South America for the class or to design a poster illustrating major exports.

The checklist on pages 162–64 describes some modifications and accommodations that are frequently used to help students compensate for learning disabilities. It is essential to employ as many of these as necessary to enable a child to participate successfully in class. It is also important to pay careful attention to scheduling so that valuable elements of a child's program do not conflict. If a student is to leave class for special help in reading, for example, every effort should be made to schedule that help during the class reading period rather than a time that would compel the child to miss enrichment activities or instruction in other subject areas. When a child must miss instruction in a content area in order to get special education, it may be necessary to release the student from some academic obligations in order to avoid overburdening him. (For example, a fifth grader who needs three hours of special basic skills instruction a day might be exempted from health education and state history lessons, neither of which would be essential to success in sixth grade.) Whenever practical, basic skills instruction and course work should be combined—as when a learning specialist uses a simplified version of the history text to teach reading, or a science lesson to reinforce math principles.

As important as they are, modifications and accommodations should never be used as a substitute for adequate teaching. "Don't let the school system get away with saying 'We've given Johnny all his books on tape, so we don't have to teach him to read,'" a special educator warns. "These supports are intended to help students keep up with class content—not to enable the school to avoid doing its job." Excessive accommodation can also rob students of the opportunities they need to practice what they have been taught; if you let Johnny dictate *all* his assignments, his writing skills will never improve. Throughout the educations of children with learning disabilities, it is necessary to strive for balance. Encourage students to do as much of the regular classwork and homework as they can. Use modifications and accommodations when disabilities prevent them from learning or demonstrating what they know, or when the academic load starts to become overwhelming.

3. THE PROGRAM MUST HELP THE STUDENT LEARN APPROPRIATE EDUCATIONAL STRATEGIES

The most heroic efforts to keep a student up with the curriculum won't count for much if they produce a young adult who cannot learn independently. That is what can happen, however, if youngsters with learning disabilities are not taught organizational and time-management skills, effective study habits, methods to improve memory, problem-solving and decision-making strategies, and self-advocacy skills. For most students, these skills are also essential to academic survival; test and homework failures can have as much to do with forgotten deadlines, books that got left at school, and failure to ask for help as with basic skills deficits or information-processing problems.

The Metacognitive Skills Checklist in Chapter 6 (pages 126–27) lists areas in which children with disabilities are likely to need special instruction. Help needs to be provided at a level that is appropriate to the student's age. For example, while youngsters can start to learn basic organizational skills (such as keeping books and school supplies in a special place, and having a regular time for doing chores or schoolwork) as young as five or six, not many are ready for work on memorization or problem-solving strategies before the fourth or fifth grade. (Keep children's memory capabilities in mind at

Modifications and Accommodations for Students with Learning Disabilities

Modifications and accommodations such as those listed below can be either formally specified on students' Individual Education Programs (IEPs) or worked out informally with teachers and school administrators. When they are specified on an IEP, all the child's teachers are legally required to comply with them. In most cases, accommodations and modifications specified on a high school IEP will continue to be honored by colleges and vocational programs. Students with documented disabilities are also allowed some accommodations on college entrance exams (SATs and ACTs) and state and national competency tests.

In the Classroom:
- Allow preferred seating (near the teacher, close to the blackboard)
- Allow extra time to answer questions and to complete written work
- Provide copies of laboratory or lecture notes (notes can be provided by either the teacher or another student)
- Allow use of a tape recorder to record lectures
- Allow use of a calculator
- Provide access to a computer
- Allow alternative activities (e.g., ask student to prepare a video instead of writing a report)
- Highlight texts and worksheets to help student locate most important material
- Provide instructions both orally and in writing
- Provide more or fewer visual aids (depending on type of disability)
- Provide ready access to math tables, lists of formulas, maps, and so on (rather than requiring the student to memorize such material)
- Assign lab or study partners to help with particular tasks or subjects
- Preview written material (discuss contents of assigned texts in advance); pre-teach key vocabulary words
- Exempt student from selected requirements or activities (e.g., memorize periodic tables; oral math drills)

Testing:
- Allow alternate settings (student may take tests in library, resource room, at home)
- Allow flexible scheduling (student may take tests after school, during study hall or resource period; test may be completed in two or more sessions)
- Extend or waive time limits
- Allow directions and test questions to be read to student
- Rephrase test questions in simpler language as necessary

- Allow student to answer questions orally instead of in writing
- Allow short-answer-only tests (true/false, multiple choice)
- Allow essay-only tests
- Allow use of calculator or math facts chart
- If student is unable to memorize, allow access to dates/facts/formulas on "cheat sheets"
- Allow tests to be taken on a computer (at school or at home)
- Allow student to circle answers in test booklet rather than use a computerized answer sheet
- Reduce number of test questions or problems (student is tested on ten division problems or vocabulary words rather than twenty five)

Homework:
- Give students their homework assignments in writing on a daily or weekly basis (as opposed to giving assignments orally or expecting them to be copied from board)
- Arrange for textbooks on tape
- Allow all or part of assigned texts to be read to student
- Allow use of computers to scan and "read" written material
- Reduce total amount of material to be read (teacher highlights key passages, for example)
- Allow assigned texts to be rewritten in simpler language
- Allow text alternatives (permit student to watch movie version of Shakespeare's *Romeo and Juliet* instead of reading it)
- Allow students to record assignments on tape rather than writing
- Allow student to dictate reports to a "scribe" (often a parent) or give reports orally
- Reduce number of questions to be answered and/or length of written assignments (answer five comprehension questions instead of ten; write a three-page rather than a five-page report)
- Allow grading policy of no points off for spelling errors
- Allow assistance of proofreader to correct spelling/punctuation errors
- Allow use of computer with spell-checker
- Allow use of Cliff Notes or prepared outlines for previewing, organizing, and reviewing text material

Overall Program Planning:
- Consider extended time to complete the educational program (e.g., five years to complete high school) in order to reduce the course load each year. Public school students are legally entitled to remain in school through age twenty-one. Students have successfully negotiated with colleges to spread four years of courses over five years without incurring additional tuition charges.

continued

- Encourage the student to take some courses in summer school and reduce course load during the academic year
- Grant exemption from foreign language requirement
- Allow computer technology courses to be substituted for higher-level math courses
- Design independent study or work/study courses to meet some requirements

home, too. Most first graders will have to be reminded to do chores. Ten- and eleven-year-olds, however, can be taught strategies for reminding themselves, such as posting notes on a bulletin board or marking the chores on a calendar.) The importance of metacognitive skills increases dramatically when students enter secondary school. For this reason, the introduction of learning-strategies instruction should not be delayed beyond seventh grade if at all possible.

Self-advocacy is among the most important skills a student with learning disabilities can master, yet teaching this skill is often overlooked. Both parents and teachers sometimes get so used to "managing" a student's program that they forget that a time comes when it is proper to step aside and let the student take over. Children need to be helped to understand their own learning strengths and weaknesses, taught when and how to ask for assistance, and encouraged to communicate and negotiate with teachers on their own behalf. Youngsters must also learn appropriate uses of self-advocacy: seeking a reasonable accommodation like extra time to finish an exam is fine, but using a disability as an excuse to avoid taking an exam altogether is not. Note that it is appropriate for secondary school students (and mature younger children) to attend IEP meetings and participate in setting educational goals. Teens especially become more cooperative and enthusiastic about their programs if they are involved in the planning process.

4. THE PROGRAM MUST HELP THE STUDENT ADDRESS PROBLEM BEHAVIORS

Students with learning disabilities often need help learning how to modify behaviors that interfere with functioning in a classroom. Most common among these are difficulties with focusing attention, staying on task, controlling impulsive behavior, and managing anger. Some shy students need help learning to become more assertive about asking for help and/or participating in class activities. Learning appropriate social skills can also pay off in improved peer acceptance of students with learning disabilities, an important (but often overlooked) element of classroom survival.

Teachers use many methods of behavior management, but the most successful tend to employ *positive reinforcement*. This involves making an effort to "catch the child being good" and rewarding desirable behavior, as opposed to giving children attention mostly when they act up or step out of line. Methods centered on punishment rarely succeed in effecting long-term behavior changes; sarcasm, ridicule, and humiliation are bad for all children and should never be used as methods of "motivation." To be most effective, systems of behavior modification need to be practiced by all the child's teachers— and also reinforced at home. Parent-teacher cooperation is often the key to real improvement. (If parents and teachers both agree to recognize and praise efforts to improve handwriting, for example, children will probably improve faster than when either parents or teachers target the issue on their own.)

For children who suffer from attention deficit hyperactivity disorder (ADHD), medication (most commonly with stimulants like Ritalin) can also play a role in behavior management. The decision to use medication must be made cautiously, however. Some experts feel that Ritalin has been vastly overprescribed and is too often given to normal, high-energy youngsters by physicians who know little about ADHD. It must also be noted that stimulant medications can have side effects that need to be weighed against potential benefits. In the box on pages 168–70 the pros and cons of medication for ADHD are discussed so that you can make an informed choice on this issue. Keep in mind, though, that medication should be viewed as only one element in a multi-level program of support.

In IEP meetings, parents may have to advocate for measures that address a student's individual needs in each of the four key areas described above. "Special education committees often suffer from tunnel vision," one mother comments. "They focus on academic goals, sometimes to the exclusion of everything else. Behavior modification might be suggested if a child is really out of control—but for a child who is quiet and doesn't speak up enough? Not likely." Social skills training and instruction in learning strategies may also not be provided unless parents specifically ask for them. Even when addressing academic concerns committees can over-focus. "My son's reading problems always got attention at IEP meetings," another mother remembers, "but I usually had to remind the committee that he needed some help with his writing too."

Since a student's program must be described in terms of written goals and objectives on the IEP document, it will help if you can state what you want for your child in the most concrete terms possible. To be effective, listed goals and objectives should have the following characteristics:

Realistic: Objectives must take into account the student's present levels of achievement, and they should describe gains that can be made within one year. "Tim will score within the average range for math computation" is not a realistic objective if Tim is a sixth-grader starting out with second-grade math skills. "Tim will complete three-column addition and subtraction problems with 90 percent accuracy and learn to use a calculator for problems involving multiplication and division" is more realistic.

Specific: "Susan will improve her vocational skills" is too vague an objective to be useful for guiding instruction. "Susan will complete the career explorations program, target an area of interest, and participate in a short internship" is a better statement of what she might be expected to accomplish this year.

Measurable: "Darnell will improve his self-esteem" may describe a worthy goal, but how will Darnell's parents and teachers judge whether efforts to help him in this area have succeeded? "Darnell will be given leadership responsibility as a crossing guard" and "Darnell will use his advanced art skills to make posters for school activities" are concrete objectives targeting self-esteem.

All the modifications, accommodations, and exemptions to which the child is entitled should also be included in the IEP document. Remember that modifications and accommodations recorded on an IEP are binding on all of a child's teachers unless otherwise specified. "May take tests orally" means a high school student can take oral exams in any class or subject.

If the student needs services in addition to those offered by regular and special education teachers, the IEP document should specify those as well. For example, a child might receive direct or indirect help from the following school specialists:

Reading or math specialists provide remedial instruction to nondisabled low achievers and also help organize and evaluate the reading and math curricula at the school. While the law requires students with learning disabilities to receive basic skills instruction from special education teachers, reading and math specialists are sometimes called in to help pinpoint problems and advise special educators on materials and methods.

Speech-language pathologists are trained to work with students who have articulation, voice, fluency (stuttering), or language development disorders. They often help screen entering students for developmental delays.

School psychologists participate in teams that evaluate students for learning disabilities. They also counsel students about a wide variety of nonacademic problems and advise teachers on behavior management and instructional techniques.

Physical and occupational therapists can assist students who have persistent coordination difficulties, in addition to providing services for students with physical handicaps.

Audiologists can determine if sound processing problems or hearing deficits are contributing to learning disabilities. These findings can be used to modify instructional approaches or student seating arrangements.

Social workers and guidance counselors are available to help families resolve issues that may be having an impact on a student's learning. They are often instrumental in helping families connect with support services or resources in the community (such as health care services or adult literacy training).

Vocational educators assist with career exploration as well as helping students learn specific employment skills. They can sometimes place students in job-training positions in the community.

If the child is to receive direct services, the duration of each service must be specified on the IEP in addition to specific objectives (it might be determined, for example, that the child will receive speech therapy for three half-hour sessions each week, and the goal is to increase intelligibility from 60 percent to 85 percent). Once services have been specified on an IEP, the school district is expected to provide them immediately (short delays are permissible if needed to

Medication for Attention Deficits and Hyperactivity

For more than fifty years, stimulant medications such as methylphenidate (Ritalin), dextroamphetamine (Dexedrine), and pemoline (Cylert) have been used to "normalize" the behavior of children who exhibit symptoms of attention deficit hyperactivity disorder (ADHD, described in Chapter 2). Studies indicate that as many as 80 percent of students with ADHD respond to stimulants positively. For these individuals, benefits include reduction in hyperactivity, increased attention span, and improved muscle coordination, all of which help students focus on and complete academic tasks. Since children using stimulants often become less impulsive, aggressive, and destructive, drug therapy can improve social acceptance as well.

Research indicates that use of stimulants to improve availability for learning can lead to dramatic short-term gains in academic achievement. Several studies have found improvement in test scores and accuracy, quantity, and speed of completing daily assignments after students with ADHD started taking stimulants. The long-term picture is less clear, but it seems safe to say that stimulant medications can help many students with ADHD perform better by improving their levels of attention, motivation, and cooperation.

The most common side effects associated with use of stimulant medications are reduction of appetite and weight loss, and difficulty falling asleep. These problems sometimes disappear after children become accustomed to the medication; if they persist, a change in dosage or type of drug may bring improvement. (Some doctors recommend medicating students during school hours only, so that stimulants won't interfere with dinner and bedtime. Others say use of Ritalin at bedtime may help children calm down for sleep.) Research also indicates that the growth of children taking stimulants is often slowed or delayed, although the growth of youngsters taking low to moderate doses of Ritalin usually "rebounds" after the first year. The growth of children taking Dexedrine or higher doses of Ritalin may be slow as long as they remain on medication, but studies indicate these students also return to normal growth patterns when drug therapy stops. Some experts advise "drug holidays" during vacation periods to allow children's growth to catch up. Others note that because not all education takes place during school hours, it may be best to leave children on medication so they can take full advantage of their learning opportunities. Children who remain on medication may be late to attain full growth, but they do catch up eventually.

Less common effects of stimulants include headaches, lethargy, irritability, talkativeness, nausea, euphoria, depression, nightmares, dry mouth, constipation, anxiety, hallucinations, nervous tics, and tremors.

Some research indicates that stimulants can bring on symptoms of Tourette's syndrome or make them worse, so treatment with stimulants should be avoided by children at risk for tic disorders. If adjusting dosage does not deal with adverse side effects or does not improve attention and concentration, parents may want to discuss alternative medications with their physicians. Clonodine (a medication normally used to treat hypertension) has helped some people who have both ADHD and Tourette's syndrome. Antidepressant drugs such as imipramine have also been found to help some youngsters who cannot tolerate or do not respond to stimulants.

Concerns about use of stimulants leading to addiction are not supported by research to date. While some stimulants (notably amphetamines) can become addictive if abused by adolescents and adults, low therapeutic doses appear to be safe for children. Children do not become addicted to these medications, nor do they become more likely to abuse other drugs later on. In contrast, there are studies suggesting that *untreated* children with ADHD may be at increased risk for alcohol and drug abuse as teens. Authorities relate the substance abuse to the high rate of academic failure and low self-esteem often found in this population.

Successful drug therapy depends on finding the right medication, as well as the lowest effective dosage for each child. Note that youngsters may remain energetic and somewhat impulsive even after starting medication; the goal is only to improve their attention, not to drug them into a zombie-like state. Since drug responses are highly individual, close monitoring and frequent adjustments in dosage may be needed at the beginning of treatment. Periodic additional adjustments are also likely to be required as children get older. In addition, parents must be alert to potential drug interactions (the antihistamines in some cold and allergy medications, for example, can neutralize the effects of stimulants). It is important to be aware that medication is a long-term treatment. The National Institute of Mental Health (NIMH) estimates that 80 percent of individuals who need medication for ADHD as children will continue to need it as teenagers; 50 percent will benefit from taking stimulant medication as adults.

Experts at NIMH also urge parents to "remember that many things, including anxiety, depression, allergies, seizures, or problems with the home or school environment can make children seem overactive, impulsive or inattentive." In addition to finding a physician knowledgeable about treating ADHD (this might be a neurologist, a psychiatrist, or a pediatrician), it is important to conduct a comprehensive educational evaluation so that all factors contributing to a student's behavior and

continued

achievement problems can be understood. Up to 40 percent of students with ADHD also have specific learning disabilities that require special education intervention. Psychotherapy, social skills training, and vocational counseling may be needed to address social, emotional, and employment issues. Sometimes dealing with these concerns effectively makes use of medication unnecessary.

make arrangements for transportation, personnel, or new equipment).

If assistance from several different specialists is recommended (a speech pathologist, an occupational therapist, and a psychologist, for example), ask who is going to be responsible for coordinating these services and monitoring the student's overall program. Too often, it turns out that nobody is. When this is the case, services can start conflicting with instruction, with recreation, and with each other, and children can become more and more confused because of all the "help" they are getting! To achieve a well-integrated program, somebody has to be watching out for interests of the whole child—and parents frequently inherit this role.

Be aware, then, that providing too many services can be as troublesome as providing too few. When children have multiple problems or disabilities, prioritizing goals and tackling a few problems at a time is usually better than trying to take on everything at once. (If a student has become very depressed about school, for example, get the academic program adjusted, involve the child in satisfying and rewarding activities, and look into counseling first; speech and occupational therapy can wait until the youngster has regained some self-confidence and enthusiasm for education.)

An issue of urgent concern for most parents at IEP meetings is "in what kind of class should my child be educated?" School districts are required to provide a broad range of educational options for students with special needs. Eight are described below. (The actual choices in your own district may be greater or more limited than those presented here).

1. The child is placed in a regular classroom full-time. The classroom teacher individualizes the environment and modifies the curriculum for the student to some extent.

2. The child is placed in a regular classroom full-time. A learning specialist visits the classroom on a regular basis to help special-needs students (the "push-in" model). Sometimes the learning specialist will also work with some non-disabled students (such as the advanced readers) in order to avoid "spotlighting" or stigmatizing children who need special education.

3. The child is placed full-time in a program in which there are special education and regular education co-teachers. Usually there will be a number of special-needs children in such a class, and several different kinds of disabilities may be represented (for example, the class may include children who are mildly retarded and/or children with emotional problems as well as typical children and children with learning disabilities).

4. The child is placed in a regular classroom, but leaves to get help from a special educator in a *resource room* for one to three periods daily. (This—the "pull-out" model—is currently the most common arrangement for students with learning disabilities.) Instruction in the resource room is delivered one-to-one or in small groups.

5. The child is placed in a self-contained special education class (a smaller class with more teaching support; all the students have special needs), but is "mainstreamed" in regular classes for subjects with which the child's disability will not have a major impact (for example, science, art, music, and gym).

6. The child is placed in a special education class full-time. Ideally this class will be located at the student's home school, but it might be necessary to transport the child to another facility. This could be a regular school where there is more in the way of staff, space, equipment, or services for students with disabilities, or a school where all students have special needs. (*Note*: School districts can contract with private schools or individuals to provide pupil services rather than provide them directly. A district *must* seek private placement or support if it cannot provide appropriate services for a special education student in a timely fashion. In these cases, the school district pays tuition and related charges. There is no cost to the family.)

7. The child is placed in a residential setting. This option is likely to be exercised only if the child has needs so unusual or severe that they cannot possibly be met locally, or has behavior problems serious enough to have involved the criminal justice system.

8. The child is schooled at home. This option is available for children who have serious illnesses, have been suspended for disciplinary infractions, or have other problems that must keep them out of

Is Home Schooling the Answer?

"Michael was born two months prematurely and has several disabilities," explains his mother, Mary. "He has very poor fine motor coordination, which affects his writing and his ability to take care of himself; all through elementary school, he needed help with things like tying his shoes and getting his coat buttoned. He also has problems with spatial awareness, some problems with reading comprehension, and attention deficits—it's very hard for him to stick to things." In his nine years of school, Michael has been assigned to several different types of special education programs. Self-contained classes provided the structure and supervision he needs, but they did not always challenge Michael to work up to his full intellectual potential. "His progress in those classes was so slow I ended up hiring tutors after school to teach him to read and write properly," Mary says. Regular classes, however, did not provide Michael with enough individual attention and guidance to keep him on track. "When we tried mainstreaming, Michael just fell apart," Mary remembers. "His behavior went all to pieces—like I suddenly had a devil-child on my hands."

For junior high, Michael was placed in an integrated program co-taught by regular and special education teachers. He did reasonably well in this environment, and a similar program was recommended for ninth grade. Unfortunately, the program was not available in Michael's home high school; he would have to be bused across the city. "I don't think the school and the neighborhood where it's located are safe," Mary explains, "especially for a kid like Michael, who has been protected and isn't that 'street wise.' I also didn't want to cut Michael off from his neighborhood friends—I think having a social support system is very important." Since nothing the school district could offer looked right for Michael, Mary decided to home-school him for ninth grade.

Mary and Michael are part of a growing trend in America. In the last decade the number of students being educated at home has more than tripled, and it is estimated that 2 percent of America's students will be home-schooled by the year 2000. It is a choice that is gaining increasing acceptance by the "educational establishment." Some school districts now have explicit policies of cooperation with home-schoolers, providing books, library privileges, testing, and other support services to parents who wish to educate their own children. A few even permit children

school for extended periods. Teachers visit the home daily to provide individualized instruction. Some parents also choose to teach their own children at home (see pages 172–73).

who are home-schooled to participate in sports and other extracurricular activities. In addition, home-schoolers can now turn to a network of local, state, and national organizations for help and information. Organizations such as the National Homeschool Association (P.O. Box 157290, Cincinnati, OH 45215-7290) keep families posted about resources, research, and legal news.

Parents who home-school cite many advantages to their way of life, including their ability to ensure high academic standards, physical safety, moral education, and an education tailored to children's individual talents, needs, and interests. Most admit, however, there is a downside to home schooling. Social isolation is one difficulty that is widely acknowledged. Some parents note that access to educational materials and resources can also be a problem, and others say they could use help with choosing educational activities and with testing. Parents who have support from their school systems, churches, families, and/or communities have fewer complaints than those trying to "go it alone." In one survey, 92 percent of home-schooling parents indicated that such support was integral to the process.

Parents interested in making the serious investment of time and energy that home schooling requires should begin by contacting their superintendent of schools for information about state and local policies. Keep in mind that federal law does guarantee access to special education services for children with disabilities who are educated at home (as well as for those educated in private and parochial schools). Available services include testing for disabilities, speech, physical, and occupational therapy, and individualized help with arithmetic, reading, and writing.

For now, home schooling is working for Michael and Mary. Mary says two things have helped make the program successful: Mary's aunt (a teacher) set up math and reading programs on a computer for Michael ("I don't have the academic background to teach reading or high school math," Mary admits), and Michael regularly participates in sports at a local recreation center ("That's where he gets exercise and connects with his friends," his mother explains). Mary is undecided, though, about whether she will continue home schooling next year. "Michael is almost sixteen, and we have to start thinking about how he's going to support himself," she says. "I expect to continue to help Michael with academic skills, but we're also looking over our options for vocational education."

Over the course of a student's education more than one of these options may be utilized. For example, a third-grade non-reader with a history of behavior problems might need the structure and low

student-teacher ratio of a self-contained special education class starting out. When his behavior stabilizes, he can be "mainstreamed" for
classes that do not require too much in the way of reading. When his
reading skills reach "survival" level, he can be placed in a regular
classroom with some accommodations, and receive continued reading instruction in the resource room. If he learns appropriate self-
advocacy and compensatory strategies, this student may well reach a
point where he can function successfully in regular classrooms with
minimal outside help.

Education experts and parents agree that the type of class in which a
child is placed is ultimately less important than what happens *in* that
class. "Attaching too much importance to the type of program a child
attends can distract parents from looking at issues that could have a
far greater impact on the child's success," says the director of a university learning clinic. "The fact is that the 'place' in which services
are offered is not a critical factor. What really count are things like
the skill and attitudes of the teacher and the atmosphere in the classroom. Is the learning environment pleasant and peaceful or is it noisy
and distracting? Do students respect one another or are they disruptive and at odds? Is the teacher organized or disorganized? Rigid or
flexible? Are the teacher's instructional style and the student's learning style compatible? All of these considerations are more important
than whether a class is labelled regular or special education." Experienced parents echo this view emphatically. "The bottom line is that
you have to locate the best teachers," a father of two children with
learning disabilities summarizes. "Nine times out of ten, it's the
teacher that makes or breaks the program."

Parents should therefore not give final approval to *any* placement
until they visit the school, talk with the teacher(s) who would be
working with their child, and observe those teachers at work in their
classrooms. Although this involves a commitment of time and effort,
it is by far the best way to determine whether or not a proposed
placement is likely to meet a student's needs. As we discussed in
Chapter 6, much of what you will look for when you observe in a
classroom will derive from your knowledge of your child and your
understanding of the types of settings, tasks, and personalities that
bring out the best in him or her. In addition, ten characteristics of an
effective school environment that benefit most children with learning
disabilities are described below:

A manageable class size. Research finds a consistent relationship between class size and academic achievement. Not only are teachers

more likely to individualize instruction in smaller classes, but they tend to have more positive attitudes about students when student-teacher ratios are low. This translates into both greater student participation and higher student self-esteem. An advantage of special education classes is that state laws require them to be small (often fifteen students or less); when class size exceeds twenty-five students, the quality of education usually declines sharply.

Limited distractions. Excessive background noise and/or clutter can compromise the learning potential of an entire class. Studies show that all students— not just those with learning disabilities—do best in relatively quiet environments with limited visual distractions. Some teachers try to limit distractions further for youngsters with learning disabilities by placing them in isolated corners of the classroom, but this practice is counterproductive (it usually results in less supervision and encouragement from the teacher). Research indicates that students with disabilities do best when seated near the teacher in the front of the classroom.

A teacher who provides effective guidance. Beware of teachers who give the class an assignment and retreat to their desks to grade papers. The best teachers for kids with learning disabilities (and for typical children as well) are those who take an active role in instruction and spend a high percentage of their time directly involved with students. When students are working independently, good teachers are found moving around the classroom monitoring individual progress, helping students stay on task, checking for understanding, and offering encouragement. Effective teachers also model and reinforce respect for others and good social manners in the classroom.

A noncompetitive atmosphere. Many teachers use "contests" like science fairs, math competitions, and spelling bees to encourage youngsters to study. The classroom's top academic performers may also be given rewards like stickers, gold stars, or special privileges. This type of motivational technique, though, is likely to *discourage* kids with learning problems. They feel they cannot possibly compete, and in addition may feel shamed and betrayed because their limitations have been publicly exposed. In general, children with learning disabilities do best in classrooms in which students work cooperatively toward shared goals. A team approach to assignments can make a student a valuable player in spite of disabilities (for example, a student who does not read well but has strengths in math might prepare the statistics for a group science report). Look also for a teacher who values personal progress over high grades; the child who moves from a D to a C in spelling ought to get the same recognition and approval as the child who moves from a B to an A.

An orderly approach to learning. Nearly all students with learning disabilities need structure. They do their best work in classes that have consistent routines, clear rules and procedures, and predictable schedules. A disorganized teacher will make it very hard for these students to do their best, as will a schedule that requires many changes of class and the need to absorb several sets of rules and requirements (the transition to secondary school is often difficult for this reason). Not only does inefficiency in the classroom compromise students' ability to perform, it also cheats them of valuable instructional time. One study of elementary school classes found that students spent 14 percent of their school days simply waiting for teachers to get organized; another found that one-third of students' time was spent waiting for teacher directions, getting and putting away materials, and lining up and moving to new activities. Time spent on task and academic achievement are clearly related, so look for a teacher who keeps noninstructional business to a minimum.

A focus on basic skills. "Enrichment activities" like field trips, music, art, and drama are valuable components of the curriculum and often offer students with learning disabilities opportunities to stand out. In some schools, however, there is so much enrichment going on that basic skills instruction has been compromised. One mother found that her son's sixth-grade curriculum had been organized around a theme of discovering other cultures. "Every month they focused on a different ethnic group," she remembers. "They really got into it—watched movies, cooked ethnic foods, dressed in costumes. I thought it was great until I realized that my son hadn't brought home one written paper all year. Later I found out there wasn't much reading going on, either." Students with learning disabilities need continuous instruction and reinforcement of their basic skills. Worthwhile goals like learning about other cultures should be tied to skill-building activities such as reading stories connected to the culture, using a computer to find more information about it, writing related reports, and/or corresponding with pen pals.

Instructional flexibility. As we have said more than once, rigidity in the classroom is toxic to students with learning disabilities. These students are limited in the ways they can understand, remember, and/or communicate information; if they are not matched with teaching styles and curriculum materials that target their strengths, they make very poor progress. In addition, because these youngsters' brains often process information more slowly than those of typical students, many need extra time to understand material and complete tasks successfully. When uncompromising time limits are imposed on instruction and testing, students with learning disabilities find it hard to succeed. One way of evaluating flexibility is to ask teachers about basic skills curricula. Does the teacher stick with one reading and math program, or (far better) select materials from several different programs according to student needs? Look also for classes that group students by skill level (groups might include students of different ages) and change groupings for different subjects (a student who is a poor reader but has great math skills should be in the top math group, and can participate in a heterogeneous group for social studies). Instructional groupings should not be cast in concrete; students should be able to move easily from one group to another as skills improve. Creative approaches like assigning peer tutors, study partners, or volunteer "mentors" to students who need extra help can also improve the options of students with learning disabilities.

Clear expectations for achievement. There are many studies that show that children rise to the occasion when teachers expect them to do well. Unfortunately, high expectations are not always extended to the student with learning disabilities. Regular classroom teachers sometimes assume special education students will do poorly; as a result, some invest less effort in these students, apply lower standards, and even avoid assigning them homework (kids don't want to hear it, but doing homework *is* clearly related to academic success). "Look for teachers who call on the low achievers as often as the class 'stars,'" one parent advises. "Also, don't allow the teacher to accept anything less than your child's best efforts. If you feel your child is capable of doing better than the work that's coming home, make an appointment to talk to the teacher about raising standards." Students with learning disabilities benefit most when goals for achievement are clear, attainable within a reasonable time period, and tied to specific learning practices. "I expect you to do better in Spanish" is not as motivating as "If you practice with the flash cards for fifteen minutes a day, you should score 80 percent or better on the Spanish quiz next week."

Effective monitoring of student performance. "My son brought home great math grades all year, so I was expecting real improvement on the year-end standardized achievement tests," remembers the mother of a fourth grader with learning disabilities. "But those tests showed he was still two years behind; he'd made very little progress. I was disappointed and angry. What happened?" What happened is that this student earned good grades on the second-grade math work he had been given, but had not been challenged sufficiently to close the gap between his math performance and that of his typical peers. The A's on his report card were therefore somewhat deceptive. Does this mean the student should have been given D's and F's? Of course not; students with learning disabilities should be graded fairly on the highest level of work they are capable of doing. Comparisons with achievement of typical students, though, should not be left until the end of the year. If this student's good performance but relative lack of progress had been noted earlier, he might have been placed success-fully in a more difficult math program and moved ahead faster. *Curriculum-based assessment* (described on page 179) is one effective way of monitoring student progress on an ongoing basis. Whatever monitoring methods are used, it is important for teachers to keep parents informed about both performance on current lessons *and* progress toward annual goals (as listed on the IEP).

Ample positive feedback. Research shows that all students benefit from being given frequent and timely feedback. Tests and papers that are returned promptly, weekly or monthly progress reports, and charts or graphs that illustrate progress toward stated goals have all been shown to have a positive effect on learning. Students with learn-ing disabilities, however, often need extra feedback and encourage-ment. Because these youngsters so frequently advance by fits and starts (two steps forward, then one back again), many have trouble understanding they are actually making progress. "These kids are very easily discouraged," says a special education teacher. "You have to keep *proving* to them that they're getting somewhere. They need cheerleaders to keep them on task, to keep them from giving up." Cheerleaders must remember, however, that students with disabili-ties can be very sensitive about feedback that isn't fair or honest. As Jeff's story illustrates, these youngsters want applause for actual achievement; they need teachers who recognize, value, and validate small steps forward and real work that has been done differently.

Recommendations for how to get a student placed in a preferred setting vary. "I hear some schools are responsive to parent requests for a particular class, but ours wasn't," says a mother who admits to

Curriculum-Based Assessment

Curriculum-based assessment (CBA) offers teachers a quick and easy method of keeping tabs on an individual student's progress, using everyday class materials. If your school's teaching team is unfamiliar with CBA, most recent books on assessment describe how it is done. Below are brief examples of how CBA can be used to evaluate achievement in particular subjects. These exercises can be repeated every three to four weeks to assess progress. CBA is very useful for determining how well certain teaching methods or materials are working for a given child.

Reading: The number of words your child reads aloud correctly in one minute is compared to that of classmates reading the same passage (children are given the correct word if they hesitate or stumble for three seconds). Since reading comprehension is closely tied to reading rate, this simple test predicts reading comprehension levels accurately for most children.

Math: The class is given three minutes to work a series of problems representative of what has been taught that year, or of what children their age are expected to know. The number of correct digits in the answers provided by your child is compared with the number in the answers supplied by other students. The percentage of correct digits will rise as comprehension of concepts and ability to compute improve.

Spelling: Twenty spelling words are dictated to the class; students have seven seconds to write each word before the next one is dictated. The number of correct two-letter sequences is counted, as well as correct first and last letters. Repeating this test can tell the teacher whether your child's spelling skills are developing, and whether development is slower or faster than other children in the class.

Writing: A "story starter" is provided; children are then asked to write for three minutes. The length of the passage (total number of words) your child has written is compared with that of classmates. Usually, length of passage and writing quality (sophistication of thoughts expressed) improve together.

"shameless manipulation" to get her son placed with the school's best teachers. "I found out *teachers* could recommend a particular class for a student, so each year I enlisted the help of my son's teachers in selecting the best class for the next year. The teachers were usually happy to cooperate because I went out of my way to be helpful to

---

JEFF

A self-employed computer software designer, Jeff struggled with dyslexia throughout his school and college years.

My mother remembers me coming home from school and saying "I am so much smarter than those guys. Why are they so dumb and they can read and I can't?" I always had a little of that constructive arrogance, you know. I never really thought I was stupid, and I think that's fortunate for me. But I remember being overwhelmed, and just downright obstinate about the way I wanted to do things . . . One thing I was very sensitive about throughout my elementary education was, you know, just evaluate me on what I *do;* don't say "Well, you misspelled nine out of ten words, but you did a great job on this one word so we'll give you 100 with two smiley faces at the top." I mean, don't lie to me in terms of my performance. I was always really aware of how I was doing, and I was also aware of how everybody else in the class was doing. I was quite on top of that . . .

I remember in fifth grade we had to do a report. The subject I chose was "Arms and Armor in the Middle Ages." My dad took me to the Metropolitan Museum in New York City and I pawed over every single piece of armor in their collection. We bought tons of books and my father read all these books to me. Then I basically created my own book. I cut up all the books Dad bought me—I cut pictures out and I cut words out and I created this report. I didn't really type anything or write anything but I took all the things I wanted to say out of all the different books and I

---

them—I could always be counted on to chaperon a field trip, sew costumes for the class play, or bake four dozen brownies for the bake sale." Other parents have found that *suggesting* a teacher for a child (and backing the suggestion up with logical reasons for such a placement) sometimes works where a straightforward request would not. "Our elementary school had a policy against parent requests for individual teachers," one mother remembers, "but if I said 'Gee, Mrs. Smith is so calm and patient, I think Harold would do awfully well with her, don't you?' the principal usually went along." Many parents swear by the "squeaky wheel" or "broken record" approach: "I just kept politely asking for what I wanted until they gave it to me," a mother explains, "I think it got so the principal got a headache as soon as she saw me coming." "I always got a better reception when I

pasted them together. It was a great report, and it was obvious that for me to accomplish this had taken enormous effort—I mean, I can't begin to tell you, hours and hours. So I handed in this report like it was nothing, like everybody hands in their report, and that's how I wanted it treated. I mean I just wanted to know if I really worked hard and did my best, how would I do? In this particular school the grades were E for excellent, then B,C,D and F. I don't know why they didn't use A, but they didn't. Everybody in the class who got an E on their reports got an E for excellent, except me. The teacher gave me an E for *effort*. I was so irate about this particular event; I mean—irate is an understatement. My parents had this medication to give me when I got out of control and after school that day I had everybody piling on top of me to get one of these pills down my throat. But I was behaving this way because of these tremendous *injustices*. It was just the most incredibly offensive thing to me at the time. I would have been happy with a B or a C, but instead I got an E for *effort* . . .

After that I decided I was not going to let this thing and these people run my life. So I began to run everybody else's life. I was very, very intrusive on other people, to the point where my sixth-grade teacher—one day early in the fall he left the classroom without saying a word. I found out later he went to my parents' home and he broke into tears and said, "I can't have this kid in my classroom. He has to go."

Interview by Jennifer Kagan

showed up at school dressed like a professional," another mother adds; "My advice? Don't go to school meetings dressed in blue jeans."

More than one mother has noticed that requests made by fathers—or by mothers and fathers jointly—sometimes carry more weight than those made by mothers alone. "It's sexist and it's disgusting but it's reality," one says; "When a man walks into the conference, people sit up and pay attention. Use it to your advantage if you can." With or without Dad in tow, many mothers say knowing their legal rights and understanding the available educational options helped them be assertive in the program-planning process when they needed to be. "When they send you this dull-looking publication about your rights as a special education parent, *read* it," one urges; "That's how I learned what it was possible to ask for. Asking for what you want is important. Frankly, I think I got more out of our school district most years than they were planning to provide."

As we discussed in Chapter 7, the school district cannot initiate special education services or change your child's placement without your permission. If you feel the program offered to your child is inappropriate or inadequate, you have the right to challenge the school district's decisions at a due-process hearing before an independent hearing officer (that is, an official not employed by the school district) who will weigh both sides of the case and issue a ruling. Due-process hearings cannot resolve all disputes—you cannot ask for a hearing because you don't like your child's teacher, for example—but the law does protect your right to be heard in the following cases:

- You feel your child has been incorrectly identified (*Example:* You think the child has learning disabilities; the evaluation team says the child is borderline retarded)

- You feel your child needs more services than are being offered (*Example:* You feel the child needs speech therapy; the district says the speech problems are not severe enough to interfere with academic performance)

- You feel the school or class placement recommended for the child is inappropriate (*Example:* You feel your child's problems with ADHD justify placement in a small class with structure and close supervision; the district recommends inclusion in a regular class with behavior modification)

- You feel the program described in the IEP is not being implemented effectively (*Example:* The IEP calls for the student to learn computer keyboard skills; due to a lack of equipment, only one period a week of computer time is being provided, and little progress has been made)

- You feel your child's rights have been violated (*Example:* Although an IEP was completed three months ago, services have not started)

Keep in mind that due-process hearings should be resorted to only after reasonable attempts at negotiation have failed. Since hearings are both time-consuming and expensive for the school district—a case must be prepared and legal representation is usually involved—it is in the district's interest to avoid one and cooperate with you if it can. Aim for compromises that get most of what you want: if the district won't provide your child with a personal computer, for instance, will they guarantee that there will be a computer he can use as needed in his classroom? Suggest making changes on a temporary or "trial" basis, such as placing the student in a regular class for three months and seeing if skills and behavior have improved at the end of that period.

Don't allow shortsightedness, shallow-mindedness, or cost-consciousness on the part of the school district, however, to result in half measures that seriously compromise your child's right to the "free, appropriate public education" guaranteed by law. If you feel your child must have a higher level or quality of support in order to achieve up to his or her full potential, fight for it. "I started out assuming the school district would know and do what was best for my son," says the mother of a boy with multiple learning disabilities, "but I soon found out differently. It seems like half the time the district doesn't know what Ryan needs, and the other half they're arguing that they can't afford to provide it. Parents of kids with disabilities have to be prepared to go to bat for them. Planning a child's education is far too important a matter to leave to educators."

9

THE ABCs OF
SUCCESS IN SCHOOL

It is no secret that children with learning disabilities must work harder than others in order to get ahead in school. These youngsters often have to be more motivated, be more dedicated, and spend more time involved with academic tasks than their classmates just to stay afloat. "It used to make me crazy when teachers criticized my writing and told me to try harder," a high school student with visual perception and fine motor disabilities remembers. "In third grade it took me almost an hour to finish a simple worksheet. I sweated out two or three of those every night, while my sisters got to watch TV. How many eight-year-olds did my teachers know who tried harder than that?"

Children can't be expected to maintain this level of discipline and motivation for long unless their efforts meet with some degree of success. It's not hard to understand why. Just imagine yourself trying to learn a new skill on the job and getting absolutely nowhere. How long would you have to fail before you give up and quit? A month? Two months? Maybe you're stubborn and you're making a little progress, so you hang in longer. But could you keep it up for thirteen years (the period we want children to remain motivated in order to graduate from high school)? Not many of us could. If we don't succeed at our work, we figure pretty quickly that we're in the wrong business. That's just what happens to our kids; if they try and don't succeed in school, they decide they're unfit for the business of education.

Unfortunately, failure to believe in your own capacity to learn is the most serious kind of learning disability there is. Students who do not believe that they are able to achieve rarely put forth the effort necessary to do so, making continued poor performance inevitable. Experience proves, however, that if you can show children with learning problems that they *can* achieve in school, their level of interest and motivation improves dramatically. While positive reinforcement and rewards can help get kids moving forward, success is the only incentive that works in the long run. Just as unrewarded effort can set up a failure cycle ("I'm no good at reading, I'm no good at school, there's no point in even trying"), achievement sets up a success cycle: it creates self-confidence and positive expectations, which in turn support more success.

The fundamental task facing adults who care about kids with learning disabilities, then, is to stack the deck so these children can experience success on a regular basis. Without that experience, you cannot expect a child to sustain the energy and attitudes necessary to overcome information-processing problems. Happily, a little success can go a long way. Children need not be successful in everything they undertake in order to keep trying, nor must they be "the best of the best" in order to feel successful. All children need *some* area of accomplishment, however, to which they can point with pride, saying, "I did that! I worked hard and I made that happen!" From these empowering experiences comes faith that effort can influence events, that obstacles can be overcome and hopes and dreams realized.

In this chapter we will discuss seven important ways parents can help children improve their level of accomplishment in school. As you review them, keep a few general guidelines in mind:

Sometimes it's best to work behind the scenes. You will note that not all of these suggestions involve providing direct assistance to the child. Whenever possible, the goal is to structure circumstances so children can succeed on their own by drawing on their strengths and abilities. The best kinds of help are those that encourage children to take responsibility for themselves and their work.

Forget the old saying, "If at first you don't succeed, try, try again." Perseverance may be a virtue, but a major source of frustration for children with learning disabilities is that they are often urged to "try harder" using unsuitable methods or materials. When reasonable goals are not being met, a change of approach may be far more effective than more encouragement, effort, or practice.

Be sensitive about how you define success. If your idea of achievement is "straight As and an admission letter from Harvard," it's time to adjust your thinking. Youngsters who have become discouraged about school need their "success cycles" kicked off and maintained with short-term, readily attainable goals. As the cartoon on page 188 affirms, little victories can mean a lot. Learn to recognize them (and to help your child recognize them).

With those principles in view, let's look at some strategies that can support success.

1. GET ORGANIZED

Most children with learning disabilities have some difficulty organizing objects and information; many also have trouble with concepts involving space and time. As a result, these children's problems with basic skills are often compounded by a host of difficulties with educational procedures. "These are the kids who forget to copy the assignment from the board," a special education teacher says, "or they copy it, but they copy it wrong. Or they copy it right, but they forget to bring the book home. Or they bring the book home and do the assignment, but leave it on the kitchen table when they go to school. . . . Kids with learning disabilities often lose points to this kind of thing even when they're on top of their lessons."

As students get older and demands on organizational ability increase (because of more classes, more teachers, and more complex assignments), youngsters with learning disabilities often find themselves at a growing disadvantage. Transitions to new schools can be especially difficult, and many students remember junior high school as a low point in their academic careers. "It took me forever to learn my way around the new building" one student remembers. "I couldn't remember the combination to my locker. I had seven teachers, and they all had different rules. I got in trouble for being late to class, for not having the right kind of notebook, for having no sneakers on gym day. . . . I felt sure the other kids were all laughing at me for being so out of it."

Because organization is not a gift that comes to them naturally, children with learning disabilities benefit from external structure. Four general areas where assistance is particularly helpful are described below.

DAVID

Parents can be very creative about making it possible for children to succeed, as David's story shows:

Fifth grade was a low point for David, an eleven-year-old with mild language processing disabilities. Although he had received special help in reading for two years, David still read slowly and had trouble keeping up with assigned work. His written work usually came back to him covered in red ink. Arithmetic was nearly as bad; David was struggling with math reasoning, and during much of math period he felt totally lost.

"About the only subject David did well in was art, and he only had that once a week," David's mother remembers. "David was making academic progress, and the resource teacher assured us he would be fine once he got on top of his basic skills, but meanwhile his self-esteem was taking a beating. He felt incompetent at everything."

David's family enjoyed visiting art galleries, and on one of those outings David saw an exhibition of watercolor landscapes. He fell in love with the delicate paintings and told his mother, "I want to learn to do that!" "I was so glad to see David motivated about *anything* that I became determined to find someone to teach him," his mother says. "But I had no luck—the art teacher at school said watercolor painting was too difficult and 'sophisticated' for kids David's age, and people who ran children's art programs in the community said pretty much the same thing. Then I saw an ad for an evening introductory watercolor course to be given at a local senior citizen center. I contacted the instructor, explained our situation, and asked if she would consider including an eleven-year-old in the class. She said if David didn't mind being in a class of retirees, she'd be willing to give it a try.

"What a blessing that class turned out to be!" David's mother continues. "Not only did David learn the fundamentals of watercolor painting—something no one else in his class could do—but he became the darling of his "classmates." It was like he suddenly inherited a dozen extra grandparents who thought everything he did was wonderful. He just bloomed. When his teacher put some of his pictures on display at school it was like the icing on the cake."

David's success with watercolors also helped keep him motivated about practicing basic skills. "He no longer felt like a total loser," his mother says. "That boost to his self confidence affected everything he did."

Providing an Organized Work Space

Students with learning disabilities often have trouble settling down to work, and frequent interruptions to look for paper, pencils, calculators, or other tools and supplies don't help their concentration any. A well-lit, uncluttered work space with adequate supplies of most-used materials close at hand will help students make the most of homework time. In planning this space, keep in mind that many children with learning disabilities are easily distracted by movement or background noise. Remember also, however, that these children often need some help and supervision with their assignments. "Don't make their work area so isolated that you can't comfortably get to it several times a night," one mother warns.

Elementary-aged children often prefer to be close to where the family "action" is when they are working on school projects. The kitchen or dining room can be fine places for homework sessions as long as noise in the general vicinity can be controlled (some students find that music helps them concentrate, so a radio or CD playing softly may be okay) and a permanent place can be made for the child's books and supplies. "We set a kitchen cabinet aside for the school stuff," one mother says. "How often do you need the good china, anyway?"

Managing Time

No work space for a student with learning disabilities is complete without a calendar with large spaces for recording school events, activities, and assignments (some families like to include family events and chores also). In the early stages of getting organized, maintaining this calendar is probably going to have to be the parents' job (if the student can't remember where he's supposed to be and what he's supposed to do. you don't really expect him to remember to write it

---

Learn to Recognize Little Victories

PEANUTS is reprinted by permission of the United Feature Syndicate, Inc.

down, do you?). "The point is to get the child in the habit of looking at the calendar," an experienced parent explains. "Check it with her every night, so she can see what's happening tomorrow and what she has to bring to school. Look ahead to see if there's anything later in the week that needs advance preparation. Don't assume your child will know how long an assignment or a project will take—kids with learning disabilities are notoriously bad at estimating time." Later, students can record assignments and events on the calendar themselves. Children are usually more responsible about doing this after they have become used to working with a calendar and are convinced of its value.

Children with learning disabilities also thrive on routine. Most benefit from predictable schedules for meals, recreation, homework, and bedtime. "These kids often have trouble with transitions," a teacher explains. "It can be hard for them to let go of one activity and get into another. Consistent routines make transitions easier. After a while, the kids know that they can play after school but must do homework after dinner, and they don't fight it."

In addition to helping students manage time at home, parents should alert teachers and other staff that children with learning disabilities may need help getting on top of schedules at school. "When your child is going to start a new schedule, walk him through it or get another student to walk him through it a few times when the building is quiet and empty," one family suggests. "Think the whole schedule through, so you can say, 'On your way from science to social studies you go right by your locker, so that would be a good time to pick up books for the afternoon.' Get that stuff worked out in advance so the child doesn't have to try to figure it out when the halls are packed with students, bells are going off, and announcements are coming over the loud speaker." Walk-throughs are especially important whenever a child starts a new school. Many students with learning disabilities have trouble with mental maps; several trial runs and extra attention to landmarks ("See, the steps you want are the ones *after* the bathroom") may be needed to help them become comfortable in an unfamiliar building.

Structuring Tasks

Many children with learning disabilities have difficulties with sequencing—that is, putting pieces of information into a logical or meaningful order. As a result, these students often have trouble breaking down complex tasks into simpler components, and figuring out which of those subtasks to tackle first. This applies equally to schoolwork and chores at home. "You can't just tell kids with sequencing problems to set the table or wash the dishes," a mother says. "With most jobs, you have to break it down and walk them through it many times before they get it right." While it can take time and patience to teach household tasks to children with learning disabilities (many an irritated parent concludes, "It would be faster to do it myself!"), experts advise that the effort is worth it in the long run. Taking responsibility for a share of the family's work can help build independence and create a sense of belonging and importance. Both are important to a child's self-esteem.

Students need help structuring school assignments, too. When asked to plan a science fair project, create a collage, or prepare a report on Uruguay, children may declare, "I can't do it!" because the project seems overwhelming in its entirety—not because it is actually beyond their abilities. When you help them break the task down into steps or phases, it often looks much easier. To organize a science fair project, for example, you might explain to the child: "First we'll go to the library and look at some books to get ideas. Then you'll choose a project that can be completed in four weeks. Next you make a list of the materials we need so we can go shopping. Then we will make a schedule for doing the experiment and set up a notebook for recording results."

Remember that *the point of restructuring tasks is to create a set of simpler tasks, each of which students can handle mostly on their own.* If students have trouble following steps even after a job has been broken down, an alternate strategy may be what is needed. A youngster who cannot yet handle a science project independently, for example, might need a modified assignment (a simple experiment with directions provided, perhaps) or to work with a partner or a team. "Flexibility is the key to success in the classroom and at home," a special education teacher says. "If the child has fine motor problems, teaching him to set the table or wash dishes may be a lost cause. That kid can handle a vacuum cleaner, though. You have to choose the tasks that allow kids to make their best contributions."

Keeping Track of Schoolwork

It is a fact of life that kids with learning disabilities lose things. But when they start losing school things, it can translate into unnecessarily lowered grades (not to mention frustrated parents, annoyed teachers, and students with reduced self-esteem). It is therefore important to work out a system for keeping track of materials that go to and from school. Parents say the following items are among the most important to keep tabs on:

Assignments. Does the child actually know what he is expected to do? Youngsters with learning disabilities sometimes do not because they could not interpret what was on the blackboard, missed the quick announcement made as the bell rang, copied the assignment wrong, or trusted themselves to remember it instead of writing it down (short-term memory is not always trustworthy for these students). To make sure that all assignments are understood, it may be necessary to ask teachers to give students their assignments in writing, or to pair students with a "study buddy" who reliably writes down test dates and homework assignments.

Books. "I left the book in school" is a familiar refrain for students with learning disabilities (second only to "I left the homework at home"). If this is a problem for your child, ask the school for a second set of textbooks to keep at home. "Saves a whole lot of aggravation," one parent says.

Homework. "Whenever a teacher said my son had missed turning in homework assignments, he was always so surprised," one mother remembers. "He'd insist, 'I did that work!' Then we'd clear out his backpack or his locker, and there the assignments would be, along with old spelling tests, gym socks, and candy wrappers." To avoid this familiar scenario, try providing the child with a heavyweight folder with pockets for each school subject (some have handy information like multiplication tables and standard weights and measures printed right inside). Label one side of the folder "Things to Hand In," and the other side "Things to Bring Home." Make sure completed homework assignments—and also items like notes to the teacher and signed permission slips—are in the correct folders before the student leaves for school each day, and teach children to check their folders for papers to hand in as soon as they arrive in class (you may need teachers' cooperation for this). Check the "Bring Home" side of the folder daily for assignments, graded work, and school announcements. "If you punch the folders and insert them in a three-ring notebook they'll be harder to lose," a special education teacher advises. "If that makes the notebook too bulky, try making two notebooks, one for the morning classes and one for the afternoon. I saw one parent color-coordinate folders and textbook covers—red for reading, blue for math, and so on." If children have chronic problems keeping track of papers, it is also a good idea to encourage them to check with teachers once a week to make sure all required work has been handed in. That way they can catch up on what's missing before the load of unfinished business becomes overwhelming.

Experienced parents add that it is also a good idea to clean out lockers and backpacks every week or two. As one mother puts it: "This greatly improves your chances of getting the note about the class trip before they actually go."

Not surprisingly, parents who have the most trouble helping their children get organized are those who are disorganized themselves. For them, however, efforts to provide appropriate support for their children can produce unexpected benefits. "Stabilizing our routines and writing everything down on a calendar helped me become more efficient and organized about my own work," one parent says. "I don't procrastinate as much as I used to, and I feel more on top of things."

2. HELP CHILDREN FIND THEIR PREFERRED LEARNING STYLES

Everyone has a preferred learning style, including the authors of this book. Lisa learns best from books and visual materials; she doesn't get much from tapes or lectures unless she takes tons of notes. She looks for the "big picture"—details bore her—and deals well with abstract concepts. She is also an introvert who prefers to work independently. In contrast, Corinne learns best by listening and talking; she likes lectures and discussions but finds reading slow going. She's superb at organizing information and keeping track of details. She is outgoing and thrives on interaction with other people.

Obviously, our learning styles are distinct and very different (between us, we figure, we have a whole brain). The only thing that distinguishes us from an individual with a learning disability is that we have a little more flexibility—Corinne does plow through mounds of printed material, and Lisa can cope with details when she has to. Youngsters with learning disabilities must stick with their preferred learning styles, however, because other means of handling information are inefficient or blocked. Yet many do not know what their preferred learning styles are; they understand only that they don't respond to the methods promoted at school.

To help children understand their preferred learning styles, you need to consider three separate areas:

Which Senses Make the Most Sense?

Some individuals learn best with their eyes; they are most likely to retain information presented in the form of visual materials (such as pictures, maps, charts, and diagrams) or demonstrations. Auditory learners, on the other hand, rely more on their ears. Educational techniques that work for them include discussions, lectures, and reading aloud. There are also children who learn best by touching and manipulating objects; hands-on experience is their best teacher.

While any student will do better when educated according to his or her strongest sensory channel, research suggests that a *multisensory approach* to education may be even better for many. A first grader who has a hard time recognizing letters, for example, may be able to learn them by saying them out loud while tracing them in sand or cutting them out of colored paper. A high school student who retains little of what she reads may benefit from creating charts, lists, and other "graphic organizers," and/or forming a study group to discuss material in the text. Many good teachers use multisensory techniques in class (especially in the lower grades), and special educators some- times use special multisensory curricula to teach reading and math. Even when teachers prove single-minded, however, students can learn to vary their own approaches to academic tasks, adding differ- ent sensory dimensions.

Abstract Versus Concrete Thinking

Albert Einstein once said that fantasy and imagination meant more to him than his ability to handle facts. This famous physicist was the quintessential abstract, or conceptual, thinker. He was comfortable in a world of theories and ideas and did not need to see or touch things in order to understand them. (Einstein, by the way, did not learn to read until he was nine. He also failed the language require- ment for admission to technical school.) Abstract thinkers can usu- ally visualize and manipulate information easily in their heads. Many like to take their time considering different aspects of a problem; they may resent being rushed or pressed for answers while they are think- ing things through.

Concrete thinkers, in contrast, are most comfortable with applied or practical knowledge. They prefer to deal with real objects and sit- uations. They learn by exploring the physical world, and are likely to be bored by abstract theories and ideas. A gifted concrete thinker was the inventor Thomas Edison, who even as a child had a driving need to figure out how things worked. (Edison proved so unsuited to tradi- tional methods of education that his mother withdrew him from pub- lic school after only three months and taught him at home.) Today, of course, Edison is known for his technical brilliance and ingenuity.

Nearly all small children think concretely; the ability to deal with abstractions develops over time. Traditional methods of education reflect this normal pattern of development. There are usually lots of multisensory, hands-on activities in primary school, but students are expected to do more and more "in their heads" as they get older. In high school, students who become accomplished abstract thinkers can expect to do well in most academic subjects. Students who remain primarily concrete thinkers, however, may find that the only classes taught *their* way are shop, home economics, and gym. These students are educationally disadvantaged. No matter how bright they are, their learning style limits their opportunities in a conventional educational environment.

Research suggests that many students with learning disabilities are concrete thinkers. It is necessary to find ways of rooting these youngsters' educations in reality. Teaching methods that work for them include interactive demonstrations; hands-on experiments; field trips; providing case studies, illustrations, and examples; and placing skills and information in a practical context (for example, you use fractions and measuring skills when you follow a recipe or build a house). When teachers fail to provide a bridge between abstract concepts and the real world, parents can sometimes build one. Everyday activities like meal planning, cooking, and shopping offer many good opportunities for helping concrete (or "experiential") learners learn and remember information.

Youngsters who are concrete thinkers also benefit from structured tasks and precise instructions. Care may have to be taken to help them understand the purpose of their lessons and assignments. "Never assume these children understand the point of work they are doing," a special educator warns. "Often they are clueless—which easily undermines their motivation. It's necessary to explain objectives carefully and draw these kids' attention to key facts and concepts as you go along. Don't expect them to make inferences or draw conclusions on their own; if it's important, spell it out for them."

Frequent reference to a lessons' goals or main ideas doesn't hurt the abstract thinker, either. Some of these youngsters overanalyze problems and become bogged down in side issues. A child who feels the need to understand *everything* in a textbook is a good candidate for early academic burnout. Explicit instruction on what is most important can help such students make more efficient use of their time and intellectual energy.

Sequential Versus Global Processing

A lot of school teachers are *sequential processors*. They take a logical approach to learning, sorting information into linear sequences and

---

Never Assume . . .

A special education teacher offers these words of wisdom to parents . . .

In the twenty-five years I have taught children with learning disabilities, I have learned to always expect the unexpected and never, NEVER assume a student has prior knowledge of a subject, no matter how old, how intelligent, or how "street wise" s/he is . . . I remember the high school student who was learning how to plan and prepare a meal in life-skills class. After the class selected burgers and fries as their main course, they had to construct a grocery list—rolls, ground hamburger, potatoes . . .

"Potatoes?" one young man inquired. "What do you need potatoes for?"

"The fries!" came the response.

"No kidding!" said the student. "Fries are made out of potatoes?"

Source: Mary Ann Coppola

---

presenting it in a methodical, step-by-step manner. They like to keep things systematic and orderly. They are good at outlining, categorizing, and analyzing. They pay attention to details. Not surprisingly, these teachers reward students who process and present information the same way.

Not everyone, however, thinks in a linear or logical fashion. Some individuals are *global processors*. These people don't learn step-by-step; they learn by making mental leaps. They grasp information intuitively (as a result they may have trouble explaining to others how they know what they know). Because they do not sort or categorize data in a conventional manner, they may perceive links between different kinds of information that are not obvious to others. Global processors hunger for insight; they tend to be impatient with details (which they consider unimportant). Often they are perceived as "jumping the gun" or jumping to conclusions. Still, their conclusions are right often enough—and even when they are wrong, these students' views are often creative and interesting.

Like concrete thinkers, global processors can be at a disadvantage in school because their preferred learning style is out of synch with the dominant teaching style. When these children don't understand something, logically minded teachers usually backtrack, slow down, and become even more systematic: for example, they'll reorganize a task into six steps instead of three. This further frustrates the global processor, who wants only to know where all this explanation is going. To reach these students, it is important to summarize the main points of a lesson *before* it is taught. As one special education teacher puts it: "You give them the answers and work back toward the questions. Once they have the 'big picture,' these students usually become more willing to attend to details and follow procedures."

This teacher adds, "You don't meet many students with learning disabilities who are sequential thinkers." The students she works with most often have styles that are abstract/global ("They get accused of being ditzy airheads," she says) or concrete/global ("They look like restless troublemakers; their motto is *'Ready, fire, aim!'*"). "It is important to teach these kids appropriately—and also to assure them that theirs is a legitimate learning style," the teacher concludes. "I always remind them that life's agenda is a lot more flexible than the curriculum at school. Once they graduate, they'll have more freedom to do things their own way."

Three additional factors that affect learning style are described below:

Attention span. Some youngsters must put so much effort into focusing attention that they tire after a relatively short time. If they keep trying to work beyond this point, their skills deteriorate rapidly. Attention problems are most obvious when children are attempting to master new skills, or are required to do work they find boring. (Motivation boosts attention, so attention levels may be good for creative ventures or for projects the child really wants to do.) For students with attention difficulties, work needs to be broken up so that it can be completed in short sessions. A list of twenty spelling words might be too much to take on at a sitting, for example, so limit spelling practice to five words a day. For difficult work, ten or fifteen minutes of concentration may be the most children can handle without a break. Length of time on task can often be increased as the work becomes more familiar. Attention-grabbing strategies—like letting children practice "writing" letters and numbers with shaving cream, or using colored highlighters to identify new or important information in texts—can also increase time spent on academic tasks.

Sociability. Some people like working alone, while others prefer interacting with other people. Successful "loners" tend to be internally motivated, self-disciplined, and goal oriented. If this does not describe your child, look for cooperative learning opportunities: team projects, discussion groups, and study partners. Socially oriented learners may have difficulty maintaining their motivation without frequent input, feedback, and encouragement from others.

Information-processing speed. Some folks grasp information quickly; their minds can absorb large "chunks" of information at a time. They seem able to keep several lines of thinking going at once, which makes it possible for them to perform mental tasks like comparing, contrasting, and analyzing very rapidly. Many equally intelligent individuals, however, process information more slowly. These people often handle information best in small chunks, and they prefer to focus on one thing at a time. It is important to avoid throwing too much information at these students too fast because "data overload" produces confusion. The best way to support these students is to reduce or eliminate extraneous material and just . . . slow . . . down. Children should also be given additional time to respond to requests and answer questions.

In addition to paying attention to their children's learning style, parents need to understand their own. If you are a visually oriented, concrete, sequential thinker, for example, your natural way of explaining things might be all wrong for your abstract, global, auditory child. "Whenever my son had trouble memorizing something in elementary school, my first thought was *flash cards*," one mother says. "I would never have made it through school without flash cards. But Terry learns best through his ears and his hands. Verbal rehearsal worked better for him—he learned his times-tables by reciting them over and over while bouncing a basketball."

A helpful book about learning style is Gail Murphy Sonbuchner's *Help Yourself: How to Take Advantage of Your Learning Styles* (New Readers Press). Written for secondary school students, this illustrated guide discusses various strategies for assisting memory, improving study skills, and handling many daily challenges.

3. KEEP ON TOP OF THE CURRICULUM

Many parents are unaware of the fact that a great many different programs exist for teaching reading, writing, math, science, and social studies. Publishers of these programs (which include student texts, teachers' guides, and sometimes workbooks, films, tapes, posters, and other learning aids) aggressively compete with each other for the dollars of America's school systems. Every school district has some kind of committee responsible for periodically reviewing newly developed curriculum materials and comparing them to materials in use. New materials may be chosen because they better address student needs— or because they have been heavily promoted by publishers and/or reflect some currently popular trend in education.

As we have said earlier, there is really no one program or type of program that is best for all children. Good teachers know this, and many use materials from several different teaching programs (as well as designing curriculum materials of their own) in an effort to reach the greatest possible numbers of students. Inexperienced or less talented teachers, in contrast, often attempt to teach classes "by the book" regardless of students' individual needs. If the curriculum materials supplied are unsuitable for some students, it is usually the students—not the publishers or the teachers—who are blamed for resulting problems.

Because students with learning disabilities are less adaptable than others in the ways they can assimilate information, the programs used in their classrooms can either speed or wreck their academic progress. It is therefore important for parents to investigate materials and methods and evaluate how well they are likely to meet children's needs. Two good ways to do this are to preview textbooks and workbooks, and to ask to see the "scope and sequence charts" supplied to teachers by publishers of different curricula. These charts describe what skills and content will be covered in the course of the semester or the year (the *scope* of the curriculum), as well as the order (or *sequence*) in which skills and information will be taught.

When you preview the curriculum, you can anticipate—and prevent—many kinds of trouble. It should be clear from the start, for example, whether text materials are appropriate for the child's reading level. Materials are appropriate if the child can read 95 percent of the words automatically (that is, without stumbling or stopping to sound them out); if they are too difficult, discuss modifications, substitute texts, or plans to find a reading partner with the teacher. If you are familiar with your child's learning strengths and weaknesses, you will also be able to spot problem areas (for example, the math class will be doing a unit on word problems, and the history materials call for memorization of names and dates) and work out methods of helping the youngster through them in advance (students may need to be assigned fewer homework problems each night when math material is difficult; open-book essays might be substituted for short-answer tests in history). If the skills of the special education teacher will be needed to help the student cover some material, you can draw both teachers' attention to this so they can plan to coordinate their efforts.

It is particularly important to explore how basic skills are being taught at your child's school. Some methods of teaching reading, writing, and arithmetic are notoriously problematic for students with learning disabilities. A few to look out for are discussed below.

"Whole-Language" Reading Programs

These have become very popular in recent years. Whole-language curricula stress recognition of entire words and textual meaning. There is little or no instruction in phonics; it is assumed that students will associate letters with sounds "naturally" as they go along. Fans of this system say it promotes appreciation for language and literature (students are introduced to good literature at an early age) and is less boring than other methods of teaching reading. These units are often taught in conjunction with whole-language writing curricula, which encourage youngsters to express themselves freely on paper without worrying about spelling, punctuation, or other conventions.

Students who have visual perception problems are very poor at whole-word recognition, and children with language processing disabilities are unlikely to connect sound sequences with written words naturally. Whole-language programs do not provide these students with alternative strategies for deciphering words they do not recognize. Children with both types of disabilities need explicit instruction in phonics (decoding words by sounding them out) in order to read successfully. Students with severe disabilities may need a multisensory approach to phonics that combines seeing, hearing, saying, and sometimes touching (cutting letters out or tracing them, for example). This type of instruction is usually available only through special education.

An additional problem may be finding age-appropriate reading materials. It may seem logical academically to use second-grade materials to teach a twelve-year-old with second-grade reading skills, but a sixth grader will find those texts so embarrassingly juvenile and boring that no interest in reading will be stimulated. There are publishers who specialize in "high-interest low-level" reading materials. These books use a limited vocabulary but focus on topics and issues of interest to older children and adolescents. They also look more like "grown-up" books—they are smaller and have smaller print than books designed for younger children, and the illustrations depict older children or adults. The school's special education staff, reading specialist, and/or librarian should be able to help you (and the child's teachers) locate such materials.

Writing Programs That Overemphasize Mechanics

Ask students with learning disabilities how to become a good writer, one researcher found, and you get answers like "practice and hope and hold your pencil right." For many of these students, writing means struggles with legibility, spelling, and grammar. These issues may be so consuming that the children give little thought to content. Studies show students with learning disabilities seldom plan what they write; many believe a successful paper simply means not too many spelling and punctuation errors.

For these youngsters (as well as many typical students), drilling mechanics is far less important than teaching them how to communicate effectively. Programs that emphasize planning, review, and revision of written work (often called *writing process* curricula) are best; they focus students' attention on what they want to say and how to say it clearly. (Note that emphasizing content does *not* mean that teaching spelling and grammar can be overlooked. This sometimes happens when teachers urge children to be creative about expressing themselves but do not help them review and revise results.) Hallmarks of a good writing process curriculum include *pre-writing activities* in which students select topics, "brainstorm" ideas for addressing the topic selected, and organize those ideas logically; *conferences* in which students read early drafts to the teacher or to another student and receive feedback; a *revision phase* in which compositions are reworked for style, clarity, and effectiveness; and a final *editing phase* in which spelling, grammar, punctuation, and so forth are corrected. These programs often conclude by producing publications of student efforts.

Note that children who have trouble with handwriting (including some students with visual perception disabilities, as well as those with fine motor problems) may find it impossible to focus on what they want to say in writing until they are relieved of the burden of trying to form legible letters. Allowing these youngsters to dictate to a "scribe," or teaching them to use a tape recorder as a pre-writing tool, sometimes improves the content of their written efforts dramatically. Many students with disabilities also find that word processors (which make revising and correcting easy) greatly reduce the difficulties involved in writing. For these youngsters, typing is a survival skill that should not be left until high school; try to get computer keyboard skills built into the student's educational program by fifth or sixth grade. (Many schools now teach basic computer skills to all students routinely, but it may be necessary to arrange an early introduction to word processing through special education).

Arithmetic by Rote

The traditional "drill and kill" approach to arithmetic is not very good for any student. Studies indicate that rote memorization of facts, rules, and formulas in preparation for tests does not equip students to handle math reasoning or higher-order problem solving. Children with learning disabilities may not even learn to handle basic computation using this system. A great many of these students have trouble with tasks involving rote memorization; the methods others use to memorize often do not work for them. Sometimes the focus on knowing math facts becomes really absurd. When the mother of a third grader who had not learned his multiplication tables suggested that he be given a calculator so he could get on with the math curriculum, for example, the teacher replied, "In third grade, memorizing multiplication facts *is* the math curriculum." (This parent got permission for the calculator from the school district's special education committee, and also asked that her son's class be supplied with concrete materials that demonstrated basic math concepts.)

Another problem that can interfere with math education is that some students with learning disabilities have trouble with abstract ideas. Young children may not even understand that numbers on paper represent real things. Until the relationship between numbers and objects is made clear, these students will see little point in paper-and-pencil addition and subtraction exercises. Hands-on activities that involve counting and manipulating real objects (such as blocks or Cuisenaire rods) are often essential to understanding basic number concepts and relationships. An explicit, tangible approach may also be necessary to help these youngsters learn about money, measurement, fractions, and time. Throughout their math educations, students with learning disabilities need instruction that emphasizes understanding concepts and reasoning (steps in problem solving). These are the things that ultimately define math competence.

Elementary school teachers are sometimes poor at explaining math concepts because they don't understand math very well themselves (unlike secondary school teachers, elementary teachers are not certified in particular disciplines or subjects). Many freely admit they teach math by rote because they learned it that way and know no other means of handling math information. "If your child has one of these teachers, look for help from special education personnel or get a good math tutor so the child can build a solid conceptual foundation," one parent suggests. "You may find—as we did—that the student actually does better in math in secondary school where teachers are better at explaining the how-and-why of it all and memorization is less of an issue."

*   *   *

Sometimes, the most practical way of keeping on top of any curriculum is simply to read a chapter or two ahead in a student's textbooks. Parents say this practice helps them spot problems and plan supplementary or enrichment activities that give students a head start. "When I saw my son had an introduction to fractions coming up, I made a point of getting him involved in some cooking activities," one mother remembers. "He did all the measuring, which helped him understand concepts like one-half and one-third." Another mother increased her daughter's interest in an upcoming unit on Roman history (and effectively previewed the subject) by taking some illustrated books about ancient Rome out of the library.

An important final word on curriculum: Do *not* assume your child's special education teacher is familiar with the programs being used in regular classrooms. Not many resource teachers have the time to keep track of how all subjects are taught in each of their students' classes. If you become concerned about the methods or materials used by a particular teacher, alert the special education teacher promptly and ask for help with intervention.

4. PAY ATTENTION TO BASIC SKILLS

Research indicates that significant delays in reading, writing, and arithmetic increase students' risk for academic failure and dropping out of school. This is why children who are making slow academic progress are sometimes encouraged to repeat kindergarten or first grade. Educators want to make sure children get the best possible basic skills foundation before they move on to more complex subject matter.

Basic skills acquisition, then, is obviously a matter of concern to any parent. What many parents do not realize, however, is that schools offer children a relatively small "window of opportunity" for learning these skills. In a typical grade school, basic skills are pretty much what the curriculum is about from kindergarten through third grade (everything else generally falls in the category of "enrichment"). In the fourth through sixth grades, however, increasing amounts of additional subject matter (science, health, social studies, and so forth) are introduced, and explicit instruction in reading is phased out. Math begins to focus on complex operations (such as working with decimals and fractions, long division, and word problems) for which knowledge of basic arithmetic is necessary. Writing instruction shifts to matters of composition, and competence with basic grammar and usage (punctuation, capitalization, and so on) is increasingly expected rather than taught. What this means is that children who have failed to master the fundamentals of reading, writing, and arithmetic by the fourth grade have substantially missed the educational boat. At age nine or ten, Johnny may be ready to learn basic skills, only to find that his teachers aren't teaching that stuff any more.

While continuing basic skills instruction is usually available through remedial and special education programs, these programs do not always provide the intensity of instruction students need, or the time and opportunities they require to practice new skills. If they do not, the gap between Johnny's skills and those of his typical peers will start to grow. As a result, Johnny will become less and less prepared to handle his academic subjects as the years go on, and find it harder and harder to maintain interest in school. This scenario is the sad experience of too many students with learning disabilities. To avoid this kind of educational catastrophe, there are several things parents can do.

Monitor Progress Frequently

Most schools give achievement tests once a year to establish how students are doing in basic skills. The progress of students with learning disabilities, however, needs to be checked more often. Failure to move forward in reading, writing, or arithmetic is a red flag signalling that intervention is needed, and children should not have to languish for a year—or even half a year—before appropriate help is provided. Understanding where your child's basic skills stand with respect to other students will also help you determine what kinds of support will be necessary to help him or her keep up in class. A sixth grader who is a year behind in reading may only need a little extra time to handle class texts, for example, while a student who is three years behind will probably need to be paired with a reader or provided with alternative materials.

It is therefore important to discuss ongoing monitoring systems with your child's teachers. Curriculum based assessment (explained in Chapter 8) offers teachers a simple way of checking on skills development using ordinary class materials. Weekly progress reports like the one illustrated on page 207 can help parents and teachers keep in touch about both academic skills and classroom behavior (an issue that is equally important to teachers). You can also keep tabs on

What About Retention?

Retention is frequently recommended for kindergartners and first graders who have not made satisfactory progress in pre-reading, writing, and counting skills. Repeating a year may also be advised for students who have not passed basic skills competency tests at various educational "checkpoints" such as third, fifth, and/or eighth grades. Does retention actually help children?

Research suggests retention is valuable in limited circumstances. Repeating kindergarten or first grade can give children who were not ready to start school or who are "late bloomers" the time they need to catch up in their academic readiness skills. Retention is therefore a viable option for students who have started school very young, and for youngsters who have relatively mild developmental delays. Children who have been deprived of *opportunities* to learn (due to illness, frequent moves or emotional stress, for example) may also benefit from repeating a year in primary school. The best candidates for retention are youngsters who are of average intelligence, show normal social and emotional adjustment, and who have moderate academic deficits (no more than one year behind in any subject). In all cases, retention is likely to succeed only if children's parents are thoroughly supportive of the idea and children themselves do not oppose it. It is important for children to understand the difference between failure and needing extra time to grow. When youngsters think they are repeating because they have failed or are stupid, sinking self-esteem is likely to wipe out any benefit an extra year of education might provide.

Studies show that youngsters with more severe academic deficits and students of below average intelligence benefit less from retention. Although they may make some gains during a repeated year, their progress

your child's progress using the basic skills charts supplied in our Appendix. Be especially watchful for lags in areas that are building blocks for higher education (spelling problems are less worrisome than trouble sequencing ideas in written compositions, for example).

If your child is not making progress in basic skills, ask for a conference with his or her special education teacher to discuss intervention. Sometimes a simple adjustment to the child's program (providing more practice with a new skill, for example) will bring improvement. At other times more drastic changes (such as placement in a smaller or more structured class) might be called for. The point is to address the issue promptly so that your child does not become unnecessarily discouraged or frustrated.

typically remains slow and so the gap between their skills and those of average youngsters often grows. Evidence suggests these students' failure to make progress is due to their need for a different type or intensity of instruction, not a need for more time. Rather than make them repeat what did not work for them before, it is better to refer these students for remedial programs or special education intervention at the earliest possible point.

Research indicates that after sixth grade the effects of retention are almost entirely negative. Repeating a year in junior high school is associated with increased rates of failure, truancy, and behavior problems. Students who have been retained in later years, retained against their will, or retained more than once are also at significantly higher risk for dropping out of school before graduation. As students grow older, potential for academic gain appears to be sharply undercut by the decline in social status associated with repeating a year of school. Other means of assistance (tutoring, remedial and summer programs, referral to special education) are therefore better choices for secondary students with achievement problems.

In the early elementary school years, the child who needs time to mature and the child who has learning disabilities look much alike. For this reason, it should not be assumed repeating a year of school will solve all a child's academic problems. Children repeating kindergarten, first or second grades should also be exposed to an expanded range of teaching methods and materials to see if they benefit from new approaches. If children have not shown satisfactory progress by the midpoint of a repeated year despite intensified efforts to reach them, an evaluation for learning disabilities should be requested without further delay.

Communicate With Teachers About How Your Child Learns

While special education departments often collect a great deal of data about how a child with disabilities learns, very little of this information (some of which is considered confidential) gets passed on to regular classroom teachers. As a result, you cannot assume these teachers know what teaching methods and materials are most likely to work with your child unless you tell them. Information that is most useful to teachers includes:

- How the child's disability might affect performance in different subject areas (the child has trouble with word problems in math; spells phonetically; has difficulty reading aloud)

- Areas of particular strength or interest (the child is talented in music; loves computers; gets along well with others)

- Teaching or management methods that have proved successful (child needs main points of lesson to be summarized in advance; does best when seated in front row; responds to "time out")

- Accommodations or special grading policies that have been approved (student may take tests in resource room; no points get taken off for spelling errors; assistance with note-taking must be provided)

Many parents schedule a parent-teacher conference to discuss these concerns—or provide this information in writing—at the beginning of each school year while children are in elementary school. Not only does this practice reduce the chances that your child will be taught inappropriately, it can help dispel the negative attitudes some classroom teachers have about students who have learning disabilities. A father explains: "Teachers have egos, too, and few enjoy working with students who don't succeed. Anything you can do to help a teacher work with your child more successfully will pay off in increased acceptance and approval."

Reinforce Basic Skills at Home

Many students with learning problems see basic skills primarily as a series of academic hurdles they have to leap—not as pathways to knowledge or tools that can help them in real-life situations. Because they fail to see the relevance of these skills, their level of commitment to learning them remains low. When children are encouraged to apply their skills in daily life, however, both motivation and performance often benefit. Not only does experience make learning more relevant, it may actually improve the child's capacity to handle new information. A growing body of research suggests that growth in different areas of the brain can be stimulated by mental exercise. Some authorities believe, for example, that living in a language-rich environment promotes neural connections in parts of the brain that are concerned with language.

Parents are in a far better position than teachers to help children place basic skills in a practical context. Some of the most valuable things parents can do follow:

Talk with children. It's so obvious that many miss it: a child's first experience with language is through speech, and those who don't learn

Weekly Progress Report

Child's Name: _____   Subject: _____   Week of: _____

Excellent   **S**atisfactory   **N**eeds **I**mprovement

Academic Accomplishment

___ Class Attendance
___ Class Participation
___ Performance on Assignments
___ Performance on Tests

Citizenship and Work Habits

Work habits:
___ Paying Attention
___ Completion of Assignments
___ Effort

Behavior:
___ Cooperation
___ Interactions with Others

Teacher's Comments:

Parent's Comments:

_____
Teacher's Signature

_____
Parent's Signature

to handle language competently at that level rarely become skilled at reading and writing. Talking with children can also help them learn to express ideas and put them in logical order.

Read to children, and help them find appropriate reading materials of their own. Reading to children builds vocabulary, encourages interest in books, and stimulates thinking (try interrupting a story and asking your child to predict what's going to happen, then read on and compare endings). As children grow older, show them that reading is a tool they can use to entertain themselves or get useful information on their own. Try subscribing to magazines that focus on areas of interest to young people (even a basketball-crazed teen might make time for a publication like *Sports Illustrated*).

Play games. Word games like *Scrabble* and *Taboo* help build vocabulary skills, while *Battleship* and Chess encourage youngsters to plan and develop logical strategies. Almost any kind of game is better for intellectual development than TV.

Let children manage money. An allowance can be a valuable math teaching tool, if you are clear about when cash will be handed over and what it is expected to cover. In Chapter 11 we will discuss guidelines for helping children with learning disabilities learn to handle money wisely.

Encourage correspondence. Exchanging letters with pen pals, writing to public officials or the newspaper about issues of importance, even writing fan letters to celebrities helps students learn to put ideas on paper. A computer-savvy father mentions that e-mail may have rescued the art of letter writing from the scrap-heap of history (kids love it because they don't have to wait a long time for replies).

Show children how you use your own basic skills. Bringing children to work can give them valuable insight into how academic skills are used on the job. Involving young people in cooking, shopping, and other activities can also show them how you use basic skills in daily life (get them to help you figure out gas mileage for the car or adapt a recipe for four to serve six).

Do remember that progress in basic skills for youngsters with learning disabilities is not always smooth. Many develop skills in bursts of learning activity separated by relatively stagnant periods. When this is the case it is important not to let either yourself or the child become discouraged. Think of these plateaus as opportunities to consolidate skills by applying them in new ways. It is also vital not to let poor performance in reading, writing, or arithmetic interfere with a child's intellectual development in other areas. Children who do not read well, for example, can be exposed to literature by other means (try listening to an actor read Mary Shelley's *Frankenstein* on tape during a long night car ride), and they can excel in almost any subject provided they learn alternative methods for gathering information. Remember that our brains keep developing into early adulthood. Possibly the greatest tragedy in education is that every year many children stop learning because adults give up and stop teaching them.

5. TAKE ADVANTAGE OF TECHNOLOGY

As one student put it, "If you have to have a handicap, this is the era to be handicapped in." He was referring to the array of technological supports that have become available to students with learning disabilities and other handicaps in recent years. Chief among these are personal computers, which now include a variety of useful programs even in the most basic packages (see "What Can a Computer Do for My Child?", pages 211–14). Some of the most helpful devices, however, are far less costly and complicated. Below is a list of some familiar electronic aids, with descriptions of how they can be used to help youngsters with learning disabilities cope.

Calculators

Research has consistently shown that use of calculators in elementary school increases skill acquisition, improves attitudes toward math, and frees youngsters to reason more intelligently about mathematical concepts. As a result, many experts now urge that *all* children learn to use calculators in math class (although teachers have resisted this recommendation). For children with learning disabilities use of calculators is even more important. Ready access to addition, subtraction, and multiplication facts via calculator enables these students to keep up with the curriculum and allows them to focus their mental energy on problem-solving strategies. Seeing correct numbers pop up over and over again also helps these youngsters learn their basic math facts (when calculating on their own, these students often produce a lot of errors). To use calculators to the greatest advantage, students should be taught to employ them to solve each step of a complex problem—not to jump straight to the final conclusion. (For example, students would use the calculator only to retrieve addition, subtraction, and multiplication facts while actually doing the process of long division by hand.)

Students with documented disabilities can be permitted to use calculators on tests, including many standardized achievement tests (make sure this modification is recorded on the student's IEP). On some tests, including the college SAT I Reasoning Test, *all* students are now allowed to use calculators. Students taking higher-level exams—like the SAT Math IC or IIC Achievement tests—should learn to use scientific and/or graphing calculators, which are used in advanced math courses.

Note that some students find the use of a math fact chart easier than using a calculator for retrieving basic math information. "Cheat sheets" may also be necessary to give students access to formulas, theorems, or equations that they are unable to memorize. As with calculators, proper use of these materials frees students to develop a better understanding of math concepts.

Watches

Some of the newest electronic watches call up visions of comic hero Dick Tracy. Many have calculators built in ("When you strap the calculator to their wrist, it makes it that much harder for them to lose it," one mother comments). Some watches can be programmed to "remember" telephone numbers and engagements, a valuable benefit for students who have difficulty keeping track of those things. These watches are not always easy to program, however, and their tiny buttons may be hard for young children and students with fine motor problems to use. Some youngsters also find it hard to tell time on digital watches—for example, students who have trouble making sense out of number sequences will probably do better with an old-fashioned big hand and little hand. Teachers add that watches with second hands are usually better for helping young children understand how the passage of time is measured, too. The consensus seems to be that programmable watches work best for older kids and teens.

Wristwatches are also great for helping kids distinguish right from left; remembering that the watch is worn on the left (or right) wrist is a trick many keep using into adulthood. "But don't invest a lot of money in a watch until you are sure your child can be responsible about keeping track of it," cautions the mother of a boy who managed to lose four wristwatches in one year. "Even then, I recommend going for a watch that's shock resistant and waterproof. That way they can wear it to gym, swimming, in the shower. . . . The less they take the watch off, the less chance of misplacing it."

What Can a Computer Do for My Child?

The father of an eleven-year-old with severe language processing disabilities sits down at his keyboard to show us some of the ways his family has been able to use a home computer for educational support. "My daughter was interested in reading *Little Women,*" he explains. "That's a great book for her age, but she would have a lot of trouble reading it herself. So we got on the Internet (*click, click*) and found *Little Women* in a university library. Then (*click*) we downloaded the book into our computer's memory—we can do that because it's not copyrighted material. Now I call the text up on our screen (*click*) . . . here's Chapter One. Okay, now we choose a voice (*click*) and the computer starts reading the text aloud." The computer does indeed start reading Louisa May Alcott's classic in a pleasant baritone, highlighting each word on the screen as it goes along. "If you like a female voice better, we can do that," our guide says, clicking away on his mouse. The computer now sounds like a woman. "You want it slower? We can do that, too (*click, click, click*). See? We're all set, and we didn't even have to go to the bookstore or the library."

Welcome to the brave new world of computers. The technology demonstrated above was included in a fairly standard home computer package. The cost of such packages in this highly competitive industry has been dropping steadily, putting computers in range of more and more American family budgets. Before you buy, however, it is important to understand the educational applications of computers and determine which (if any) would be useful to your child.

Computers' usefulness in education falls in three basic categories: they can be used for drill and practice, for instruction, or as tools. All three can have value for youngsters with learning disabilities, but applications must be carefully chosen with individual students' specific needs in mind. Each of these uses is discussed in more detail below:

Drill and practice. Youngsters with learning disabilities often need extra drill and practice to master new skills. Game-like computer programs can make drills in math or vocabulary skills more fun, thereby increasing the time students are willing to spend on these tasks. On the downside, students may find the graphics in some programs too confusing, distracting, or overstimulating to be helpful. Rapidly paced programs will be inappropriate for some students' information-processing speeds and reaction times. In addition, use of the keyboard and joysticks requires a fairly high level of manual dexterity.

Instruction. You can find tutorial programs that teach a huge range of subjects at a variety of levels. Because the child controls the speed at

continued

which information is introduced (lessons can be stopped and repeated at any time), these programs can help students with learning disabilities learn new material at their own pace. Some programs use sophisticated graphics and sound effects to introduce new skills and concepts in creative ways. Students particularly like simulation programs, which take a "you are there" approach to subject matter (the computer simulates a road test to help a student learn driving skills, for example, or allows students to decide moves in an important historical battle). The best of these programs teach more than content: they also help students learn such important problem-solving skills and strategies as forming and testing a hypothesis, planning ahead, evaluating risks, analyzing clues, interpreting directions, and using maps. Not all programs, however, are well designed and educationally sound—many offer more flash than substance. Overreliance on computer instruction is also a problem at some schools. If your child is using a computer in the classroom, make sure this instruction is being used to reinforce what a teacher has taught, not as a substitute for professional teaching assistance.

Tools. Computers can be used as tools for communicating; for finding, organizing, and storing information; and for solving many kinds of problems. Given the right kinds of software, for example, you could use a computer to access library materials and research a report, organize and file your notes, write the report, and illustrate it with charts, graphs, and pictures (sophisticated graphics programs even make animation possible). At many colleges you can submit your report to professors electronically instead of on paper. When you are finished doing that, you can e-mail a few friends, pay your bills, and play a game of chess or backgammon, all without leaving your keyboard. As we have already seen, computers can be used to assist students who have learning disabilities with reading (computers equipped with scanners can read from textbooks and other printed materials, as well as from computer discs). There are also voice-activated writing programs that enable computers to take dictation (originally developed for busy executives, these programs were rapidly adapted for special education). The wizards of the world of microchips seem to be coming up with additional applications every day.

Of all these tools, by far the most useful to students is word processing—in fact, some parents say it is worth buying a computer for word-processing capability alone. Good word-processing programs offer a host of advantages to youngsters with learning disabilities. By making manipulation of text easy, they facilitate brainstorming ideas, making outlines, writing rough drafts, and making improvements and corrections. Modern programs come equipped with spell-checkers and a thesaurus (which helps students develop their vocabularies). Some programs even advise students on issues of grammar and style—for example, the computer might indicate that sentences are too long or that certain words have been overused. All these features greatly reduce the agony involved in getting ideas down on paper, and can therefore improve the overall quality of student work. Of course, a teacher is still necessary to help students learn the basic principles of organization and good writing!

If you are convinced a computer can help your child, it is important to research this investment carefully. Prices and the types of equipment included in different packages vary, and not every system will meet your needs. Some important questions to ask when looking for a home computer set-up are listed below:

Will the system do everything I want it to do? Try to think through all the ways different family members will use the computer in advance. If you are interested in computers that can read aloud, for example, you need a machine equipped with a particular type of sound card. To use a scanner you must also have optical character recognition (OCR) software. (Always listen to computers "talk" before you buy; voice quality varies considerably.) Students interested in creating computer graphics usually want high-resolution color monitors and top quality printers. Families interested in e-mail and other online services will need access to telephone lines by means of a modem. Computer salespeople can demonstrate different options and help you separate the necessities from the frills.

Is the memory provided adequate? Expandable? To run today's complex programs and games with high-tech graphics, a minimum of 8 megabytes of random access memory (RAM) is recommended. Memory capacity affects speed at which word-processing and other programs run. Buying an expandable system will make it possible for you to update your machine to handle new programs and applications.

What equipment is included in the system? Does the package price include a color or a black-and-white monitor? Speakers? A printer? A modem? A mouse? Can a scanner be added later? Find out what the cost of upgrading or adding components would be, and shop around for the best prices. (The high-volume, low-overhead companies that advertise in computer magazines sometimes offer good deals.)

What software is included? To make packages more attractive, dealers sometimes "throw in" programs with the machines. If they are programs you actually want, you can save hundreds of dollars. Word-processing programs usually have to be bought separately and must be investigated

continued

carefully—some are much easier to use than others. To learn more about word-processing and other software, check your library and newsstand for magazines that review software created for the home market. Catalogs describing available educational programs should also be available at local bookstores. Computer-savvy teachers and parents are among the best sources of software reviews and recommendations; those associated with learning-disabilities support groups are often knowledgeable about special education applications.

Who will I call when things go wrong? Sooner or later, something will. If you have a friend or relative who is computer-wise, great. If you don't, forget about mail-order sales. Buy your system from a reputable local store that has an accessible and well-informed staff.

Note that when use of a computer has been determined to be essential to a child's educational development, school systems must provide a computer and appropriate software for the child's use at school. Students who have severe or multiple handicaps are the most likely to qualify for this type of assistance (a child whose learning disabilities are compounded by severe speech problems, for example, might need a computer in order to communicate). Access to computers at school can also be negotiated for specific situations (for example, a student with learning disabilities might be permitted to take notes on a computer in the classroom, or take tests in the school computer lab). If students intend to carry work on computer discs to and from school, making sure your home computer is compatible with the system at school could be important.

Be aware, however, that checking out systems at school may lead you into the heart of a fiery computer controversy. Apple (the manufacturer of Macintosh systems) has very successfully marketed its products to schools for many years. IBM personal computers (PCs) and their compatible cousins, however, have developed an increasingly firm grip on the home market. As a result there are some good educational programs that only run on Apple systems, and some popular word-processing and data management programs that run only on IBM-type machines. If you're new to the computer game, veterans suggest you choose the *programs* that best meet your needs first, then look for value in a machine that runs the software you have selected.

Tape Recorders

Tape recorders can be valuable tools for students with many types of learning problems. For example, youngsters can record lectures in addition to taking notes and use tape recorders to complete assignments (students might answer some homework questions orally and submit a tape to the teacher instead of a paper). Tape recorders can also be used as a pre-writing tool. Students who feel paralyzed at the thought of writing a paper sometimes find it easier to begin by dictating their thoughts into a tape recorder; the tape is then played back, and the ideas written down.

Students who learn best through their ears can also use tape recorders as a study aid. Young people who have trouble understanding what they read, for example, may improve their comprehension if they read text material aloud into a tape recorder, then play the tape back and listen to it. Tape recorders can also be used to help students review class material and prepare for tests. Dictate (or have the student dictate) questions into the tape recorder, then count slowly to five before recording the answer. When the tape is complete, the student listens to each question, pushes the "stop" button and writes the answer, then restarts the machine to see if the answer was correct.

For students who have reading disabilities, tape recorders can be used to record textbook chapters and other printed materials—something some parents do for children on a regular basis. It should be understood, however, that simply transferring material to tape may not be enough to help these children learn. Most children with learning disabilities also need help organizing information and determining which material is most important. Experts recommend use of the following guidelines when preparing tapes for children:

- Read at a comfortable rate and in a natural tone of voice.

- Provide a short advance organizer or "preview" of what is to come ("This chapter concerns the first European explorers to reach South America. The explorers we will learn about are . . .")

- Do not record chapters verbatim. Instead, read key sections and summarize or paraphrase sections of lesser importance.

- Insert questions and reminders that will encourage the listener to stop and think about what has been read ("Why were the kings and queens of Europe interested in South America? What was their view of the people who already lived there?").

Parents of students who are poor readers may also want to look into professionally taped materials. Organizations that record materials for the blind (such as Recording for the Blind in Princeton, NJ; the American Printing House for the Blind in Louisville, KY; and the National Library Service for the Blind at the Library of Congress in Washington, DC) can provide textbooks, newspapers, and magazines on tape as well as popular nonfiction books and novels. Commercial publishers also produce books on tape, some of which are read expertly by professional actors. Many of these materials—which can do a great deal to sustain children's interest in reading and literature—should be obtainable through your public library.

Electronic Spellers

These clever gizmos were originally developed for crossword puzzle fans, but they rapidly found a larger market. When students type a word into the hand-held device, a list of correctly spelled words resembling what has been typed appears on a small screen. The machines can also recognize fragments of words (if a student types in the first three or four letters, for example, the machine will start scrolling possible word choices). Most youngsters will tell you this beats thumbing through a dictionary hands down. Electronic spellers can be very helpful for students who spell phonetically (the spelling of youngsters with auditory processing problems may be too irregular for the machine to recognize). Students must also be able to recognize the word they want when they see it. Parents say spellers are good buys for younger children; once students plug into computers, word-processing programs take over the correction of spelling errors.

Electronic Notebooks and Laptops

These miniature data managers range from pocket-sized electronic address books and calendars to mini-computers that can do anything their larger relatives can. They are designed for people on the go (most of whom are already users of full-size personal computers). The latest laptops run on rechargeable batteries and are no bigger than large textbooks. This makes them completely portable and easy to use in any location—they can be taken to class, to the library, or away on holidays. Laptop computers make wonderful tools for high school and college students with many types of learning disabilities, but at present they are priced beyond the reach of many families. As with most electronic gadgets, however, prices are dropping steadily. By the time today's first graders reach high school, laptops may be a far more familiar sight in the classroom.

Note that none of these devices—personal computers included—can take the place of good teaching. There is no substitute for human warmth and skill, for example, when it comes to planning lessons, selecting appropriate learning materials, and offering encouragement.

At its best, however, technology *can* reduce the penalties for having a handicap and help students adapt tasks to fit their strongest learning styles. As a college student puts it: "As long as I can get to a computer, I can wipe out 80 percent of my learning disability. My written work looks terrific. My life would be perfect if only the thing could help me meet girls and find the things I've lost in my room."

6. AVOID HOMEWORK TRAPS

Let's be clear about one thing up front—*no* parent should have to spend all evening, every evening helping a child do homework. Mom and Dad need some time for themselves, for each other, and for their other children. Yet parents of kids with learning disabilities often find themselves parked at the kitchen table night after night, helping frustrated, teary-eyed youngsters through piles of reading comprehension checks, vocabulary lists, math problems. . . . Then there are those special evenings when big projects like book reports and term papers are due (often made even more memorable by the fact that the student has procrastinated and left everything until the last minute). "I remember a night when my husband and I were both up until three in the morning helping our son finish a paper on the Civil War," one mother says wryly. "At any given point in the evening two out of three of us were hysterical."

How do parents get entangled in this sort of mess? That's easy to explain: parents love their children and they don't want the kids to fail. But over-involvement in homework rapidly becomes counterproductive. First, when you regularly sit down and do homework with your child you start to blur the issue of whose responsibility the work is. Some youngsters become expert at exploiting confusion in this area. Many a parent, for example, has heard a child whine, "I'm going to *flunk* this test Mommy, because you're not *helping* me!" "That really gets the guilt machine going," a mother says. "Before you know it I'm convinced my daughter's grades really *do* depend on me!" The truth, of course, is that satisfactory completion of schoolwork is the student's obligation, not the parent's. The presence of a learning disability does not alter this basic fact. (This mother eventually learned to respond to her daughter's manipulation by saying, "The spelling test is not a problem for me, sweetheart; I've already passed fifth grade!")

A second problem is that students who receive a great deal of "help" may become increasingly convinced they cannot swim on their own academically. As their self-esteem plummets these youngsters become increasingly dependent on adults (who often respond generously to their obvious neediness, thus reinforcing an unhealthy pattern). Young people who become hooked on excessive academic nurturing can become truly panicky at the thought of tackling anything on their own. They are at high risk for failure in college or on the job—if in fact they find the courage to attempt higher education or apply for employment.

A third problem is that parents don't always make good teachers— and even when they do, children would usually rather have them act like parents, instead. The bottom line is most mothers and fathers are too emotionally involved with their children to teach them effectively. Parents often take setbacks personally. They become frustrated and disappointed (and show it) when they try to explain something and students don't "get it." Sometimes their fears for their children's futures lead them to increase academic pressure, urging youngsters to shape up, try harder, put in more time . . . (parents who are high achievers themselves are most likely to exhibit this kind of response; fathers are observed to be somewhat less patient than mothers with short attention spans and forgetfulness). Of course it's all for the children's own good (parents say), but children rarely see it that way. What children want most from their parents is emotional support and help structuring an environment in which they can function successfully. If they get chronic tension and discontent over school issues instead, they may react by developing a distaste for learning, by withdrawing from parents emotionally, and/or by rebelling against parental authority.

What, then, is a concerned and caring parent to do? Experts (including experienced parents) offer the following guidelines for helping youngsters with homework appropriately.

Make Sure the Homework Is Doable

If it is taking a child all night to struggle through one or two assignments, the solution is not necessarily to provide more help. It might be more appropriate to discuss the problem with the student's teacher(s) and see what can be done to modify assignments and/or cut down on the total work load. "Teachers may not even *know* that it takes a child twenty minutes or more to work a certain kind of math problem, or that the combined assigned reading from several classes has become overwhelming," a parent says. "There is no limit to the amount of work any child should be asked to do in a night."

How much time is a reasonable amount to spend on homework? A special education teacher suggests that an hour a day is the most children in first through third grades can handle. Students in the third through sixth grades should be able to manage sixty to ninety minutes a day (a bit more, perhaps, when they are working on a special project). Students in the seventh through ninth grades can be expected to work on homework for two to three hours a night, and motivated tenth to twelfth graders can apply themselves for three to four hours (the level of effort invested by many ambitious typical students). Means of modifying assignments for students who are overburdened with homework include reducing the number of problems to be solved or questions to be answered (for example, do ten selected problems from each math unit instead of all twenty-five), reducing reading to the essentials and/or providing other means of keeping up with text (such as asking teachers to highlight the most important areas or pairing youngsters with a "reading buddy"), providing alternative strategies (dictating or illustrating a story instead of writing one), and eliminating some types of work entirely (for instance, exempt the student from answering questions at the end of social studies chapters so more time can be invested in math). Your child's special education teacher can help you negotiate these adjustments with regular classroom teachers. *Remember that the purpose of homework is to practice or reinforce what has been learned in class.* Homework should not be assigned to introduce new important information or to cover content that students have missed.

Set Aside a Regular Time for Homework

Having a predictable homework period accomplishes several things. First, most children with disabilities find security in routine (these youngsters don't much like surprises, and many find changes of schedule unsettling). Second, a daily homework period communicates to children that homework is considered important and is not optional. Third, this practice gives parents some control over the amount of time they are going to turn over to providing academic assistance. "My kids knew I'd be available between seven and nine," a mother explains. "After that they could keep working, but I was on my own time." Experienced parents add that it is a good idea to involve children in decisions about when homework time will be. This avoids creating the impression that parents are being unreasonable or arbitrary about imposing rules and restrictions.

Be Specific About What Kinds of Help You Will Provide

Many kids will let you do as much of their work as you're willing to do, and some are adept at sucking parents into providing much more assistance than they had planned. It is usually best, however, if parents establish some clear boundaries about what they will and will not do; this helps young people understand and face their own responsibilities. The best types of assistance are those that leave the "thinking" part of schoolwork to students. Appropriate roles for parents include the following:

Help getting organized. This includes checking calendars and assignment notebooks, making lists of things to do, going over directions, and making sure assignments are understood. Students may also need help prioritizing tasks and breaking down complex assignments (like writing a research paper) into steps or stages. In general, it is best to encourage children to do the most difficult work first—when their energy level is highest—and to complete each assignment before moving on to the next (as opposed to jumping from assignment to assignment, which kids sometimes do when they are frustrated).

Help managing time and staying on task. Youngsters with learning disabilities often have difficulty estimating how long tasks will take, and so they may need help planning their study time. (Typically, the time needed to complete assignments or prepare for a test is underestimated, so work tends to pile up at the end of the day, the week, or the semester.) For children with limited attention spans, homework may need to be scheduled in short sessions, with mini-breaks in between. Frequent feedback may also be needed to help children stay on course—but don't let the child trap you into continuous involvement. Some children find soft music or "white noise" (like the hum of a fan or air conditioner) helps them concentrate; you might see how they like commercially available tapes of nature sounds (waves, wind in the trees, rain falling . . .). Some youngsters also find that rhythmic or repetitive movement helps them focus their attention. If their pencil- or toe-tapping drives you nuts, see if chewing gum or squeezing a soft ball provides the same benefits.

Reading aloud. The job of reading assigned material aloud to the student or into a tape recorder often falls to parents—and many enjoy it. Do make sure, however, that students do as much of their own reading as they can; they cannot learn this skill without practice. If you do not enjoy this kind of activity or lack time to do it consistently, there are other ways to meet the child's needs: ask teachers to match the student with a peer reading partner or hire a high school student to read to the child, for example. You may also find that a family member (such as a grandparent), a church member, or members of local community service organizations would be willing to take on the job of recording text materials on tape.

Serving as a secretary or scribe. Students who have trouble getting words on paper sometimes have an easier time explaining what they know if they are allowed to dictate to someone. As with reading, it is important to encourage students to write out as much of their own work as they can (students can often manage short assignments on their own, but they may need help with long written projects like reports). When serving in this capacity, it is important to record students' words faithfully—it can be very tempting to make "improvements" as you go along. Note that a common problem for children with weak handwriting skills is lining up the numbers in math problems correctly; this sometimes leads to needless confusion and errors. Some parents address this problem by writing out homework problems for students in large numerals. Also try writing out math problems on lined paper turned sideways to create vertical columns, or on graph paper.

Reviewing and proofreading written work. Students with learning disabilities are notoriously bad about checking their own work. Sometimes this is due to their disabilities (students with visual perception problems, for example, may be unable to identify spelling errors), and sometimes it is because when a difficult or boring assignment is done, students never want to see it again! By helping students check over their work, however, parents both provide some "quality control" and communicate to children that they are expected to meet high standards. Just make sure that these standards are attainable and that students are not unnecessarily penalized for making improvements. You might offer to type a corrected composition, for example, rather than asking a child to copy it over (for many students with disabilities, copying is a task that involves generating a whole new set of mistakes).

Students with learning disabilities may also need to have information that they couldn't understand from books or lectures reviewed and/or interpreted for them from time to time, but parents are not always the best people to do this. "Working with my son took the patience of a saint," a mother confesses, "and half the time I didn't understand his homework either. Usually I contacted his teachers when he had trouble understanding something." This sensible policy also helps teachers figure out which materials and methods work best for children and which give them trouble. If teachers are unable to give children the individual attention they need at school, finding a competent tutor may be preferable to tying up all the time you and your child have together with schoolwork or leaving yourself no free time. Even when students have learning disabilities, schoolwork should not be allowed to consume all a family's energy.

Look into Study Buddies

Peer study partners (these partnerships are usually brokered by teachers) can assist youngsters with learning disabilities several ways. Partners can help children record assignments in a notebook or on a calendar, help copy material from the blackboard into notebooks correctly, share class and/or lab notes, and quiz or drill each other in preparation for tests. In addition to providing direct assistance, peer study partners serve as positive role models in the classroom. Students who are good choices for partnerships are those who are well organized, have good social skills, and have a firm grasp on class subject matter. It is also best if the partner volunteers for this duty (there is usually no shortage of volunteer helpers in classes where teachers recognize and praise cooperative effort). Partners who are required to work with a student who has learning problems may be too resentful to offer much in the way of patience and understanding. Children with learning disabilities can also benefit from working with older student "mentors." A fifth or sixth grader, for example, might provide valuable one-on-one instruction for a fourth grader who is struggling with long division. (Educators know this kind of relationship is usually good for the older student as well; teaching helps them consolidate and expand their own knowledge.)

With teachers' permission, youngsters can also team up to tackle tasks like research reports; this practice helps keep students who have trouble working independently in the game, and it also helps reduce big projects to manageable proportions. Take care, however, that students do not coast through group projects on the coattails of energetic achievers. In the best cooperative ventures, each participant has well-defined responsibilities.

Note that homework hassles are frequently related to emotional issues. Homework makes a convenient battlefield, for example, for a student intent on challenging parental authority. If this appears to be the case, parents need to back away from the power struggle—pounding away at the issue will only make matters worse. "Refuse to fight over homework," a teacher advises. "If your child is avoiding it, talk to teachers about your concerns and let them work on the kid for a while. Continue to express support and willingness to help if asked. Once the pressure is off, most students realize that doing well in school is in their own best interests." If conflict over homework is part of a larger pattern of rebellion that includes defiance of authorities at school—or if a student has become withdrawn and apathetic about nonacademic activities, as well as schoolwork—the situation is more serious. These circumstances signal an emotional crisis and call for prompt intervention from a mental health professional.

7. GIVE YOURSELVES A BREAK

Many conscientious parents who have stuck with us to this point are probably feeling fairly panic-stricken by now. "Good Lord!" some will be thinking. "How am I going to check up on my child's basic skills, build her a study corner, tape-record her textbooks, find her a mentor, preview the curriculum, hold down a job, and take care of my other children, too?" Relax. You're not going to do all those things today, or probably even this year—and your child can still grow into a splendid human being if you don't ever do all of them. What we have provided in this chapter are suggestions for things parents can do to help children academically *as opportunities arise*. We wouldn't advise anyone to rush out and try them all immediately.

Instead we want to warn parents here of the hazards of becoming overly focused on academic performance. In today's achievement-oriented culture, this is a problem many families face. While any child can suffer from too much scholastic pressure, there are some special risks for students who have learning disabilities.

The greatest danger of academic "tunnel vision" is that children will be required to spend so much time and effort struggling with what they do badly that they have no energy left over to do what they do well. Many children with learning disabilities find that their spheres of success—the areas of activity or endeavor that are most satisfying to them and give them the most confidence in themselves—lie outside the academic arena. These children may be unusually creative and able at expressing themselves through art, music, or drama, for example. Some are exceptionally sensitive to the feelings of others and demonstrate strong leadership skills or commitment to their communities. They may be skilled craftspersons, gifted with machines, talented athletes, enterprising entrepreneurs . . . the list of what these youngsters *can* do goes on and on. But if adults over-focus

SARAH

Sarah is a 21-year-old college senior who has an auditory processing disability. She began studying the flute in fourth grade.

It's funny: I have a very hard time remembering things people say to me, but remembering music is no problem. I've always loved it. Some years music was the only thing that kept me going to school. For example, when I was in middle school I did very poorly academically. I don't mean in just math or English; I was doing horribly in *everything*. I was unhappy and unmotivated—except in band and chorus. I made an effort for my music teachers, and they gave me a lot of encouragement. When I was in eighth grade, the high school band director came and auditioned all the kids who wanted to play in the band the next year. It seemed like besides me, there were about a hundred other kids who wanted to play the flute, and we all had to play solos. The director chose me for the second seat in the high school band! That success lifted my self-esteem tremendously. I was a lot less afraid of high school, knowing I had such a good place in band waiting for me . . .

In high school, music turned my life completely around. I eventually became involved in the Pep Band, the Marching Band, and the Concert Orchestra; I participated in three different choral groups and sang and acted in musical theater performances. I won awards for musical achievement—when our concert band was invited to play at the Epcot Center at Disney World, I even got to play the featured solo. The amazing thing, though, was the way success in music carried over to my other studies. At some point it clicked that I was successful in music *because I worked at it*—and that working hard could make a difference in my other classes. I started to apply myself, and my grades went up. When I graduated, my first-choice college awarded me an academic scholarship.

Music did wonderful things for me socially also. I would guess that 85% of the people I feel close to and keep in touch with today are friends I met through musical theater or band. Looking back, it's easy to see that without music my high school career would have been nothing. Music gave me friends and teachers who supported and believed in me. It taught me the value of effort and self-discipline and gave me self-confidence. It think I would be a very different person now if my family and my school hadn't supported my love of music the way they did.

on what children *cannot* do (reading, writing, or arithmetic), children may not find the opportunities they need to explore these other areas of achievement. Even when opportunities are provided, children whose lives have been dominated by disability may lack the courage and self-confidence to risk trying something new.

Another by-product of academic overkill is that children end up leading unbalanced lives. All children need exercise (children with ADHD need it more than most), time to be with friends, and time to "veg out" and rest. Children who are never allowed to forget that they are doing poorly in school, however, may be shortchanged in any or all of these areas. Should we really be surprised when such children display explosive tempers or rebel against authority's heavy hand? Note that pressure to excel in school does not come only from parents. Teachers and guidance counselors also issue dire warnings about finding a job or getting into college—and ambitious youngsters who are competitive by nature sometimes do a great job of pressuring themselves. Parents may have to help children like this learn how to relax, lighten up, and enjoy life.

A third consideration is that overemphasizing school achievement can start to warp relationships between adults and children. When school concerns dominate the time parents and children have together, children may come to see their parents as demanding taskmasters instead of sources of warmth, acceptance, and support. It is therefore important to distinguish between encouragement to achieve ("I know you can do it") and behavior that sounds encouraging but carries a heavy subtext ("I know you can do it, and if you don't do it quick we're all going to be really fed up and disappointed"). In Part IV of this book we will discuss how parental behavior influences motivation and learning in greater detail. The point to keep in mind here is that if you made a list of what children with learning disabilities need most from their families, help with schoolwork wouldn't even make the top ten. Do *not* allow your concern about school performance to prevent you from playing with your child, talking with your child, enjoying outings, and sharing activities that have no "academic" value whatever. Those are the times that make meaningful memories—not the hours you spend helping the child look up vocabulary words.

Realistically, what all this means is that parents of children with learning disabilities must often make choices. Allow the child to go to the movies or insist that she finish her history homework? Hire a piano teacher or a math tutor? Can the teen handle Chemistry given three hours of soccer practice every day? If not, should the Chemistry or the soccer be given up? Sometimes the choices are very tough: should a student who is falling significantly behind, for example, be signed up for summer school or abandon the college-preparatory curriculum? Although parents sometimes feel unprepared to make these decisions, they are usually the persons best qualified to do so, because choices like these have to be made with the whole child in mind. Teachers and school officials can usually be counted upon to push for academic achievement; it's Mom and Dad who know how much music means to the child, how much soccer has done for the student's self-confidence and self-esteem, how much the youngster needs relief from academic stress. At the bottom line, academic potential should never be nurtured at the expense of a child's emotional security and well-being. What children need most is parents who will make humane decisions on their behalf—and teach them to establish healthy priorities and make sensible decisions for themselves as they get older.

The director of a parent-professional support group in New York (herself the mother of a successful college student with learning disabilities) adds that young people aren't the only ones to feel the pressure in our competitive society. Parents can also be tripped up by unreasonably high expectations of themselves. "Perfectionism is an awful trap," she says. "Expecting ourselves to be perfect parents is hard on us and hard on the kids, too, because perfect parents are supposed to produce perfect children. Sometimes I think the best thing we can do for our kids is relax and accept ourselves. My kids have seen me screw up a million times—and I'm glad, because that's what tells them they don't have to hate themselves if they try something and don't succeed."

What else has this authority learned from working with hundreds of parents over the years? "Hold on to your sense of humor!" she says. "The mothers who I see making it are the ones who know how to laugh. Certainly, that's been my own experience. My daughter's junior high school years were a nightmare—not only was she failing several courses and hanging out with a dangerous crowd, but her father walked out on us and I ended up in the hospital facing major surgery! We're much stronger as individuals and as a family for having survived all that, but part of the reason we did survive was that even at the worse times, we could laugh a little."

Part IV

A QUALITY LIFE

10

SOCIAL AND EMOTIONAL GROWTH

Although parents understandably fret about school performance, research finds that "book learning" often has less to do with achievement in life than personal attributes like optimism, ambition, adaptability, willingness to work hard, and persistence in the face of difficulty. These qualities make the difference between average and outstanding performers, and often characterize exceptionally resilient individuals who rise above disabilities and oppressive circumstances again and again.

Social competence also has an impact on how comfortably an individual functions in the real world. Not only does the ability to form and maintain relationships improve quality of life, it is a basic building block of self-esteem. Among teens, for example, connecting with a peer group is an essential part of establishing an identity. So important is having friends at this age that child guidance experts view adolescent "outsiders" as extra-high risks for emotional disturbance. Significantly, teens and adults with learning disabilities consistently cite social life as an area with which they most want assistance. In surveys, this concern is often ranked as more important than finding educational opportunities or employment.

This is not to suggest that schoolwork is unimportant; educational achievement does affect students' career choices and prospects for higher learning. There is no doubt, however, that social and emotional development are equally important to a student's success and sense of well-being. There is also no doubt that the most powerful influence on a young person's social and emotional growth is the family. Much of children's feelings about themselves and other people are formed long before they start school. As they grow, the attitudes and expectations of parents and other family members continue to have an enormous effect on how students interact with others, approach difficult tasks, and view their own abilities. For an example of the impact family can have on achievement, we need look no further than the current generation of Southeast Asian immigrants to the United States. In part because of strong family support systems that emphasize the value of hard work and education, many children who endured tremendous hardship to reach this country, lived much of their lives in poverty, and started school speaking no English at all are now leading their classes at high school and college campuses across the nation!

It is important for parents to recognize the crucial role they play in helping children develop aptitudes for living and learning. It is also important for parents of children with learning disabilities to understand that information-processing problems can affect social and emotional growth. Learning disabilities often have as great an impact on life at home and in the community as they do on performance in school. One expert suggests these handicaps should really be called "living disabilities" because their effect is so pervasive. Yet parents do not always connect "problem" behaviors like bad table manners, difficulty completing chores, chronic inability to be on time, or a tendency to go bananas at Grandma's house with the neurological irregularities that cause trouble with reading or writing. As a result, some children with learning disabilities get punished for laziness, carelessness, and disobedience at home as much as they do at school. Accusations and repeated family clashes, of course, help erode these youngsters' self-esteem and add to their burdens of anger and anxiety.

Even when the link between learning disabilities and personal problems is clear and families are eager to offer support, parents may feel uncertain about how to help youngsters cope with many of life's challenges. Finding appropriate assistance with reading, writing, and arithmetic can seem simple compared with figuring out how to help a child who has trouble with language to learn how to make conversation, or to teach a teen with no sense of direction how to drive a car! Some parents find themselves keeping children with learning disabilities close to home in an effort to protect them from failure, hurt, or rejection. These good intentions can backfire, however, as over-sheltered children tend to remain immature and often lack confidence in their own ability to survive independently.

Also challenging for parents is managing the impact a learning disability has on family dynamics. How to deal, for example, with differences of opinion with a spouse over spending savings on tutoring or private school tuition? With siblings who are resentful that the child with learning disabilities does fewer chores while grabbing *all* of Mom's free time for help with homework? Or with the grandparent who insists that what the child needs is "a little less spoiling and a lot more discipline . . ."? When and how to apply discipline can become a divisive family issue that may find mother and father on opposing sides (about the only thing the family may agree on is that no known form of discipline seems to work). As one mother put it: "Learning disabilities are really a family affair. The stress and the emotional fallout have a ripple effect. One way or another, the problem touches everyone."

Obviously a discussion of learning disabilities cannot end with a summary of the child's needs at school. In this section we will therefore look at some of the nonacademic factors that contribute to a quality life. In this chapter we will discuss stages of development and talk about how learning disabilities can influence social and emotional growth. In Chapter 11 we will discuss some strategies for helping young people maintain their self-esteem, develop a sense of responsibility, and form healthy relationships, both in- and outside of the family. In Chapter 12 we will look at skills that are necessary for independent living, and talk about helping young adults make the transition from school and home to the world of work or higher education. Along the way, we think you will discover that many of the problems that afflict children with learning disabilities and their families are avoidable. While living with these youngsters may never be stress free, a little understanding can go a long way toward finding solutions that preserve everyone's sanity and dignity.

LEARNING DISABILITIES AND CHILD DEVELOPMENT

On their way to maturity, all children go through a series of fairly predictable stages, each with its own set of needs and characteristic behaviors. Children with learning disabilities, however, do not always move through these stages at the same rate as their typical peers. Just as cognitive, verbal, and motor skills are often delayed among these youngsters, lags in emotional development and social

CHAD

When Greta remarried, she was delighted how well her eight-year-old son, Chad, related to his stepfather. Greta married Chad's father young; he was a high school dropout and a "rebel" who deserted her soon after Chad was born. Mike was a totally different kind of man: responsible and kind. The family lived on a farm, and Chad followed Mike everywhere, begging to be allowed to help with chores.

Over the next two years, however, Mike and Chad's relationship changed. "I tell Chad what I need help with but he doesn't follow through," Mike complained. "I can't trust him." Privately, Greta thought Mike's perfectionism was contributing to the problem. "Take it a little easier on him," she suggested. "He's just a kid, and he already has enough people on his case at school." Chad's grades could have been a lot better, and his fourth grade teacher was always nagging him. "Take it easy!" Mike replied. "I'm giving him the simplest jobs as it is. He's just goofing off!"

Greta felt hurt that Mike was so rough on Chad, but Mike was hurting, too. "Lately Chad avoids me," he confided to Greta later. "I try to make time for him and show him how to do things, but it seems like he wants nothing to do with me." When Greta urged Chad to spend more time with his Dad, however, Chad only replied, "He's not my Dad," and retreated to his room with a video game.

At the end of the school year Chad's teacher said he had made so little progress that he ought to be tested for a learning disability. He was eval-

skills can occur. As a result, the thinking and behavior of children with learning disabilities may sometimes seem babyish or resemble that of younger children (causing exasperated parents to exclaim "Why can't you act your *age*?").

In addition, many children with learning disabilities seem to enter the world with intense personalities that challenge parents to the max (it has been observed that children with learning disabilities are just like other kids—only more so). These children may be *extra*-energetic, *extra*-sensitive to their surroundings, *extra*-moody, or *extra*-insistent on doing things their own way. As a result, their behavior at any given stage of development may seem magnified. While virtually all kids go through a "no" stage at around age two and a half, for example, an intense child's "no" may seem resistant to all forms of persuasion or be accompanied by hour-long tantrums.

It is important to understand that children cannot be hurried

uated over the summer, and found to have language processing problems that interfered with both reading and understanding verbal directions. With help, his performance in school improved in fifth grade, but relations at home became even more strained. Mike became increasingly irritated with the boy's "carelessness and irresponsibility," while Chad's mother felt obliged to defend him. They argued about what Chad should be expected to do on the farm, and how to punish him if he failed to do it. When Mike lost his temper and told Chad he could sleep in the barn if his chores weren't finished by suppertime, Greta responded by packing a bag and taking Chad to her sister's apartment.

Neither Mike nor Greta realized that Chad's learning disability accounted for much of his problem with chores. He could not remember the lists of jobs Mike told him about, nor follow all the instructions for how to do them. (If *shown* how to do something Chad usually got it right, but Mike's teaching style leaned toward long, detailed explanations.) Aware that he was disappointing his much-admired stepfather, Chad dealt with his growing sense of inadequacy by withdrawing and masked his feelings with a hostile "attitude." Because it was assumed that a learning disability was exclusively an *educational* problem, everybody in the family was miserable. Fortunately, this family's crisis led them to get counseling which helped them identify these issues. The lesson remains: it can be perilous to address learning disabilities at school but ignore them at home.

through basic stages of development. A great deal of stress can be created when cognitive or social expectations are far beyond children's levels of developmental readiness. Just as important, it is necessary to understand that some elements of personality are difficult to modify. Scientists now believe that many aspects of our temperaments are genetically programmed. The traits listed on pages 236–37 are those most likely to be inherited and therefore resistant to change. While environment can influence these traits to some extent, fundamental transformations are unlikely. (In other words, you can help a very shy child learn good social skills, but you cannot turn that child into a gregarious extrovert.) Parents who are not respectful of temperamental differences sometimes end up labeling a child whose approach to life is different from their own as "wrong" or bad—an attitude that can strain parent-child relationships. We will talk more about temperament in Chapter 11. For the time being, remember that a great deal of conflict and aggravation can be avoided by learning to work *with* a child's basic temperament instead of struggling against it.

Maturation is also affected by personal circumstances. A. H. Maslow, a psychologist who studied motivation, observed that as they grow, human beings attempt to get their needs met in a particular order; his hierarchy of human needs is presented on page 238. Maslow believed that all of an individual's needs at one level must be met before he or she can succeed on the next level. (Maslow also observed that if several needs are present at once, people will devote their energy to meeting the needs that are most basic first.) In other words, while everyone needs affection and acceptance, children who lack shelter, safety, or family stability often have a harder time attaining them than children who are securely provided for. Similarly, if teens are unable to find acceptance in a peer group, their ability to develop self-respect and set goals for themselves may be compromised. Maslow's hierarchy reminds us that concerns like safety, stability, and acceptance are not merely "early childhood issues" or "adolescent issues." These needs remain important throughout our lives. Whenever circumstances or disabilities interfere with getting basic needs met, social and emotional progress can be delayed.

With these general ideas in mind, let's look at how children behave at different stages of their development.

The Preschool Child

A remarkable amount of social and emotional development takes place during the first three years of life. It is during this critical period, for example, that children discover whether or not it is safe to explore their environments and trust other people. The quality of a child's relationships at this stage can have a significant impact on his or her emotional outlook. In general, children who have secure, stable relationships with their adult caretakers are most likely to be attentive, motivated, and responsive to challenge. Even at age three or four these fortunate youngsters appear to have optimistic expectations and a certain amount of self-confidence. Children who have not had consistent nurturing from adults, on the other hand, are more likely to be passive, easily discouraged, withdrawn, and/or fearful of new situations. Research indicates that these early attitudes can be very persistent, enduring into the school years and even into adulthood.

The ability to play cooperatively with others typically develops at around age three (before that, children tend to play *near* each other rather than *with* each other). From this age on, peer relationships (as well as relationships with adults) present the growing child with opportunities to learn and practice social and language skills. Since children who are open, enthusiastic, and outgoing are attractive to other children, they often garner more social opportunities than those who are more shy or passive. By the time they start school, these socially advantaged youngsters have a significant head start over children whose social and language skills are less developed. Students who are good communicators, comfortable with both peers and adults, and confident of their own abilities usually make good students, sometimes outdistancing peers of higher intelligence academically.

Preschoolers who have learning disabilities benefit no less than others from loving support from their parents and appropriate opportunities to interact with peers. Children who have these advantages are typically more resilient and able to compensate for their disabilities than those who are socially isolated or whose family systems are disengaged, rigid, or chaotic. Youngsters who have immature or unevenly developing nervous systems, however, can be challenging to raise and sometimes present their parents with special problems. As infants, for example, these children are sometimes irritable and hard to comfort. They may defy all efforts to settle them into a schedule for eating and sleeping and react to attempts to play with or cuddle them by screaming or turning away. These behaviors usually leave parents feeling helpless, incompetent, and rejected. As a result, parents do not always "bond" with these infants as successfully as they do with their other children. Indeed, Mom and Dad may not be able to help actively resenting the baby who keeps them up night after night and refuses to respond to their loving efforts to relieve the child's discomforts.

Children with learning disabilities can continue to be challenging as toddlers. Difficulty processing verbal or visual information makes it harder for them to follow directions, remember rules, or play games; delays in learning to talk, dress, or feed themselves may also disappoint and frustrate parents. Children who are hyperactive often seem completely out of control as pre-schoolers. Many cannot seem to avoid mayhem when taken out: parents watch helplessly as supermarket displays tumble; the company picnic becomes a shambles as the child climbs all over the table, upsetting everyone's food; grandmother's furniture and carpets sustain new damage with every visit. Even when parents go out alone, they may spend their time worrying about what kind of catastrophes are befalling the babysitter at home.

Genes and Personality

While much of human behavior is learned, some aspects of temperament are inherited. Responses in the areas listed below can be particularly resistant to change.

Intensity. Very intense children commit 110 percent of their energy to everything they do: even as infants, they never whimper—they wail loud enough to wake the neighbors. Their emotional responses are dramatic; they are passionate about what they like (and what they don't). Less intense children appear more reserved. Parents may have to tune in to subtle facial expressions and body language to judge how these youngsters feel (for example, a little muscle tension may be the only sign that they are very upset).

Persistence: Once "locked in" to an activity, idea, or emotion, persistent children pursue it to the limit—and even then they have trouble giving it up. These kids will not take "no" for an answer and are not afraid to assert themselves. Less persistent children are more easily redirected; they are also more easily "turned off" when things don't go their way and may need extra encouragement to follow through on difficult tasks.

Sensitivity to environment: Some youngsters are very sensitive to noises, smells, light, and textures. They are easily overwhelmed in "busy," noisy, or crowded situations, and can be very picky about their food and the comfort of their clothing. These children also can be extraordinarily sensitive to others' moods (they may know how you're feeling before you do). Less sensitive youngsters will eat anything and sleep through fireworks—but plan to *tell* them when you're getting angry or stressed out (they won't notice that you're gnashing your teeth).

Adaptability: Slow-to-adapt children don't like change. They are distressed by variations in their schedules and often have difficulty with transitions (both shifts from one activity to another and changes of environment). They really hate surprises (*don't* expect these kids to be happy about getting a cherry popsicle when they were expecting grape). These children have a greater need for routine than more flexible youngsters, who change activities and settings with relative ease.

Distractibility: "Distractible" children are in fact ultra-perceptive; they are very attentive to details in their environments and often see things others miss (who else would notice that the little stain on the ceiling is shaped like the state of Texas?). They may be so interested in their surroundings, however, that they have trouble following through on tasks.

Less distractible youngsters are usually better at focusing their attention. (They may also be so intent on homework that they completely miss the sunset glowing outside the window.)

Regularity: Very regular children become hungry and sleepy at predictable intervals; even as infants, it is easy to settle them into schedules. Other children seem wired to a different kind of clock: you never know when they're going to sleep or want food. Irregular children can resist all attempts to establish routines; their parents' most frequent complaint is that they will *not* sleep through the night. (The mother of an irregular teenager says, "Take heart; eventually they learn to amuse themselves at 2 A.M. and they don't wake you up any more".)

Activity level: Even when they sleep, very active children aren't still; they creep all over the bed, tangling their covers or dumping them on the floor. They are typically curious and "into everything"; they shift rapidly from one activity to another and don't stop until they drop from fatigue. When required to sit (as at dinner or at church) they fiddle, tap, and squirm. Less energetic children are more likely to sit quietly absorbed with a book or game. Since they are by nature less exploratory, however, parents may have to make an effort to expose these youngsters to new activities and areas of interest.

Mood: Some children are upbeat and optimistic by nature; they look for each cloud's silver lining and usually express satisfaction with their lot in life. For others, however, life is a more serious matter. These "Eeyores" focus on the flaws and drawbacks in every situation. They may try parents' patience with their gloomy observations and endless lists of criticisms. There is an up side to a "down" personality, however. Think: which of these kids would you rather have with you when you test-drive a used car?

Openness to new experience: Children vary considerably in the way they approach new people, places, and things. Some instinctively withdraw or turn away from anything unfamiliar; they need time to observe and "warm up" before entering into a new activity, talking to a stranger, or playing with a new toy. Others charge into new situations—sometimes forgetting to look before they leap. Like the other traits on this list, this one can persist into adulthood. Reticent children may become cautious adults, while their more outgoing opposites often continue to embrace (or even restlessly seek) novelty.

Maslow's Hierarchy

Psychologist A. H. Maslow ranked human desires according to importance. Individuals who are unable to satisfy basic needs (at the bottom of the pyramid) have a hard time attaining "higher order" goals. Maslow's principles are sometimes used to explain why economically disadvantaged children are often less self-confident and successful than more privileged youngsters.

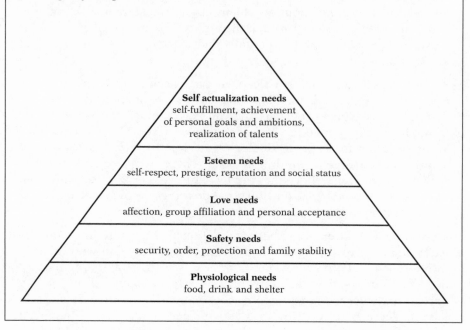

Self actualization needs
self-fulfillment, achievement
of personal goals and ambitions,
realization of talents

Esteem needs
self-respect, prestige, reputation and social status

Love needs
affection, group affiliation and personal acceptance

Safety needs
security, order, protection and family stability

Physiological needs
food, drink and shelter

Parents of hyperactive children often come to feel increasingly isolated from friends and extended family members—all of whom may be generous with advice on child management without fully understanding the realities of the situation. If parents disagree about how the child should be "handled" or blame each other for the child's behavior, the stress can undermine a marriage and family stability as well as parent-child relationships.

Sadly, in circumstances such as these parents and children sometimes become increasingly estranged. Research finds that parents of children with learning disabilities often feel more negatively about these youngsters then their other children and behave toward them in a harsher or more remote manner. Sometimes parental affection is transferred to a more successful or less troublesome sibling, effec-

EDEN

Eden is a seven-year-old girl of average intelligence from a middle-income family. Every child in her family has inherited a language processing disability which results in serious reading delays. Eden's family is supportive, understanding of her disability, and hopeful about her future. Her parents have formed a cooperative relationship with Eden's teachers at school, and Eden is making steady progress. In her family picture, Eden shows her father presenting flowers to her pregnant mother, while Eden plays ball with her older sister. Her self-portrait (top left) shows a happy little girl. When she was given incomplete sentences to finish, Eden's answers reflected satisfaction with her family and high self-esteem: *Boys think I am* . . . Pretty; *My father never* . . . Shouts; *I know I can* . . . Read; *My family is* . . . Important to me; *People are always* . . . Nice; *Other children* . . . Play with me.

tively rendering the child with disabilities "odd man out" in the family group. As the drawings on this page and the next illustrate, parents' feelings about their children directly influence how children feel about themselves. Kids who become labeled "family screw-ups" or "family troublemakers" usually end up with poor self-concepts and low opinions of their own abilities.

Some pre-schoolers with learning disabilities are also at a disadvantage when it comes to establishing peer relationships. Toddlers

REBECCA

Rebecca is the same age as Eden and has the same type of learning disability. Her mother and father are both physicians, and her older brother is a straight-A student. Rebecca's parents are unable to accept her disability. They are angry about her poor academic performance and have demanded that the school do something to "fix" their disappointing daughter. Their dissatisfaction and lack of respect for Rebecca's teachers has spilled over to Rebecca, who is ambivalent about investing energy in her schoolwork. In Rebecca's family picture the cats are more animated than the people. Rebecca's parents and brother are together, but Rebecca is segregated, looking in from a doorway. Her self-portrait in the corner is angrily scribbled out. In response to questions about her drawing, Rebecca stated: "I'm pretty stupid"; "I'm sad because my Mom and Dad yell and scream"; "My brother's mean to me"; and "My Mom and Dad wish for me to get away for real and in the picture."

Source: Smith, C. R. *op. cit.*

who are maturing slowly, for example, may remain in the possessive "mine" stage longer than usual, making them unpopular with peers who are learning to take turns, cooperate, and share. Youngsters who are impulsive human whirlwinds are usually no more welcome at nursery school or the playground than they are at the family dinner table. Pre-schoolers who have trouble processing verbal or visual information can have a hard time understanding the rules of even the simplest games, and they may be impatient with activities that other children enjoy. A child with auditory-processing problems, for example, is likely to be restless and disruptive during "story time" and may be frustrated to the point of tears by games like "Simon Says." As games and play activities selected by others become more complex and language-based, children with learning disabilities sometimes get left behind. By the time they start school, therefore, many are doubly disadvantaged; not only do they have problems with academic tasks, but they have not yet learned to interact with other children successfully. Even when youngsters come from very supportive families, the combination of poor school readiness and unsuccessful peer relationships can test children's emotional defenses to the limit. Unless appropriate social opportunities are provided along with academic help, the result can be plummeting self-confidence.

Elementary School

During the elementary school years, friendships play an increasingly important role in children's sense of success and well-being. At school, matters of who sits next to whom at lunch, who gets invited to which birthday parties, and who gets selected as a best friend often get at least as much attention as reading, writing, and arithmetic. Social relationships in elementary school are increasingly governed by unwritten "rules," and conformity to these rules is expected if one wants to "belong." Rigid codes may be developed for behavior, language (use of slang), and dress. This is an age when fads sweep the school with predictable regularity. A particular haircut or shoe style initially identifies peer leaders and others "in the know"; when everyone else catches on a new trend is embraced or invented.

Throughout these years same-sex friends are typically preferred. Research finds that younger and older children have somewhat different expectations of friendship—as do girls and boys. Six- to eight-year-olds, for example, say a friend is someone to play and share with, while nine- to eleven-year-olds increasingly value friends' ability to help one another and be loyal and dependable. As they approach middle school, an important element in girls' friendships is trying to *look* like one another. Boys, on the other hand, look for friends who enjoy similar pastimes—guys to "hang out" with.

Elementary-aged children become very astute at "reading" the requirements and values of the different groups they interact with. A fifth grader, for example, can recognize not only that peers and adults have different attitudes about clothes, entertainment, and grades but is also capable of distinguishing attitude variations among several different peer groups (what's "in" at one's own school, for example, may be different from what's "in" at a cousin's school or at summer camp). Desire to conform to a chosen group's standards typically becomes stronger as students get older. By the end of fourth grade most children are choosing their clothing and amusements with the opinions of other children—not their parents—uppermost in their minds. The lust to possess what "all the other kids" have can seem quite maniacal at this point. Some weary parents report almost daily requests for popular collectibles, the latest style in a particular brand of sneakers or jeans, the newest thing in electronics, and/or other items pertaining to some currently "in" activity. Even what goes into the lunch box may be accepted or rejected on the basis of peer tastes and preferences!

Clearly, children who look "different," who are not skilled at popular sports and games, or whose behavior is erratic or unpredictable are at a disadvantage in the elementary school environment. Many youngsters with learning disabilities fall into these categories. Children who are immature or who have visual perception deficits, for example, are often *socially imperceptive;* they do not pick up on "cues" in their environments as easily as others do. Not only do these youngsters fail to appreciate the finer points of fifth-grade fashion, they may be totally unaware of the fact that appearance influences popularity! These children also have difficulty recognizing the effect their behavior has on others. A child who is describing the plot of a television show in tiresome detail, for example, may miss facial expressions and body language indicating that her audience is becoming bored or that others would like a chance to speak. Caught up in her own excitement she rattles on and on—then wonders why no one wants to sit next to her on the bus. Frequent failure to observe social conventions can lead to a child becoming labeled "dumb," unfriendly, or "weird." Among youngsters with learning disabilities, however, the problem is more often ignorance of what the prevailing social conventions are, or difficulty applying social skills correctly (for example, a child may remember to say "please" when asking for something, but still annoy others by interrupting frequently with small requests).

Some children understand social rules but nevertheless have a hard time following them. Youngsters who are poorly organized, for example, may endanger friendships by inability to remember names and phone numbers, frequent tardiness (thereby holding up group activities), or failure to return borrowed items ("I have your hat? Uh, what does it look like?"). Children who are impulsive (a common characteristic of Attention Deficit Hyperactivity Disorder) exasperate others by speaking and acting without thinking about consequences. They blurt out embarrassing observations, try to insert themselves into activities that are already underway, and reach for what they want without regard for whom it belongs to or whose turn it may be to use it. (These children may later realize they have caused offense, but honest regret does not prevent them from blundering and barging in again and again.) Young people can also alienate peers with their rigidity and need to do everything one way (theirs), or their emotional immaturity (they may be so intolerant of losing, for example, that they will cheat or overturn the checkerboard rather than allow someone else to win). Not surprisingly, youngsters such as these are avoided and sometimes ostracized; eventually many come to expect rejection. Frustration over their inability to connect positively with peers can have a corrosive effect on these children's self-esteem. Hostile attitudes ("I'll reject you before you have a chance to reject me") are sometimes adopted to mask feelings of personal inadequacy or self-hatred.

Youngsters who have difficulty processing language also encounter a variety of social problems. Not only do these children have trouble following and participating in conversations (a problem that typically gets worse in group situations) but they may appear to lack humor because they fail to appreciate word-play or recognize the point of jokes. They make embarrassing social gaffes because they choose the wrong words or misunderstand explanations and instructions (the child who fails to grasp that the rules of "Musical Chairs" call for sitting down *after* the music has stopped may feel like the laughing stock of the birthday party whether she is or not). Learning the rules of games can be such a problem that children avoid games altogether—which of course deprives them of valuable social opportunities. ("Klutzy" kids with poor muscle coordination and children with severe perceptual disabilities can also find themselves shut out of sports and games.) Often youngsters with language disabilities cope by adopting the role of passive followers in a crowd. They find they can achieve a certain amount of acceptance by hanging watchfully around the fringes of activities, copying others' behavior. The price of this acceptance, however, may be a feeling that it is not all right to be oneself or to strive for positions of leadership.

Because of their sensitivity to issues of social status, elementary aged children may display increasing reluctance to participate in special education classes as they get older. To escape the stigma of a special education "label," middle school students sometimes try to refuse to participate in these programs altogether, and many young people attempt to hide their disabilities from classmates. In surveys, students voice a variety of concerns about "going public," from risking the ridicule of poorly informed peers ("Some tease you and think you're really stupid for being in there. They just think it's for retards . . ."*) to jeopardizing chances for success with the opposite sex ("If I go out with a girl from another class, she'll ask 'What classes do you have?' If I say I have LD classes that's one thing that clicks them off right there. . . ."*). Concerns of this kind do need to be taken seriously. The way teachers are managing classes may be contributing to the problem, and a more sensitive approach at school may improve the child's comfort level. It is equally important, however, to probe children's own understanding and attitudes. Do they think they need special education because they are stupid, bad, genetically defective, or otherwise "messed up"? This is often the case when students lack information about their learning disabilities. Students who have a thorough understanding of their strengths and weaknesses, on the other hand, are more likely to express confidence in themselves and their ability to overcome negative stereotypes ("Everybody has a disability and problem with some subject. I'm not embarrassed. . . . I just do everything with everybody. . . . Nobody ever says anything or that I can't go anywhere. They just say 'Let's go!'"*). Research reveals that the secondary and college students who are most successful are those who have accepted their disabilities, know how to compensate for them, and have learned to identify situations in which they can prosper. Helping children understand learning disabilities and empowering children to deal with them is therefore a better strategy than cooperating with efforts to hide or deny handicaps.

Note that both children and adults with learning disabilities are often observed to be somewhat egocentric. Their preoccupation with themselves and their own concerns is often interpreted as an irritating lack of sensitivity or failure to appreciate the needs and concerns of others. It is important to remember, however, that people who are literal or concrete thinkers do not easily generalize or transfer information from one set of circumstances to another. Just as children sometimes have difficulty seeing that basic number principles can be applied to word problems in math, they can have trouble placing themselves in another person's shoes. It may therefore be necessary to *explain* to them what others are thinking and feeling—even when you'd think it would be obvious. For example, a fourth grader might

---

* Quotes from a study by Beverly R. Guterman; *Exceptional Children*, October/November, 1995.

be capable of being very considerate and compassionate once you tell him "Cindy is feeling very sad now because her grandmother died." Fail to provide that information, however, and he may try to tell Cindy his latest joke the moment she returns from the funeral! This is one area where understanding the child's thinking process can significantly improve family relations. If those who are close to the child get in the habit of spelling out how they feel and what kind of behavior is expected, everyone may be amazed at how sensitive and helpful the child has suddenly become!

Adolescence

During adolescence typical youngsters experience a "cognitive leap" that makes it easier for them to understand and reason about the world around them. It is during this time, for example, that most young people become capable of distinguishing between objective and subjective realities. They start to recognize that what you see is not always what you get, that what you are told is not always true, and that different people sometimes see things different ways. As a result, teens usually spend a great deal of time comparing their own thoughts, feelings, and experiences with those of others. This process eventually leads to the formation of independent views and opinions.

Parents—who are all too aware that their values and judgment are being scrutinized and questioned—often feel during this stage that their children are pulling away from them. Typical teens, however, want not so much to terminate as to re-negotiate their relationships with their families, placing these relationships on a more grown-up basis. Often teens seem more eager to claim adult privileges than adult responsibilities (which they do not yet fully understand). What the adolescent most longs for, however, is respect for his or her emerging individual identity.

The road to an adult identity can be rocky, however. Along the way, teens must resolve some major developmental issues. On the adolescent agenda are such tasks as

- learning to accept one's changing body
- becoming comfortable with one's sexuality and learning to express it in a safe and responsible manner
- learning to become less emotionally dependent on parents through the development of closer relationships with peers of both sexes
- selecting a career and preparing for economic independence
- developing an ethical code or set of values by which to live

This is a tall order, and these goals are seldom achieved without a certain amount of *angst* and inner conflict. Typically, teens are excessively self-conscious and self-centered, wary of adults (whom they judge harshly, having only recently discovered that we can be fallible, hypocritical, or otherwise imperfect), and committed to the concept of their own "specialness." Most adolescents—including those who sincerely love and respect their parents—also develop a passion for privacy and a desire to keep the worlds of family and friends separate. Affiliation with a peer group becomes a matter of urgent importance at this stage. Friends provide the often-insecure teen with social status, a place to "belong" outside the family, and a transitional support system that helps the child face those all-important issues: "Who am I and where am I going?". Studies suggest that teens who do not develop close peer-group attachments have difficulty answering these questions satisfactorily. Such young people often remain either inappropriately dependent on their parents' support and authority or end up separating from their families prematurely, without a reliable "inner compass" to guide them. Strong peer relationships, therefore, play a crucial role in enabling teens to grow into responsible, self-respecting adults.

Of course, the yearning to "belong" has its down side, too. Because their need to find acceptance among peers is so compelling, adolescents are exceedingly vulnerable to social pressure. To achieve "popularity" even basically level-headed youngsters may sometimes engage in behavior that is foolish, harmful, or illegal. By far the most common reason teens cite for using alcohol and drugs, for example, is a desire to "fit in with the crowd"; even children who understand and fear the consequences of drug and alcohol abuse (car accidents, arrest, addiction . . .) may fear being ridiculed or rejected by friends much more. Desire to achieve the status of having a boyfriend or girlfriend—as well as longing to experience the romance and passions glorified in movies and on television—also stimulates widespread sexual experimentation among teens. Recent polls indicate that a majority of adolescents (girls as well as boys) are sexually active by eleventh grade. Sadly, many of these young people do not protect themselves against pregnancy and sexually transmitted disease. As a result, one in ten girls between the ages of fourteen and nineteen becomes pregnant, and chlamydia—a virus that often produces no symptoms but can damage the reproductive system and cause sterility—now infects teens in epidemic numbers (it is estimated that 25 percent of girls and 15 percent of boys are affected). Even more tragic, teenagers have become this country's fastest-growing risk group for AIDS. Since

1989 the number of reported HIV infections among adolescents has been doubling approximately every 14 months. Heterosexual activity accounts for the great majority of new cases.

Teens who have stable family support systems are most likely to negotiate the hazards of adolescence successfully. It is therefore critically important for parents to strive to appreciate teens' fears and concerns, to keep lines of communication open, and to uphold their own value systems by both word and deed. Adolescent children do continue to rely on their parents for guidance, security, and affection, even when their behavior suggests otherwise. Children also rely on their parents for information. Accurate facts about sex (including the risks of sexually transmitted disease, pregnancy, and sexual abuse) and about drug and alcohol use need to be provided in a tactful, non-judgmental manner. To avoid this responsibility is, in essence, to leave a child's education in these matters to other children and the media. Recommended reading for parents who want to learn more about adolescent issues and how to address them is *Your Child's Emotional Health: Adolescence,* prepared by the Philadelphia Child Guidance Center (available in paperback from Macmillan). This easy-to-read guide includes suggestions for discussing sensitive issues with teens and also lists warning signs of dangerous adolescent crises that require intervention, including substance abuse, sexual abuse, eating disorders, and depression. (Making an effort to learn about child development at any stage is a good investment in your family's mental health. You may be relieved to discover how much "strange" behavior is normal!)

For the child with learning disabilities, the risks of adolescence can be significantly magnified. Slow-to-mature teens, for example, may find themselves in hazardous situations that they lack the cognitive awareness, emotional maturity, or basic good judgment to handle. An immature girl, for example, may fail to understand that boys could interpret friendly touching as a sexual come-on. A boy who has not yet reached the stage of mature moral reasoning may be unable to think through an older friend's invitation to go joyriding in a "borrowed" car (how annoying and unfair to cut the evening short by being arrested!). Youngsters who are particularly naive or socially imperceptive may even become the butts of cruel humor or abuse. One mother recalled her sixteen-year-old daughter dressing carefully for a "date," only to be driven to a parking lot and told how to perform oral sex. "Fortunately she had enough self-confidence to say no," Mom reports, "but she was humiliated and heartbroken because she thought this boy really liked her."

Sometimes teens with learning disabilities become relatively eager participants in their own undoing. Those who have not yet established successful peer relationships, for example, may now be driven to extreme behaviors to find a place among other adolescents. A ticket to acceptance in the drug culture or party crowd is relatively easy to obtain (as one young man put it: "A friend with weed is a friend indeed"). Habitual use of alcohol and other drugs can also blunt the pain of loneliness and provide escape from other uncomfortable realities. The search for "love" can lead to sexual promiscuity among teens who have low self-esteem; some girls in this group actually hope for pregnancy, believing that a baby will provide focus for an aimless existence and fulfill their longing for someone to love and belong to. There are also teens who seek thrills and excitement as a means of escaping unpleasant or humdrum lives; they are attracted to risky behaviors (such as fast driving, gambling, and shoplifting) and seem to go out of their way to generate crisis in their personal relationships and affairs. Experts speculate that risky or otherwise highly stimulating activities are particularly rewarding to some individuals with ADHD because they help focus attention in a way ordinary experience cannot. Unfortunately, individuals who do not learn to channel their need for excitement productively often find themselves at odds with the law. Thrill-seeking young men with ADHD and other learning problems are significantly over-represented in the prison population and juvenile justice system—a fact increasingly recognized by authorities who hope to improve methods of crime prevention and rehabilitation.

As with typical teens, young people with learning disabilities rise to the challenges of adolescence best when they have informed, supportive parents who model responsible behavior. Parents whose beliefs, values, and personal habits are under frequent attack from adolescents do not always find it easy to be supportive, however! (It can be even harder to be understanding when the children are also blowing off family obligations and doing poorly in school.) In addition, many fathers and mothers feel threatened by the repeated assaults teens launch on their authority and their own self-esteem. In an effort to regain control, some parents become rigid and didactic and "lay down the law"—a strategy that usually succeeds in escalating the level of conflict. Teens who are both in conflict with their families and unable to find support among their peers are very high risks for emotional disturbance. This helps explain why research finds higher than normal rates of depression, anxiety, and anti-social or hostile conduct among adolescents with learning disabilities, as well as higher rates of failure to complete school. Alienated adolescents who are doing poorly in school are among the most likely to drop out. Too many teens with learning disabilities (including some who never got identified) fit that sad profile.

Even teenagers who have family support and avoid these emotional extremes may develop defensive strategies to mask the shame of not fitting in. For example, a child who is "out of it" at school may respond by

- becoming angry and aggressive ("Move out butt-face! This is my seat!")

- cutting up or becoming the class clown ("Just wait to see what happens when Mrs. B. opens her purse . . .")

- claiming that school is too dumb or boring to bother with ("Algebra is so stupid, like who's ever going to need it?")

- shifting blame or adopting the role of a victim ("Nobody ever gives me a chance . . . they don't know how to teach . . . this family sucks . . . it's not my fault"!)

- becoming manipulative ("Do it for me just this once! I really need your help, pleeeeeeeeeeeease!")

- creating distractions ("Look Ma! I dyed my hair blue!").

Creative and resourceful youngsters may also use verbal intellectualism or performance in areas of relative strength to distract attention from a disability ("I'm an artist! I don't need to read; I need to express myself . . ."). These self-protective postures do help youngsters cope with the pain of failure or rejection, but they can become self-defeating in the end. Children are not likely to give these behaviors up, however, unless they are provided with alternate tools and strategies that address their needs (this is why nagging, bribes, and threats are so rarely effective). Remember that teenagers can not take responsibility without learning the skills (communication skills, reasoning skills, organizational skills . . .) that are the foundations of responsible behavior. Just as they often need special help with reading or math, teens with learning disabilities may need to have social and emotional growth opportunities tailored to their special needs.

Young Adults with Learning Disabilities

Leaving home and entering the larger worlds of college or career can be difficult and stressful for any young person, and we should not be

MARTIN

Martin is a 44-year-old commercial baker. His Attention Deficit Hyperactivity Disorder (ADHD) was identified last year. Experts estimate that up to 50 percent of individuals with unaddressed ADHD abuse alcohol and/or other drugs at some point in their lives.

I had a lot of problems in school from the beginning—I flunked first grade. Later on I had trouble focusing on what I was reading and I could not take notes . . . I did real well on some quizzes and short-answer tests, but essays and writing papers, that was something else. No way I was going to college . . . By the time I graduated from high school I thought I'd never amount to anything.

I was an angry kid, too—I had a real bad temper and I got into a lot of fights. I always felt like other kids were laughing at me. Later on, when I tried to get close to girls, I'd try to get intimate too fast so of course I got rejected a lot. But I didn't understand what I was contributing to the problem. I just thought everybody hated me and that helped feed this terrific anger I felt all the time.

When I was a senior in high school I discovered alcohol and drugs and I felt like my troubles were over. I liked booze and I *loved* marijuana—it calmed me right down. Before you knew it I was partying all the time. The only problem was, alcohol made me completely crazy. I was always getting into trouble. I couldn't work steady—I kept getting mad at my bosses and quitting. I drifted from job to job, working on assembly lines, driving fork lifts, doing maintenance—whatever I could get. At night I'd go to bars and get into fights . . . Or I'd buy everybody drinks, like I was trying to buy friends.

One good thing did happen in those years: I met my wife. She was a nurse at this nursing home where I worked as a security guard. Claire has been a real miracle in my life. She's always believed in me, even though I put her through a lot. She used to say, "Marty, there's something going on with you that we don't understand yet;" she sensed that there was something behind all this restlessness and anger. But back then we'd never even heard of ADHD—so of course it never occurred to us that I could have it.

Meanwhile, drugs and alcohol started taking over my life. I was smoking pot all day—I smoked on the job when I could. At night I'd drink and pick fights with Claire so I'd have an excuse to storm out of the house and run around the bars. At one point things were so out of control I thought I was losing my mind. I went to a psychiatrist, who said I was paranoid schizophrenic. He put me on anti-psychotic drugs, which made everything even worse (especially when I mixed them with pot and booze). I ended up locked in a psych ward for three days. The docs told my wife "We'll look after him; go get yourself another life . . ." She didn't buy it, thank God—she signed me out of there and we went looking for another counselor. This therapist said "Marty, you better get yourself to Alcoholics Anonymous, and if you don't there's not much point in coming back here."

I stopped drinking with AA in 1984, but it took me almost three years longer to give up the marijuana. It's hard to explain how much I loved that stuff; it just relaxed me and made me feel all right about things . . . But in the end pot twisted me and started making me even *more* hyper and nervous—yet I couldn't quit. I checked into a treatment center to get help for my drug addiction in 1987, and with the support of AA I haven't used a drink or a drug since.

After that my life got better in a lot of ways. I was able to work steady and got a job in a commercial bakery. My mom taught me how to make bread when I was a kid and my dream has always been to have a bake shop of my own. But I was still disorganized—the house was always a mess and I had a lot of trouble remembering where I was supposed to be and being on time for things. I also had a hard time managing money. Then my wife's aunt read a book about ADHD and said, "Marty, this sounds like you." I read the book and it was like they were telling my story! I found a psychiatrist who specializes in ADHD. She recommended medication.

At first I was afraid—I was worried that I would become addicted to the medication like I had been addicted to alcohol and marijuana. But the doctor said she would monitor me carefully, so I decided to give it a try. It took a while to find a medication that worked without sideeffects, but what a difference the right medicine makes! It's like giving my brain a tune-up. I can organize myself. I write appointments down and get places on time. I pick up after myself and put things away. I can sit still. I can listen. I can read! And so far I have no desire to abuse the medication at all—I take it exactly as directed.

Best of all, I have started my own business. It's part-time now—I bake Italian bread at home and deliver it to restaurants—but my customer list is growing. We're saving our money so that one day my dream of having my own shop will come true. Claire and I just celebrated our 23rd anniversary, and it feels like everything is finally coming together. Claire says she loves coming home to the smell of bread baking. She says that when I'm baking, I smile all the time.

surprised that it is sometimes even harder for the young adult with learning disabilities to make this transition successfully. Continuing problems with academic skills, organization, taking responsibility, and establishing a personal support network can all undermine the individual's attempts to achieve economic and emotional independence. Poor self-image often exacerbates the problem. Studies find that young adults with learning disabilities often have lower expectations for their futures than typical peers. They are less likely than others to complete college, and more likely to live at home with their parents into their twenties and thirties. When they work (and many do not—studies find that only half to three quarters of young adults with learning disabilities are steadily employed) they are more likely to work part-time, or at low status minimum-wage jobs. Individuals with severe language disabilities, attention deficits, and/or hyperactivity are generally found to be the highest risks for low educational achievement and underemployment.

Yet many young people with learning disabilities do manage to function successfully in demanding jobs and in institutions of higher learning. Studies of these productive young adults find a number of factors that appear to relate to sustained good performance. Among the most important are:

Self-awareness. The students with learning disabilities most likely to succeed in college are those who recognize their strengths and understand and accept their weaknesses. Based on this understanding, they set realistic goals, seek appropriate accommodations, and identify situations in which they are likely to perform well. Realistic understanding of disabilities is also linked to successful employment. Adults who have this insight choose appropriate careers and are resourceful about modifying tasks or developing other compensating strategies on the job.

A strong work ethic. Successful adults with learning disabilities usually frankly admit: "I had to work harder than everyone else to get where I am today." These high achievers are characteristically ambitious, goal-directed, determined, and creative about overcoming obstacles. They accept the necessity of putting more time and effort into completing some tasks than others (they may not like having disabilities, but they have put resentment and self-pity largely behind them).

A positive personality. The personal characteristics of optimism, adaptability, curiosity, and tenacity are strongly associated with both academic achievement and success on the job. Research finds that self-confidence (defined as belief in one's own ability to bring about change) also has a tremendous impact on performance. Individuals who have a strong work ethic and a "can do" attitude have been known to become successful in spite of severe disabilities and limited educations. While some aspects of personality are inborn, self-confidence and attitudes about work are most often learned from parents and other role models.

An effective support network. The support and guidance of family and/or significant others (teachers, counselors, girlfriends/boyfriends, and other mentors) is frequently cited by young adults with learning disabilities as essential to their success. Families are very influential in helping young people develop visions for their futures, set reasonable goals, and make specific plans for achieving objectives. Both family and friends provide advice and emotional support when young adults encounter obstacles or become discouraged. The availability of this kind of support often separates individuals who "bounce back" from setbacks or defeat from those who give up.

A positive school experience. Research finds that satisfaction with one's high school experience is related to expectations for the future and enthusiasm for higher education. Students who have achieved a certain measure of success in secondary school are most likely to see themselves as competent and in control of their own destinies. Academic achievement, extracurricular activities, and social interactions all contribute to school satisfaction (a student who has the lead in the class play, a position in student government, and many friends, for example, may feel successful in spite of spotty grades.) As Jeff's story shows, however, individuals who are flexible, upbeat, and willing to work hard can transcend school situations that are disastrous.

Even a glance at this list makes it obvious that young people with disabilities who grow up in families that model positive values, support children's individuality and autonomy, and advocate for children appropriately have a tremendous edge on success. Research indicates that these youngsters often manage to succeed even where the destructive forces of poverty, discrimination, poor health, and limited educational opportunity are at work. Sometimes individuals who lack family support are able to find mentors and role models elsewhere (young people with upbeat personal characteristics are particularly good at attracting people who want to help them). Individuals who do not feel loved and accepted and who lack effective advocates and advisors, however, often continue to struggle uphill in many aspects of their adult lives.

JEFF

Self-confidence (defined as belief in one's ability to influence events), persistence, and willingness to work hard are important contributors to success among young people with learning disabilities. Here, Jeff (a dyslexic adult whom you met in Chapter 8) describes how he went about getting into college:

In my last couple years of high school, the whole idea of college seemed incredibly out of reach. Everybody sort of had the attitude that "Well, you're a bright guy, but, you know college is just not in the works for you." But that never sat right with me. Maybe it was because my father is Dean of a university, but I don't think that's the only reason. I just had ideas about what I wanted to do in life and they were going to require that somehow or other I get a handle on using my mind. But I had no study skills, and even after five years of high school I could not write. I had no clue as to where a period went or what commas were for. I had sort of got reading understood, but writing was overwhelming . . . So my senior year wound down and out of the blue I decided to call the new headmaster of a boarding school for students with learning disabilities where I had gone for seventh and eighth grade. I introduced myself and told him I had been a student at the school, and I didn't have a good plan for next year. And he said, "Well, come on down and we'll talk about it." So I hopped on a bus and spent the weekend at this school and we threw around some ideas. And the plan we came up with was that I would work at the school as a janitor, and they would give me a small salary plus room and board and tutoring from the faculty so I could take courses at the local community college.

In my first semester at the college I took two courses. It was an incredible experience, because I really started to feel that "Hey, I can do academic things." I never had that academic confidence in high school. I don't think my school had a very good idea of where they were going academically, let alone where they were going with someone who had disabilities. There was no plan, and when they saw I wasn't making progress they just let me do whatever I wanted. So high school was pretty much a lost situation. But my two years at the community college were great. They changed the way I perceived myself as a thinker. I took basic writing—like a pre-college writing course—and I really enjoyed it.

Sadly, young adults with learning disabilities sometimes have as much trouble with personal relationships as they do with higher education and employment. Some feel so inferior and so fear rejection that they become socially isolated and withdrawn. Others plunge into

We talked about structure—things like an introduction, and argument paragraphs and a conclusion. I found out once I had a *system* for writing I could do it. Another good thing I learned was to have someone proofread so I got credit for what I was saying and didn't get an inordinate number of points deducted for misspelling every other word (this was pre-computer for me, so I had to type everything out, which was a remarkably cumbersome process). I started getting A's and B+'s and learned that I could think, and that made me more confident. I liked working at the boarding school, too. The next year they gave me a position as a dorm master; I lived with thirty kids. They were all learning disabled one way or another and some had been so protected by their environments—well, they all had low self-esteem but some were completely incapable of handling basic tasks, like how to make a bed or get your shoes on the right feet or take a shower. So that was challenging, but I felt good because I could identify with these kids and the incredible satisfaction they got from learning to do things on their own. . . .

Then one of the teachers at the community college who had worked with me a lot suggested, "You know, you ought to apply to some four-year colleges." We wrote away and got some applications to some great schools. A lot of them seemed pretty overwhelming but I sent several in and went to one interview, which was actually very useful. I mean, a lot of students going through high school have everyone grooming them for college, but I had no clue. So this interviewer gave me a lot of tips about the application process, which was great. Still, I did not get into this very selective small college I wanted. When I got the rejection letter, I called the Dean of Admissions and I just said, "I'd like to drive there tomorrow and review my application with you." And to my total surprise he said, "Sure, what time will you be here?" So I met with him, and explained really simply that I had worked harder to have the opportunity to just sit down with him than any other student he would be accepting this year, and that no matter how carefully he screens all those applications somebody is going to drop out. So what did he have to lose? The worst thing that could happen was I would be one of those . . .

Anyway, halfway through the summer I got a letter from the college. And they accepted me.

Source: Interview by Jennifer Kagan

one relationship after another, but their immaturity, insecurity, and emotional instability defeat partner after partner, and the love and acceptance they long for remains ever beyond their reach. The most common complaint expressed by this group is loneliness; even those who are successfully employed often say they need help learning to meet people and make friends. Finding appropriate recreational activities and helping individuals with learning disabilities learn social and "courtship" skills is therefore an important part of helping them make a successful adjustment to adult life.

Clearly, experiencing success at home and in the community are as important to a child's future as experiencing success at school. Fortunately, parents do not require college degrees or teaching certificates to provide what children need most from them. As we shall see in the next chapter, common sense and parents' own nurturing instincts are the best qualifications for helping children reach a healthy, happy maturity. Remember that children with learning disabilities are *children* first. They need what all children need: love, understanding, acceptance, responsibility, and discipline. The point is to not let the child's disabilities interfere with a family's ability to effectively provide those things.

11

STRATEGIES FOR PROMOTING PERSONAL SUCCESS

While quality of schooling may determine how skilled a child becomes at reading, writing, and mathematics, it is families who provide children with the self-confidence, determination, and resourcefulness they need to put their skills to effective use. Children's homes are also the laboratories in which they learn (or fail to learn) such important survival skills as how to set goals and make plans, how to evaluate choices and make decisions, and how to solve problems and resolve conflicts. Competence in these areas can ultimately have a greater impact on a young person's success in life than the ability to read or write.

Parents are therefore a child's most influential teachers. While this is the good news (parents can help youngsters overcome the negative effects of poor schooling), some parents may wonder if it isn't the bad news, too. Many mothers and fathers find the responsibilities of parenthood sobering (if not flat-out overwhelming) and worry that they are not equal to the job. This insecurity is not hard to understand. After all, nobody taught us in school how to raise children. Most of us don't even have a wise old aunt or grandfather in the neighborhood to help us over the humps (an advantage often enjoyed by earlier generations). We therefore go through much of our parenting careers as on-the-job trainees—a role that can present some serious challenges to our own self-confidence. There is nothing like spending a night with a baby who will not stop crying to make one feel like a complete incompetent (although taking a teen who has just pierced her nose and shaved her head to your mother-in-law's for Thanksgiving dinner probably comes close). No matter how many parenting books we read, children have a way of presenting us with situations that make us feel like we have no idea what we're doing.

Mothers and fathers of children who don't grow up "by the book" often feel even more uncertain of their parenting abilities. We note that the neighbor's little boy does better somersaults than our son, and we start to wonder where we went wrong. When a youngster's deficits prove to be more severe—for example, the child is still struggling to decipher the alphabet in second grade, or is not "college material" according to the guidance counselor—parents often assume they are responsible and suffer enormous guilt. In an achievement-oriented culture where many parents wear their children's accomplishments like merit badges ("Johnny got elected captain of the baseball team!" "Great! Susie got a scholarship to Princeton!"), parents of children with learning disabilities sometimes feel like failures or second-class citizens. The well-intended (and frequently conflicting) suggestions these parents receive from others often serve only to fuel the fires of doubt and confusion.

Before we discuss ways to help children maintain their self-esteem, therfore, we would like to offer a reminder for parents who may be struggling to hold onto their own. Learning disabilities are physiological problems that can occur in any kind of family. They are not reflections of your lifestyle, your intelligence, your skill as a parent, or your worth as a human being. There is therefore no reason to let anyone trap you into feeling ashamed of yourself or your child. As for those who offer unsolicited advice or try to engage you in games of parental one-upsmanship, try to forgive them their arrogance and their ignorance. If you don't get defensive and continue your search for creative solutions, you and your family may discover opportunities for personal growth that average achievers never dreamed of. As one mother put it: "My sister's children get good grades in school, and sometimes I'm jealous that so much comes easily to them. But I know her children don't know half of what my son knows about courage, and I think my sister is sometimes jealous of the close relationship Chris and I share."

Refreshed by this reality check, let's look at what parents can do to help children with learning disabilities grow up feeling like winners.

1. BELIEVE IN YOUR CHILD

Parents' attitudes about children's capabilities have a powerful effect on how children regard themselves. Youngsters who see themselves as essentially able and responsible usually have parents who see them the same way. Research finds, however, that children with learning disabilities sometimes have parents who view them as bumbling, helpless, fragile, or otherwise incompetent. Not surprisingly, many of these children seem to approach life as if it were a war that they have already lost.

It is not hard to fathom how parents come by these damaging attitudes. By the time their problems are identified, many children with learning disabilities have established a losing streak both at school and at home. These are the kids who can't seem to do anything right: in addition to bringing home disappointing grades, they spill orange juice all over themselves at breakfast, forget to feed the gerbil for days on end, and lose three lunchboxes in a month. After the family has been made late for the hundredth time because the "problem child" can't find his jacket (or his glasses, or his shoes), even basically patient parents may erupt with messages to the effect of, "You dimwit! Why must you screw up *everything?*"

When the child's learning disability is identified, parents may regret these earlier accusations, but they do not necessarily adjust their basic perception of the child. Some accept the learning disability as an excuse for continued poor performance and irresponsibility. Earlier expectations for achievement may be lowered and the amount of work the child is expected to do at home and at school reduced. Children absorb the view that they are helpless and hopeless all too readily. Surrounded by low expectations, young people quickly settle into a pattern of low achievement, and may even stop trying to do things they can do well.

Parents who are fearful about children's ability to cope in a world that can be insensitive to people with special needs sometimes kill their children's self-confidence with kindness. Very protective mothers, for example, sometimes run so much interference for their offspring that the children never get an opportunity to advocate or care for themselves. In the saddest of these cases, Mom may start to build her identity around being the child's champion. She may so "need to be needed," for example, that she actively resists others' efforts to help the child become more self-sufficient—this resistance often takes the form of repeatedly rejecting or finding fault with professionals, on the grounds that they don't understand what the child really needs. In this pathological twist on the scenario of the genuinely supportive parent (who usually welcomes professional assistance), youngsters tend to develop low opinions of their own abilities and become progressively more dependent. All too often, children like these grow into adults who are passive, friendless, and virtually unemployable.

Obviously, it is important to avoid being overwhelmed by children's problems and stay positively focused on their *abilities*. Some suggestions for helping you keep your outlook optimistic follow.

Strive for a More Positive Vocabulary

What words do you use when you describe your child? When dealing with a youngster with learning disabilities, words like *difficult, stubborn, wild, obnoxious*, and *impossible* are sometimes among those selected. Negative labels like these can hurt children even if they are never spoken aloud. Words influence perception, and when we use words like these we render ourselves incapable of seeing our children in their best light. Educator Mary Sheedy Kurcinka—herself the parent of a boy "who could scream for forty-five minutes because his toast had been cut in triangles when he was expecting rectangles"— notes that changing the words we use can help us think of our children more positively. She suggests we begin by thinking of our "difficult" children as "spirited," then go on to select new words for as many spirited traits as we can. Some alternatives suggested in Kurcinka's book, *Raising Your Spirited Child*, are as follows:

Instead of saying the child . . .	*Try saying the child . . .*
is wild	is energetic
is demanding	has high standards
is stubborn	is tenacious
is anxious	is cautious
is picky	is selective
is explosive	is dramatic
is loud	is enthusiastic, full of zest
is aggressive	is assertive

The more negative labels you can replace with neutral or positive ones, the easier it will be for you to appreciate your child's spirit and individuality.

While you are working on your vocabulary, take a good look at the words your children are using also. Siblings can be vicious to each other when they are angry, and children with learning disabilities sometimes get into the habit of using derogatory words to describe themselves. Parents need to take the lead in teaching children that name-calling and put-downs are an unacceptable way to express feelings. When children put themselves down, it is important to confront and correct them gently, offering positive views to replace negative ones ("I know you are disappointed about your grade on the spelling test, but you are not stupid. Spelling is very hard for you. I'm proud of the effort you put into studying. You're a hard worker!")

Look for the Positive Side

The very word *disability* focuses attention on what the child cannot do. It is easy to forget that children with learning problems sometimes develop unusual strengths. Many excel in art, music, and other creative endeavors. Some who have difficulty with reading and writing become verbal virtuosos who can talk their way into—or out of—anything. (These "natural salespeople" excel in politics and sometimes become successful entrepreneurs.) The compassion some children with learning disabilities develop for people who are "different" or who struggle with hardship is remarkable; these young people are often attracted to volunteer service and the helping professions, where their sensitivity is an asset. Because of their slightly skewed way of looking at the world, many young people with learning disabilities also have a delightful, offbeat sense of humor.

Speaking to a Massachusetts chapter of Children and Adults with Attention Deficit Disorder (CHADD, a national support group) Dr. Edward Hallowell, coauthor of the popular book *Driven to Distraction: Recognizing and Coping with Attention Deficit Disorder from Childhood Through Adulthood*, explained there are hidden benefits to this kind of problem, too:

> ADD people are highly imaginative and intuitive. They have a "feel" for things, a way of seeing right to the heart of matters while others have to reason their way along methodically. . . . This is the man or woman who makes million-dollar deals in catnip and pulls them off the next day. This is the child who, having been reprimanded for blurting something out, is then praised for having blurted out something brilliant. . . . It is important for others to be sensitive to this "sixth sense" many ADD people have and to nurture it. If the environment insists on rational, linear thinking and "good" behavior from these

kids all the time they may never develop their intuitive style to the point where they can use it profitably.*

A mother suggests: "Try sitting down and making a list of ten things about your child that you *like*. I do that when I'm feeling discouraged, and it helps me keep things in perspective." In addition to keeping her own thinking positive, this parent has found a good way to give her child a head start on self-esteem. What parents value in their children, the youngsters usually come to value in themselves. By thinking about why she likes her son, this mother gives him a fresh and frequently updated list of reasons to see himself as a great guy.

Learn to Put Failure in Perspective

Inventor Thomas Edison made about a thousand light bulbs that *didn't* work before he made one that did. When asked how it felt to fail that often, Edison is reported to have replied: "I didn't fail one thousand times; the light bulb was an invention with one thousand steps." Like most scientists, Edison knew that discovering what doesn't work can help you figure out what does. Progress is often a matter of trial and error, and people who are afraid of making mistakes limit their opportunities for advancement.

Unfortunately, children are often taught in school to fear failure and to take it personally. In many classes, learning is not presented as a matter of interest or exploration, but as a tournament in which students must prove their worthiness. To the victors go the spoils; the esteem of teachers and other students, college acceptances, and scholarships. Failure restricts youngsters' options and reduces their status. Rarely are students encouraged to analyze failures and learn from them.

If children are to learn that failure can be educational, therefore, they are probably going to have to learn it at home. In order to help them, parents must examine their own attitudes about making mistakes. How do you react when a youngster botches a chore or an assignment? Do you berate the child ("What's wrong with you, Johnny? We've told you a hundred times the trash goes out on Friday, and here you've forgotten again!"), or do you take a neutral position, helping the child backtrack and discover what went wrong ("You seem to be having trouble remembering this chore. Let's talk about how we can

---

* Thanks to Carson Graves and the Concord Special Education Advisory Council in Massachusetts for posting Dr. Hallowell's comments on the Internet.

get around that problem.")? Children who frequently get the first kind of treatment will eventually learn to see themselves as incompetent losers. The second approach eliminates the emotional penalty for failure and encourages youngsters to see themselves as creative problem solvers.

Emphasize Education

"My parents never talked about 'If you go to college,'" says a sophomore psychology major. "It was always, 'When you go to college.' They said that even when my grades were bad. When we found out I had a learning disability, the position became, 'We'll have to look carefully for the *right* college.' Not going to college was never considered."

This young woman's parents helped her keep her sights set high—a fact that almost certainly helped seal her success. Research indicates that parental attitudes about education have a tremendous impact on students' expectations. One study determined that the most significant predictor of adult occupational status was parents' attitudes about school. (Occupational status and income are closely linked to the number of years of school completed. Parents who encourage children to finish high school and go on to attend postsecondary education programs therefore help boost them into better jobs.)

While college-educated parents are among the most likely to encourage their offspring to pursue higher education, many teachers, doctors, and lawyers recall parents who worked long hours at blue-collar jobs so that their children could get advanced degrees. "My mother could barely speak English, but she checked all my homework every single night," a social worker remembers. "I'm not sure how much of it she understood, but I sure got the idea that homework was important." Students like this always have an advantage over those whose parents are indifferent to school performance. It is the respect, interest, and enthusiasm parents convey for education—not the parents' level of educational achievement—that make the point.

For students with learning disabilities, high expectations must be coupled with careful planning based on a solid understanding of youngsters' strengths and special needs. As we shall see in the next section, self-esteem plummets when children are presented with expectations they cannot hope to meet. Parents must also recognize the difference between having high hopes and attempting to impose their will on children. The third-generation businessman who insists that his son carry on in the family tradition (even though the boy dreams of a career in the arts) is both interfering with his child's growth and endangering their relationship. Young people usually apply their greatest efforts toward goals they set themselves. The wise parent therefore combines enthusiasm for education with a certain amount of open-mindedness as to what the ultimate objective of that education ought to be. (For more on college and career planning, see Chapter 12, where we discuss preparing for life after high school in greater detail.)

2. ESTABLISH REALISTIC EXPECTATIONS

No parent would intentionally ask a child to do the impossible. We know, for example, that babies can't ride bicycles and first graders can't read advanced physics texts. When children's personalities, stages of development, and/or learning capabilities are poorly understood, however, parents may unwittingly establish expectations that are almost as unreasonable as these examples. Children with learning disabilities are especially vulnerable to this kind of misplaced confidence. Since they look "normal" and are able in many areas, it's easy to forget these kids can't do everything like other children their ages.

Unrealistic expectations set children up for failure—and when children fail, they can suffer tremendous guilt for letting Mom and Dad down. (Since children assume that adults know what they are doing, they almost always blame themselves in these situations.) If they let their parents down a lot, young people often come to see themselves as intrinsically inept and unworthy. To protect children's self-esteem, it is therefore essential for adults to keep what they ask in line with what youngsters are capable of delivering. The bottom line is that kids don't *know* enough to say, "Sorry, Mom and Dad, I don't have the cognitive ability to manage that request at this stage of my development." They trust us to be aware enough to make that judgment for them.

There are three areas where it is especially important for parents to know their children well enough to align their expectations with the children's capabilities: temperament, moral development, and learning style.

Temperament

Some aspects of temperament have a genetic component and therefore resist change (for a description of these traits, see Chapter 10). Parents who do not understand this may overestimate children's ability to adjust to different circumstances and environments. Mom and Dad may look forward to showing their talented five-year-old off at a family reunion, for example, only to be disappointed when Johnny whimpers and turns away from people he doesn't recognize (which is just about everyone). As Johnny becomes increasingly overwhelmed and irritable, they may find themselves urging him not to be such a tiresome crybaby. When they are forced to take their quickly disintegrating son home early, we hear Mom muttering, "You've ruined the day for all of us being such a brat!" In addition to being tested beyond his limits by overexposure to new faces, Johnny now knows his inability to cope has made his mother unhappy—an emotional double whammy.

If this naturally reticent child has been born into a family of outgoing socializers, variations on this scenario may be repeated many times over the years. Eventually Johnny may well become convinced his inability to mix comfortably means there is something seriously wrong with him. Even though he may have largely outgrown his fear of new situations by the time he enters junior high school, if he accepts his family's labels (Johnny is a loner, Johnny is antisocial), he may not even try to make friends. Such a child ends up paying a heavy price for his parent's failure to recognize and respect his basic personality.

Researchers have found that when a child's temperament is very different from a parent's, the level of stress and conflict in the household often increases. In the story on page 266, the result is tragic. How different Norman's life might have been if his father had been able to accept the differences between his son and himself, instead of rejecting the boy and branding him a failure!

Parents who are sensitive to their children's temperamental needs can both establish realistic expectations and help manage their environments so that the youngsters are not unduly pressured. Johnny's parents, for example, might warn relatives that he will need time to warm up to them at the family reunion (children like this sometimes need to be defended from overeager huggers). They might also decide not to subject him to an entire day of festivities—or find a comfortable place on the sidelines until Johnny is ready to approach the crowd. In this way, they would set their son up for success rather than failure and frustration.

Awareness of temperamental characteristics also helps parents appreciate their children as unique human beings, especially if they are able to recognize positive aspects of temperamental traits. (The flip side of Johnny's "shyness," for example, may be that he forms considered judgments about people and chooses his companions

NORMAN

Norman was seen at age seventeen by one of us (S.C.), who had followed him since age four and a half because of persistent behavior disturbance. At age seventeen, he had already dropped out of two colleges in one year, and was planning to go abroad for a work-study program. He was in good contact but dejected and depressed. He was extraordinarily self-derogatory, said he could not finish anything he started, was lazy, and didn't know what he wanted to do. "My father doesn't respect me, and let's face it, why should he?" He talked of "hoping to find myself" in a vague, unplanned way.

Norman had always been a highly distractible child with a short attention span. Intelligent and pleasant, the youngest in his class throughout his school years due to a birth date, he started his academic career with good mastery. However, at home his parents were impatient and critical of him even in his preschool years because of his quick shifts of attention, dawdling at bedtime, and apparent "forgetfulness." By his fifth year he showed various reactive symptoms such as sleeping difficulties, nocturnal enuresis, poor eating habits, and nail tearing. Year by year his academic standing slipped. His father, a hard-driving, very persistent professional man, became increasingly hypercritical and derogatory of Norman. The father equated the boy's short attention span and distractibility with irresponsibility and lack of character and willpower. He used these terms openly to the boy and stated that he "disliked" his son. The mother grew to understand the issue, but no discussion with the father as to the normalcy of his son's temperament and the impossibility of the boy's living up to his standards of concentrated hard work succeeded in altering the father's attitude. He remained convinced that Norman had an irresponsible character and was headed for future failure—indeed a self-fulfilling prophecy. There were several times when the boy tried to comply with his father's standards and made himself sit still with his homework for long periods of time. This only resulted in generalized tension and multiple tics and Norman could not sustain this effort so dissonant with his temperament—another proof to himself and his father of his failure. Direct psychotherapy was arranged in early adolescence, but Norman entered this with a passive, defeated attitude and the effort was unsuccessful. His subsequent development was all too predictable.

Source: Thomas, A., and Chess, S., (1977). *Temperament and Development.* NY: Bruner/Mazel.

wisely—character assets most parents would value.) To help children make the most of their temperaments, it is also important to understand that personalities do not always match traditional cultural roles. If shyness is seen as acceptable for girls but a mark of cowardice in boys, for example, half the shy people in the world will be condemned (and feel guilty) unnecessarily.

Moral Development

Children's ability to judge what is right and what is wrong develops in stages. Mothers and fathers who do not understand moral development sometimes find themselves trying to enforce rules that are beyond children's comprehension and/or punishing youngsters who don't understand what they have done wrong. Misinterpretation of youngsters' motives can also convince parents that children are sinful or wicked when their behavior is actually normal and innocent.

Let's take a brief look at how a child's morality develops. Experts agree that children under the age of two have no real sense of right or wrong; their controlling principle is pretty much "If it feels good, do it." At this stage of their development, children are not capable of understanding "rules." Punishing toddlers for behavior deemed unacceptable (such as touching their genitals or breaking fragile knickknacks) is therefore pointless and cruel. A more appropriate strategy is to distract the child from behavior you don't like, or to eliminate temptations. (If offering a toy doesn't keep the baby from playing with the buttons on the VCR, remove the baby—or the VCR—to another room.)

As they grow older, children learn that some behaviors are acceptable and others are not. Children younger than seven or eight, however, don't have the reasoning ability to understand *why* a particular behavior is right or wrong; their moral code is borrowed whole from parents and other authorities. This tends to result in a black-and-white view of the world and a very rigid interpretation of rules—for example, a five-year-old will tell you that lying is always wrong; suggesting that it might be okay to tell a "white lie" to avoid hurting someone's feelings will only confuse her. It is necessary to explain rules and expectations clearly to these youngsters; without adult input, they have no idea how to behave. (Children who have not received consistent adult guidance can be expected to behave inconsistently.) Appropriate discipline for this age group is often more a matter of education than punishment. Lecturing early elementary-aged youngsters is ineffectual, but they do understand concrete consequences closely tied to events ("These markers belong to the store. You are not allowed to bring things home from the store unless you pay for them. We are going to take the markers back now.")

MATTHEW

Understanding a young person's level of moral reasoning can be the key to effective intervention:

Thirteen-year-old Matthew had an explosive temper. When things didn't go his way, he often took out his feelings on furniture—he overturned desks and chairs and once threw a wastebasket through a window. Unfortunately, Matthew was often unhappy in eighth grade. His difficulty maintaining attention and his problems with written language had been recognized late; this year was Matthew's first experience with special education classes. He resented being separated from his friends, some of whom teased him about having to go to a reading class with "retards and dummies." His attitude toward his resource teacher and the other students in his reading group was hostile at best. On his bad days, Matthew's behavior was so aggressive and disruptive that the teacher had no choice but to send him to the principal's office.

The middle school principal made many efforts to reason with Matthew. She pointed out that his behavior interfered with other students' right to learn and also set back his own education. None of these talks had much impact. Matthew's mother also tried to reach him; she was a religious woman and made it clear that his destructive outbursts violated the teachings of their faith as well as the rules of the school. Matthew loved his mother and wanted to please her, but her words didn't help him deal with the anger that kept building up inside his small, wiry body. Giving Matthew detention didn't work either—in fact, being forced to stay after school and miss playing ball with his friends made him even more angry. On his way into his most recent detention, Matthew deliber-

Around the time they enter third grade, children begin to use their own judgment instead of relying entirely on adult guidance. Whereas "being good" is primarily a matter of pleasing adults for younger children, youngsters eight and older also consider rules and standards established by their peers. This divided loyalty sometimes presents them with ethical dilemmas ("Mom says I should invite Emily to my birthday party because she lives next door, but my friends at school think Emily is a pain."). Discussing problems like these gives parents an opportunity to share values. Although children younger than twelve deal poorly with abstract concepts and prefer simple solutions, they are capable of understanding that the "right" choice can

ately swept three students' books off their desks and "accidentally" over-turned the teacher's coffee.

In a last-ditch effort to avoid suspension, Matthew was referred to a guidance counselor. The counselor recognized that generalized appeals to Matthew's instincts for good citizenship were not going to modify his behavior. Matthew was immature in several respects (his favorite television programs were cartoons, for example); this suggested the need for a more concrete approach to managing his anger. The counselor offered a deal: if Matthew would come to the counselor's office to talk when he got angry instead of disrupting class, a red star would be placed on the cover of his folder. When Matthew had five stars, the counselor would take him out for a pizza at lunch time. When he got ten, Matthew would get two tickets to a movie of his choice.

The system worked. By the time he got his movie tickets, Matthew had built a trusting relationship with the counselor and begun to learn how to talk out his anger instead of attacking property. Once he settled down in class, his resource teacher was able to help him understand his learning disabilities. Matthew became less hostile when he understood that you could have a learning disability and still be smart. He started to apply himself, and his academic skills improved. The key to these positive outcomes was the counselor's understanding of Matthew's level of moral development. Although most thirteen-year-olds are beginning to develop a "social conscience," Matthew's development was somewhat delayed. His thinking was more like that of a fifth or sixth grader, and children that age are motivated by tangible rewards. The counselor's point system was therefore successful where attempts to reason "maturely" with Matthew had failed.

depend on circumstances. Children this age often need help thinking different aspects of a problem through, but should be encouraged to make their own decisions whenever possible. Parents who arbitrarily impose their own judgments ("You have to invite Emily, or there's no party!") rob children of opportunities to practice thinking and acting maturely.

Elementary school-aged youngsters do test the rules. Since most do not yet reason logically, concrete rewards and consequences remain the best means of modifying their behavior. When it is necessary to discipline children, an explanation of the punishment is appropriate (even if they do not fully understand your judgment, children need to know you have a reason for what you are doing and are not acting on a whim). You can spare them lengthy analyses and philosophical observations, however—short and to the point works best. At any stage of development, it is important to distinguish between criticizing a child's *behavior* and criticizing the *child*. Criticizing behavior ("Hitting is not all right. Hitting hurts people!") establishes boundaries, but criticizing or shaming the child (*"You bad boy! Why are you so mean?"*) is a form of character assassination that can leave lasting scars.

By the time they reach junior high school, most children understand that rules arise out of mutual consent and involve a certain amount of give and take. They no longer think exclusively in terms of good guys and bad guys, and they understand that real justice takes mitigating factors into account. (This insight sometimes gives them an incentive to try excuses; these are the kids who insist, "Really, Mrs. Jones, the dog ate it!"). As a result, teenage children want to *negotiate* rules and consequences. Parents have to make sure they don't become inflexible in response to these challenges; experts find that a certain amount of debate and negotiation is characteristic of healthy family systems in which generations respect one another. During the teenage years children also start to develop a "social conscience." As they mature intellectually, teens begin to appreciate abstract ideas like altruism, brotherhood, and patriotism, and these concepts reinforce their desire to become good citizens.

Parents must note, however, that children's moral judgment is not yet fully developed. Young teens' respect for the law, for example, is still based partly on fear of being found out and punished; they may be tempted to break rules if the risk of being caught is small. It is not until late adolescence that children fully understand that laws preserve society, and that compliance is necessary to maintain the social order (youths who feel victimized by the established social order will not be highly motivated by this consideration). Wise parents therefore continue to provide teenage children with structure and help them think their actions through. Since slip-ups tend to generate their own consequences at this age (shoplifting can get you arrested; unsafe sex can result in illness or unwanted pregnancy), threats of punishment may be superfluous. When parents act like advisers instead of police officers, adolescents often find it easier to see that responsible behavior is in their own best interest.

To be effective, efforts to discipline children must be based on their stages of moral readiness, not their ages. Children who are slow to mature (including many children with learning disabilities) are sometimes punished unfairly because parents misjudge their ability to understand rules and evaluate consequences. As Matthew's story illustrates, treating children as if they had the social judgment and moral reasoning ability of a child two or three years younger is sometimes the key to bringing successful solutions within a young person's reach.

Learning Style

In Chapter 9, we discussed how learning preferences affect students' performance in school. Since parents also have a great deal to teach, insight into how children learn is just as important at home. Yet, as one mother puts it: "It's amazingly easy to forget about learning disabilities when you're trying to get the kid to clean up his room. Even though I know my son doesn't deal well with verbal directions, I still tell him to do things sometimes and get angry when he forgets."

Too often, parents don't consider how a child's learning style might affect behavior at home at all. When this is the case, expectations for the child are likely to be unrealistic; family friction usually follows when the child fails to perform. To avoid this unhappy situation, parents may want to keep a few basic guidelines in mind when trying to teach tasks to children with learning disabilities:

It takes them longer to learn. The task that your typical five-year-old learned after one explanation may take your eight-year-old with learning disabilities longer to master. Some can only attend to tasks for short periods at a time, which slows their rate of learning. In addition, most of these children need to practice a new skill many times before they are comfortable with it. Parents who expect quick results from children with learning disabilities are often disappointed. If you plan to invest two or three weeks in teaching your youngster to set the table, on the other hand, you can probably count on results you and your child will both be proud of.

You have to show them as well tell them. Many children with learning disabilities have difficulty following verbal directions. Some process language poorly. Others have difficulty visualizing information; no matter how many times you explain a sequence of events, they have trouble "picturing" it. Nearly all children with learning disabilities do best when new skills are demonstrated as well as explained. In the box on page 273, a noted special educator suggests a teaching sequence that is usually very successful.

You need to break big jobs into little ones. No child welcomes an order to "clean up your room," but most can handle it without a great deal of supervision. To a child who has trouble with sequencing or visualizing what an orderly room looks like, however, a task like this presents too many bewildering choices. Pick up the toys first or put away the clothes? Deal with the trash or make the bed? Without help, the youngster cannot devise an efficient strategy, so the job drags on and on. To help youngsters complete a complex job like this, break it down into a series of simpler tasks (put dirty clothes in hamper, collect and throw out trash, put toys and books on shelves, and so on). Older children can be given a list to follow; younger ones (and children with short attention spans) may need you to check results after each subtask has been completed.

You must teach memory strategies. A frequently heard complaint from parents of children with learning disabilities is that the kids are forgetful; they forget the time, their chores, and where clothes and possessions were left or last seen. (On page 274, we have a note from a child who hopes the Tooth Fairy can overlook the fact she's lost her lost tooth!) Carelessness is not the issue here; most children with learning disabilities have difficulty entering some kinds of information into their memory banks. It is therefore important to teach memory-boosting strategies such as writing commitments on a calendar, posting daily lists of things to do on a bulletin board, putting possessions away promptly, and/or wearing a watch with an alarm that warns of upcoming appointments. Even when using these techniques, however, the child with learning disabilities is likely to remain the least organized member of the family. Sanity sometimes lies in accepting our "free spirits" the way they are—and developing family strategies to compensate for their disorganization, such as allowing ample time to get ready for events.

Reward direction, not perfection. Children with learning disabilities are often frustrated by their own inability to achieve perfect results. Help them see that progress—not perfection—is the point. When children do a job partly right, praise what was done well before showing them what was overlooked. Children who understand that they are getting somewhere are far less likely to get fed up and quit.

3. GIVE THE CHILD RESPONSIBILITY

Research indicates that giving children responsibility is very important to their overall development. Many studies have found that chil-

Teaching New Tasks to Students With Learning Disabilities

Parents! Ask yourselves, "How many things do I do for my child every day . . . tasks that I complete out of habit . . . tasks that are within the child's range of ability?" Do you still iron for your fourteen-year-old? Do you continue to ban the sixteen-year-old from the power tools?

If so, consider this simple sequential approach to teaching the child with learning disabilities. This four-step method can be applied to nearly any common task. We will use teaching Jimmy to make his bed as an example.

STEP 1: Do it for him
Make the bed while Jimmy observes you. Carefully point out the stages of the task while you complete each step. Encourage him to ask questions. Continue to do this daily until he is ready for Step 2.

STEP 2: Do it with him
Slowly integrate Jimmy into the process. Have him assist you with various stages of the task. Praise and encourage his increasing involvement. Continue this step daily until he is ready for Step 3.

STEP 3: Watch him do it
For a few days, watch Jimmy make his bed. Provide encouragement and gently point out any mistakes he may make. (This will prevent bad habits from forming.)

STEP 4: Have him do it
Now that the task has been mastered, require Jimmy to make his bed every day. Make this part of his routine. Often parents will make a great effort to teach children a skill and then not allow them to *use* that skill. Do not fall back into the old unproductive habit of making Jimmy's bed for him!

Source: Richard D. LaVoie.

dren who do helpful work in their homes and neighborhoods gain both skills and self-esteem. For example, a long-term study that followed a group of individuals with learning problems on the island of Kauai, Hawaii, found that those who were given useful work (usually in middle childhood and adolescence) were most likely to grow into caring, competent adults. The young people's work typically involved helping parents out at home and assisting neighbors or needy members of the larger community.

Learning to take responsibility for oneself is another key to successful independent living. Unfortunately, research finds that often adults do not encourage youngsters with learning disabilities to think or do things for themselves. As a result, many of these young people feel unable to influence events and so drift passively from day to day rather than making plans or decisions that might improve their lives.

Parents sometimes sabotage their children's initiative with the best of intentions. Presented with a disorganized child who is struggling with simple tasks, it's natural to offer help. As children with learning disabilities grow, help with eating and dressing and getting to the top of the jungle gym flows naturally into help with homework, help with housework, help with money, and so on. Before we know it, helping

---

Note to the Tooth Fairy

Dear toothfairy
I Lost My
tooth can
you still
Giveme
Money

from
you
toothless
Kid

Source: Lee Anne Hoffman

has become a habit that neither we nor our children are very moti-vated to break. The children enjoy the attention (and are not averse to having us do their work for them); we want to protect them from failure—and besides, it's really easier to do their laundry than to teach them to do it themselves.

A habit of helping, however, can eventually become a destructive cycle. The more parents do, the less children accomplish; the less they accomplish, the more persuaded parents become that the chil-dren are basically helpless and incompetent. This often leads to the parents becoming even more protective and "helpful" (although ef-forts to shore up the child sometimes start to be tinged with resent-ment). Escalating parental involvement continues to prevent children from analyzing or solving their own problems. By the time the kids reach adolescence, a pattern of "bawl them out and bail them out" may have become established (parents bawl children out for their failures, then jump in to "fix" the situation). The teens resent Mom and Dad's interference and lack of trust in them—but they have never learned to take care of themselves, and by this time have real doubts about their ability to do so. Nobody sees the future as promis-ing.

Although children with learning disabilities need energetic advo-cates, it is important to avoid doing for young people what they *can* do for themselves. A number of proactive steps parents can take to help children become more responsible and independent are out-lined below.

Give Children Regular Chores

As we pointed out in the last section, it can be harder to teach house-hold tasks to children who have learning disabilities. Enabling these children to contribute to the work of the household, however, pays off several ways. First, children who feel they are helping their families enjoy a boost in self-esteem. These youngsters feel more capable and more valuable to their loved ones than kids who are always on the re-ceiving end of assistance. Second, children who pitch in at home learn skills that are essential for independent living. Since youngsters with learning disabilities usually need more practice than others to master new skills, it is wise to start teaching both boys and girls about cooking, cleaning, shopping, and other aspects of household management as early as possible. Third, when children with learning disabilities do a fair share of the family work and are expected to meet the same obligations as their brothers and sisters (for example, writing thank-you notes, ironing their own clothes, and taking a turn walking the dog), sibling relations improve. A common complaint of siblings is that children with learning disabilities get less work and more help doing it—a perception that is often accurate.

It is sensible, of course, to assign chores with a child's strengths and special needs in mind—you would probably not want a child with fine motor problems dusting your collection of antique porcelain figurines, but mowing the lawn should be no problem for her. You may also have to modify tasks from time to time in the interest of fairness (a thirteen-year-old with weak handwriting skills was allowed to type forty thank-you notes on a computer following his bar mitzvah). At other times, however, you will have to accept that children with disabilities must work a little harder. It is going to take a poorly coordinated teen longer to iron a shirt than it would his sister, for example, but that doesn't mean you should do it for him. He's going to have to know how to iron a dress shirt when he's living on his own, and will feel more self-confident for his ability to do it. (Of course, introducing the young man to permanent-press and wrinkle-free knits is also a good idea.)

Let Children Handle Money

Money management is a particularly common stumbling block for young adults with learning disabilities. Poor math skills, lack of experience with planning, and impulsive temperaments can all lead to overdrawn notices from the bank. This essential life skill is seldom taught successfully in school. The bottom line is that the best way to learn to manage money is to manage it; young people who handle their finances responsibly usually learn to do it at home.

Like others, children with learning disabilities benefit from receiving a weekly allowance. (Experts advise that to be an effective learning tool, the allowance should not be tied to chores, behavior, or academic performance; it should be an income the child can count on.) They may need more help than their brothers and sisters, however, in learning to spend it. It may not occur to these youngsters to compare prices, for example; the addition and subtraction involved in comparison shopping may be too much for them. (Try shopping together with a calculator in hand until children can use the calculator themselves.) Impulse shoppers—the ones who didn't know they needed a purple-spangled pixie wand until they saw it—need encouragement to look around and explore what different things their money will buy. You might point out, for example, that the cost of the pixie wand is about the same as a poster, a package of barrettes, or a box of modeling clay. This gives the child practice considering her options and making decisions.

Involve children in spending your money, too. One family asked their children to propose how $1,500 might be spent on a family vacation; the suggestions—accompanied by price estimates for food, lodging, and entertainment, as required—ranged from a theater weekend in the city to two weeks of wilderness backpacking. While parents are sometimes reluctant to talk to children about income and household expenses, doing so can help youngsters develop realistic expectations and understand the point of establishing a budget. Financial candor, however, should not be taken to the point of frightening children or burdening them with adult concerns. Letting kids know the amount of the monthly car payment is fine, but telling them you're having trouble making it because Dad is late with the child support again creates unnecessary anxiety and adds nothing to the children's education.

As children acquire experience handling cash, trust them with larger amounts. A quarterly clothing allowance can be educational for secondary school students (one mother says that her daughter learned all about discount stores within days of being put on a clothing budget). Since most students this age have some impulse control and can delay gratification, this is also a good time to start encouraging saving. Most students become motivated to save only after identifying a desirable item that is within reasonable reach. Since some youngsters cannot delay gratification very long, you may want to start off discussing purchases that could be made after saving for only a few weeks. Some parents like to add incentives at this point— for example, a fourteen-year-old was told that if he could save $150 toward a mountain bike, Dad would match it.

Consider providing high school students with a checking account and/or debit card (it's better not to allow students to use credit cards until they prove able to plan a budget and stick to it). Students with long-term savings goals need to explore various financial instruments (savings bonds, certificates of deposit, mutual funds, and other types of investments) for helping their money grow. It's a good idea to have these tools in place *before* a child starts working; paychecks that get cashed rather than put in the bank have a way of evaporating quickly, leaving little of value behind. Some parents expect working teens to pay some of their own expenses, such as gasoline, auto insurance, and telephone bills. If you do, think about establishing separate accounts in children's names so they can become familiar with paying monthly bills (and, if necessary, with the loss of service that comes with failure to pay them). Beware of overbudgeting, however—if kids don't have some "play money" left after bills are paid and savings goals are met, they rapidly lose interest in working.

Most youngsters with learning disabilities will need to be taught how to keep financial records, and they will have to be walked through the process of balancing their accounts several times before they can manage this task on their own. Monthly bookkeeping sessions can be a good time can to review goals and spending habits. ("Did you plan to spend fifty dollars on pizza last month?") Youngsters who receive this kind of guidance become educated consumers and gain confidence in their ability to make financial decisions. It doesn't guarantee that they'll never bounce a check, but it makes it much more likely that they will be able to live within their means down the road.

Help Children Get Around on Their Own

Nearly every parent remembers the gut-wrenching anxiety that accompanies taking the training wheels off the bicycle, putting a teen behind the wheel of the family car, or seeing a child off on her first solo trip on the subway or the bus. For parents of children with learning disabilities, it's worse. In addition to the fears all parents face when letting go, we think about how easily the children are distracted, how rotten their sense of direction is, how confused they are by noise, and so on. Sometimes we scare ourselves so much with these considerations that we decide not to let the children go after all.

There is no question that teaching young people with learning disabilities to get around on their own can be a challenge. General immaturity and specific skill deficits (such as poor coordination, short attention span, and/or difficulty judging speed and distance) often delay the age at which they can learn to ride a bike, drive an automobile, or use public transportation safely. Achieving this kind of independence is so important to growth and self-esteem, however, that parents should make every effort to help children learn the basics of transportation as soon as they are ready.

As with any other skill, teaching a youngster with disabilities to ride a bike or interpret a bus schedule or a city subway map takes time and patience. Parents should be prepared, for example, to take several trial runs on the bus to likely destinations, answering questions and pointing out landmarks (gradually, have the child start pointing landmarks out to *you*). Learning to ride a bike may take hours of supervised practice. (Older children struggling to learn this skill may fear ridicule and want to practice out of public view—or at least out of the neighborhood—until they can stay upright.)

Deciding to trust a teen with the car is a more complicated issue, because driving requires both skill and good judgment. Skill issues for young people with learning disabilities include trouble reading signs, right-left confusion, difficulty coordinating hand and foot movements, and problems with estimating speed and distance. Situations that call for integrating several of these skills quickly (such as looking left and then right upon approaching an intersection, or checking street signs and judging the speed of oncoming traffic before making a left turn) can be particularly challenging. Young people with attention deficit hyperactivity disorder (ADHD) present some additional concerns. These teens often have trouble keeping their minds on the road; they are easily distracted by the music on the radio, the airplane overhead, the blonde on the sidewalk, and so forth. When impulse control is poor, these adolescents may also be tempted to drive too fast and too aggressively—tailgating, weaving in and out of traffic, and cutting other drivers off—placing themselves and others at risk for accidents. When problems such as these are severe, it is best to delay teaching teens to drive (be prepared for vigorous objections from your sixteen-year-old). Coordination and judgment may improve when the nervous system matures (although some individuals with severe learning disabilities never become good driving risks). It is important to make sure that teens and young adults who do not drive know how to make efficient use of available forms of public and private transportation.

Young people with mild to moderate disabilities can usually learn to drive successfully, given appropriate instruction and support. In the box on page 280, parents share some helpful tips for putting teens behind the wheel.

Before youngsters are allowed to travel alone by any means, of course, you must make sure they know how to conduct themselves safely among strangers. Some young people with learning disabilities are very trusting and affectionate—a charming trait at home, but potentially dangerous for a child out on his or her own. Anticipate and discuss situations and approaches that should make children wary, and explain exactly what they should do if they become uneasy. If you have doubts about a youngster's maturity, you may want to encourage a more limited kind of freedom (such as allowing the child to visit selected stores in the shopping mall alone while you wait in the snack area). These intermediate steps toward independence help build self-confidence while protecting children's safety.

Tips for Teaching Teens to Drive

- Invest in professional driving instruction. Individual instruction may be a better bet than the group instruction that is available through many high schools. Make sure the driving instructor understands the nature of the child's disabilities and how best to approach them.
- Forbid use of the radio/tape deck until driving basics have been mastered. (If youngsters are very distractible, keep the car radio off permanently).
- Tape labeled arrows indicating left and right on the dashboard.
- Spend extra time studying the section on road signs in the drivers' manual (many can be identified by shape and/or color and do not have to be read).
- Drive with your child through the neighborhood and along most-used routes (to school, to friends' houses, to the mall, and so on), pointing out landmarks, road signs, and areas where extra attention is needed (such as awkward intersections or a stop sign partly hidden by trees).
- If children have to drive someplace new (as to a job interview or to pick up a new date), study the route on a map and/or take a few "trial runs" so they can familiarize themselves with the roads and drive with confidence on the big day.
- Do *not* assume children understand what the dials and indicators on the dashboard mean, auto maintenance ("Check the oil? I thought the car ran on gas!"), how to read a road map, or what to do in the event of an emergency or an accident. Take the time to review each of these things before your teen hits the road.

Remember that passing a driving test does not make a child a good driver. Parents need to make their *own* rules and standards for safe driving clear, and ride with children until they are certain these rules are understood and regularly observed. A mother adds: "Having friends in the car can be a major distraction for teenage drivers. We didn't allow our children to carry passengers until they had several months driving experience and we were sure they knew how to stay alert and drive defensively."

Encourage Decision-Making

Many youngsters with learning disabilities don't realize that decision-making involves a number of steps, such as establishing priorities, identifying and examining options, researching and ruling out alternatives, and testing several solutions to see what works best. Children who lack awareness of this process usually make choices on impulse or by guessing. When these strategies produce poor results, children often conclude that they are unlucky, incompetent, or both. Eventually many give up trying to influence events and adopt a passive approach to life.

To avoid this situation, it is important to teach decision-making strategies to children. Unfortunately, many schools actively *discourage* decision-making (in authoritarian classrooms, for example, it is passive compliance that is valued and rewarded). Students with learning disabilities are sometimes perceived as even less competent to make choices than their typical peers. Quite often these young people are excluded from discussions (such as IEP reviews) that have a direct bearing on their futures.

To help children learn decision-making skills, it is important to encourage them to make their own choices, starting with small ones and working up. Too often, when children ask us what we think they should do, we make the fatal mistake of telling them (sometimes we tell them even before they ask us). Instead, try helping children think through their alternatives. Expressing confidence in the child's initiative is vital ("The sweater and the jacket are both nice. The jacket is warmer; have you checked the weather report? Either way, you're going to look terrific!"). For big decisions, children need to be encouraged to do things like brainstorm possibilities, write down priorities, research alternatives, and make lists of pros and cons. ("Let's make a list of the things you most want in a college and rank them according to importance. Okay, now we can compare that list with these books and decide which campuses to visit.") The more children are walked through this process when they are growing up, the greater their chances are of making effective decisions when they are on their own.

The hardest part of teaching children about decisions is that sometimes you have to let them take the consequences of bad ones. As Julie's story (page 284) reminds us, experience is sometimes the only teacher a youngster is willing to respect. Although the temptation to rescue children from mistakes can be great, it can be wiser (if the situation is not life-threatening) to let young people play their choices out. An important aspect of taking responsibility is accountability; children who are protected from the consequences of their choices seldom learn to be accountable for their actions.

4. IMPROVE SOCIAL SKILLS AND OPPORTUNITIES

Research indicates that winning social acceptance can be even more important to children's self-esteem than achieving good grades in school. The ability to make friends and hold up one's end of a relationship is also one of the keys to making a successful adjustment to adult life. Among the most important things parents can do for children with learning disabilities, therefore, is to help them learn and practice social skills. Parents can also support children's development by learning to identify the environments in which youngsters are most likely to succeed, and structuring social opportunities accordingly.

What do we mean when we talk about social skills? Much is a matter of simple good manners: being on time, playing fair, respecting others' rights and property, and considering others' feelings. Conforming to group standards in these respects provides an important foundation for social interactions. Studies of school-aged children, however, find that other factors influence personal popularity as well. Among them are the following:

Appearance. Children who are perceived as unkempt or unfashionable are more likely to be excluded than children who are neat and clean and dressed like their peers. It is therefore a good idea to teach good grooming habits, and to help youngsters keep their wardrobes up to date. Since children with learning disabilities are often slow to pick up on fads and fashion trends, you may have to sharpen your own awareness of what's "in" at school. (Other children, such as siblings and neighborhood pals, make good consultants in this regard).

Attitudes. Youngsters who are enterprising and enthusiastic are generally perceived as more attractive than those who act gloomy or helpless. While you cannot change a child's basic temperament (some kids are naturally more "up" than others), encouraging your child to maintain a positive outlook on life will improve his or her social outlook, too. Note that school-aged children are drawn to others who make them feel good about themselves, and children who express interest in others are viewed as more friendly than those who are self-absorbed. Encouraging your youngster to notice and comment positively on what other children are doing ("You did a good job on the science project," or "I liked your sculpture in art") can help boost acceptance.

Ability to express thoughts and emotions. Children who lack the ability to put their needs and feelings into words are more likely to make

Questions That Help Children Set Goals

Asking youngsters the following questions can help them assume greater responsibility for their futures:

- What would you like to do, have, accomplish?
- What do you wish would happen?
- What would you like to be able to do better?
- What do you wish you had more time for? More money for?
- What more would you like to get out of life?
- What are your ambitions?
- What makes you tense or anxious?
- What do you need to complain about?
- What misunderstanding needs to be straightened out?
- Who would you like to get to know better?
- With whom would you like to get along better?
- Where do you need to make a change?
- What takes too long?
- What are you wasting?
- What is too complicated?
- What blocks or "bottlenecks" exist in your life?
- What wears you out?
- What would you like to organize better?

Once a goal has been identified (e.g., "I wish I had a bike"), children may need help examining alternatives and forming a realistic plan ("Let's find out how much bikes cost and figure out how long you would have to save your allowance. . . . Let's talk about how you could earn some extra money to save faster.") Don't take on too much! Most youngsters do best if they focus on one goal at a time.

Adapted from Canfield, J. and Wells, H.C. *100 Ways to Enhance Self-Concept in the Classroom.*

themselves unwelcome by barging in or acting out when things don't go their way. It is therefore important to encourage youngsters to use language to ask for what they want, resolve conflicts, and express emotions. Learning to express anger appropriately can be a particular challenge. Asking kids to take "time out" to cool off and providing a safe means of releasing anger physically (such as a punching bag or a big soft ball to kick) are often helpful—some children need to do this before they can talk. Educator Mary Sheedy Kurcinka advises

JULIE

The summer before she entered high school, Julie announced that she was no longer in need of special education. She said reading was not a big problem for her any more—and her reading skills had indeed improved considerably in the five years she had received special education help. Julie was still poorly organized, however, and lacked study skills. This compromised her written work; Julie's compositions and reports were not well researched and showed little evidence of logical thought. It had therefore been recommended that she continue to receive help in the resource room for one period a day in ninth grade.

Julie became more and more adamant about her decision to abandon the resource room as the opening day of school came closer. Her parents thought they knew what was going on. Over the past two years, Julie had become increasingly sensitive about being "different" in any way. It had been hard for her to make friends at the junior high school, and she blamed her special education label for this (although her parents thought Julie's shyness probably contributed more to her social isolation than the fact she needed help with basic skills). It was obvious that Julie wanted to start at the central high school with a clean slate. By shedding the special education label, she hoped to put herself on an equal footing with her peers.

Still, Julie's parents were frustrated by her obstinacy. They pointed out all the ways special education had helped her in the past: not only had she received instruction in reading and writing, but the resource teacher had helped negotiate extra time for tests and assignments when

that a wordless "Tarzan yell" (complete with beating one's chest) can discharge a lot of tension without causing specific offense. Once youngsters have calmed down, help them find words for what they are feeling. A playful approach ("How mad are you? Mad enough to bust a brick? Mad enough to bite a bear?") sometimes helps kids put things in perspective. Be careful not to belittle children's emotions, though. Children whose feelings are not taken seriously learn to repress their emotions—a habit that can lead to depression.

As children approach adolescence, planning and decision-making skills become an important part of the social tool kit (there is no point asking for a date, after all, if you can't decide where to go). Teenagers also need to learn to be appropriately assertive and to handle stress. The box on page 286 lists fifty social skills that have been identified as

needed. Did she want to give that up? These reasoned arguments only made Julie angry. "You don't think I can do it on my own!" she accused her parents through tears. "You don't have faith in me!" Bewildered and uncertain as to what course to take, Julie's parents called her junior high school resource teacher and explained the situation. "I think you should let her try it her way for a year," the teacher suggested. "Tell her to give it her best shot, and in June you'll re-evaluate the situation."

"That ninth-grade year was rough," Julie's mother remembers. "Julie was swamped with homework every night. Her midterm grades were awful; she failed history and English. There was a week she had three research papers due when she did nothing but cry. She had no *time* for a social life. All she did was work, work, work." At the end of the year, Julie had B's in math and Spanish, a D in English, and an F in history. "She knew it was the essays and research papers that had hurt her in English and history," Julie's mother said. "She hadn't done badly on short-answer tests."

Julie took history again in summer school and passed with a C (all the tests were multiple choice). She offered no objections to a resource period in tenth grade, and used it to work on her research and written composition skills. "The hardest thing I ever had to do was watch Julie bottom out in her freshman year," her mother recalls, "but letting her try it her way was the right thing to do. She learned what kind of help she needs, and I learned something, too. I learned I've got a spunky kid who doesn't give up easily. Her determination and willingness to work hard earned our respect. In tenth grade those things really paid off; with minimal help, she finished the year with A's and B's."

important during adolescence. In addition to facilitating social relationships, these skills support responsible behavior in school and in the workplace, so they remain important throughout adulthood.

Because young people with learning disabilities cannot be counted upon to learn correct social behavior by observation alone, a direct approach to teaching social skills and repeated reinforcement may be needed to help them learn to act appropriately. Role-playing and rehearsal ("Let's imagine we're at Grandma's and you want something to drink. I'm Grandma. What do you say?") and what-if games ("What if you were over at your best friend's house and he offered you alcohol? How might you react?") are both useful ways to help youngsters practice responding to different kinds of social situations. Noticing and rewarding good behavior ("What a great job you did staying quiet through the whole church service! You must be ready to

Social Skills

Group I. *Beginning Social Skills*
1. Listening
2. Starting a conversation
3. Having a conversation
4. Asking a question
5. Saying thank you
6. Introducing yourself
7. Introducing other people
8. Giving a compliment

Group II. *Advanced Social Skills*
9. Asking for help
10. Joining in
11. Giving instructions
12. Following instructions
13. Apologizing
14. Convincing others

Group III. Skills for Dealing with Feelings
15. Knowing your feelings
16. Expressing your feelings
17. Understanding the feelings of others
18. Dealing with someone else's anger
19. Expressing affection
20. Dealing with fear
21. Rewarding yourself

Group IV. *Skill Alternatives to Aggression*
22. Asking permission
23. Sharing something
24. Helping others

25. Negotiation
26. Using self-control
27. Standing up for your rights
28. Responding to teasing
29. Avoiding trouble with others
30. Keeping out of fights

Group V. *Skills for Dealing with Stress*
31. Making a complaint
32. Answering a complaint
33. Sportsmanship after the game
34. Dealing with embarrassment
35. Dealing with being left out
36. Standing up for a friend
37. Responding to persuasion
38. Responding to failure
39. Dealing with contradictory messages
40. Dealing with an accusation
41. Getting ready for a difficult conversation
42. Dealing with group pressure

Group VI. *Planning Skills*
43. Deciding on something to do
44. Deciding what caused a problem
45. Setting a goal
46. Deciding on your abilities
47. Gathering information
48. Arranging problems by importance
49. Making a decision
50. Concentrating on a task.

Source: Goldstein, A., Sprafkin, R., Gershaw, N., & Klein, P. (1980). *Skillstreaming the adolescent: A structured learning approach to teaching prosocial skills.* Champaign, IL: Research Press.

cut loose—how about a trip to the park?") play a vital role in cementing new skills into place.

*   *   *

To do a really effective job of social education, it is necessary to make an effort to understand the peer value system at school—if you don't, you won't know what social situations to prepare your child *for.* One mother was shocked to learn, for example, that some youngsters were sexually active in junior high; (she'd assumed that she had until high school to deal with sex education). Another discovered that athletes were the social aristocrats of the local high school (the school had a tennis team, so she encouraged her eleven-year-old to take lessons). Among the best sources for this kind of information are kids a few years older than your own; a respectful relationship with a neighborhood teenager can be well worth cultivating if you want to know what really happens at school.

Peers can also help youngsters with disabilities learn social skills. Some high schools match youngsters who have learning and other types of disabilities with volunteer "coaches" who introduce them to a variety of activities, answer questions, and serve as models for appropriate social behavior. Programs like this offer the advantage of providing teens with guidance when and where they need it most. If your school does not have such a program, consider approaching student organizations that promote service and leadership (such as the student government or the National Honor Society) about starting a peer mentoring project.

What else can parents do to promote social development? Three important strategies that can help children grow in the right direction are described below.

Turn Off the TV Set

Many American children spend more time watching television than on any other activity except sleeping. Four or five hours of television viewing a day is not unusual, and some children regularly watch even more. Experts object to excessive TV watching on a variety of grounds. One is that television introduces children to questionable content and values. It is estimated, for example, that the average American child will have witnessed 13,000 killings and more than 100,000 other violent acts on television by the age of eighteen. This has been connected to a rise in both anxiety and aggression among young people, as well as to increased indifference to human suffering. While there is more diversity on the small screen than there used to be, racial and sexual stereotyping remain rampant. Many shows perpetuate the idea that life rewards only those who are young, beautiful, and white (a message that saps the self-esteem of a majority of people in the viewing audience).

Wait; it gets worse. Television viewing also has been connected to weaknesses in verbal fluency, reading ability, and creative thinking. Low school achievement has been associated with watching as few as ten hours of television a week. Even "educational" shows have questionable value. Some authorities believe, for example, that fast-paced children's programs like "Sesame Street" reduce attention span and reinforce hyperactivity. (Slower-paced shows like "Mr. Rogers' Neighborhood" do a better job of encouraging reflective thinking.) A study of a small Canadian town before and after television reception became available found that reading fluency and community participation both dropped after TV was introduced to the community. Verbal and physical aggression among children went up.

Even if all programming were acceptable, television would still interfere with social development because it robs children of social opportunities. The most compelling reason to unplug the TV set may be a brief list of what children are *not* doing while they are glued to the tube: learning to play cooperatively, learning to make decisions or solve problems, having conversations and developing language skills, or getting exercise. They are not doing anything, in fact, that will improve their health, their intellects, or help them interact effectively with other human beings. So while children are sure to object, the evidence suggests that restricting television is in their best interests. As we shall discuss shortly, other kinds of activities have much more to offer them.

Promote Social Awareness

Youngsters with learning disabilities are often less aware of social issues than others their age. Research finds that current events and hot topics like AIDS, drug abuse, racism, violence in the media, sexual harassment, environmental issues, homelessness and poverty, and religious intolerance are less likely to be discussed in special education classes. When these topics are discussed in regular classes, students with learning disabilities are more likely to be absent (getting special education help) or unable to participate because information is not presented in a form they can use. As a result, these young people frequently either are ignorant of these issues or have opinions that have been heavily influenced by the entertainment media.

This general lack of awareness contributes to the impression that kids with learning disabilities are "out of it," and it can also lead to behavior that is viewed as inconsiderate, irresponsible, or just plain offensive (efforts to act like Hollywood tough guys, for example, are rarely appreciated by teachers). To prevent this situation, parents may have to make an extra effort to help children become more aware of the world around them. Some suggestions follow:

Keep children abreast of current events. Discussing what is going on across the country and around the world helps students develop their awareness of such important issues as civil rights, religious freedom, economic inequality, and environmental safety. It can also help children appreciate cultures other than their own. To help kids tune in, watch TV news with them and ask their opinion on controversial issues. Subscribe to newspapers and news magazines (which are preferred by some students because they are illustrated), and invite youngsters' comments on events of local, national, and global importance. Even if children do not read the news themselves, discussing it with you will increase their awareness; it will help develop their thinking and language skills as well. You might also encourage your child's teachers to subscribe to one of the "junior" news publications produced for schools (*Time for Kids*, an illustrated weekly digest of events reported in *Time* magazine, is slick enough to appeal even to teenagers).

Involve children in community service. There is no better way to learn about the important issues facing our own communities than becoming a volunteer. Not only does volunteer work help youngsters find a focus outside themselves, but being helpful to others can provide a big boost to self-esteem. In addition, young people who volunteer regularly often acquire skills that help them later on the job (learning to be on time, to operate computers and other office equipment, and to deal with the public in person and on the telephone are likely benefits). In most communities there are many service opportunities, ranging from helping out in museums to staffing soup kitchens and assisting with environmental education and political action campaigns. For ideas, check your local list of United Way agencies. Many of these nonprofit organizations welcome reliable volunteer workers.

Relate issues to personal conduct. Concrete thinkers will not automatically apply general observations about issues like sexism, racism, and religious tolerance to personal behavior (a youngster who knows that racism is wrong, for example, may still thoughtlessly repeat racial slurs he has heard used on television or at school). It is therefore necessary to make the connection explicit. When talking about environmental concerns, for example, emphasize how the

---

Sexual Survival Skills

Learning to behave in a sexually responsible manner is an important part of growing up. Parents need to make sure their adolescent children know how to do the following:

- Turn down unwanted sexual advances in a manner that suits the child's personality and the situation at hand (this skill is equally important for girls *and* boys)
- Display romantic interest in someone in a respectful, nonintimidating manner
- Recognize and respect someone else's rejection of romantic or sexual advances (understanding that the phrase "Let's be friends" is usually a turn-down, for example)
- Convey relationship expectations to a partner openly and honestly (rather than behaving in a way that is offensive or misleading)
- Elicit the relationship expectations of a partner in direct conversation (instead of guessing them and/or being misled)
- Negotiate dating activities that are mutually agreeable as well as reasonably safe and responsible (for example, that don't involve a high risk of being stranded somewhere or winding up in unwanted company)
- Establish terms of intimacy with a partner that are physically safe, responsible, and respectful of both parties (if not abstention from sex, then the practice of safe sex)

Adapted from Philadelphia Child Guidance Center with Maguire, J. (1994). *Your child's emotional health: Adolescence.* Macmillan.

---

child can personally address the issues (such as by assisting in recycling efforts or conserving water). Be equally explicit about behavior the child should avoid (such as littering or buying disposable or over-packaged products.) This promotes social awareness at a personal level.

As youngsters approach adolescence, it is particularly important to connect social responsibility and sexual behavior. While courtship rituals can be tough to figure out for any teen, socially imperceptive adolescents have an even harder time understanding how to behave properly around the opposite sex. A list of sexual survival skills is presented in the box on page 290. These issues need to be discussed with youngsters before they leave junior high school (earlier may be even better; preteen children are often more open to discussing sexual matters with parents than teenagers are). To be effective, it is important to go beyond talking about what to avoid ("Make sure that boy respects you and keeps his hands to himself!"); you must also talk about how to avoid it ("Let's imagine he wants to get physical before you're ready; what are some ways to say no? What if he's not listening?"). This kind of preparation can both reduce the risk of embarrassing blunders and help insure teens' sexual safety.

Encourage Outside Interests

Getting involved with hobbies, extracurricular activities at school, sports, and/or community-based programs like scouts or 4-H clubs can increase a child's opportunities for social contact. Shared interests also provide a basis for friendly interaction (two baseball fans or coin collectors usually have no trouble finding something to talk about, for example, even if their conversational skills are limited). Improving opportunities for quality interaction is important, because research suggests that the better children come to know each other, the more they get to like each other, regardless of differences in their academic achievement levels. Participating in sports and recreational programs can also help develop children's skills and boost their self-confidence. On pages 292–93, Benjamin Strick, a college student with learning disabilties and a son of one of the authors, describes the benefits that came from running with his high school track team (an activity he needed more than a little "encouragement" to join).

Studies show that recreational pursuits can also ease the transition to adulthood. For example, the landmark study in Kauai, Hawaii, cited earlier, found that most of the individuals with learning disabilities who coped well in adulthood took pleasure in interests and hobbies that relieved stress when other things in their lives fell apart. Most of these people had participated in cooperative recreational programs (such as cheerleading, 4-H clubs, and YMCA programs) as teenagers.

Obviously, there is a great deal to be gained from these endeavors beyond physical fitness and fun. To involve youngsters with learning disabilities in these activities successfully, however, it is helpful to observe guidelines such as these:

Take the time to prepare the child for the activity, and the activity for the child. Many children with learning disabilities are somewhat

BEN

Ben is an anthropology major and an officer of the photography and outing clubs at Bates College. His hobbies include fly fishing, drawing, ballroom dancing, mountain biking, and guitar (an instrument he says helps him make friends wherever he goes).

When I started high school, my father insisted that I go out for a team sport. It was part of his scheme to get me involved in my new school. I remember feeling very disgruntled about being forced to occupy my time according to my father's plans. I was tall, gangly, not in terribly good shape, and certainly not interested in organized physical activity. I saw myself being hit by balls, crushed by three-hundred-pound freaks with no necks, and being told to grin and bear it when I was in pain. My interests strayed more toward the arts spectrum, where my coordination could be put to use in a manner that did not involve damaging my limbs. But for me it was a sport I must choose, or risk the wrath of my father standing tall and dark above me.

I consulted my gym teacher. She introduced me to her nephew Joe, a senior who had run on the cross-country team since middle school. Joe introduced me to his coach, who told me to show up for practice the next day with shorts and running shoes. Thus my career as a runner began.

When I showed up for practice, the coach sent me out on a five-mile run. I woke up the next morning hardly able to walk. When I hobbled into school, the muscles in my legs felt like they were being flayed by red hot pokers. Other members of the team noticed and sympathized with my condition. Older team members encouraged me to keep running and told me it would get better.

As I continued to attend practices, I discovered that I was not so different from these other runners. Yes, there were some stereotypical "jocks" on the team, but there were also artists, drama enthusiasts, and mathematicians participating for various reasons. Some of us ran for fun, some ran for fitness, and some ran for scholarships. We all hurt at the top of the hill, and when the race was done.

Often experienced members of the team would help new members. They offered encouragement when exhaustion set in and passed on bits of advice about warming up, reducing fatigue, getting rid of cramps. I liked the fact that even if you weren't a "star," you were accepted and respected as a member of the team. I remember one runner who was obese. Every year he ran to lose weight. He wasn't any good—in fact, he usually came in last—but he always finished. And every time he crossed the finish line, his teammates would clap and cheer.

As I began to get in shape, my times started coming down. I became more interested in how I was running; I enjoyed setting personal records and breaking them. I wasn't running because my father said I had to any more—I was running because I liked it. I developed a friendly rivalry with another freshman as we competed for the same spot on the team roster. I found myself wanting to win. I made sure I got plenty of sleep before race day and ate spaghetti for dinner so I would have plenty of energy.

At the end of my first semester, I made varsity. My mother had promised me that if I earned a varsity letter, she would get me a jacket like some of the older members of the team wore. We went to the mall, picked out the jacket, and had it monogrammed. At home, Mom sewed on the bright orange letter. The next day I felt great wearing that jacket to school, like I'd made the big league! Looking back, I guess I must have looked pretty funny, a skinny freshman "art geek" in a size-too-big varsity jacket. But I felt proud of earning it, and that jacket still keeps me warm on autumn days.

I know now my father was right to have me go out for a team. In addition to becoming a source of confidence and personal pride, the team offered a great way of getting to know people. My high school is the most culturally diverse in our city. Its population includes African-Americans, Latinos, Native Americans, Middle Easterners, and Asians. Unfortunately, the school is fairly socially fragmented, and people of different races and nationalities do not always mix. People from nearly all these groups run, however, and on the track team there were fewer cliques. Because of my participation in a sport, I developed a much wider base of friends.

From joining the team I also learned to be more open-minded about trying new things (and maybe to listen to my dad). I discovered that if I want to be part of something, I can't just wait to be invited in. I didn't intend to join a club or activity when I started high school, but after I started running I realized how much I could learn from extracurricular endeavors. I went on to become involved in many other school activities. I joined the ski club. I helped build sets for the drama club and eventually worked up the courage to audition for parts in the school plays. I became a photographer—and ultimately photo editor—for the yearbook. Each of these activities involved a different kind of teamwork, and each gave me opportunities to make new friends. These experiences added so much to my enjoyment and growth in my high school years that I really hate to think of what they would have been like for me if my father had not insisted that I become a member of a team.

fearful of new situations and anxious about their ability to succeed. Some children also have difficulty learning new procedures and rules. Before starting a new activity, give your child as much of a "preview" of what is going to happen as you can. (Before the first Girl Scout meeting, for example, arrange to meet the troop leader, visit the site where meetings take place, and read some Girl Scout literature together.) It is also important to tell group leaders about the child's learning disability so they can help youngsters do their best and avoid placing them in embarrassing positions. (Mentioning to the coach that a child has trouble hearing directions against background noise, for example, could make the difference between an ice hockey player's success and failure.)

Choose activities on the basis of interest, not age. Having friends is important to self esteem, but there is no rule that says all of your friends have to be the same age you are. Because children with learning disabilities can be slow to mature, they are sometimes most comfortable with people somewhat younger—or older—than themselves. A twelve-year-old who is too impulsive and distractible to play baseball with other seventh graders, for example, might have a great time gardening with a group of adults or working on a model railroad with a ten-year-old neighbor. A youngster who builds a rock collection with his grandfather both benefits from the special attention and develops a body of knowledge with which he can impress his peers. By encouraging cross-age activities, you can often improve a child's social opportunities considerably.

Avoid cutthroat competition. Cooperative activities that emphasize enjoyment, individual growth, participation, and making a contribution to a shared endeavor tend to be the best confidence boosters for children with learning disabilities. Many youngsters prefer individual or recreational sports such as swimming, tennis, golf, skating, or skiing to more competitive team athletics. If your child does want to play a team sport (in many communities these are high-status activities, especially for boys), make sure the coach is interested in building up the individual player as well as the team.

When it comes to friends, keep in mind that it's quality—not quantity—that counts. Many children with learning disabilities are most comfortable sharing an activity with one or two special people; larger groups may overtax their receptive or expressive language capabilities or provide too many distractions. A youngster who has a couple of regular buddies is probably doing fine, and he or she may need no more. Hobbies and group activities still provide wonderful opportunities for exercise and intellectual stimulation, of course, so whatever your children's interests, look for opportunities that will help them follow through.

5. BE CONSISTENT ABOUT RULES AND LIMITS

All children need the security of a system of rules and limits. The way rules are established and enforced, however, can have a significant impact on both family relationships and the child's self-image. Let's take a look at three types of child-raising practices which are particularly common:

Strict parents. These parents communicate high standards to their children and tolerate little in the way of deviation. Energy is typically focused on correcting negative behaviors. Standards are enforced by power measures (threats or punishment), unaccompanied by explanation or discussion. Children are given few or no choices. Obedience is seen as a virtue and valued for its own sake.

Authoritative parents. These mothers and fathers also have firm standards for obedience, school performance, and responsible behavior at home. They explain the reasons for their rules, however, and are willing to listen to children's point of view. Parents recognize and reward good behavior as well as punishing wrongdoing. Children are given a limited range of choices. Independence and initiative are traits that are valued.

Permissive parents. These parents are very accepting of their children's behavior and impulses. They are often warm and affectionate, but they do not insist on standards or limits; any rules are rarely enforced. Freedom is valued. Children are given many choices but little support or guidance in making them.

Research indicates that it is the authoritative parents who are most likely to inspire trust and respect, and to have offspring who are responsible, self-reliant, cooperative, confident, and creative. Strict parents are more likely to inspire fear and resentment; their children are often withdrawn, distrustful, and discontent. Children of very permissive parents tend to be the least self-controlled and self-reliant of the lot. Lack of structure and effective role models frequently leaves them irresponsible, disorganized, and drifting.

Studies of children with learning disabilities find that their problems can be made worse by parenting styles that are either overly strict or overly permissive. Over-indulgent parenting, for example, has been observed to aggravate hyperactivity. Parents who are in-flexible about their standards frequently set youngsters with de-velopmental differences up for failure; loss of self-confidence and motivation usually follow. In contrast, authoritative parents give children with learning disabilities two of the things they need most: structure and encouragement. Following are some experts' sugges-tions for those who would like to make their parenting style more productive.

Keep Rules to a Minimum

Too many rules create a repressive family atmosphere. Parents end up acting like parole officers—ever vigilant for wrongdoing—their kids become either fearful or sneaky (depending on their ages and per-sonalities). Either way, the children feel devalued. Don't issue man-dates when friendly give-and-take will do, or for chores that enforce themselves (you really don't have to tell children to do their laundry, for example; they'll do it when they run out of clean clothes). Lay down the law only for important matters, such as insisting that your children keep you informed about where they are and/or call to tell you when they are going to be late. Rules like these let children know parents value and care about them.

Remember also that the point of rules is to regulate behavior—not thoughts or feelings. Attempts to dictate matters of personal taste or opinion are usually unwise. Telling children what they can wear or whom they may have as friends, for example, invites unnecessary conflict and risks your relationship with your child. So even if you hate your son's earring and ponytail, try to live with them. (He prob-ably thinks your personal style is pretty weird, too.)

Seek to Educate and Negotiate Rather Than Dictate

Educating children about standards and negotiating mutually ac-ceptable solutions to problems can be a much more effective means of improving their behavior than punishment. Consider the case of a five-year-old who snatches a toy from her baby brother and knocks him over. We could yell at Susie or punish her for her aggressive be-havior, but instead let's ask her what went wrong. Ah! It appears the doll Susie snatched was her own, and she didn't like baby brother chewing on its head. If we hear Susie out, we may realize she was rougher than she meant to be and is frightened that she may have hurt the baby badly. Clearly, there is little to be gained from sending the little girl to her room; what she needs is a strategy for dealing with this kind of situation in the future ("Now that the baby can crawl, it's best not to leave your toys on the floor. Maybe we need a special shelf for your things. If you are feeling angry with the baby, come tell me and I will help you solve the problem").

As they get older, it becomes increasingly important to involve children in establishing standards and rules. Attempts to control them with arbitrary commands ("You'll do it because I said so!") both convey a lack of faith in the child's judgment and make rebellion his or her only option for expressing individuality. Even when their views seem outlandish it is essential to hear youngsters out. Listening communicates respect and interest in them as people. Children who feel respected and understood are most likely to trust their parents' opinions. You may therefore find young people become much more open and flexible once they have had their say.

Learn to recognize the point at which negotiation starts to deteriorate into a power struggle, however. When discussions degenerate into accusations and character bashing, nobody can win. If you or your child is "losing it," declaring a time out can be a sanity-saver. Sometimes a quiet meal, a warm bath, or a night's sleep can do wonders to restore one's perspective and ability to appreciate children's better qualities. Remember, too, that the final responsibility for making and enforcing rules does rest with adults (*don't* let kids talk you into the idea that family issues should be decided "democratically"). If reasonable attempts at discussion and negotiation have failed to produce a workable compromise, it is appropriate to tell your children, "Thank you for your input; here is my decision," and put an end to further discussion.

Apply Logical Consequences

Sooner or later, all kids test the rules. Ignoring these violations is not in the best interests of the child; authoritative parents respond promptly when rules are broken. Following a brief discussion in which the rule is reviewed (and children are given a reasonable opportunity to explain their behavior), discipline is carried out.

Whenever possible, consequences for wrongdoing should be logically connected to the misbehavior. If a child is chronically careless about where he leaves his bicycle, for example, it is logical to take the bike away for a period of time; this punishment is likely to be more effective than a lecture or a spanking. (Hitting children rarely accomplishes anything other than humiliating them and stimulating a desire for revenge). Try to explain punishments in a way that is respectful to the child. "I see you are not old enough to be responsible for a bicycle yet, so we will put it away until next month" does not call the child's character into question. In contrast, "How can you be so careless! Your father paid good money for that bike, but obviously you don't appreciate it!" implies that the child is a bad person who is undeserving of his parents' love.

When undesirable behavior produces its own unpleasant consequences, the best strategy is sometimes simply not to interfere. If a child forgets to return library books, for example, a whopping fine from the library may be all that is needed to encourage her to change her ways. If the consequences children face are not really dangerous, resist the impulse to "rescue" them from these helpful learning experiences. Note also that enacting logical consequences can be a much more effective motivator than nagging. If children are having trouble remembering to put dirty clothes in the hamper, for example, don't browbeat them about it. Don't wash anything that isn't in the hamper, either; they'll get the point.

Generally speaking, the best time to determine penalties for breaking rules is before wrongdoing takes place. When you establish an expectation (that Johnny's junk will be removed from the kitchen on Saturday, for example) also establish the penalty for failure to comply (no social engagements will be allowed until the job is done). This helps prevent misunderstandings, and it also spares you from trying to think of a fair punishment when you are angry—a time when life imprisonment at hard labor may seem reasonable. If you discuss consequences in a calm moment, children can sometimes be surprisingly helpful. "When I asked my seventeen-year-old son what the penalty for being late to dinner should be, he said, 'Well, Ma, I guess I should cook my own dinner,'" a mother remembers. "Sounded reasonable to me. From then on the rule was that if he hadn't come home or called by 5:30, I didn't cook for him."

Remember that whatever consequences are established, you are the one who is going to have to enforce them. Don't set up consequences that are harder on you than they are on the child! Forbidding a teenager to use the car for a month may seem like an effective penalty, for example—until you realize that you are now stuck with driving the child wherever she needs to go. Similarly, if assigning extra chores puts you in the position of nagging children to do them and/or standing guard to see that they are done right, the punishment may be more grief than it's worth. Since rules are pointless unless they are enforced consistently, the best consequences are simple and easy to execute. (Grounding a teenager on Saturday night for break-ing curfew may be as effective as grounding her for a month, and you will only have to listen to her complain for one day instead of thirty).

Use Positive Reinforcement

One of the most powerful tools for changing children's behavior is to "catch them being good" and reward them for doing right. Positive feedback also boosts self-esteem because it helps children see them-selves as capable and responsible (frequent punishment tends to un-derscore the idea that children are irresponsible or inherently bad). Taking a youngster out for dinner to celebrate a good report card, or posting an improved spelling paper proudly on the refrigerator, is usually a more effective motivator than nagging about homework. Similarly, telling a teenager that "You look sharp today!" is often worth more than a week's worth of "Don't tell me you're leaving the house dressed like that!"

Offered the wrong way, however, rewards can actually undermine children's motivation. Children who are given indiscriminate posi-tive feedback, for example, sometimes become "praise junkies"—the point of performance becomes getting attention and recognition, per-sonal satisfaction in achievement declines, and performance falls off as soon as praise is withdrawn. Children may also find themselves so impatient to receive a promised reward that they have trouble focus-ing on the task at hand. A child who is told he will be given popcorn after he finishes his math homework, for example, may rush through the assignment and do a worse job than if no incentive were offered! Youngsters who perceive rewards as an attempt to coerce their com-pliance (and therefore limit their choices) are also likely to find their motivation slipping. Praise that is vague and unrelated to specific be-havior (such as "You were a good girl today") can leave children feel-ing uneasy and insecure (what exactly did they do that was "good," and what if they forget to do it tomorrow?).

To make positive reinforcement effective, experts advise following the guidelines outlined below:

Use rewards only when they are needed. Don't offer rewards if a child's level of motivation or satisfaction in an accomplishment is already high; let success be its own reward whenever possible. By all means acknowledge children's achievements ("I'm so proud of how well you've done in math"), but be aware that offering additional incen-tives ("Here's ten dollars for getting an A") may only complicate and confuse the issue.

Tie praise and rewards to specific behavior. Children need to know *exactly* what they have done right if you want them to do it again. "I noticed you took a time out when you started to get angry—that was smart!" will therefore have a more powerful effect on behavior than the more general "It's nice to see you and Steve are getting along better these days." Whenever possible, link rewards to the particular type of effort being made. If a child is working hard in art, for example, rewarding her with art books or a generous supply of paper, paints, and brushes is the most meaningful way of expressing your approval.

Use the least powerful incentive that is effective. Research shows that a little encouragement can go a long way. A study of high school students, for example, found that praise worked best when offered sparingly (5 to 10 percent of the time); if it was used more often, the kids stopped hearing it. (Young children usually need more frequent reinforcement than teens). Excessive rewards can also undermine pride in accomplishment and set up expectations for bigger and better "prizes." If the effort to pass math in a given year is aimed at getting a new bike, for example, what's the point of continuing to work hard in math next year? A hug and a sincere "Well done!" is often all a youngster needs (for some alternative ways to say "Well done," check the box on page 301).

Respond promptly. Praise and rewards do a good job of reinforcing desirable behavior only if they are provided close to the time that the behavior occurs. If you have promised your son a banana split if he improves his citizenship grade, don't put the trip to the ice cream parlor off until next week—go the day he proudly brings his report card home.

Reward effort and initiative as well as achievement. Working hard and being persistent are as praiseworthy as outstanding performance. For children with learning disabilities, they may be especially worth celebrating; these youngsters often need extra encouragement to "hang in there" and see difficult or frustrating tasks through. When a child with attention deficits has put in a solid thirty minutes on a task, he deserves praise even if the task isn't finished. Remember that it's *behavior* you want to reinforce; rewards can never guarantee results.

A special educator adds, "Showing a sincere interest in what a child is doing is often even more effective than praise." The most valuable reward a parent can bestow, after all, is *time.* Asking a child to play you that new song she has learned on the violin or show you

50 Ways to Say "Well Done!"

Your hard work is paying off	You've learned a lot
You made my day	You remembered!
How clever of you!	I really like that
You're on the right track	Good try
You're good at that	Wow!
Much better!	Look at you go
I knew you could do it	You're a hard worker
A big improvement!	Congratulations!
Now you have it	Nice job
Beautiful!	Good thinking
Good idea	You did it yourself!
You haven't missed a thing	A new record!
Good start	You're almost there
That's what I like to see!	That's it!
A first-class job	Couldn't have done it better myself
The best yet	You're right on target
Good for you!	Yes!
I'm proud of you	You got it
Way to go!	Outstanding!
Very original	Good move
Super!	You've outdone yourself
Coming along nicely	A lot of effort went into that
You're really on top of it	Creative!
I'm impressed!	You're really applying yourself
You must have been practicing	Let's celebrate!

his stamp album clearly states, "I'm proud of who you are and what you have done."

6. TUNE IN TO FAMILY DYNAMICS

I don't think the stress of coping with a child who has a learning disability would cause a couple to split up, but it sure will open up any cracks in the relationship that are already there. My husband and I have fought about a lot of things having to do with both education and discipline. For instance, my husband says I spoil Justin and help him too much with things. But I think my husband is too critical—he hasn't put in the time with Justin that I have, and I don't think he has a realistic idea of what Justin can do. We fought over giving Justin piano lessons. My husband said Justin would only quit (which he did), but I thought he deserved the same chance to learn to play as his sisters. The most difficult time in our marriage was when we were trying to decide if we should move into the city. We had our dream house in the country, and we loved the space and being able to have animals. But the school district was in the Dark Ages where services for learning disabilities were concerned—we had to fight for every single thing Justin needed, and it seemed like all his teachers hated him. They have a lot more experience with his kind of learning problems in the city schools, but that would mean a smaller house, higher taxes, a tiny yard. . . . Even if it was best for Justin, would a move be fair to the girls? We argued about it for a year. In the end we did move, but even now we don't always agree that it was the right thing to do.

The speaker is the mother of a fourteen-year-old boy who has language processing disabilities and attention deficits. Her story highlights some stresses that are very common in families of children with learning disabilities: ambivalence about how much to expect of the child at home, frustration over the difficulty of securing adequate help at school, and guilt about the impact of the disability on nondisabled children.

Although she may not realize it, this mother is also describing a pattern of family interaction that is common: the "problem child" has formed an alliance with one parent against the other. It is often (but not always) Mom who becomes the child's protector, while Dad gets to be the bad guy (the one whose job it is to set standards and find fault with household policies and educational plans). Sometimes the family becomes increasingly locked into these roles as time goes by. If Mom feels she is the only one who really understands the child, for example, she may invest more and more of her time and energy in meeting the child's needs. When this happens, Dad—who feels like no one is listening to his point of view—often responds by becoming even more demanding and critical.

Nondisabled children in families like these sometimes adopt roles, too. Some that are seen frequently follow:

The super-kid. These children get good grades, star in sports or other extracurricular activities, and generally strive to do everything right—almost as if they are trying to compensate for their siblings' problems and failures.

The troublemaker. This child keeps parents involved with him or her by having one problem after another. If attention is diverted to other children, this one may respond by producing a crisis of some kind.

The mediator. These kids are exquisitely sensitive to other people's feelings and invest a lot of energy in trying to patch up arguments and smooth out problems so that stressed family members will feel better.

The clown. They keep us laughing with their antics or distract us from our worries by being generally winning and adorable.

Each of these roles represents a bid for parents' attention and a place of importance in the family. To some extent, these youngsters are all trying to compete with the child with disabilities, whose family role is being dysfunctional.

While roles such as these are seldom entirely comfortable, over time a family can become so habituated to them that change poses a significant threat to the family system and the identities of the individuals within it. If one member of the family tries to change—Dad attempts to become more supportive of Mom, for example—other family members may display considerable resistance or even initiate counterbalancing tactics. (If Dad becomes more supportive, Mom doesn't get to be the child's "savior" anymore; if she is unwilling to give that role up, she may go out of her way to provoke disagreements and arguments. Likewise, a child who fears losing Mom's undivided attention may attempt to regain it by becoming even more "disabled" and helpless.) These reactions are instinctive attempts to protect what is familiar; often, the family members who are following these scripts have little conscious awareness of what they are doing. The problem with patterns of this kind is that they allow little room for individual growth. Family members trapped in roles are also unlikely to work together to solve problems—indeed, if the family has become organized around a problem, members may fight to keep it in place.

Awareness is the first step toward addressing this and other damaging patterns that occur in families with "problem" children. Before we discuss prevention, let's look at a few other familiar family traps:

Scapegoating the child with disabilities. This occurs when a family focuses on a child's dysfunction as a means of avoiding other painful issues. Virtually everything that goes wrong in the family is laid at the "difficult" child's door. For example, the fact that all children in a family are doing poorly in school might be blamed on the presence of an "out of control" hyperactive teenager; the facts that Dad is abusive and Mom drinks too much remain safely buried. (If these secrets are discovered, the alcoholism and anger may be blamed on the teen, too.) This pattern confers a spectacular amount of guilt upon children with disabilities, who often come to believe they really are responsible for all of the family's problems.

Giving in to denial. In this scenario, one or more family members refuse to accept that a disability exists, then pressure the rest of the family into playing along. The person leading the parade is most often a parent ("There's nothing wrong with my son! Those teachers just don't know how to deal with a boy who has real spunk!") or a grandparent ("Please don't tell anyone about this evaluation; I don't want people to think she's retarded. I'm sure it's wrong, anyway—it's obvious that Bonnie is perfectly normal"). If the individual in denial holds a powerful position in the family, help for the child may be blocked or delayed. Alternatively, the learning disability may be acknowledged in some family settings but not in others ("Don't tell Grandma . . ."). Denial is frequently rooted in guilt and fear; ("Everyone will think it's my fault . . . I can't bear to give my mother-in-law one more thing to hold against me"). Concerns about social status may also play a role. Cooperating with denial, however, protects adult egos at children's expense. It often convinces young people that having a learning disability is bad or shameful.

Slighting sibling interests. The primary complaint of brothers and sisters of children with learning disabilities is that Mom and Dad expect more of the siblings while giving them less time and attention. Even when parents bend over backwards to be fair, unavoidable inequities can breed resentment and strain sibling relationships, as Eli describes (see box). Siblings of youngsters with learning disabilities can also experience a lot of ambivalence. For example, a girl may feel protective of a brother with disabilities but also feel embarrassed about his behavior when friends come to call, and she may fear peer rejection on his account. A boy might become a super-achiever, then feel guilty about succeeding where the sibling with disabilities cannot. Younger children may fear "catching" a learning disability, or try to copy "disabled" behavior in an effort to win attention (the latter problem can be unwittingly reinforced by teachers, who sometimes expect less of siblings of youngsters known to have learning problems). When learning disabilities are severe, nondisabled children may worry about becoming responsible for siblings after parents die. All these stresses can take their toll; studies have found up to 25 percent of siblings of children with disabilities experience significant emotional problems. If siblings have no safe means of resolving their rivalries, jealousies can also erupt into vicious open family warfare. The risk for emotional distress is greatest when parents are so intensely focused on a child with disabilities that siblings' concerns are ignored or devalued ("How can you complain about being late to a silly soccer game when your brother has slammed his finger in the car door again!").

What can be done to avoid these snares? The key is often effective family communication. An effort may have to be made, however, to break counterproductive habits. Four strategies that can help get families headed in the right direction are discussed below.

Avoid Blame

When we are feeling frustrated or angry about a problem, we often start looking around for someone to blame. After all, if we can figure out whose fault the problem is, we can demand that they fix it! In the families of children with learning disabilities, you often see blame being sprayed all over the place. Dad blames the school and the incompetent teachers who have mismanaged his child's education. Mom blames Dad's genes ("Just look at his side of the family"). Big sister blames her brother for complicating her life and her parents for neglecting her needs. The child with learning disabilities blames everybody for misjudging him and himself for making his family miserable.

This kind of behavior, of course, can be very hurtful. But an even bigger drawback of the blame game is that it inhibits action. Since the problem is always the *other* guy's fault, no one takes responsibility for solving it. Describing this state as "the paralysis of analysis," one mother recalls:

> When he was in eighth grade, my son brought home a note that said he was failing science because he had handed in less than half of his homework assignments. I was horrified! Science was his favorite subject—how could this have happened? Maybe it was my fault; that year we were encouraging Jay to take more responsibility for himself and I'd supervised his homework less than usual. Or maybe the science teacher was disorganized and had forgotten to check that Jay had his assignments written down. . . . Surely the resource teacher should have been on top of the situation and not let things get this far! Or maybe the issue was simply that Jay had started spending a lot of time on the phone talking to girls. . . . After several days of fretting I realized that analyzing the problem was getting us no closer to a solution.

ELI

Being the younger child is not easy—especially in a family of two boys. My memories are filled with competition and jealousy. In some ways, my older brother's learning disability made our relationship even more complicated and difficult.

I admit, when I was first told my brother had a learning disability I was thrilled. He's two years older than I am and had been ahead of me in almost everything. Now *I* was going to be better at a few things! When I was angry with my brother (which was pretty often), I sometimes felt like taunting him with his handicap: "I'm smarter than you are in school! You have brain damage and I don't!" I never said it; I knew it would be a low blow. I thought it, though, and I think he knew I did.

But at times I had trouble believing in this disability. I couldn't see anything in my brother that was "different." At my elementary school there were a lot of students with disabilities, and he didn't look or act like any of them. He didn't have distorted features or make odd noises or need a wheelchair or walk with a tilt. He looked about as normal as a big brother can get.

I watched for signs of his handicap. It was taking him a long time to learn his times tables, but I knew lots of kids who were bad at math. Nobody was making excuses for them! I began to wonder if having a learning disability wasn't more of an advantage than a disadvantage. My brother got to use a calculator for math tests (blatant cheating, it seemed to me) and was given extra time for some assignments and exams. He didn't even have to take a language in high school. Hey, I had some trouble with social studies and Spanish, but nobody was giving me any breaks! At one point in high school, my brother and I landed in the same math class (I was a year ahead in math, and he was a year behind). I

Jay needed to make up his missing homework and learn to keep better track of his assignments—everything else was a distraction.

When a family has gotten into the blaming habit, it can take considerable effort to re-route energy along more constructive lines. It's useful to begin by recognizing that when a family has a problem, everyone has a stake in solving it regardless of the problem's origin. Instead of asking who *should* resolve a difficulty, try asking who *can* contribute something that might help. This helps family members refocus their attention and encourages them to work together cooperatively.

worked hard and got 90s while he got 70s. My parents seemed equally pleased with those grades (because the learning disability made math especially hard for him, they were happy my brother had passed). They expected each of us to do our best and maybe that was the fairest way to look at it, but it sure didn't feel right to me at the time.

When my brother got extra time to take his college SATs, I thought, "These learning disabilities sure are handy!" It seemed like I was going to have to do twice the work to get into college that he did. One day when I was swamped with homework, I remember telling my mom I wished I had a learning disability so I could get all kinds of help and forgiveness if I screwed up. (Nobody was happy with *me* when I brought home a C on a test!) She told me to be grateful that I could succeed in every class if I worked hard—small comfort to a kid who thought he had too much to do.

Today I can think of my brother's learning disability with a little more compassion. It couldn't have been easy for him, sharing a class with a cocky younger brother. Looking back, he handled that situation with an amazing amount of dignity. I understand also that I do have more options than he does. When I look at my college catalogue, for example, my choices are unlimited, and there are no roadblocks between me and my choice of a career. My brother has a lot of talents, so I know he will succeed, but I wonder if he'll have to explain learning disabilities to his employers. That's going to be a lot harder than explaining to teachers at school. I know from experience how difficult it is to make people believe in something they can't see. No matter how much my mother told me about learning disabilities, the extra help and attention my brother got always seemed unfair. I was never 100 percent sure he wasn't just fooling everybody and coasting.

Don't Keep Secrets

"My mother said I shouldn't tell the neighbors about needing help in reading," recalls a dyslexic adult. "It was like I had this awful secret. We didn't tell my grandparents or my cousins, either. I felt like if anyone found out about me being in special education, it would bring shame on my entire family. Even now I'm not really comfortable talking about it."

No child should suffer shame or guilt for having a learning disability, but when parents attempt to hide these conditions from friends or family members, youngsters almost always do feel ashamed. Most children assume that what can't be talked about is either painful, dishonorable, or both. The best policy, therefore, is to talk about learning disabilities openly and honestly, emphasizing positive aspects of the situation. A matter-of-fact acknowledgment ("Johnny has a learning disability and has been getting some extra help in reading. We're so proud of how hard he's been working!") tells both the listener and Johnny that his good qualities are admired and his learning disability is no big deal.

When you adopt this open approach, you may have to learn to deal with the occasional insensitive individual ("A learning disability? How awful! My neighbor's son has one of those; he's in jail now"). A mother advises: "Try not to get defensive when you run into one of these clods. I usually say, 'Ah! I see you don't know very much about learning disabilities,' and smile. If they really want to know more, they can ask me. If not, we change the subject. Either way, we've communicated that we're not ashamed and we've gotten out of my son's personal business."

Sometimes parents will be honest about a child's learning disability with everybody except the child. Behind this policy is usually fear that telling children the whole truth about their disabilities will be hugely harmful to their egos. In fact, keeping youngsters in the dark can do far more damage. Children who lack knowledge about their learning disabilities often assume they are stupid (why else would they be having such trouble in school?). Without accurate information, these young people also cannot devise efficient compensatory strategies, which effectively intensifies their handicaps. Don't be afraid to tell children about learning disabilities; the news that they are different hardly ever comes as a surprise to them, and learning *why* they are different often comes as a relief ("You mean I'm not retarded?" is a fairly common response). The kids will take their cues about how bad the news really is from you. If you talk to them through tears, sighing "My poor, poor baby" at odd intervals, they will probably be worried. If your approach is accepting and optimistic ("It's good we know about this; now we can find better ways of teaching you"), they will very likely share your positive attitude.

Remember that there is a difference between talking frankly about learning disabilities and *harping* on them. Educators sometimes meet parents who are so worried about their children's school problems that they talk about learning disabilities obsessively, ignoring the children's many charms and virtues. These unbalanced monologues can frighten children or leave them feeling humiliated and guilty for causing so much concern. If you are frightened and worried yourself, it is best to talk to professionals without your children present. Put off talking to the child until you have learned enough about his or her learning profile to talk knowledgeably about strengths as well as weaknesses.

Give Siblings an Even Break

Children with learning disabilities often need more time, more attention, more help, and more encouragement than their typical siblings. If tutors, private school, or special equipment like computers are needed, the child with disabilities may also require a larger share of the family's financial resources. This situation is to some extent unavoidable, and it is therefore necessary for all the children in the family to accept it. The question is, will they accept it with equanimity—or with jealousy and resentment?

Siblings will almost certainly react with resentment if they are given no reason for differences in treatment. It is therefore important to explain learning disabilities to all children in a family. Avoid making the child with learning disabilities an object of pity, however; "Poor Mary isn't as good as you are at reading" invites Mary's siblings to look down on her—an attitude you can't expect Mary to tolerate serenely. (Comparing kids almost always promotes jealousy and rivalry.) "Mary has a learning disability that makes it hard for her to recognize sound sequences" puts a more neutral spin on the discussion.

As children get older, they normally ask plenty of questions about perceived inequities ("Why do you write out Mary's math problems for her? How come you type Mary's papers and not mine?"). These occasions make good teaching opportunities. Providing straightforward answers to questions ("Because of her learning disability, Mary has difficulty with small print . . . It is hard for Mary to control a pencil; next year she will learn to type for herself") works better than becoming defensive ("You know I love you both! Didn't I bake brownies for you last week?"). Try to avoid scorekeeping—it invites kids to keep tally sheets and become manipulative. Children who constantly whine "It's not fair!" usually do so because there's a payoff in it for them somewhere. If you stop rewarding this behavior ("All right, I'll buy you one, too!"), the whining stops eventually.

Siblings are also less likely to be resentful if parents help them to understand that being fair does not necessarily mean treating all children the same. A more mature view is that being fair means everyone gets what he or she most *needs*, and that it is unusual for different people to need exactly the same thing. For example, Mary's sister,

Sue, needs recognition and encouragement for her achievements in track, so Mom and Dad make an effort to attend every meet and help organize the athletic awards dinner at the school. Mary's brother, John, has a passion for music, so he is the one being given piano lessons. Mary needs help doing better in school, so the family invests in a computer primarily for her use. Although the time and money being spent on the children may not be exactly equal, these parents are being fair.

Siblings who feel that Mom and Dad are tuned in to what's most important to them are least likely to complain about what other children in the family get—but this means that parents must learn to recognize and honor their children's priorities. Perhaps your eleventh grader's agony over whether to wear a short or a long dress to the junior prom seems insignificant compared with the fact that her brother is flunking out of school; if this decision is very important to *her*, however, it deserves your respectful attention. If you devote the weekend to helping her find that perfect dress, she probably won't care if you spend the next two weeks trying to straighten out your son's school problems.

As we mentioned earlier, siblings' perception that children with disabilities "get off easy" when it comes to housework is a frequent cause of resentment, so an effort does need to be made to involve children equally in chores. Parents sometimes wonder if this policy is entirely fair to the disabled child. Is it reasonable to ask these kids to wash dishes and take out the trash even though it takes them longer to do their homework? Sure it is. The fact is, individuals with learning disabilities often have to work harder to meet all their obligations, and those who are successful eventually accept this. When you exempt children from responsibilities in an attempt to "equalize" their loads, you set up unrealistic expectations for the future. (The child's employers are *not* going to say, "Hey, take the afternoon off, buddy, I know you have a lot of laundry to do.") Of course, if children are really swamped you can always do them a favor ("I'll walk the dog for you, honey, so you can keep up that good work"), but be equally sensitive when your nondisabled child has a term paper due. (Sometimes kids devise their own ways of adjusting work loads. One mother recently overheard her son offer to do his sister's laundry if she'd correct his spelling and type his book report.)

A final caution: if parents give siblings too much responsibility for the care of children with disabilities, considerable resentment can develop. Older girls in a family are most likely to be drafted as caregivers, but boys may also be enlisted or urged to "take your brother along" when they go out. "My mother had no concept of how embarrassing it was to have this hyperactive kid around when I was with my friends," a college student recalls. "A couple of times she made me take him along to the movies; he went back and forth to the popcorn stand ten times, disturbing the whole row. After that, when my friends went to the movies, I just said I couldn't go." While it is reasonable to ask older siblings to help with child care, it is important to limit the number of hours that care is expected, and to give older children some choices about how they provide this help (the teenager quoted above said he wouldn't have minded taking his brother to the park once or twice a week; he just didn't want the child bothering his friends). If the amount of child care you need starts to limit siblings' ability to pursue their own interests or significantly interferes with their social relationships, consider hiring a babysitter. This is sometimes the best investment you can make in family relations.

Note that some parents of youngsters with learning disabilities establish unrealistically high expectations for achievement for their nondisabled children. Since they do not have handicaps, these siblings are expected to perform perfectly and fulfill all the hopes and dreams that the child with disabilities cannot. While this pressure may not create sibling hostility, it can threaten parent-child relationships and seriously undermine the self-esteem of the nondisabled children. Remember that each child in the family deserves a chance to explore his or her own interests and make a fair share of mistakes and wrong turns. Children should never be pressed to achieve in order to make up for the perceived failures of a sibling, to repair a family's social status, or to bolster parents' own sagging sense of self-worth.

Learn How to Listen

Parents are often much better at talking to kids than they are at hearing what children have to say. Similarly, when husbands and wives discuss problems, each is sometimes so bent on getting points across that no real effort is made to listen to the other's views. The problem is that people who don't feel heard rarely feel understood or respected. Those who don't feel heard over an extended period of time have a limited number of options: they can quit trying to communicate and withdraw (often silently nursing a growing list of grudges and resentments); they can become more aggressive about pushing their opinions; or they can flee this frustrating situation. Counselors sometimes see all three responses at work in troubled families (a father and son launch escalating attacks on each other nightly, Mom hides in the bedroom, and the boy's brother runs off to party with friends). Once these habits are entrenched, it becomes very hard for the family to address problems, so difficulties tend to compound (the brother starts abusing drugs; Mom becomes clinically depressed). Eventually, professional help may be needed in order to restore the family's health and stability.

When families do seek help, listening skills are often among the first things family members are encouraged to learn. Learning to listen can help prevent problems, too. Three suggestions for parents who want to help keep family members in close and respectful contact with one another follow:

Take time to debrief. In previous generations, families didn't need to make time to talk; they gathered around the table for a meal at least once a day, and as often as not everyone spent the evening at home. Today, though, it is not unusual to find family members heading off in several different directions at night; dinner may be eaten in shifts in front of the TV. The result is less conversation and less information being shared. The smaller trials and triumphs of everyday living may not be communicated at all. Only relatively urgent matters may cause family members to seek one another's attention, giving conversation a frenzied quality.

If you can't reliably remember the names of your children's friends . . . if you don't know who their most and least favorite teachers are or what musical groups they like . . . or if most of your conversations seem to fall into the "Mom, I've gotta have poster board and a report cover for tomorrow" category, you need more time to debrief. Successful debriefing involves four steps, described in the box on page 314. For children with learning disabilities, regular debriefing is especially important. These sessions provide youngsters with opportunities to practice their language skills in a safe, supportive environment (essential for the development of linguistic confidence).

Polish your listening skills. Listening involves more than being quiet so your partner or child can have a say. A good listener also makes an effort to understand the speaker's feelings and opinions and lets the speaker know that he or she has been understood. This is easy enough to do when you're in agreement with views being expressed; in the middle of an argument, however, it can be much harder. A listening exercise that can be used in times of conflict is described on page 315. Try it and see if the level of cooperation among family members improves.

Listen to the feelings, too. Children who can talk about how they feel are usually more resilient than those who keep their emotions stuffed inside. They are also less likely to resort to inappropriate behaviors as a means of expressing themselves (a child who can tell his sister how angry he is, for example, is less likely to punch her out). Many children grow up, however, with the idea that some emotions are bad and should not be expressed. Anger and fear are among the feelings most likely to be judged unacceptable. Parents who react to emotional outbursts with phrases like "Stop making a scene!" or "Stop being such a baby!" are usually the architects of the belief that getting mad or being scared is wrong.

To avoid this pitfall, encourage young people to talk their emotions out. When your son comes home and denounces his math teacher with a string of unprintable adjectives, for example, try to tune in to the feelings as well as to the inappropriate behavior. Saying "I don't like that language, but I can hear that you're really mad—what happened?" gives him room to keep talking. Telling him "I won't tolerate cursing! Go to your room immediately!" may make him feel that anger and swearing are both wrong. Similarly, saying "Don't be silly! There's nothing to be afraid of!" to the child who is anxious about going to overnight camp invites her to shut her emotions down (not only will this kind of "encouragement" fail to reassure her, it labels her feelings as wrong). Asking her to sit down and talk about what's worrying her helps your daughter confront her fears—the first step toward overcoming them.

When children talk about problems, they don't necessarily want adults to "fix" them. What youngsters often need most is a sympathetic listener who will allow them to vent. Once intense feelings have been discharged, children's perspectives often improve to the point that they can once again manage life's challenges on their own. "I remember a day my son came home mad as a hornet," a mother remembers. "He exploded as soon as he got inside the door—his English teacher was unfair, the lunch aide was a jerk, he hated the girl who sat behind him in social studies; it went on and on. . . . After about twenty minutes he wound down. Finally he said, 'Thanks, Mom; I appreciate talking things like this over with you,' and went outside with his basketball. Through the whole episode I hadn't said

Debriefing

Debriefing is a method of keeping up with what is going on in your children's lives without making them feel like they are victims of an inquisition. The objectives are to learn more about your children's experiences, to help them explore feelings, to identify problems, and to set goals. Successful debriefing consists of four steps:

1. Provide an opportunity for relaxed togetherness (a walk after dinner, a leisurely Sunday breakfast, or something similar). You need to find a time when you won't be interrupted or feel pressed about getting other things done.
2. Ask *specific* questions ("What's your favorite class this year?" works better than the more general "So how are things going at school?"). Avoid questions that imply criticism or judgment; this is not the time to ask if the child's math grades are improving. To make the most of your time, keep questions focused on one area—don't try to cover school, dating, and career goals in one lunch.
3. Keep the child talking by being a good listener. Sometimes a nod and a sympathetic "Mm-hmm" are all that is needed to keep the ball rolling. At other times you may need to offer supportive feedback ("I bet that made you mad," "Sounds like this really excites you," "How did you feel when she said that?").
4. Acknowledge what you have heard. This involves reflecting children's thoughts and feelings back to them in your own words ("Sounds like what Gail said to Naomi made you wonder if Gail is really your friend"). At this stage, letting children know you have listened and understood them is much more important than analyzing their problems or offering advice. Indicate that you are willing to help solve problems, but don't push. This tactful approach conveys respect for the child's own problem-solving abilities, and makes it more likely the child will want to talk things over with you again.

one word!" Even so, this parent was communicating with her child very well. By avoiding advice, she told him she believed in him. By listening to his feelings, she told him she cared.

7. LOOK FOR OUTSIDE SUPPORT WHEN YOU NEED IT

Independence is a virtue that is much admired in America. Although few of us grow our own food or build our own houses these days,

Listening Exercise

This exercise is especially useful when trying to resolve a disagreement:

Three Yesses

The ground rules are that each party will be given a turn to talk without interruption for up to five minutes. At the end of this period, the listener must summarize the main points of what he or she has heard in a *minimum* of three sentences, each of which will be acknowledged with a "yes" if correct. The listener must keep trying until three "yesses" have been received. It is then the listener's turn to talk.

Let's imagine that a mother has been arguing with her teenage son about how little work he does around the house. They have reached an impasse, and have agreed to use Three Yesses. The boy speaks first. After he is finished, Mom attempts to summarize her son's side of the argument as follows:

"You think I don't appreciate how much time it takes to keep on top of schoolwork and sports."

"Yes."

"You believe you already do more around the house than most kids you know."

"Yes."

"You think I'm the meanest mother on the planet."

"Wait a minute! I never said that!"

"Okay. You think I'm a clean freak and my expectations are unrealistic."

"Yes."

It is now Mom's turn to talk, and the boy's turn to listen and respond.

Families who try this exercise often say that listening carefully enough to get three "yesses" can initially be a challenge, but that the effort pays off. Once everyone feels heard and understood, tempers usually cool down, and solving problems often becomes much easier.

---

many of us do believe we should be able to handle our children without assistance. Some parents are therefore very reluctant to seek outside help for family problems. These adults sometimes find admitting that they cannot manage their own affairs so shameful that they deny problems exist, or convince themselves that "it's just a phase—he'll outgrow this behavior any day now."

Experts advise, however, that the ability to turn to others for help and support is a strength that can contribute significantly to quality of life for adults and children alike. For example, several studies have shown that individuals with learning disabilities who build support networks are happier and more successful than those who try to go it alone. For parents, finding appropriate support can make the difference between getting bogged down in unproductive (or counterproductive) habits and managing family matters effectively. Generally speaking, there are three kinds of support available to children with learning disabilities and their families. Each is discussed below.

Public Services

Federal law requires a variety of services to be made available to the families of children with disabilities in addition to those provided by school districts. For example, communities are required to provide support services for preschool children (and, in some states, infants) who have disabilities or developmental delays. Early intervention services help children who need assistance with social or emotional development, communication, or cognitive skills before starting school. Physical, occupational, and speech therapy can also be provided to preschoolers who need them.

The agencies responsible for screening children and providing services vary from place to place. This information should be available from your school district or state department of education. (For the address and telephone number of your state department of education, as well as other key agencies in your area, request a free "State Resource Sheet" from the National Information Center for Children and Youth with Disabilities by calling 1-800-695-0285. NICHCY is a treasure trove of information about disabilities and services; ask them to send you a list of their publications.)

Under some circumstances, families can get federal support for adaptive technology for a child with disabilities. Under the Technology-Related Assistance for Individuals with Disabilities Act —also known as the Tech Act—support may be provided for devices that enhance personal independence (such as augmentive communication devices), medical equipment, and/or equipment that makes it possible for an individual to participate more fully in school or on the job (such as electronic readers and computers). Training in the uses of adaptive technology can also be provided. Generally speaking, financial support is reserved for individuals with severe disabilities who lack the financial resources to purchase equipment on their own, but information about the uses of adaptive technology is available to all. To find out more, contact your state's Tech Act office. Additional information about locating sources of funds for adaptive technology is available from the National Rehabilitation Information Center (NARIC) by calling 1-800-346-2742.

Career planning and job training services are available to eligible young adults with learning disabilities under the federal Rehabilitation Act (also known as the Rehab Act) and coordinated state programs. The purpose of the Rehab Act is to maximize employment options for individuals with disabilities and help them become economically independent. Individualized programs are facilitated by a vocational rehabilitation counselor; career exploration, vocational counseling, skills development, work-study opportunities and help learning independent living skills can all be provided. In some circumstances, tuition for higher education can also be provided through the Rehab Act. NARIC (see the telephone number above) can put you in touch with the agencies that administer rehabilitation programs in your area. An excellent free guide to rehabilitation services is also available through the Higher Education and Adult Training for People with Handicaps (HEATH) Resource Center, a program of the American Council on Education; call 1-800-544-3284 and ask for *Vocational Rehabilitation Services: A Consumer Guide for Postsecondary Students.*

In some communities, federally funded parent training and information programs such as the Technical Assistance for Parent Programs (TAPP) are available to qualified families. (Help with parenting skills may also be available through schools and other local agencies; contact your department of social services for information.) These programs are designed to help parents learn how to support healthy child development, handle discipline effectively, and access community services that the family needs. Parent Training and Information Projects (PTIs) is a federally funded organization that provides training in advocacy and special education issues specifically for parents of children with disabilities. To locate a PTI in your state, contact the National Center for Learning Disabilities (NCLD) at (212) 545-7510, or write 381 Park Avenue South, Suite 1420, New York, NY 10016. A private, nonprofit organization, NCLD operates a free information and referral service that can help you locate other resources in your area as well.

Note that children identified as economically or educationally disadvantaged (this includes many children with learning disabilities in both urban and rural areas) may be eligible for a much broader range of support services than those listed here from federal, state, and local agencies. Your school district's department of pupil services and local department of social services are good places to start looking for information. Services that provide support to children from birth to age five—as well as to their families—are particularly important. Many experts feel that assistance at this critical stage can prevent many future problems.

Parent Support Groups

Local parent support groups may be chapters of national support organizations like the Learning Disabilities Association of America (LDA), Children and Adults with Attention Deficit Disorder (CHADD), or the Orton Dyslexia Society, or they may be independent organizations. A primary focus of these groups is to introduce families of children with disabilities to one another for the purpose of sharing information and providing mutual support. Some groups offer much more. For example, support groups may provide the following:

- Speakers and newsletters
- Resource centers with libraries of books and tapes of interest to parents and children
- Access to computers and computer instruction
- Parenting classes
- Professional tutoring
- Babysitting co-ops and/or respite care
- Legal guidance
- Help with advocacy at school
- Recreational programs for children
- Information and referrals to other services in the community (everything from vocational rehabilitation services to dentists who are good with children who can't sit still)

Some groups are also involved in political activism and work with legislators and education professionals to improve services for children and adults with learning disabilities at the local, state, and national levels. Your school district's department of special education should be able to guide you to support groups in your area. For information about reaching the national organizations mentioned above (and a number of other specialized support organizations), turn to the Appendix. Some assistance (newsletters and other publications, referrals, information about conferences) can be provided directly by these groups' national headquarters.

Individual, Marriage, and Family Counseling

There are times when individuals and families need more assistance than self-help groups and public support systems can provide. The situations described in the checklist on page 320, for example, call for prompt evaluation by a mental health professional or other qualified counselor (such as an alcohol or substance abuse counselor, marriage counselor, or appropriately trained clergy). Families need not wait until matters have become this urgent to take advantage of counseling, however; those who seek help for mild to moderate emotional strain can often prevent these tensions from exploding into major problems. Among the things families can learn from a professional counselor are communication skills, techniques for reducing stress, and methods of resolving conflicts. Counseling can also help individuals resolve persistent feelings of anger, guilt, anxiety, and/or depression. Family counselors can help parents identify unproductive or destructive habits, devise systems of rules that work, and improve methods of discipline. Reviewing this list of potential benefits, it is obvious that there are very few families who would *not* benefit from professional help at some point in their lives!

The chief drawback of counseling is that it can be expensive. Many health insurance policies offer benefits that provide for some types of counseling, however, and in most communities there are mental health clinics and other counseling agencies that have flexible fee schedules based on family income. Research finds, furthermore, that many problems can be addressed successfully with short-term therapy; no longer does counseling automatically involve a commitment of many months or years. Troubled families without health insurance coverage should therefore not assume that counseling is beyond their reach. Subsidized programs may be found listed under "Mental Health Services" and/or "Clinics" in the yellow pages of your phone book (individual practitioners will be listed under "Counselors," "Social Workers," "Psychologists," and "Psychiatrists"). Free or low-cost counseling may also be available at a local university or hospital, through your synagogue, parish, church, or diocese, or through your child's school.

Two important factors contribute significantly to the success of a counseling experience: willingness of family members to participate, and finding a good "fit" between the family and the counselor. The

When to Look for Help

It is important to recognize when family problems have worsened beyond the average parent's ability to cope. The following situations are unlikely to improve on their own and call for prompt evaluation by an appropriately qualified professional:

- Parents have become locked into adversarial roles and cannot agree on methods of family management, or family members have lost the ability to communicate without fighting
- A child persistently ignores or violates all household rules and/or fails to respect the rights of others
- You are unable to maintain control of your own behavior in confrontations with your child
- A child exhibits symptoms of severe depression or talks about suicide
- A child has become excessively or irrationally fearful of particular persons, places, or situations
- A child has developed a sleep or eating disorder, or other chronic health problems
- You suspect a child is abusing or addicted to a drug (including alcohol)
- Your child is unable to stop tormenting or abusing another child, either within or outside of the family
- A child's school performance is irreversibly deteriorating
- A child is unable to break a pattern of illegal or antisocial behavior (e.g., lying, stealing, vandalism, truancy)
- A child is repeatedly absent from home or school without explanation, or has attempted to run away from home
- You are often afraid of your child

It is also wise to seek help if you sense that something is seriously wrong, but you're not exactly sure what the problem is. These intuitions are often accurate, and a counselor can help you identify the issues that need to be addressed.

Adapted from Philadelphia Child Guidance Center, *ibid.*

first factor applies even if counseling is being sought for an individual. As any professional counselor will tell you, it is very difficult to treat a child if parents refuse to become involved. Adolescents or adults dealing with emotional problems or substance abuse can also have a hard time addressing these issues in isolation; the support of family members sometimes makes the difference between successful treatment and failure. Furthermore, as we discussed earlier in this chapter, one person's difficulties can eventually entangle other family, members in inefficient or destructive patterns of behavior. Addressing individual problems may therefore require everyone to make some changes. If a lot of negativity has built up inside the family, some members may initially decline to become involved in counseling ("Don't ask *me* to waste my time with a headshrinker! I haven't got any problems—*he's* the one who's messed up"). If this is the case, go ahead and make a start with whoever is willing to participate. You may find the naysayers become interested in joining you when they see others learning improved coping strategies.

Finding the right counselor can sometimes be a challenge. First, there are several different kinds of professionals working in the mental health field, including psychiatrists, psychologists, and social workers. Some work primarily with individuals, some work with children and families, and some work with groups. Then there is a bewildering array of therapeutic specialties: psychoanalytic therapy, systems therapy, psychodynamic therapy, behavioral therapy, and cognitive therapy, just to name a few (many family counselors draw from more than one type). The kind of professional or brand of therapy you choose, however, will ultimately be less important than finding a counselor with whom you feel comfortable communicating, and whom you feel you can trust. If you regularly come out of a counselor's office feeling demoralized rather than hopeful, you're in the wrong place, no matter how many credentials are displayed on the wall. You may have to interview more than one counselor before you find someone who "feels" right. Usually, that will be a professional who does the following:

- Appears to be genuinely interested in you and your child

- Listens respectfully to your views of your family's situation

- Exhibits knowledge about the types of stress faced by children with learning disabilities and their families

- Listens to and answers questions

- Offers a coherent intervention plan that addresses your concerns

Parents at your local support group may be able to recommend counselors who have worked successfully with children with learning disabilities and their families in your community. Your child's school counselor or pediatrician may also be able to refer you to competent professionals. Whatever route you choose, don't be embarrassed about seeking help. There is certainly no shame in wanting to provide a brighter future for your child, or in wanting to improve your own parenting skills.

Family counseling often improves parents' ability to support and nurture each other as well as helping them care for their children. Enabling Mom and Dad to work together more productively, in fact, is one of the better ways of addressing children's concerns. When parents are divided, young people often invest a lot of energy in manipulative strategies designed to get one parent or the other on their side. So much effort may go into these schemes that children never learn more appropriate and effective ways of getting their needs met. For example, the boy who knows that Mom will ride to the rescue if only he acts helpless and pathetic enough (no matter what Dad says) is not learning tools that will serve him well in the future. Similarly, the girl who counts on Daddy to defend her whenever she fights with Mom about homework or rules may eventually come to feel dependent on male support (and develop questionable ways of getting it). When parents present a united front, however, manipulative strategies like these become ineffective. Once these bad habits have been broken, more successful methods of dealing with life's challenges can be taught.

Parents who really want to help their children therefore need to find the courage to face their own differences and examine their own roles in the family system. This process may require you to confront control issues or painful memories of your own younger years. Those who are willing to take the risk, however, may be surprised at the benefits in store. "I never thought I'd say I was grateful for my daughter's problems," says a mother who sought family counseling when her rebellious sixteen-year-old refused to return to school, "but helping Sandy compelled everyone in the family to grow. Because we faced that crisis together, our family is closer and stronger than ever before."

Albert Einstein once said, "In the middle of difficulty lies opportunity." Parents who keep looking for those opportunities in hard times teach their children the value of positive thinking and persistence. As we have seen in this chapter, those are qualities that help support both achievement and self-esteem. In the next chapter we will see how a third element—planning—can help young people maximize their opportunities and face the future with confidence and enthusiasm.

12

LOOKING FORWARD TO
THE FUTURE

In many families, anxiety mounts as a child nears the age of sixteen. At this point many questions that used to be hypothetical start to become real and pressing. What is the child going to do after high school? How will he or she earn a living? Does the youngster have the academic interests or the intellectual potential to go to college? Is he or she mature enough to live away from home?

Parents of students with learning disabilities often face these questions with an extra measure of concern. In addition to having incomplete academic skills, our adolescents sometimes appear to lack maturity and motivation. They may approach the end of high school without having given much thought to what they want to do in the future. Parents who are becoming increasingly worried about how a child will survive after leaving school sometimes mistake this failure to look ahead as a deficiency of ambition. More often, however, it is lack of experience with planning and decision-making that is the problem. Students who struggle in school (and have many decisions made for them) often develop a survival mentality; what is important to them is getting through each day without humiliation or disaster. Over a period of years, these students become "future impaired"—the concept of next year, or two years from now, has little real meaning for them.

Extra support and careful planning may therefore be necessary to help young people with information-processing problems make a successful transition to the world of work or higher education. In recognition of this fact, federal law requires an Individual Transition Plan (ITP) to be developed for students with learning disabilities no later than age sixteen (some states require the transition planning process to be initiated earlier). Research indicates, however, that the transition plans developed in many high schools offer too little, too late. As a result, many students with learning disabilities leave school without marketable skills or a coherent, realistic plan for the future.

Parents need to take the lead in the transition planning process rather than leave this important matter entirely to the staff at the child's school. Authorities agree that age sixteen is too late to begin transition planning; most recommend making a start in ninth grade or even earlier. Furthermore, although transition services are improving in many areas, youngsters with learning disabilities are still frequently shortchanged in the college and career guidance process. Guidance counselors are sometimes largely ignorant of the special needs of individuals with learning disabilities and the programs and services that are available to assist them. Monitoring and advocacy are therefore more important than ever as the child approaches graduation in order to make sure that students are exploring a full range of options. (An important objective in high school is also to bring the student more actively into the planning and advocacy processes.)

In this chapter, we will discuss the three most important questions families must address in order to help young adults with learning disabilities face the future with confidence. We conclude the chapter with a transition-planning timetable that suggests appropriate goals and specific activities for junior high and each year of high school.

1. DOES THE CHILD HAVE A PLAN FOR CONTINUING EDUCATION OR SPECIFIC JOB TRAINING AFTER HIGH SCHOOL?

Research makes it clear that young adults who leave school without marketable skills will have a hard time finding meaningful work. Some will not even be able to find steady employment. Individuals who do not finish high school face the bleakest economic outlook: not only do dropouts face higher rates of unemployment, but those who do work make one-third less than high school graduates. A recent study found that fewer than 25 percent of high school dropouts with learning disabilities earned enough to pay all their own living expenses one to four years after leaving school. These young adults are often limited to minimum-wage jobs that offer little in the way of benefits or opportunities for promotion. Employment prospects are particularly grim for dropouts in urban areas, where technical or clerical skills are increasingly required for entry-level jobs. Young women without skills typically fare even worse than young men when it comes to achieving economic independence. Studies find that female dropouts with learning disabilities usually occupy the lowest rungs on the occupational ladder, are more likely to work at part-time or temporary jobs without benefits, and earn even lower hourly wages than their male counterparts.

When students complete high school and pursue postsecondary education, however, the picture brightens considerably. Studies find that the employment rates of people with learning disabilities who complete vocational education programs compare favorably with those of job-training graduates without disabilities. A study of college graduates with learning disabilities found more than 80 percent employed in professional or managerial positions. Obviously, it is critically important to encourage young people to examine their career options and to get as much education as possible to prepare for the jobs of their choice. If they have already left school, young adults need to be encouraged to explore other means of improving their skills and continuing their educations (see box on pages 326–27).

For many parents, the critical question at this point is whether it is realistic for their child to consider college. The good news is that young people with learning disabilities are attending colleges and universities in record numbers, thanks in part to an explosion of programs and services designed to support them. (Federal law requires all institutions of higher learning to make "reasonable accommodations" for students with learning disabilities; the range of additional services available varies from school to school.) At some campuses, the number of students identified as having learning disabilities has increased more than tenfold in recent years. An administrator at Brown University recalls, for example, that in 1983 the school provided assistance to six students with learning disabilities. In 1996, assistance was provided for 175 undergraduates with learning disabilities at Brown, as well as to 25 graduate students.

Some authorities feel that the number of students with learning disabilities on college campuses would be even greater if these youngsters were given better guidance in high school. Since many guidance counselors know little about college programs for students with

Getting Back to School

High school dropout rates for students with learning disabilities are alarmingly high, approaching 40 percent in some studies. These young people often leave school before eleventh grade—the point at which transitional planning begins at most schools—and many lack both basic skills (reading, writing, and arithmetic) and specific job skills. It is important to encourage individuals who left school before graduation to explore options for improving their skills and continuing their educations. Here are some suggestions that can dramatically improve their employment outlooks.

The General Educational Development (GED) test. The GED program, sponsored by the American Council on Education, gives adults a second chance to obtain a high school credential. Each year, approximately 70 percent of those taking the GED exam succeed in earning a high school equivalency diploma. In recent years the number of GED applicants with learning disabilities has quadrupled. Special testing accommodations (including extended time, help with reading, and alternative recording methods) are allowed for individuals with documented disabilities. For more information about GED classes and tests, call the toll-free 24-hour GED hotline at 1-800-626-9433.

Adult literacy programs. Programs that teach adults to read better—either one-to-one or in small classes—exist in many communities. Most are free. The toll-free National Literacy Hotline (1-800-228-8813) connects you to a 24-hour bilingual (English/Spanish) service that provides information about literacy programs and other educational opportunities. Ask for their learning-disabilities brochure.

Adult education courses. Evening courses in typing, computer skills, and other vocational subjects are offered by many school districts, as well as by some colleges and universities. Most welcome beginners of all ages. Contact public school districts in your area for information, or call the Learning Resources Network (1-800-678-5376) for help locating providers of adult continuing education.

Community colleges. Most community colleges offer courses in both basic writing and study skills, which can be lifesavers for adults who hope

learning disabilities, these students are sometimes not encouraged to consider higher education or to sign up for college preparatory classes. Students who have uneven academic records and/or standardized test

to enter college. Some also have alternative admissions procedures for adults who do not have high school diplomas and offer extensive support services for students with learning disabilities. For more information, contact the coordinator of learning-disability services at your local community college. In some circumstances, support for college tuition can be provided for students with disabilities by the state's rehabilitation services agency (see below).

Job training through state rehabilitation services agencies. The Rehabilitation Act of 1973 (Rehab Act) required each state to establish services to help individuals with disabilities become more employable and independent. The act continues to provide federal support for these services. Eligible individuals can receive career counseling, on-the-job training, and/or financial support for education (technical and trade school or college courses). Help with independent living skills (such as planning and living on a budget) is also available. For information about services and eligibility, contact your state's vocational rehabilitation agency. If you cannot find this agency under state government listings in your telephone book, you should be able to get the number from your public library or high school guidance office, or call the National Rehabilitation Information Center (NARIC) at 1-800-346-2742 and ask for a state agencies list.

Note that the student with learning disabilities who moves smoothly through four years of high school followed by four years of college is the exception rather than the rule. Research reveals that these individuals frequently need extra time to complete their educations, either because they fail some courses or because they choose not to take on a full course load, to attend school part-time, or to take periodic "breaks" from the stresses of formal education. It is important for both parents and students to avoid becoming discouraged if educational goals are not met "on time." Taking longer to graduate from high school or college should not be viewed as a failure as long as students are willing to keep trying. Taking formal education in small doses is a sensible strategy for many young people with learning disabilities; sometimes, this approach is the most successful route to a diploma or a degree.

scores may also assume that no college will accept them, so they fail to explore college options. To help parents assess children's potential for success in college, experts suggest applying the following guidelines:

Students who have mild to moderate learning disabilities and average or above average intelligence should be encouraged to consider college. Students most likely to succeed are those who can function successfully in regular high school classes with appropriate accommodations, have adequate self-advocacy skills, and do not have serious attention, organizational, or interpersonal problems. Given appropriate academic preparation in high school, students like these often do well in college with minimal help. Most, however, will need some modifications and accommodations in order to compete successfully. Typical accommodations used by these students in college are additional time for tests, help with taking notes, books on tape, and access to a writing center for use of word-processing equipment and assistance with planning and preparing long papers.

Motivated students with moderate to severe disabilities can also succeed in college, but they will require more assistance. It is important to research educational options carefully and identify institutions that can provide the kind of structure and intensity of support that these students will need (individual tutoring, assistance with study skills, help with advocacy, and specially trained advisors for academic planning and career counseling may all be required, for example). There are now a number of college guides published especially for students with learning disabilities; these are good places to start investigating the services and support programs available at different institutions (if these guides are not available at your high school guidance office, check your public library or local bookstores). Students with multiple or severe disabilities may also want to investigate other means of moderating academic pressure, such as attending college part-time. (Check sources of financial aid before making this decision; some apply only to full-time students). Note that these students may also require extra support and/or extra time in high school to meet college entrance requirements.

College will probably not meet the needs of youngsters who have significantly lower than average intelligence, major interpersonal problems, and/or very severe language, cognitive processing, or attention deficits. College is also not the best choice for the student who has developed a strong aversion to formal education. (This may sound obvious, but parents sometimes become so fixed on college as a goal that they fail to consider their children's feelings about the matter. Children who are forced to attend college are rarely successful, regardless of their intellectual potential.) Postsecondary planning for these young people needs to focus on building functional social and vocational skills and/or providing mental health support. Parents may have to be assertive to make sure that appropriate guidance and services are provided for these young people, both in high school and afterward. Youngsters with severe learning disabilities—who are often unable to live and work on their own immediately after high school, but may be perceived as not "disabled" enough for programs serving the handicapped in the community—are among the most likely to fall between the cracks of the education and social service systems.

If college has been identified as a goal, begin by obtaining a copy of *How to Choose a College: Guide for the Student with a Disability,* a free booklet from the HEATH Resource Center (call 1-800-544-3284 to request a copy). This valuable publication helps students assess their own readiness for college and identify what to look for in an institution of higher learning. Next, make sure that your child is taking the most rigorous academic program he or she can handle in high school. Under federal law, colleges cannot refuse to admit students because they have disabilities, but they are under no obligation to admit students who have failed to take an adequate college preparatory program, or whose grades and test scores do not meet their standards (see box on pages 332–33). Finally, start exploring college options early. Success depends on finding a good match between the college and student, and this process takes time. A thorough college search typically involves reviewing college guides; sending for information from specific institutions; comparing admissions requirements, academic programs, special services, and financial aid options; and making a personal visit to top-choice campuses. The parent of two college students (one of whom has learning disabilities) advises:

> Don't make college visits over the summer. "You don't learn much about a school from touring empty buildings. Visit when classes are in session, and arrange for the student to sit in on an introductory-level class in an area of academic interest. Ask about overnight visits. Our son found that spending a night in a dorm and talking to students informally gave him a much better idea of what went on than the typical campus tour. At one small school that had excellent academic programs, he discovered that the most popular recreational activity for students was smoking pot. That wasn't a social standard he wanted to conform to; we kept looking.

If your child comes across much better in person than on paper (this is often the case with young people who have learning disabilities), also try to arrange an on-campus interview. This gives your child a chance to impress an admissions officer with his or her intelligence and motivation, as well as an opportunity to explain why that math score or foreign language grade is so low. If special support for learning disabilities is going to be needed, it is also important to talk to the person in charge of providing these services during your visit. The box on pages 334–36 lists some critical questions for which answers should be found before choosing an institution.

For young people who are not yet ready to leave home or attend college full time, community colleges offer some excellent options. Many have open admissions policies and provide extensive services for students with academic weaknesses; most are used to accommodating part-time students. Investigating specific support for students with learning disabilities at community colleges, though, is just as important as checking out other institutions. As Barbara Cordoni, an experienced coordinator of special education support services for university students (as well as the mother of two children with learning disabilities) warns, "Do not, repeat, do not send him to a community college near home to 'get his feet wet' unless the college has an LD [learning disabilities] support program. The most difficult time we have at my university is with those students who go to community colleges without support programs and who do not do well. They enter the university with poor grades, and by their junior year they are supposed to choose a major. However, most majors require a minimum grade point average, which the student may simply not have because of those community college grades that are averaged in."* The bottom line? Wherever they go to college, it is important that students start out with access to all the support they need, and receive informed guidance so they do not bite off more than they can chew. As attention deficit hyperactivity disorder expert Dr. Edward Hallowell puts it:

> It doesn't make sense in your first semester of college to take four laboratory science courses, or five humanities courses, all of which require two forty-page papers, or three courses on the novel, each course requiring ten books to be read . . . so that the student must read some 12,000 pages during the semester just to satisfy the minimum requirement. (Don't think this sort of thing doesn't happen—I've had patients who have signed up for all of the above.) Encourage your child to sign up for a challenging academic load, but one that he or

---

* Cordoni, B., *Living with a learning disability* (Rev. ed.). (1990). Southern Illinois University Press.

she can handle. It's easier to add on later, rather than frantically dropping courses that are burying you.*

Some students fear that being honest about their learning disabilities during the college application process will prejudice admissions committees against them and hurt their chances of getting in to the school of their choice. This is unlikely, since discrimination against individuals with disabilities is prohibited by federal law. Disclosing a learning disability can, however, help explain discrepancies or weaknesses in the high school record that might otherwise be puzzling. We think being open about a learning disability therefore offers more advantages than disadvantages. (Our experience is that students who are hesitant to disclose their disabilities often hope to make a "fresh start" in college and get by without any special help. While their desire to be "normal" is understandable, these hopes are also naive. Heavier work loads and harder course content make appropriate support more important than ever in college—another reason why honesty is usually the best policy.)

If students do not intend to go to college, the focus switches to career planning and preparation. In some ways this can be more challenging than locating the right college program. Although public and private career training opportunities abound, few instructors in vocational education programs are knowledgeable about learning disabilities. (Many have no background in *education*; their experience relates primarily to the skill or trade they are teaching.) Little in the way of formal support may therefore be available for the student who needs help with reading diagrams or manuals, taking notes, or taking timed paper-and-pencil exams, all of which may be required. Vocational education programs designed for special populations often target the needs of individuals with limited intelligence, or those who have a history of truancy or juvenile delinquency—needs that are quite different from those of a youngster with information-processing problems. Finding a suitable program can be complicated by the fact that young people either have no idea what they want to do, or have ideas that are unrealistic (the child may dream of becoming a basketball player or a newspaper reporter, for example, despite lack of athletic or writing ability). Youngsters' organizational abilities, work habits, and interpersonal skills may also be so weak that parents wonder if there is *any* workplace where the child will fit in.

---

* Hallowell, E. M., and Ratley, J. J. (1994). *Answers to distraction*. Bantam Books.

What About College Entrance Exams?

Colleges do not waive basic admissions requirements for students who have learning disabilities. Youngsters interested in colleges that require SAT or ACT scores must therefore plan to take these tests. Students with documented disabilities *are* permitted some special accommodations on these examinations, including extended time and testing in alternate settings (to minimize distractions). Note that special test administrations must be arranged in advance; the student cannot simply show up and ask for accommodations on test day. Information about test accommodations and instructions for documenting disabilities for the SAT and ACT exams should be available at your high school guidance office, or it can be requested directly from the following sources:

SAT Services for Students with
Disabilities
P.O. Box 6226
Princeton, NJ 08541-6226
(609) 771-7137

ACT Test Administration
P.O. Box 4028
Iowa City, IA 52243-4028
(319) 337-1332

The more familiar youngsters are with the examination format and with test-taking strategies (such as knowing when it's a good idea to guess at an answer and when it's best to skip a tough question), the better they will do on these tests. Commercial study guides, computer programs, and test preparation courses are all widely available to help young people sharpen their test-taking skills. College-bound students should also plan to take required tests more than once if possible; scores

Because preparation for employment touches on development in so many areas, career planning should be viewed as a long-term process beginning as early as middle school. Thorough career preparation usually involves several phases, discussed below (note that these activities are also appropriate for students who hope to attend college).

Career Awareness and Career Exploration.

Many students' notions of the world of work are very narrow or borrowed largely from the entertainment media. Some young people don't even know what their parents do at their jobs! Career planning therefore begins with developing youngsters' awareness of the great variety of things people can do to earn a living. Formal career explo-

often go up the second or third time around. (Colleges usually use the highest scores earned, regardless of when the test was taken.)

Students may find that they are better suited to one exam or the other. Some youngsters with learning disabilities like the ACT, for example, because it is a more straightforward test of knowledge (students say it is less "tricky" than the SAT). The ACT's relatively long reading passages, however, can work against youngsters with reading comprehension problems. Students with significant strengths in math may be better off with the SAT (math skills account for half of the total score on the SAT, but only a quarter of the total score on the ACT exam). Since many colleges accept either test, students may want to take both the SAT and the ACT exams and submit the better set of scores.

Families should be aware that when ACT and SAT scores are sent to colleges, results of tests given under nonstandard conditions are flagged. This essentially identifies the applicant as having some kind of disability (there are very few other reasons for special test administration). While colleges cannot legally refuse to accept a student because he or she has a disability, some students fear stigmatization or prejudice, and so prefer to keep their learning disabilities confidential. These students presently have two choices: take the tests without modifications, or focus on colleges that do not require ACT or SAT scores. (Even some selective private institutions—Bates and Bowdoin Colleges, for example—have made submission of test scores optional.) Applying to institutions that do not require admissions tests may also improve the chances of students who have good grades but consistently perform poorly on standardized exams.

ration programs (which involve visits to a variety of work sites in the community and events like "career fairs," in which representatives of various trades and professions make presentations) are usually available in junior high and high school to help with this process. Families can also do a great deal to improve career awareness on their own. Take children to your workplace, and talk about what you do there. Direct children's attention to some of the different things other people do for a living (at the doctor's office, for example, the child may see one or more nurses or physician's assistants, a receptionist, secretaries who make appointments and manage records, a person who handles billing and bookkeeping, and laboratory or X-ray technicians in addition to the doctor). Encourage children to "interview" people in their communities who perform jobs the student

Key Questions for College Applicants

In addition to the usual questions students have about colleges (about admissions requirements, academic programs, and social atmosphere, for example), students with learning disabilities need to make some additional inquiries of college administrators. In most cases you will get the most accurate information from the school's coordinator of services for students with disabilities.

What (if any) special programs and support services are in place here for students who have learning disabilities? While colleges are required by federal law to make "reasonable accommodations" for individuals with disabilities, some do little more. Ask specifically about the types of assistance you are most likely to need. What arrangements are made for students who need help taking notes, for example? Is assistance with writing papers available, and on what basis (a special class, individual tutor, or writing lab)? If a book is not available on tape from the library, will the college find someone to record it? How long would this take?

Are support services and/or tutoring included in the tuition, or do they cost extra?

How long has your learning-disabilities support program been in existence? Students looking for extensive services should seek out a college with an established track record.

How many students with learning disabilities have received services here in recent years? What percentage of those students graduate? Very low numbers may indicate a weak level of support for students who have learning disabilities.

What documentation must I provide in order to obtain services? Documentation must usually be based on an evaluation by a qualified professional and describe specific types of learning disabilities, as well as recommended accommodations. (A letter from your grade-school principal stating that you're "dyslexic," for example, won't cut it.) Many colleges will accept a high school IEP. Others may require a recent psychoeducational evaluation that includes test results and a detailed description of learning strengths and weaknesses.

What is the procedure for negotiating accommodations and modifications with instructors? Are students on their own, or is help with advocacy available? If there is a conflict with a professor, what is the procedure for resolving it?

What is the minimum number of credits per semester required to be considered a full-time student? Limiting one's course load is one key to college success, but some types of financial aid are available only to full-time students.

Are courses available in basic writing and study skills? Do they earn academic credit?

What is the average class size in my areas of academic interest? What is the usual format of these classes (lecture, laboratory, or discussion)? What kind of tests are given most frequently?

Does the college (or the proposed major) have a mathematics or a foreign language requirement? If these subjects present a problem, is it possible to substitute other courses (such as international studies courses, American Sign Language, or computer courses) to satisfy these requirements? Note that colleges and universities are *not* required to waive or change these requirements to accommodate students with learning disabilities. They may refuse to do so if changing the requirement amounts to altering the nature of the program or relaxing academic standards.

What is available in the way of work-study programs and internships? Many young people with learning disabilities learn best by doing, and so benefit from programs that go beyond the classroom. Find out if academic credit can be granted for these experiences.

Is tutoring and academic and career counseling handled through the learning disabilities support center or through academic departments and general counseling offices? How much experience do advisors and tutors have with students who have learning disabilities?

What kind of technical support is available? How easy is it to get access to a computer? Do you have to walk nearly a mile to the library to get online, or are computers scattered throughout the campus? (One Ivy League university lends laptops to students with disabilities for use in class!)

What grading options are available? Can any courses be taken on a pass/fail basis?

If noise and distraction are a problem, what housing options are available? Are there "quiet dorms" or "quiet floors" (loud music and partying are not allowed after certain hours, or not allowed at all)? Can I get a single room? Do single rooms cost extra?

finds interesting. The librarian at your local library can also help you find age-appropriate books on different career areas.

As a youngster's career interests develop, seek opportunities for hands-on experience. Job shadow, job trial, and work-study programs, internships, volunteer work, and summer or part-time jobs can all help students develop realistic expectations for what it takes to make it in fields that appeal to them. Research has also found that students who get this kind of experience are most likely to develop good work habits and become responsible employees in their adult years.

Remember that it is typical for young people—with and without disabilities—to change their minds frequently during their teenage years about what they want to do. If you expect this, you will not be disappointed or frustrated when your daughter abandons her idea of becoming an astronomer (after you went to great lengths to set up the summer internship at the planetarium for her) or decides midway through her computer keyboarding course that she likes retail sales better after all. Do not be discouraged; experts advise that no education or job experience is ever really wasted. Even if youngsters change career plans several times, their accumulated experience will help expand their understanding of employers' expectations, improve their skills and their ability to work with people, and ultimately enhance their employability.

Vocational Assessment and Career Counseling.

If students have reached high school without having developed some ideas about what they might want to do for a living (this is not unusual for students with learning disabilities, whose time and attention may have been occupied with basic academic survival), a formal vocational assessment and/or professional career counseling may help them focus their interests. Vocational assessments also attempt to measure students' aptitudes for different kinds of jobs. If pursuing a vocational assessment, it is important to make sure your child receives a multi-disciplinary evaluation coordinated by a psychologist or counselor who is knowledgeable about learning disabilities. Such an assessment would involve interviews, hands-on activities, and observation in simulated job settings, as well as tests to measure the student's aptitudes, interests, dexterity, and academic achievement. Vocational assessments should be available through your school district (ask the department of special education what can be provided). For young adults who have left school, assessments and career counseling may be available through the state vocational rehabilitation agency, local community colleges or vocational-technical schools, nonprofit community-based organizations that serve people with disabilities, or private agencies and providers. Since cost and quality of service can vary considerably, it is important to investigate exactly what a vocational assessment will include, the credentials of professionals involved, and the range of services the agency can provide. Look for an agency that works closely with local employers. Career counselors should be up to date on the local economy and on "growth occupations" in which employees are needed in your part of the country.

Career Preparation.

Career preparation includes both learning the specific skills necessary to perform a certain type of work, and also developing job search skills such as preparing a resumé, reading and responding to want ads, filling out applications, and conducting job interviews. Sixteen-year-olds who have isolated an area of career interest can often benefit from vocational education programs in high school. (Note that many of these classes require good reading and/or math skills, and that instructors may have little experience working with students who have learning disabilities. It is therefore wise to meet with instructors in these programs in advance to review texts and instructional methods and discuss accommodations the student is likely to need.) High schools should also be able to provide guidance in the job-finding process (via the special education department, the guidance department, or the department of vocational education), but parents may have to ask for this help. Make sure that specific steps in career preparation—such as preparing a resumé, or completing a particular work-study program—are included among the written objectives in the student's Individual Transition Plan (ITP).

Some youngsters with learning disabilities avoid vocational education in high school because they are not comfortable in these classes (which sometimes have a reputation of being little more than day care programs for dead-end kids and troublemakers), because they lack the skills needed to compete in these classes, or because they remain unsure about what they want to do. As a result, the challenge for many families is finding appropriate job training *after* high school (several years later, in some cases). Young adults with mild to moderate learning disabilities can often take advantage of industry-sponsored apprenticeships and career training provided by the military, community colleges, and trade, technical, or business schools. Those whose disabilities are more profound—or are complicated by very poor social skills, severe attention deficits, and/or mental health problems—need more structure, support, and supervision than these traditional sources of vocational education can provide, however. Transition programs (which are designed to help individuals with disabilities make the transition from living at home to living independently) are appropriate choices for some of these young adults. Transition programs may be either residential or day programs; some offer an academic component, while others focus primarily on developing self-care and employment skills. Private, public, and charitably supported programs all exist.

Experienced parents caution, though, that quality transition programs often have waiting lists; it is therefore a good idea to begin looking for a transition program as soon as you recognize that one is likely to be needed. Your school district's special education department, your state vocational rehabilitation agency, and community mental health agencies are among the best places to start looking for information about transition programs. The HEATH publication *Young Adults with Learning Disabilities and Other Special Needs* also lists a variety of established transition programs across the country. To request a free copy of this helpful guide, call 1-800-544-3284.

Job Placement.

Most postsecondary educational institutions (both colleges and vocational schools) offer their graduates some help with job searches and placement. Services may include help with preparing a resumé, practice with job interview skills, and placement in summer jobs, work/study positions, and internships, as well as referrals to employers who are interested in applicants with particular types of training. Agencies that serve individuals with disabilities can often place young adults who have difficulty finding work in the competitive job market in special apprenticeships or sheltered employment positions (jobs that provide additional structure and supervision for workers with disabilities) in the community. Families may find, however, that most sheltered jobs are designed primarily to meet the needs of individuals with physical handicaps or those who are retarded. Job coaching (a service in which a government-funded job coach works one-on-one with a new employee at his or her work site until essential job skills have been mastered) may be a better way to help the young adult with learning disabilities get a solid foothold on the employment ladder. For information about special placements and job coaching, contact your state vocational rehabilitation agency.

*   *   *

Note that self-employment is a career possibility that should not be overlooked. Many individuals with learning disabilities flourish operating their own services or businesses. The appeal of entrepreneurship is that it allows energetic people to maximize their skills and creativity while delegating organizational tasks—as well as those involving math, reading, and/or writing—to others. If your child dreams of becoming his or her own boss, you may therefore want to give the idea of starting a business some serious consideration. Make sure youngsters understand, of course, that creative people do need business experience and education (as well as partners or employees who can handle matters like billing, scheduling, accounting, book-keeping, inventory, reports, and contracts) in order to succeed. A high level of motivation and sincere interest in the type of work being considered—whether it is fashion merchandising or lawn care—are also helpful for keeping a small business going.

Research finds that substantial numbers of individuals with learning disabilities do not achieve economic independence until they are in their middle to late twenties, and that their education and employment histories are often characterized by many wrong turns and false starts. While watching youngsters flounder can be frustrating and sometimes frightening, parents must remember that many of these young people learn best by trial and error; they simply don't know what they like or can do until they try it. As Dale's story reminds us, young people with learning disabilities *do* get better at tasks that are hard for them if they are willing to keep applying themselves. (This story also reminds us that a cheerful countenance and good work habits can help compensate for many problems.) So instead of seeing abandoned jobs or uncompleted educational programs as failures and becoming discouraged, try looking at them as necessary steps in the growth process. Parents who have this perspective are best at helping children maintain the motivation they need to keep trying until they find a niche in which they are truly comfortable.

2. DOES THE CHILD UNDERSTAND HIS OR HER LEGAL RIGHTS AND ADVOCATE FOR HIMSELF OR HERSELF APPROPRIATELY?

Throughout this book, we have referred many times to the Individuals with Disabilities Education Act (IDEA), the package of federal legislation that protects the rights of students who have disabilities in

DALE

Dale Brown works for the President's Committee on Employment of People with Disabilities and writes frequently about learning disabilities. Her own perceptual deficits were not recognized until she was in college. Here, Dale recalls her first job:

The first day of my senior year in high school, I eagerly applied for jobs. A drug store manager hired me as a waitress. I was very excited. Minimum wage seemed like a fortune to me! On my first day at work, my first impression was of noise and brightness. Cash registers clattered. Dishes crashed. Silverware clanged. Pam, a slender young woman, explained the system.

"First you take the order," she said, handing me a green pad. "Just watch me." Pam approached a customer and said: "May I take your order, please?" The customer told her, and she wrote it down. "One hamburger!" she shouted to the cook.

"Now we have to make the tuna salad," she said. "Here's the scoop. You put the lettuce on the plate like this, then put the tuna on top. Then you put the tomato here."

We had to lean close to the counter to avoid being hit by a man carrying trays. I tried to watch her as she put the order together, but I could barely follow. "Show me how to make the tuna salad again?" I asked. "I can't until we get another order for it," Pam said. "Now we clean up the counters by putting the dishes down here . . ." She spent the whole day talking to me and telling me detail after detail. I tried to listen, but the other conversations, the sizzling of the grill, and the rushing of water distracted me. "How do you take an order again?" I asked. "It's *easy*," Pam replied. "Just write down what they say and look up the prices!"

The next day, my own section was assigned to me. A man and woman were waiting expectantly. The man asked for a hamburger and a coke. The woman asked for a tuna salad and a root beer. I wrote down the order, but I didn't know the prices.

"How much is a hamburger?" I asked Pam.

"Eighty-five cents."

"How about a coke?"

"Was it large or small?"

"I didn't ask."

"Better find out. Look at the menu next time; it has all the prices."

I went to make the tuna salad. I couldn't find the scoop. The plates had disappeared. I had to interrupt Pam again. . . . Then I couldn't make the lettuce lie flat. I couldn't get the tuna out in a ball. Finally, I spooned the tuna onto the lettuce and hoped it was enough. I gave the woman her salad and got the drinks, using the first paper cups I found. I couldn't easily see the difference between large and small, and I had forgotten to ask which they wanted anyway.

"Where's my hamburger?" asked the man.

I'd forgotten to tell the cook! "I'm sorry," I told him and shouted, "One hamburger!" As I served it to him, two more customers came in. They wanted hot dogs and tea.

"Where's our check?" asked the first customer. I gave it to him.

"How much are we supposed to pay?" he asked. I took the check back. I had forgotten to put on the prices! Panic hit. How much were the cokes? I made up a price, then concentrated on adding everything up right.

"Where are our hot dogs?" asked my second customer.

"You overcharged us for the cokes!" said my first customer.

"Sorry!" I said. I approached the huge cash register. I had forgotten how to work it.

"Pam," I said, "please show me how to work the cash register."

"I showed you that yesterday."

"I'm sorry; you need to show me again." Pam rang up my order, without explaining what she was doing. Then I told her, "Wait, I charged them too much for the cokes!"

She glared at me. "Now we have to make up a *void* slip." She turned on a small microphone. "Mr. Connors, please come to the counter . . . Dale, don't you have other orders to take care of?"

I nodded. But I had lost my order slip. I checked my pad, my pockets, the floor—I would have to ask my customers what they wanted again. But which ones were they? I couldn't remember their faces! How did Pam do this? She moved along efficiently and effortlessly, taking orders, preparing food, and ringing things up. I must have looked as lost as I felt, because Mr. Connors came over and looked at me sympathetically. "You'll catch on soon," he said. "Don't worry; it's only your second day."

But more days passed in a blur of confusion and errors. The other employees were kind at first, but rapidly grew impatient with all my questions. I couldn't memorize the prices—even after taking the menu home—and I kept on forgetting where things were located. Preparing food was difficult, even after being shown several times. (For example, to make a coke you mixed syrup and seltzer, but I couldn't tell the difference between the syrup knob and the seltzer knob on the machine. Each time, I had to squirt a little liquid in the cup and see which one it was.) I could never figure out the sequence of putting an order together. It was not clear to me that you started with the cooked items and worked on the other food while they were cooking (and no one explained it), so I was always giving my customers their food at different times.

continued

I had trouble working in the confined space between the counter and the food preparation area. I often bumped into other workers and dropped things—once a whole tray of glasses. And because of my difficulty remembering faces, I often confused people's orders. (Sometimes I wrote reminders on my order slips. One customer laughed when she found "blonde hair, blue eyes" on her check.) Gradually I mastered the cash register, although I had a tendency to punch the wrong numbers and end up with $13.80 instead of $1.38. The tax table we used was so small that sometimes I guessed the tax or forgot it altogether.

My favorite job was going to the stock room to get ice. The other waitresses hated it, but I volunteered for it. I would walk downstairs with two buckets. Then I'd sit on a carton for a few minutes and calm myself. Then I'd fill the buckets, and take them upstairs to the ice bin.

Because I was cheerful, reliable about being on time, and conscientious about trying to correct my errors, my boss liked me and kept me on in spite of all my problems. Sometimes he kidded me about all my void slips, but he was very patient. My coworkers, on the other hand, were the ones who had to put up with most of my questions and correct many of my mistakes. Even though I took care of a lot of unpopular jobs, they found me difficult and were undoubtedly glad when a change in bus schedules forced me to leave.

Later, I had many jobs. I was a salesgirl in a department store during Christmas rush. You can imagine the problems! In college, I woke up at six o'clock in the morning to clean the dormitory kitchens. I loved that job, because I worked alone, at my own pace. Later I became a cafeteria worker and served food, washed dishes, and helped the cooks. Each job I did better than the last.

Condensed from "Learning to Work: A Story by a Learning Disabled Person," by Dale S. Brown.

public schools. It is important for young adults with learning disabilities (and their families) to understand that once students leave high school, the protections of IDEA no longer apply. Colleges, vocational schools, and other postsecondary institutions are *not* required to offer special education programs for people who have disabilities. Institutions of higher learning are not obliged to adjust admissions criteria or modify academic standards for these students. Employers cannot be compelled to change basic job descriptions to accommodate individuals with disabilities; nor must employers excuse individuals with disabilities from duties or training activities that are

Ten Suggestions for Employees with Learning Disabilities

These tips are suggested by Dale Brown

1. Be prepared to spend extra time learning the job, even if you are not paid extra. Bring information such as price lists home to memorize. Practice filling out forms. If you are working at a chain of restaurants, go to a different restaurant within the chain and watch the workers. If you are slower, be willing to take extra time to finish your fair share of work.

2. Ask for help as you need it. Even though other employees and supervisors may act impatient, it's better than making errors.

3. On the other hand, never ask for help if you don't need it.

4. In most jobs, accuracy is more important than speed. Take the time to do it correctly, even if people pressure you to go faster.

5. Take full advantage of your first few days on the job. During this "honeymoon period," you can ask questions. Try to find someone who will watch you do the job correctly. Repeat information. Say, "Please listen to me tell you, so I can be sure I understand." Don't let them interrupt you and tell you what to do. Be sure they are listening to you. Some people like helping others; try to find them.

6. Offer to do tasks which you can handle but that others consider unpopular. Then, you can ask others to assist you with jobs you can't do.

7. Develop ways of remembering important facts. Everyone has a particular technique. Write things down, or say them aloud when you are alone. Or ask your friends or parents to drill you.

8. When you make mistakes, apologize and correct them immediately.

9. Report on time. If you have trouble being on time, try to arrive an hour or two early.

10. Try hard, and *appear* to make an effort. Sometimes, when one makes mistake after mistake, it gets tempting to act indifferent or as if you are doing it on purpose. That isn't helpful. Make your effort obvious. That means:

- Appear to pay attention. Look everyone in the eye, and nod your head occasionally as they speak. Respond to what they have said.
- Look at your work as you do it. Don't let your eyes and mind wander when you are on the job. Walk purposefully from place to place.
- Always work, except during breaks or lunch.
- As you improve, tell your supervisors and coworkers. Say, "Thank you for your help. As you can see, I did it correctly this time."

Reprinted by permission of Dale S. Brown

essential to their jobs, even if these assignments are difficult for the disabled worker.

Employers and institutions of higher learning may not *exclude* qualified people who have disabilities, however, or operate programs in a way that makes it unreasonably difficult for these individuals to do their jobs or get an education. People who have disabilities (including learning disabilities) are protected from this kind of discrimination by federal civil rights legislation. It is vitally important for youngsters to understand what they can expect under civil rights law, and how to go about getting the modifications and accommodations the law mandates in higher education and job settings. To begin, they must recognize that once they leave school, a significant shift in responsibility takes place. Under IDEA, schools are responsible for identifying children who need help as well as for initiating services. Under civil rights laws, however, assistance is provided *only* to individuals who disclose their disabilities and *ask* for it (documentation of the disability may also be required). Young people who lack understanding of their disabilities—or lack the confidence to explain what they need and ask for assistance—therefore risk losing support to which they are legally entitled. Because schools have traditionally done a very poor job of educating students about their legal rights and obligations, parents must take the lead in preparing children to advocate for themselves appropriately in college or the workplace.

Young adults with learning disabilities need to become familiar with the provisions of two particular packages of federal legislation: the Rehabilitation Act of 1973, and the Americans with Disabilities Act (ADA) of 1990. Both are civil rights acts that require organizations to provide equal opportunities to people who have disabilities. Section 504 of the Rehabilitation Act (often referred to simply as Section 504) applies primarily to educational institutions. Specifically, Section 504 states the following:

> No otherwise qualified person with a disability in the United States . . . shall, solely by reason of . . . disability, be denied the benefits of, be excluded from participation in, or be subjected to discrimination under any program or activity receiving federal assistance.

Section 504 broadly defines "person with a disability" as "any person who (i) has a physical or mental impairment which substantially limits one or more of such person's major life activities; (ii) has a record of such an impairment, or (iii) is regarded as having such an impairment." (Since learning is a "major life activity," this description has been determined to cover learning disabilities.) Under Section 504, colleges and universities that receive federal money may *not* do any of the following:

- Limit the number of students with disabilities that they admit

- Make pre-admission inquiries about whether or not a student has a disability

- Use admissions tests or other selection criteria that do not make provisions for individuals with disabilities

- Exclude qualified students with disabilities from any course of study

- Limit eligibility for scholarships, financial aid, fellowships, internships, or assistantships on the basis of a disability

- Use methods of evaluation that adversely affect persons with disabilities

In addition, Section 504 requires institutions receiving federal funds to provide services and accommodations that enable individuals with disabilities to take full advantage of available programs. Colleges and universities are granted some flexibility in determining how to meet each student's needs. (If a student with learning disabilities needs to use a computer, for example, the college can fulfill this need by providing access to a computer center during certain hours; it does not have to provide a personal computer for the student's use.) Note that colleges need *not* make accommodations that would reduce academic standards or alter essential elements of a program. (A university can legally require students to have a C average to be accepted into a major, for example, or insist on foreign-language mastery for participants in an international studies program.) If a student with a disability can meet the standards of the institution or perform essential tasks of the program using modifications to compensate for the handicap, however, Section 504 states that the modifications must be provided.

Section 504 also prohibits discrimination in employment practices by employers receiving federal funds (principally federal contractors and the federal government itself). The rights of a much larger number of workers, however, are protected by the Americans with Disabilities Act. This sweeping legislation prohibits any organization with more than fifteen employees from discriminating against people with disabilities in the areas of access, hiring, or promotion, and it also requires employers to make "reasonable accommodations" to help workers with disabilities do their jobs. (Religious organizations are excluded from this legislation.) The ADA's provisions also apply to institutions of higher learning, and so they expand and reinforce the rights of students set down in Section 504. Among the provisions of the ADA are the following:

- A qualified person cannot be excluded from a program or job on the basis of having a disability

- Reasonable modifications in policies, practices, and procedures must be made in order to avoid discrimination

- Employment and program participation should be in the most integrated setting possible

- Examinations and courses must be accessible

- Surcharges to cover the costs of accommodations may not be imposed solely on persons with disabilities

- There may be no harassment or retaliation against individuals who are accessing their rights under the law

The ADA also requires organizations to actively recruit individuals with disabilities for open positions; to change qualifying examinations, interview procedures, and/or training policies that unnecessarily restrict the rights of these applicants; and to provide technology that will enable employees with disabilities to be fully functional within the employment setting. Under the provisions of the ADA, therefore, it would be reasonable for a worker with a learning disability to request such accommodations as these:

- Written directions for work to be performed

- Access to word processors with spell-checkers for written tasks

- Access to calculators to assist with tasks involving math

- Work settings that minimize distractions

- Assistance with reading technical or training manuals

Although these laws have been in place for some time, young adults with learning disabilities should not assume that their teachers and job supervisors will understand the provisions of Section 504 and the ADA and comply with them automatically. Research finds that many employers and educators in institutions of higher learning have very limited understanding of these acts. Some don't know that civil rights laws cover individuals with learning disabilities as well as persons with more visible handicaps (such as vision or hearing impairments or limited physical mobility); others know next to nothing about the impact of learning disabilities. (Some years ago, an Iowa judge ruled that a plaintiff could not have a learning disability because he had a driver's license, normal intelligence, and was capable of responding to questions in court!) Therefore, in addition to knowing what they are entitled to, young people must be prepared to courteously educate teachers and administrators about learning disabilities and the law whenever they ask for accommodations. Youngsters who lack self-confidence, lack information about their disabilities, or have personal styles that are less than assertive are at a disadvantage in these situations. Some of these young people will be most successful in programs where the needs of individuals with disabilities are already fairly well understood (on college campuses that have established learning-disabilities support programs, for example).

Assertive or not, all individuals with learning disabilities need to know where they can turn for help with advocacy and/or resolving disputes when they need it. Colleges and universities are required to appoint Section 504 compliance officers to help handle complaints. Under the terms of the ADA, employers and educational institutions must also establish a grievance procedure for individuals who believe their rights have been violated, and they must make information about this procedure available to anyone who asks for it. Initiating a formal grievance, however, should be considered an action of last resort. Most disputes can be resolved through informal negotiation. Parents need to be alert, however, since young people sometimes need backup from family, counselors, special-needs support staff, community agencies serving the disabled, and/or legal representatives in order to get a fair hearing.

It must also be acknowledged that there are borderline situations in which the law is not entirely clear on what an individual with learning disabilities is entitled to. For example, does a student with relatively mild disabilities qualify for support, given the language of the law (which refers to "substantial" impairments)? Must employers provide costly equipment to accommodate individuals with disabilities if doing so significantly reduces profit margins? How much writing help can be provided to a graduate student with a Ph.D. dissertation, given that writing a dissertation is an established degree requirement? Can an otherwise qualified individual be denied promotion to a supervisory position on the basis of inability to read or write required reports? Questions like these are being addressed in America's courtrooms, where new cases involving individuals with learning disabilities are heard annually. While the courts struggle to interpret the finer points of the law, however, individuals must continue to negotiate for what they need as best they can. This usually involves striving for cooperative, mutually respectful relationships (as opposed to adopting an adversarial stance and making blunt demands). Young people who are perceived as hardworking and sincere are most likely to get the support they ask for. If polite negotiation fails, though, families should not hesitate to initiate formal procedures to protect a youngster's legal rights in the classroom or on the job.

Note that many individuals fear that disclosing their learning disabilities in the workplace or at institutions of higher learning will lead to stigmatization and social and/or professional rejection. These fears are not entirely unrealistic. Myths about learning disabilities abound, and ignorant individuals sometimes assume that people with these conditions are incompetent and irresponsible. Young people who wish to keep their disabilities confidential are of course entitled to do so. (The Family Educational Rights and Privacy Act, sometimes referred to as the Buckley Amendment, protects the confidentiality of young people's school records. Information about their learning disabilities or participation in special education programs cannot be disclosed to outside parties without written consent.) Under these circumstances, however, special accommodations and modifications cannot be expected. Good compensatory skills and hard work (possibly including many hours of extra unpaid effort) will likely be required of the individual who wants to succeed.

Try to involve teachers and counselors in the process of preparing students to advocate for themselves after leaving school. The best way to do this is to include the development of self-advocacy skills on the student's Individualized Education Plan (IEP) and/or the Individual Transition Plan (ITP), which must be added to the student's IEP no later than age sixteen. Throughout high school, students should also practice self-advocacy by negotiating their own program modifications with teachers whenever possible. (Parents and resource teachers can provide support if needed.)

3. IS THE CHILD READY TO LEAVE HOME?

Concern about children's readiness to live on their own is not limited to the parents of youngsters with learning disabilities. Most parents experience some anxiety when a child prepares to leave home for college or that first apartment. Worries range from simple concerns about the child's health and welfare ("Will she eat balanced meals?" "Will he wear his boots when it snows?") to serious doubts about the child's maturity ("Can he face up to peer pressure?" "Is she savvy enough to conduct herself safely among strangers?"). Apprehensions about our own well-being may also be aroused when a child leaves home ("Am I losing him?" "How lonely I will be without her!"). For many parents (mothers especially), the exit of adult children marks the end of a significant phase of their lives and leaves them wondering, "What will I do now?"

For parents of children who have learning disabilities, all of these feelings may be particularly acute. Since our youngsters are sometimes late to acquire the skills that support independence, they may look less ready than most to leave the nest at age seventeen or eighteen. In addition, we may find ourselves unusually entangled emotionally with these children. Because parents so often serve as advocates, mentors, teachers, coaches, and cheerleaders for youngsters who have learning disabilities (and sometimes as their best friends as well), involvement with these children can become very intense. Separation may therefore be a painful and difficult process for parent and child alike. This process can be complicated by the fact that young adults with learning disabilities sometimes need extra time to become economically and emotionally self-sufficient. When adult children continue to look to Mom and Dad to get many of their needs met, parents often find their feelings ping-ponging back and forth between "It's time for this child to go!" and "How will this kid ever survive without me?"

To assess a child's readiness for independence, it is important to realistically evaluate general maturity as well as academic and occupational skills. The checklist on pages 350–51 presents some important indicators of maturity. While few children will be performing well in all these areas at age eighteen (indeed, many of us continue to struggle with some of these skills as adults), difficulties in many areas suggests a young person still needs a protected environment, regardless of his or her age. Giving such children an extra year or two to grow up and improve their ability to meet the challenges of daily liv-

---

Is Your Child Ready to Leave Home?

The checklist below presents some important indicators of maturity. Young adults whose self-management skills are good in most of these areas are probably ready for independent living. (Note that even the best-prepared youngsters will not start out functioning well in *all* areas.) Those who lack ability in many areas, however, may need to live at home or in another supervised environment until their skills improve.

Mature young adults:

- Can set reasonable short-term goals and make plans to achieve them (can plan a social engagement or make a realistic list of chores for the day, for example)
- Can stick to their principles and stand up to peer pressure
- Have reasonable impulse control; can delay gratification when appropriate (they can balance "what I want to do" and "what I need to do" most of the time, for example)
- Understand their own strengths and limitations; can identify situations/settings/modifications that make it possible for them to do their best
- Can manage day-to-day personal finances (make deposits, write checks, pay bills, keep simple accounts, keep spending within budget guidelines)
- Can stick to a schedule (get up and go to bed at reasonable hours; get to work/meals/class on time)
- Have developed "memory methods" for keeping track of appointments, assignments, chores, and other obligations

---

ing makes much more sense than propelling them into a job or educational program for which they are not ready. As they become better able to take care of themselves and communicate with others, young adults' self-esteem usually grows. This growth in pride and confidence will eventually help support success in everything they do. Some skills on the checklist are likely to improve as the child grows older, broadens his or her experience, and completes stages of development that have been delayed. For others (shopping and meal preparation, for example), the child will need explicit instruction.

Determining where a young adult should live and receive this continuing support, however, can be a thorny problem. Although research indicates that many young people with learning disabilities continue to live at home into their twenties, availing themselves of

- Can shop for and prepare simple meals
- Have good health and grooming habits: dress appropriately for the weather, know how to keep selves, clothing, and living spaces clean; are reliable about following doctors' orders (including taking medications on time); understand the consequences of drug and alcohol abuse and the importance of practicing safe sex
- Can drive or use public transportation safely
- Can monitor their own behavior (are usually aware of the impact their behavior has on others; can identify when their behavior has been irresponsible, inappropriate, or offensive)
- Are accountable for their own actions; take pride in their successes and responsibility for their mistakes
- Can respond appropriately to emergencies (know what to do in case of injury or medical emergency, fire, power failure, etc.)
- Can ask for help and locate appropriate sources of support when needed. Can accept supervision and constructive criticism
- Can follow directions and work independently for reasonable periods of time (do not have an excessive need for praise, monitoring, or other forms of attention)
- Usually interact courteously with supervisors, teachers, coworkers, and service providers
- Can initiate and maintain appropriate social relationships with peers
- Know and practice healthy methods of reducing stress (such as exercise, talking problems over with others, meditation, hobbies, sports, and other recreational activities)

parental assistance while completing their educations and/or settling into a job, this is not the best option for every family. Parents may doubt their ability to provide children with the guidance they need, or may themselves be in need of a respite from the responsibilities of child-rearing. Children may *want* to leave home and try their wings (this is a normal desire for people approaching the end of adolescence). Children who have become overdependent on parents may need to leave home in order to develop some confidence in their ability to care for themselves. These are only a few of the considerations that can have parents looking for a supportive environment away from home.

For young people who have adequate academic preparation, college can provide the transitional setting they need if the program is

Estate Planning for a Child with Disabilities

Parents who want to provide for a child's housing, health care, or education in the future, or who hope to supply long-term support for a child with disabilities, need to plan their estates carefully. If a child is receiving government benefits—or is expected to need them in the future—it is important to pass assets on in a way that does not affect his or her continuing eligibility. The child's level of maturity and ability to manage money must also be considered. When preparing wills, parents have four basic options, outlined below.

1. *Disinherit the child.* No state requires parents to leave money to a child, disabled or not. If your assets are limited and your child's needs are great, it may be wisest to disinherit your child so that he or she will be eligible for federal and state benefits after your death. Instead of complete disinheritance, you may want to leave your child a gift of modest but sentimental value, such as his or her bedroom furniture. The value of this gift will be small enough not to affect government benefits, but will indicate your love and concern.

2. *Leave the child an outright gift.* For example, your will might read, "I leave my son Tom $10,000," or "I leave one-half of my estate to my daughter Susan." If the child is not expected to need government benefits, this may be the most desirable course. If you question a child's competence or ability to handle financial responsibility, however, an outright gift is not a good choice. A trust is a better means of providing for the child's future.

3. *Leave a morally obligated gift to another of your children.* Suppose parents have two children: James (who has severe learning disabilities) and Mary. The parents leave all their assets to Mary. But they also instruct Mary before their deaths that half of this money is to be used for James' benefit in whatever way she thinks best. The money has been left to Mary so that James will not lose his government benefits, and because Mary can be trusted to think of appropriate ways to help her brother (such as taking him on vacation trips, or paying for health care not covered by his benefits). This arrangement is a *moral* obligation because it has no legal force; once she has the money, Mary can do whatever she wants with it. There is therefore some risk that the parents' wishes will be ignored. (Even if Mary is honest, unforeseen circumstances could

make it difficult for her to carry out her parents' plan. If one of Mary's children falls gravely ill, for example, she might feel a greater obligation to save her child than to support her brother. Or the money might be lost in a settlement if Mary divorces.) Morally obligated gifts can be a reasonable solution, however, if parents have a modest amount of money to distribute and do not expect to provide lifetime care for a child with disabilities. Be sure to seek input and approval from the obligated sibling before committing to this plan.

4. *Establish a Special Needs Trust.* The purpose of a Special Needs Trust is to manage resources in a way that provides limited income over a long period of time, preserving a child's eligibility for government benefits. Assets are managed by a trustee, who is given authority to determine how and when funds will be distributed to the trust's beneficiary. There are two kinds of trusts: the *testamentary trust*, which goes into effect when parents die, and the *intervivos trust*, which is activated when parents are still living (parents may serve as trustees during their lifetimes). Each offers distinct advantages and disadvantages which should be discussed with an attorney experienced in estate planning for individuals with disabilities. The services of a financial planner may also be needed to help families examine their resources and determine how best to fund a trust. Again, it is essential to find a professional who is familiar with Special Needs Trusts, which are quite different from Family Living Trusts and other modern estate planning tools. Although they are more difficult to set up, Special Needs Trusts are regarded as the most secure way of providing for the long-term needs of a child who has disabilities.

Experts advise that, in addition to preparing a will, parents should prepare a *Letter of Intent* that summarizes their wishes for their child's future in such areas as housing, education, religious upbringing, employment, social environment, behavior management, and medical care. This information will help guide your child's advocates when you are no longer there. This letter (write it *now* and update it periodically) has no legal status, but it can give people who may not know your child well valuable insight into his or her history, values, personality, goals, and needs.

Adapted from "Estate Planning," *NICHCY News Digest*, a publication of the National Information Center for Children and Youth with Disabilities.

carefully selected. (Immature children need more structure and supervision than others, and social as well as academic support is often needed. This kind of support is most often found at colleges with well-established programs for students with learning disabilities.) For young people who are not ready for college, parents may wish to consider such options as boarding schools (some "prep" schools specialize in assisting older adolescents who want to improve their academic skills and go to college eventually; others focus more on vocational and independent living skills) and residential transition programs (including group homes). Arrangements in which the child lives with another relative—such as grandparents or an older sibling—or moves into an apartment but continues to receive some income and assistance from parents (with shopping and bill paying, for example) may also meet the young adult's need for increased independence while providing some continuing support. Experienced parents advise that several arrangements like these may have to be employed before a young adult is ready to live on his or her own. It is important to avoid becoming discouraged during this extended separation process (the great majority of young people with learning disabilities *do* become able to care for themselves eventually) and to be persistent about seeking placements that respect the child's dignity and status as an emerging adult while offering adequate protection.

What if it appears that a child will never be able to become fully independent? This may be the case if a child's learning disabilities are very severe or complicated by mental health problems. Since these young adults may find it difficult to work steadily or to find jobs that provide health care benefits, it is of urgent importance for parents to help them explore what government assistance may be available. Individuals with documented disabilities may be eligible for Supplemental Security Insurance (SSI) or Social Security Disability Insurance (SSDI) benefits from the Social Security Administration. Note that parents' income or job status does not necessarily affect eligibility for federal assistance (parental income is not considered for SSI applicants over the age of eighteen, for example). Recipients of these benefits are permitted to work and earn money within limits, as well as allowed to receive some money from their families. In some states, individuals receiving income from SSI are automatically eligible for additional benefits such as health insurance (Medicaid) and food stamps; in others, a separate application has to be made for these and other services (such as job counseling, support for education and subsidized housing). Your local Social Security Administration office and the state department of social services are the places to start gathering information about the support available for adults with disabilities in your community.

Parents may also wish to arrange their affairs so that continuing provisions are made for a child with disabilities after the parents die. The box on pages 352–53 outlines some estate planning options. Note that if a child receives government benefits (or is expected to need them in the future), it is very important to pass assets on in a way that does not affect his or her continuing eligibility for assistance. The guidance of an expert in estate planning for persons with disabilities should be sought when making a will. The National Information Center for Children and Youth with Disabilities (NICHCY) has produced an excellent publication for parents covering this and other aspects of making long-term provisions for the support of an adult child. For a free copy, contact NICHCY at 1-800-695-0285 and ask for the "Estate Planning" issue of their *News Digest*.

Ultimately, our ability to provide appropriate support for our sons and daughters as they make the transition to adulthood depends on our ability to find the support—and the courage—we need to enter into a new phase of our own lives. We cannot do a good job of helping our children leave the nest if we feel we have little to look forward to after they have gone! Similarly, if we are afraid of relinquishing control, fearful of facing up to difficulties in our marriages, anxious about being alone, or insecure about our value if nobody "needs" us any more, we can find ourselves holding on to our children a little too tightly and a little too long.

Because it is so easy to confuse the legitimate needs of a child who has disabilities with the needs of a mother or father who has difficulty letting go, it is important for parents to put some thought and effort into mapping their own transition to the future as children get older. What new opportunities will relief from the day-to-day responsibilities of child care open up for you? What obstacles to your happiness exist, and how can you go about overcoming them? What support will you need to accomplish your goals and cope with new challenges? Where can you find that support?

Parents who seek answers to questions like these will be in the best position to deal with the feelings of loss that inevitably accompany a child's departure from home. These parents also teach, by example, that growth is a lifelong process. Among the many lessons we teach our children, this is possibly the most important. All young people— not just those with learning disabilities—need to know that there is no time limit on learning or achievement. If we haven't met our goals by age eighteen (or thirty, or fifty), we get not only second chances, but third, fourth, and fifth chances—as many chances as we need.

As our children spread their wings and prepare to fly, then, we must look to our own paths and practice what we preach. We must trust that it is never too late to learn, to ask for help, or to reach for dreams. And as we move forward, we need to remember this Chinese proverb as well as teach it to our children:

> Be not afraid of growing slowly;
> Be afraid only of standing still.

Timetable for Transition Planning

Junior High School

• *Take advantage of career exploration programs and activities.* Expose students to as many different career options as possible. Improve career awareness by visiting different kinds of work sites and encouraging children to talk to people with different occupations about what they do.

• *Make a list of the student's personal strengths and interests.* Use it to make some preliminary choices about career paths (a student who is outgoing, enjoys working with people, and has good math skills might be encouraged to look into various forms of sales, for example).

• *Identify what kind of educational preparation is necessary for top career choices.* Will the student need college? Vocational education? On-the-job training? A combination of these approaches?

• *Make a list of challenges that will have to be met.* The student interested in becoming a police officer will need to write well enough to prepare a coherent crime report, for example, and may have to work on those skills. A would-be boutique owner will need some sales experience as well as a basic business education. Start to rule out choices that are hopelessly inappropriate. (The youngster who frequently transposes numbers and letters, for example, would probably not succeed at computer data entry.)

• *Meet with the guidance counselor to discuss high school course selection.* Students hoping to go to college should take as many college preparatory classes (as opposed to special education classes) as they can, using accommodations as necessary. Research finds that ability to achieve in regular high school classes is a strong predictor of college success. Instruction in study skills, time management, and test preparation should also be sought now if it has not been already provided. Students not planning on attending college need to ask about options for career education. Note that many vocational education classes require relatively high functional abilities in reading and math; if students' skills in these areas are below the fifth- or sixth-grade level, continuing remedial instruction needs to be provided in high school. Students in college preparatory and vocational educational programs both need to become computer literate.

• *Promote independence and decision-making at home.* Gradually begin to decrease the level of guidance and supervision you are providing in areas like homework and recreation, and encourage children to rely more on their own initiative. (Continue this process through high school.) Living away from home for short periods—visiting out-of-town

continued

relatives, traveling with youth groups, or going to overnight camp—can help boost youngsters' confidence and self-reliance.

Ninth Grade

• *Work on self-advocacy skills.* Students need to develop an understanding of learning disabilities in general, and the nature of their own disabilities in particular. (One way to do this is to ask the resource teacher or school psychologist to review the most recent evaluation with the student, explaining strengths and weaknesses in nontechnical language). Youngsters should learn to describe their preferred methods of working, their specific learning disabilities, and the settings, instructional methods, and accommodations that make it possible for them to do their best. Students should start participating in IEP meetings and academic planning sessions with guidance counselors now if they are not already doing so.

• *Learn about the legal rights of individuals with disabilities.* Many teachers and employers—and many students—do not fully understand that many accommodations for people with disabilities in public school, in the workplace, and in institutions of higher learning are required by federal law. Students need to learn about how the Individuals with Disabilities Education Act (IDEA) and civil rights laws (particularly Section 504 of the Rehabilitation Act, and the Americans with Disabilities Act) apply to them.

• *Explore recreational opportunities.* Look for leisure-time activities at school and in the community that will put youngsters in touch with others who have similar interests. Spectator sports, community volunteer work, church activities, recreational athletics, crafts and exercise classes, and special interest clubs (like gardening, bowling or bird watching) can all provide a basis for rewarding relationships as well help youngsters make productive use of their free time. *Note that the more developed students' interests become, the easier it will be for them to make friends after leaving school.* For example, a youngster who is a competent chess player, sings with the church choir, knows his way around political election campaigns, and is a pro football fan has a basis for meeting people almost anywhere he goes.

• *Look for ways of getting work experience.* Research shows that work experience during high school is closely associated with future job success. Internships, "job shadow" and work-study programs, volunteer work, and part-time or summer jobs are all good ways of gaining work experience. These activities can help students explore their career interests, develop realistic job expectations, improve their skills, and boost their levels of self-esteem, responsibility, and independence. Students with demanding academic schedules, though, must be careful to avoid becoming overloaded. (For them, summer jobs and internships are often the wisest option.)

• *Continue to define career options.* Throughout high school (and college), students change their minds frequently about what career paths they want to follow. This is normal, and continuing career exploration should be encouraged. The high school curriculum needs to be planned in a way that preserves the greatest possible range of choices. (If students have the intellectual potential for college, for example, college preparatory courses should be taken even if the child does not presently plan to go.)

Tenth Grade

• *Refine or revise goals based on work and school experience.* The student who thought she was interested in medicine may feel differently after volunteering at the local hospital for a month. The student who hoped to be a high school athletic coach may be brought up short by low grades in college preparatory classes. As youngsters' interests and aptitudes become clearer, goals need to be redefined and plans adjusted.

• *Begin to explore postsecondary education opportunities.* As students' goals become more focused, start to gather information about institutions that provide training in careers of interest (two- and four-year colleges, apprenticeship programs, trade schools, and the military may all be options). Identify admissions requirements, including tests that may have to be taken (such as the SAT and ACT exams for college). Review high school course selections with the high school guidance counselor in light of these requirements and make necessary adjustments.

• *Practice self-advocacy skills.* Students should take over the process of explaining their learning disabilities and negotiating for accommodations or modifications with their teachers and employers as much as possible (parents and resource teachers can provide backup if needed). Young adults who are most successful in college and on the job are those who can clearly articulate their own interests, abilities, and needs.

• *Increase the student's level of responsibility for self-care at home.* Has the child learned to keep track of appointments and take medications without prompting? To do laundry? To use public transportation? To budget money? If not, now is the time to start encouraging him or her to take on these and other tasks essential for independent living. Research indicates that this is one of the most neglected aspects of transition planning.

continued

Eleventh Grade

• *Develop a written Individual Transition Plan.* Federal law requires schools to prepare an Individual Transition Plan (ITP) for students with disabilities no later than age sixteen. (Some states require ITPs to be prepared earlier; parents can also request earlier transition planning). This plan is to be developed by an interdisciplinary team; representatives of community agencies (such as the state vocational rehabilitation agency) should be included if students expect to access these services after graduation. The ITP document should describe the student's educational and career goals, as well as outline the specific steps necessary to achieve them. It is important for students to participate in developing the ITP. The job of the transition team is to help students figure out how to meet their own goals, not tell students what they should do.

• *Seek out vocational assessment and education opportunities.* Students who have not yet identified career goals may benefit from a formal vocational assessment (which can help pinpoint occupational strengths and interests) and/or the assistance of a career counselor. Ask the department of special education where appropriate services can be obtained. Students who have targeted an area of career interest may be eligible to begin taking technical or other vocational courses now. Since few vocational education teachers are knowledgeable about the needs of students with learning disabilities, check these courses out carefully in advance and discuss accommodations that a student might need with instructors.

• *Prepare a "short list" of colleges or other educational institutions.* Students should begin to narrow their choices of colleges or other postsecondary institutions, using criteria such as size, location, affordability, quality of programs in areas of interest, social atmosphere, and availability of support services for students with learning disabilities. Commercial college guides (available at bookstores, public libraries, and many high school guidance offices) can be very helpful in this process; there are now several guides published specifically for college applicants with learning disabilities. Write to request catalogues and applications, and make plans to visit and interview at top-choice institutions. Overnight visits that include sitting in on one or more classes, a chance to talk informally with students, and an opportunity to sample campus social life are highly recommended.

• *Take the SAT and/or ACT exams (if the student is applying to colleges that require them).* Preliminary college aptitude tests (the PSAT and the PLAN) are administered early in the junior year. (The results of these tests are not reported to colleges, but scores do determine eligibility for some national academic scholarships.) If preliminary test results are less than satisfactory, make a plan for improving test-taking strategies by means of review books, computer programs, or classes. Many students take college entrance exams in both their junior and senior years. Test modifications are available to students with learning disabilities, but non-standard testing must be arranged in advance and documentation of the disability provided. Careful attention to test schedules is therefore required. Schedules and forms for signing up for the SAT and ACT exams will be available from the high school guidance office.

• *Begin to assemble a personal transition file.* To receive accommodations after leaving high school (in college or the workplace), young adults will have to request them—they will *not* be offered automatically—and in some cases document their eligibility (that is, prove that a learning disability exists). Families should start gathering this documentation now. Contents of the file should include the most recent diagnostic test results and evaluation reports, medical records (if applicable), a copy of the student's most recent IEP (which should include a description of all modifications and accommodations used or allowed), and a copy of the student's Individual Transition Plan. High school transcripts, ACT or SAT scores, employment evaluations, awards, letters of recommendation, and information about extracurricular activities and other outside interests may also be useful to counselors attempting to help students select an appropriate program. If the student's most recent evaluation is more than two years old, ask the school district to complete a new one in the child's final school year. Some institutions will not grant accommodations without an up-to-date evaluation.

• *Explore summer opportunities.* Some colleges (and some boarding schools for students with learning disabilities) offer summer programs that combine improving academic skills with an introduction to living away from home. For a current list of pre-college programs for students with learning disabilities, contact the HEATH Resource Center at 1-800-544-3284. Students not attending in summer school programs should seek summer jobs or internships in areas related to their career interests, if at all possible.

Twelfth Grade

• *College-bound students need to start writing college application essays, securing letters of recommendation, and filling out application forms as early in the school year as possible.* Pay careful attention to deadlines. It is a good idea for students to ask their guidance counselors to review applications for completeness and accuracy two to four weeks before they are due (neatness counts, too). Use of the Common Application Form— now accepted by a large number of colleges and universities—can save

continued

students a great deal of time and essay-writing. Copies of the Common Application (and a list of institutions accepting it) should be available in the high school guidance office.

• *Investigate technical and trade schools that offer instruction in areas of interest.* While some of these institutions provide excellent training, commercial career education is also a field that is rife with scams, so programs have to be checked out carefully. Ask your Better Business Bureau and local vocational rehabilitation agency about any programs you are seriously considering. Beware of "counselors" who are salespeople in disguise (they recruit students on commission rather than on the basis of ability or aptitude), of promotions featuring "talent tests" or celebrity instructors, and of "bait and switch" lures (students answer a help-wanted ad, only to be told certain courses must be taken to "qualify" them for the job; or they are told that the free or discounted course they applied for is full, but they are eligible for others). Ask about the length and costs of training and how the curriculum addresses the specific needs of local employers—there is not much point in preparing practical nurses or computer programmers if the local job market is oversaturated with them. Do instructors have experience working with students who have learning disabilities? If tutoring in math, reading, or writing is needed, is it available? Read all contracts carefully (or have a lawyer review them) before signing.

• *Job-seekers need to prepare a resumé, obtain letters of recommendation, and practice job interview skills.* These objectives should be included on students' ITPs. A summary of the information typically called for on job applications (including dates of previous employment, Social Security number, and names and addresses of references) should be prepared and taken along when students visit prospective employers, since many will want applications filled out on the spot.

• *Identify sources of financial support.* High school guidance counselors can provide assistance with college financial aid forms. If families intend to explore resources available through the state vocational rehabilitation system or the Social Security Administration, intake interviews to establish eligibility should be arranged with those agencies now.

• *Identify options for children who are not yet ready for work or higher education.* For students who lack the skills or the maturity to attend college or hold down a job, a transition program may be the answer. These range from boarding schools that provide an extra year of high school for students who want to improve their chances of getting into college to group homes that help young adults with severe learning disabilities learn self-care, social, and employment skills. Some transition programs are private and tuition-based; others are supported by public funds or charitable organizations—your school district's department of special education, local support groups, and the state vocational rehabilitation agency are good places to start looking for information. Remember also that students are entitled to remain in public school until age twenty-one. Students aren't usually crazy about this option, but willingness to commit an extra year or two to high school can sometimes make the difference between leaving school with a special education certificate and graduating with a high school diploma.

After High School

• *Continue to monitor youngsters' progress.* Young people with learning disabilities frequently have difficulty adjusting to new environments. The increased freedoms and responsibilities that come with leaving high school can make the transition to college or the workplace particularly rocky. While it is important to avoid being overprotective (students must try their wings and make some mistakes in order to learn), be alert for signs of excessive stress, anxiety, or depression. These are signals that some changes need to be made, or additional supports provided.

• *Help young adults build a personal support network.* Young people with learning disabilities who make successful transitions to independent living often rely on the guidance and encouragement of mentors and "coaches." It is therefore important to urge youngsters to make positive connections with teachers, tutors, counselors, academic advisors, and job supervisors and take advantage of help that is available from these quarters. Parents and other family members can be effective mentors (and often continue to coordinate different aspects of children's programs for several years after high school), but it is important for young adults to explore sources of support beyond the home as well.

• *Provide loving acceptance and encouragement.* In studies, young people with learning disabilities frequently say that the emotional support and encouragement of family members was indispensable for helping them maintain their motivation, especially when things were not going well or their lives were not proceeding as planned. The road to success for young people with learning disabilities often looks more like a zigzag path (interrupted here and there by landslides, swamps, and bogs) than a straight route to the top. A parent's most important job as children negotiate this course is to prevent them from becoming discouraged, losing faith in themselves, and giving up. In this way, parents graduate from serving as their children's physical guardians to becoming the protectors of their children's hopes and dreams.

Appendix A

BENCHMARKS OF NORMAL DEVELOPMENT

BENCHMARKS OF NORMAL LANGUAGE DEVELOPMENT

There is wide variability in the ages at which different children reach the following milestones. Therefore, these benchmarks should be interpreted loosely, giving children time to develop at their own pace. If delays continue for too long, however, professional consultation should be sought.

AGE	RECEPTIVE LANGUAGE	EXPRESSIVE LANGUAGE
6 months	• Attends to spoken voices and discriminates those of strangers • Responds to different facial expressions and comprehends parental gestures • Plays peek-a-boo • Turns to the source of sounds • Responds appropriately to friendly or angry voices	• Vocalizes using a number of different sounds • Babbles; imitates inflection patterns, sounds, and syllables • Vocalizes to an adult's social smile and when talked to • Pleasure, displeasure, eagerness, satisfaction, and anger are evident in vocalizations

AGE	RECEPTIVE LANGUAGE	EXPRESSIVE LANGUAGE
6 months (con't)	(such as smiling in response to friendly "baby talk") • Turns when name is spoken	
1 year	• Nods or shakes head to simple questions ("Want a cookie?") • When requested, points to nose, eyes, or mouth • Responds to "give me" requests and directions such as "put the spoon in the cup," "stir," and "no-no"	• Babbles sound similar to adult inflection patterns • Imitates several syllables and words after adults ("baby," "more," "up") • Unintelligible speech, with the exception of a few words • Vocabulary of ten words soon after first birthday ("bye-bye," "mama," "dada")
1½ years	• Responses indicate accurate perception of others' emotions • Points to objects when named • Understands most simple questions • Shakes head yes/no appropriately	• Vocabulary of up to 30 words, including "all gone," "more" • Uses meaningful gestures such as pointing to make wants known • Says two words in a single utterance • Beginning to identify objects or pictures when asked, "What's this?"
2 years	• Responds to simple one-part directions ("Give the doll her milk") • Comprehends approximately 300 words • Listens to simple stories • Points to pictures of objects or parts of a doll on request • Discriminates between similar requests ("Give Ben the cup" versus "the plate")	• Vocabulary of approximately 50 words • Combines two or three words ("mommy go bye-bye") • Speech is 65% intelligible • Verbalizes "no" • Attempts to describe immediate and past experiences • Uses words to make wants known ("cookie," "milk")

AGE	RECEPTIVE LANGUAGE	EXPRESSIVE LANGUAGE
2 years (con't)		• Responds to biographical and simple informational questions ("What is your name?" "What does the doggie say?") • Negation is expressed ("no bed") • Possessive is emerging ("daddy car") • Uses pronoun and name for self ("me Tommy")
2½ years	• Comprehends approximately 500 words • Identifies pictured objects by function ("Show me the one you eat/wear") • Carries out two-part commands ("Pick up your book and put it on the shelf") • Understands the concepts "one," "all" • Listens to 5- to 10-minute story	• Vocabulary of approximately 200 words • Speech is 70% intelligible • Repeats up to 7-syllable sentences • Indicates age by holding up fingers • Sentences contain subjects and predicates ("mommy going," "bottle fall down") • Uses sentences of 3 to 4 words (average sentence is 3 words) • Begins to use pronouns (he/she) • Tells how common objects (fork, car) are used • Begins to name objects by use ("What do we eat with/ride in?") • Answers "where," "what . . . doing" questions • Verbalizes toilet needs • Tells his/her sex • Counts to three • Uses articles "a" and "the" • Uses "-ing" form of verbs ("Mommy going" replaces "Mommy go") • Regular plural form emerging (cat/cats)

AGE	RECEPTIVE LANGUAGE	EXPRESSIVE LANGUAGE
2½ years (con't)		• Uses "in," "on" • Irregular past tense emerging (is/was, go/went)
3 years	• Comprehends approximately 900 words • Listens to 20-minute story • Understands concepts of in/on/under/big/little	• Vocabulary of 500 words • Speech is 80% intelligible • Sentences contain subjects, predicates, and objects (average sentence is 3 to 4 words) • Recites nursery rhymes • Plays with sounds in words or nonsense syllables ("deanut dutter danwich") • Uses no/not in sentences • Answers simple "who," "what," "why," "where," "how many" questions ("What do you do when you're hungry/sleepy/cold?" "Where is Daddy?") • Asks simple questions ("What's that?") • Asks yes/no questions ("Is he sleeping?") • Uses adjectives ("ball is red") • Uses regular past-tense verbs correctly ("walk/walked") • Uses 's for possession ("mommy's car") • Uses pronouns ("I," "me," "you," "mine") • "Not" emerging
3½ years	• Comprehends 1,200 words • Understands concepts of in front of/behind, hard/soft, rough/smooth, circle/square	• Uses 800 words • Combines 4 to 5 words in sentences • Asks mainly "what" and "who" questions

AGE	RECEPTIVE LANGUAGE	EXPRESSIVE LANGUAGE
3½ years (con't)	• Responds to commands involving 3 actions or objects ("Put your sandwich, your cookies, and your juice in the bag.")	• Supplies the last word of a sentence ("The apple is on the . . .") • Counts three objects and points to each • Uses "is" at the beginning of questions • Uses present progressive ("girls are running") • Uses regular plural ("cat/cats"); irregular plural emerging ("child/children")
4 years	• Comprehends 1,500 to 2,000 words • Understands if/then ("If you touch the stove, then you will get burned.") • Recognizes at least one color	• Uses pronouns "he," "she" • Uses conjunction "because" • "was," "were" questions emerging ("Was he there?")
4½ years	• Points to shapes when named • Understands between, above/below, top/bottom • Understands the concept of the number 3	• Combines 4 to 7 words in sentences • Speech is very intelligible • Responds to "how far" questions • Counts 4 objects • Rote counts to 10 • Repeats 4 digits when dictated • Uses "what," "does," and "did" questions • Uses irregular plurals, "could," "would" • Comparative "-er" emerging ("smaller") • Passive voice emerging ("The dog was killed by the car.")
5 years	• Comprehends 2,500 to 2,800 words • Follows more complex three-part directions • Tells if two words rhyme	• Vocabulary of 1,500 to 2,000 words • Combines 5 to 8 words in sentences (average 5 to 7 words)

AGE	RECEPTIVE LANGUAGE	EXPRESSIVE LANGUAGE
5 years (con't)	• Recognizes primary colors • Comprehends heavy/light, loud/soft, like/unlike, long/short	• Names several colors • Answers simple "when," "how often," "how long" questions • Asks meanings of words • Tells long story accurately • Counts 10 objects • Can name first, middle, and last object in a series • Uses "will" to form future tense ("I will go") • Adjectives and nouns agree • Uses noun derivation "-er" ("painter," "farmer")
6 years	• Comprehends 13,000 words • Understands opposites: fast/slow, same/different, yesterday/tomorrow, most/least, some/many, before/after • Comprehends number concepts to 10 • Points to penny, nickel, dime, quarter • Points to half, whole, right, left • Sorts objects by shape or color	• Can answer "what happens if" questions • Counts 12 objects • Rote counts to 30 • Names all letters of the alphabet • Describes similarities and differences between objects • Describes location or movement: "through," "away from," "toward," "over" • Names position of objects: "first," "second," "third" • Names days of the week in order • Adverbial endings emerging ("slowly") • Articulates /f/ clearly
6½ years		• Articulates /v/t/l/th/zh/sh clearly
7 years	• Understands 20,000 to 26,000 words • Understands rough time intervals and seasons • Aware of others' speech errors	• Combines 7 or more words in sentences • States preceding and following information in a series ("What comes before 5?" "What day comes after Wednesday?")

AGE	RECEPTIVE LANGUAGE	EXPRESSIVE LANGUAGE
7 years (con't)	• Differentiates left from right	• Uses slang • Rote counts to 100 • Perfect tense emerging ("have," "had seen") • Consistently correct grammar (including passive voice, irregular past tense, comparative as in "bigger," adverbial word endings as in "slowly")
7½ years through adolescence	• Learns to use nonlinguistic cues to help interpret a speaker's intent: speed, loudness, tone, quality, stress patterns, duration of individual words, intonation, pauses, context, gestures, posture, facial expressions, eye contact, and body movements • Learns to understand homonyms, words with dual meanings, idioms, metaphors, and proverbs	• Articulates /z/s/r/ clearly • Learns to adjust speech to the particular person being spoken to, what was just said, the topic of conversation, the goal of the discussion, the time, and the setting

BENCHMARKS OF NORMAL PERCEPTUAL-MOTOR DEVELOPMENT

There is wide variability in the ages at which different children reach the following milestones. Therefore, these benchmarks should be interpreted loosely, giving children time to develop at their own pace. If delays continue for too long, however, professional consultation should be sought.

AGE	FINE-MOTOR	LARGE-MOTOR
6 months	• grasps and lifts objects • reaches with both hands • transfers object from hand to hand • rescues an object after dropping it	• rolls over • crawls with abdomen touching floor • supports full weight when held vertically • holds trunk erect momentarily when placed in a sitting position
9 months		• holds trunk erect indefinitely in sitting position • in creeping position, supports weight on toes • Pulls self into a standing position but has insufficient motor control to lower self
1 year	• holds objects between finger and thumb, replacing the palm grasp • well-coordinated reaching • uses crayons to make marks on paper	• goes from sitting to lying down and back to sitting position unassisted • pulls self to standing and walks holding onto furniture • walks alone between 1 and 1½ years
1½ years	• throws and retrieves objects • opens doors • manipulates and drinks from a cup • takes off shoes • makes a tower of 3 to 4 blocks • turns pages of a book, several at a time	• walks sideways and backwards

AGE	FINE-MOTOR	LARGE-MOTOR
2 years	• places circle, triangle, square in foamboard puzzle • makes a tower of 6 or 7 blocks • aligns two or more blocks to make a train • puts on and takes off pants • removes coat or dress unassisted • uses fork and spoon appropriately	• runs well • jumps • goes up and down stairs placing both feet on each step • kicks a ball on the floor between 2 and 3 years • throws ball overhand
2½ years	• obtains own drink of water with cup • dries own hands • stacks five rings on peg by size • copies vertical line with pencil	
3 years	• dresses self • makes a tower of 9 blocks • places 10 or more pellets into a bottle using one hand • copies circle, horizontal line with pencil	• walks up stairs using alternate feet, descends with both feet on each step • rides tricycle • balances on each foot for 2 seconds • dribbles ball short distance
4 years	• copies cross, diagonal line • draws person with at least 2 parts or features	• performs somersaults • hops on one leg • walks up and down stairs • one step per foot • balances on one foot for up to 10 seconds
4½ years	• can manage buttons • cuts accurately, pastes • copies triangle, square	• walks on a straight line or beam • gallops • skips and catches a bounced ball between 4 and 5 years

AGE	FINE-MOTOR	LARGE-MOTOR
5 years	• ties shoes • copies X, triangle • draws person with head, hair, eyes, nose, mouth, ears, body, arms, hands, legs • brushes teeth • begins to brush hair appropriately	• catches tossed ball with both hands
6 years	• copies diamond • cuts soft food with knife	• jumps rope • gains balance on a bicycle

Appendix B

COMMON ASSESSMENT
MEASURES

INTELLIGENCE MEASURES

Wechsler Intelligence Scale for Children—III (WISC-III)
(ages 6–16 years 11 months)

In most cases, the WISC-III is the intelligence test of choice. It does a good job of measuring the ability to process both verbal and visual information. The child has opportunities to demonstrate strengths and weaknesses in several areas: interpretation and problem solving with words or visual images, speed of information processing, planning and organization, attention, and short-term and long-term memory. Because over half of the subtests award extra points for speed, the scores of children who work slowly will be negatively affected.

Wechsler Preschool and Primary Scale of Intelligence—Revised (WPPSI-R)
(ages 3–7 years 3 months)

The WPPSI-R is an easier version of the WISC-III, designed for younger children. Six- and seven-year-olds generally score higher on the WISC-III. Six- and seven-year-olds who are below average intellectually, however, have more of an opportunity to demonstrate their range of problem-solving skills on the WPPSI-R than on the WISC-III.

Wechsler Adult Intelligence Scale—Revised (WAIS-R)
(ages 16–74)

The WAIS-R, designed for older teenagers and adults, is a harder version of the WISC-III. Although the WAIS-R will score about 4 points higher than the WISC-III, the test of choice for 16-year-olds is still the WISC-III because it offers a larger number of valid subtest items to which the teenager can respond.

Stanford-Binet Intelligence Scale: Fourth Edition (SB:FE) (ages 2–32½)

The SB:FE contrasts verbal comprehension and knowledge with ability to reason about nonverbal, visual information and quantitative reasoning. Short-term memory is also assessed with a variety of tasks that require focused attention, planning, and rehearsal strategies. The SB:FE is good for children who are slow information processors because it contains only one timed subtest. This lack of timing, however, may make the testing session exceedingly long. In addition, the SB:FE may score substantially lower than the WAIS-R for very bright people age 16 and older. Caution must be used in interpreting SB:FE results because some subtests don't really measure what they are designed to measure.

Kaufman Assessment Battery for Children (K-ABC) (ages 2½–12 years 6 months)

The K-ABC measures problem-solving ability using a variety of tasks requiring sequential processing (arrangement of stimuli in serial order) or simultaneous processing (spatial and organizational problems that require the processing of many stimuli at once). Mental Processing Composite subtests minimize reliance on verbal ability or previously learned information. Verbal skills are measured on an Achievement Scale, which also measures fund of learned information, reading decoding, reading comprehension, and mathematical abilities. The scores of children with attention deficits and short-term recall difficulties may be negatively affected by the Mental Processing Composite's heavy reliance on attention and memory. The K-ABC should not be the primary instrument used to measure intelligence for several reasons: it puts too much weight on simultaneous processing, it is not hard enough to validly assess gifted children, it does not tabulate language skills (a significant predictor of achievement) into the Mental Processing Composite, and it can yield a significant discrepancy between mental processing and achievement scores that is entirely caused by test construction rather than the child's learning patterns.

DEVELOPMENTAL MEASURES

Tests of Language Development

Peabody Picture Vocabulary Test—Revised (PPVT-R) (ages 2½–40 years 11 months)

The PPVT-R measures vocabulary by having the student point to the correct picture (from among four) that depicts a dictated word. Children who have poor visual comprehension of pictures, or who tend to respond impulsively, may earn low scores on the PPVT-R despite adequate language skills. Because the PPVT-R assesses only one aspect of language development, it should be used in conjunction with tests that measure other aspects of language ability, such as comprehension of grammatical structure and oral communication skills.

Test of Auditory Comprehension of Language—Revised (TACL-R) (ages 3–9 years 11 months)

The TACL-R tests auditory comprehension by having children point to the correct picture (from among three choices) when the examiner dictates single words, words with modifiers, short sentences that vary in grammatical form, and complex sentences. As on the PPVT-R, weak perceptual discrimination in analyzing the pictures and impulsivity may reduce a child's score, even if language comprehension is good. The TACL-R should be supplemented with tasks that measure the child's expressive language abilities.

Goldman-Fristoe-Woodcock Test of Auditory Discrimination (ages 3–84)

The Goldman-Fristoe-Woodcock assesses speech-sound discrimination under quiet background noise conditions. Individual words are presented on an audiotape, and the child is asked to point to one of four pictures that depicts the word. Like most tests of auditory discrimination, the Goldman-Fristoe-Woodcock has poor reliability and validity. It should be used only as a crude indicator of auditory discrimination abilities.

Test of Language Development—2 Primary (TOLD-2 Primary) (ages 4–8 years 11 months)

The TOLD-2 Primary measures the younger child's semantic abilities (picture vocabulary and oral vocabulary), syntax (understanding sentence structure, repeating dictated sentences, and using appropriate grammatical forms), and phonology (word discrimination and articulation) through both receptive and expressive channels.

Test of Language Development—2 Intermediate (TOLD-2 Intermediate) (ages 8½–12 years 11 months)

The TOLD-2 Intermediate measures semantic ability and syntax by means of combining sentences, oral vocabulary, ordering words within sentences, understanding of abstract relationships, recognition of grammatical sentences, and correcting ridiculous sentences.

Test of Adolescent Language—2 (TOAL-2)
(ages 12–18 years 5 months)

The TOAL-2 helps determine areas of relative strength and weakness in language abilities by means of several tasks: choosing the picture that depicts a
dictated word, indicating which sentences that differ grammatically have the
same meaning, making up and repeating sentences, choosing words that belong together, writing sentences containing specific words, and combining
two sentences into one when writing. While the overall score may be accurate, some of the area scores have questionable validity because they are
comprised of only two subtest scores.

Test of Language Competence (TLC)
(ages 9–18 years 11 months)

The TLC measures sophisticated semantics, syntax, and conversational skill
by means of several tasks: the student reads a sentence that could mean more
than one thing and identifies both meanings; the student reads two related
statements and then chooses inferences that are appropriate; the student creates a sentence given three words and a picture; the student must explain
what sentences with metaphors mean.

Tests of Visual-Perceptual and Motor Development

Bender Visual-Motor Gestalt Test
(ages 5–9½ years: Koppitz Scoring System)

The Bender measures visual-motor ability by presenting nine geometric figures for the child to copy, one at a time. The products are scored for distor-
tions of shape, rotations, integration difficulties, and perseveration (for
example, extra lines or too many dots). Because most 8- to 9-year-old children can reproduce all the designs perfectly, beyond age 8 the test is useful
only for distinguishing whether a child's perceptual-motor maturity is below
that of an 8-year-old.

Developmental Test of Visual-Motor Integration—Third Revision
(VMI-3) (ages 4–17 years 11 months)

The VMI measures perceptual-motor ability by having the child copy up to 24
geometric forms within a drawing booklet. The VMI tends to produce higher
scores than the Bender, perhaps because performance is facilitated by VMI
designs being presented within a structured space with the child copying designs in adjacent areas.

Motor Free Visual Perception Test (MVPT)
(ages 4–8 years 11 months)

The MVPT measures visual perception by having the child select the correct figure during five types of tasks: spatial relationships, visual discrimination, figure-ground relationships, visual closure, and visual memory. The MVPT has questionable validity but may yield some information of value when used in combination with a copying measure such as those described above.

Bruininks-Oseretsky Test of Motor Proficiency
(ages 4½–14½)

The Bruininks-Oseretsky measures large- and fine-motor functioning on subtests that sample running speed, balance, coordination of limbs, muscle strength, visual tracking, speed of motor response, coordination of eye and hand movements, hand speed, arm speed, and hand and finger dexterity.

ACHIEVEMENT MEASURES
General Achievement Batteries Used for Screening Purposes

Woodcock Johnson Psychoeducational Battery—Revised (WJ-R)
(ages 2–90+)

The WJ-R includes subtests that measure decoding of isolated letters and words, ability to read nonsense words that follow English structural and phonetic patterns, reading comprehension, knowledge of synonyms and antonyms, calculation ability, the ability to solve practical mathematical problems, mathematical conceptual understanding, spelling, punctuation, capitalization, written expression, and knowledge in science, social studies, and the humanities. The reading disabilities of children who don't recognize words rapidly but can sound out words if given time may not be evident on the WJ-R, because the child can take as long as necessary during the test to figure out a word. In addition, little information is gained on reading fluency because the examiner listens only to how a child reads single words, not sentences or paragraphs. On the WJ-R, the reading comprehension task is unlike real-life comprehension demands (the child is asked to fill in a missing word in a sentence that is read silently). Writing ability is also judged by limited information (the quality of individual sentences that are produced, rather than the quality of paragraphs).

The WJ-R includes 12 subtests that are supposed to measure cognitive ability. Thinking skills of children with learning disabilities often are underestimated on the WJ-R Tests of Cognitive Ability. These tests should not be used to replace intelligence tests such as the WISC-III.

Wechsler Individual Achievement Test (WIAT)
(ages 5–19 years 11 months)

The WIAT measures achievement in all areas specified in the federal law's definition of learning disabilities: oral expression (while looking at pictures, children describe scenes, give directions, and explain steps in a process), listening comprehension (children identify the picture that corresponds to an orally presented word and respond orally to questions about orally presented passages), basic reading skills (children are given 10 seconds to read each word on a word list), reading comprehension (children read passages and respond to oral questions), written expression (children write spelling words and a short passage), mathematics calculation (children work math problems), and mathematical reasoning (children respond to practical questions involving math reasoning).

Kaufman Test of Educational Achievement (K-TEA) (grades 1–12)

The K-TEA measures decoding of letters and individual words, spelling, reading comprehension (children answer questions orally after silently reading short passages), mathematics computation, and the ability to answer math conceptual and reasoning questions. The K-TEA is useful after first grade but has too few lower-level items to adequately assess a first grader with poor achievement.

Peabody Individual Achievement Test—Revised (PIAT-R) (ages 5–18 years 11 months)

The PIAT-R measures knowledge of general information, decoding of individual words, reading comprehension (children choose which of four pictures depict the content of a sentence they have read), mathematics (children choose which of four answers is correct), spelling (children choose the correct spelling from four choices), and written expression (children copy letters, write from dictation, compose a story). Due to the multiple choice format on three subtests, the PIAT-R is attractive for use with students with speech and fine-motor weaknesses. The scores gained from the multiple choice format can be misleading, however, as they are not comparable to classroom tasks that require students to produce, rather than simply recognize, information. In addition, the writing subtest is to be used with caution because of low reliability.

Wide Range Achievement Test—Revised (WRAT-R) (ages 5–74)

The WRAT-R measures the ability to read individual letters and words, spell from dictation, and work math calculations. In contrast to tests that allow unlimited time to decode words, the WRAT-R allows only 10 seconds. Therefore, the WRAT-R is likely to identify children with reading disabilities who take a long time to recognize or sound out words. A disadvantage of the WRAT-R is the absence of reading comprehension and math concept subtests. In addition, it may overestimate the achievement of young children who experience academic difficulties.

Woodcock Reading Mastery Tests—Revised (WRMT-R)
(ages 5–75+)

The WRMT-R measures word identification, pronunciation of nonsense words that follow English structural and phonetic patterns, word comprehension (the child completes antonyms, synonyms, and analogies), and reading comprehension (the child reads a passage silently and supplies a key word that is missing). Form G of the test also includes a subtest that measures the child's ability to identify letters presented in common and uncommon type styles, and a subtest that measures ability to associate abstract visual symbols with familiar words and then "translate" sentences built from these symbols. Criticisms mentioned earlier for the WJ-R regarding reading comprehension procedures pertain here as well. The WRMT-R does impose a 5-second limit for decoding words on the word list. The weaknesses of children who are slow yet accurate decoders will therefore be reflected in the test score.

Diagnostic Achievement Tests Used for Instructional Planning

The Brigance Inventories
(birth–grade 12)

Several versions of the Brigance Inventories are available for different age levels. These inventories present excellent lists of developmental, reading readiness, reading, math, and writing skills that a child should be developing. The Brigance Inventories are specific enough to suggest detailed programming objectives, and are also useful in monitoring progress toward these goals. Because the Brigance Inventories have not been standardized, they should be used only as useful checklists of essential skills. Scores should not be assigned to a child's performance. The grade-level indicators on the record sheet are merely educated estimates as to the grade at which children typically learn each skill. In your child's school, expectations for what is to be learned at various grade levels may be quite different.

Gray Oral Reading Test—Diagnostic (GORT-D)
(ages 5½–12 years 11 months)

The GORT-D measures a child's speed and accuracy when reading paragraphs aloud, ability to respond to comprehension questions about these paragraphs, ability to sound out and blend nonsense words that follow English structural and phonetic patterns, ability to find smaller words within larger words, word identification and comprehension skills, and the ability to deal with compound words, contractions, and inflectional endings. Because many of the GORT-D subtests use nontraditional formats, the score may not reflect the student's classroom performance.

• **Gray Oral Reading Test—3 (GORT-3)**

• **New Sucher-Allred Reading Placement Inventory**

- **Classroom Reading Inventory**
- **Standard Reading Inventory**
- **Diagnostic Reading Scales**
- **Eckwall Reading Inventory**
- **John's Basic Reading Inventory**
  (vary from grades 1–12)

These and other reading inventories ask the student to read word lists and passages of increasing difficulty aloud. The child's reading rate and accuracy are measured, and reading errors are analyzed. Following each passage, comprehension questions are asked that require identification of the main idea in the passage, facts, sequence of events, vocabulary definitions, ability to make inferences from the passage, and critical thinking ability. Scores may be used to indicate the child's independent reading level (the child is able to read this material without aid and with good comprehension), instructional level (material is challenging but not overly difficult), and frustration level (the child has difficulty recognizing words or comprehending much of what is read). Some inventories also measure comprehension after students read silently or listen to material being read to them. Contrasting oral reading comprehension with silent reading and listening comprehension is helpful in terms of suggesting classroom interventions. Parents should be cautioned that grade-level scores are not necessarily accurate.

Gallistel-Ellis Test of Coding Skills (G-E Test)
(grades 2–6)

The G-E Test assesses the child's ability to decode and spell the basic phonetic patterns in the English language. Reading and spelling of irregular patterns are sampled to a small degree. G-E Test results can be very useful in planning reading remediation.

Lindamood Auditory Conceptualization Test (LAC)
Rosner Perceptual Skills Curriculum
(kindergarten–adult)

The LAC and Rosner are extremely useful for determining if a child's reading problems are related to difficulty perceiving the number and order of sounds in words. While these skills are usually well developed by second grade, persistent weaknesses are found even in high school students and adults with reading disabilities. On the LAC the student uses blocks to demonstrate how sounds are added, subtracted, and changed around within nonsense words. The Rosner transformations are done orally and with real words (such as "say *slip;* now say *slip* but leave out the *l*").

Test of Written Language—2 (TOWL-2)
(ages 7½–17 years 11 months)

The TOWL-2 measures strengths and weaknesses in written language by having the student write a story in response to a picture. The child's thematic maturity, vocabulary level, accuracy of grammatical structure, spelling, punctuation, and capitalization are measured. In addition, the child is asked to write sentences using specific words, spell words accurately, punctuate and capitalize, rewrite illogical sentences, and combine several sentences into one. Scores derived from unusually short samples may be suspect.

Key Math Diagnostic Arithmetic Test—Revised
(ages 5–15 years 11 months)

The Key Math assesses the student's knowledge of basic mathematical concepts (number knowledge, fractions, decimals, percentages, geometric shapes, and principles), operations (addition, subtraction, multiplication, division, mental computation), and applications (measurement, time, money, estimation, interpreting data, and problem solving).

Enright Diagnostic Inventory of Basic Arithmetic Skills
(grades elementary through middle school)

The Inventory provides a task analysis of the student's computation errors using whole numbers, fractions, and decimals. It also identifies areas in which the student demonstrates mastery.

Test of Written Spelling—3 (TWS-3)
(ages 6–18 years 11 months)

In the TWS-3, spelling words of various levels of difficulty are dictated to the student. Diagnostic observations are aided by the format: half of the words are predictable (conform to usual spelling rules) and half are unpredictable (do not follow the usual rules and therefore must be memorized).

SOCIAL AND EMOTIONAL ADJUSTMENT MEASURES

Adaptive Behavior

Vineland Adaptive Behavior Scales
(ages birth–18 years 11 months)

The Vineland assesses social competence by interviewing a parent or teacher who is very familiar with the behavior of the student. Adaptive behavior is measured in four areas: spoken and written communication, daily living skills and behavior in the community, sensitivity to and socialization with others, and gross- and fine-motor coordination skills. A Maladaptive Behavior section score is also provided. The Expanded Form of the Vineland has sufficient numbers of items to assist specific intervention planning.

Scales of Independent Behavior (SIB)
(ages 3 months–adult)

The SIB is an interview instrument that asks the parent very specific questions about the child's development in several areas: gross- and fine-motor skills, social interaction, language comprehension, language expression, eating, toileting, dressing, personal self-care, domestic skills, time and punctuality, money and value, work skills, and home/community functioning. Parents indicate whether the behavior is exhibited never/rarely, about ¼ of the time, ¾ of the time, or almost always.

Brigance Inventory of Essential Skills
(grades 1–middle school)

The Brigance samples basic knowledge, academic skills, and daily living skills essential for independent living as an adult. The inventory's detail is very helpful in intervention planning.

Behavioral Questionnaires

Child Behavior Checklist (CBCL)
(ages 2–16)

The CBCL contains a list of behavioral problems that are rated by the parent as not true, somewhat true, or very true. Children are compared with same-age peers on behaviors such as anxiety, depression, uncommunicative, obsessive-compulsive, somatic complaints, social withdrawal, hyperactivity, aggression, and delinquent behavior. Self-report and teacher report forms also are available. As with any behavior checklist, it is helpful to obtain input from both parents and several teachers. Behavior, as measured by these scales, is in the eye of the beholder—that is, each parent and teacher is likely to view the student differently. Therefore, the best perspective on the child's usual behavioral tendencies is gained by comparing multiple viewpoints.

Connors Parent Rating Scale
(ages 3–17)

Connors Teacher Rating Scale
(ages 4–12)

The Connors Scales are checklists on which parents and teachers rate a variety of behavior problems on a four-point scale. Behavioral characteristics include conduct disorder, anxiety, restless-disorganized, learning problem–immature, psychosomatic, obsessional, antisocial, and hyperactive. Several versions of these scales are available; the 48-item parent scale and 39-item teacher scale have adequate standardization. As many of the items on the hyperactivity scale involve acting out and annoying behaviors, this scale may not identify the child with an attention deficit and hyperactivity who is well socialized.

Personality Inventory for Children (PIC)
(ages 6–16)

The PIC uses a true/false format and asks the parent to rate 600 items pertaining to the child's adjustment, achievement, intelligence, developmental skills, psychosomatic complaints, depression, family relations, delinquency, withdrawal, anxiety, psychosis, hyperactivity, and social skills.

Projective Measures

- **Thematic Apperception Test (TAT)**
- **Children's Apperception Test (CAT)**
- **Educational Apperception Test (EAT)**
- **Roberts Apperception Test for Children**
- **Sentence Completions**
- **Human Figure Drawings**
- **Kinetic Family and School Drawings**

Projective tests are designed to measure emotions that the child projects into stories told in response to pictures on "apperception" cards, words used to fill in blanks in sentences (such as "Mothers should _____"), or pictures drawn about the family and classroom. Validity is poor because evaluation of the child's responses involves a great deal of subjective interpretation by the examiner, and interpretations will differ from examiner to examiner. When results from these measures are shared with you, ask to see your child's responses so you can add your own interpretations.

Self-Concept Measures

- **Piers Harris Children's Self-Concept Scale (grades 4–12)**
- **Martinek-Zaichowsky Self-Concept Scale for Children (grades 1–8)**
- **Coopersmith Self-Esteem Inventory (ages 8–15)**
- **Myself Checklist (grades 1–12)**
- **Primary Self Concept Inventory (grades K–4)**

Self-concept measures generally ask the child to read a statement (such as "I am an unhappy person") and indicate whether they agree or disagree with that statement. Sometimes open-ended sentence stems also are completed, and the child may be asked to list his or her strengths and weaknesses. While useful information can be derived from these scales, the positive and negative intent is obvious to children, and often they will respond the way they think others expect them to respond. Scores can be derived for overall self-esteem or sub-areas such as appearance, athletic skills, intelligence, academic skills or social skills.

Appendix C

THE DEVELOPMENT OF READING, WRITING, AND MATH SKILLS

THE DEVELOPMENT OF READING SKILLS

Kindergarten

Points to/names upper and lowercase alphabet letters; recognizes some commonly seen words (e.g., STOP, McDonald's, Sesame Street); begins to associate letters with their sounds; matches simple words to corresponding pictures; rhymes; growing awareness of whether words begin or end with the same sound; developing ability to break spoken words into syllables; blends dictated sounds to make a word; recognizes that reading proceeds from left to right and from top to bottom on a page; interprets picture stories; recognizes/compares/contrasts facts in a story; aware of time sequence in a story and predicts outcome; recognizes poetry; distinguishes reality from fantasy.

First Grade

Identifies consonants in all positions in a word; reads long and short vowels, some vowel teams (e.g., ee, ea), and consonant diagraphs (e.g., ch, sh, th); growing ability to break dictated words into individual sounds; reads word families (e.g., cat, hat, rat); growing sight vocabulary; aware of root words, endings, compound words, contractions; recognizes main idea and cause/effect in story; draws conclusions; follows simple written directions; aware of author, title, table of contents, alphabetical order; recognizes a play; interprets maps and globes

Second Grade

Mastery of harder phonetic skills (e.g., kn, wr, gh, ck, lk, ir, ur, oi, au, oa); sounds out unfamiliar words based on individual letter sounds, familiar spelling patterns, root words, endings; identifies words from contextual clues; less confusion with reversible letters; varies pitch, stress, volume when reading aloud; aware of syllabication rules, prefixes/suffixes, changing y to i or f/fe to v before adding ending; compares/evaluates information; recognizes character, setting, motive, resolution of a story; uses library for simple research purposes; interprets graphs; uses dictionary

Third Grade

Reading focus shifts from decoding to comprehension; rapid extension of sight vocabulary and word-analysis skills (e.g., igh, eight); interprets homophones (e.g., *way, weigh*) and homographs (e.g., grizzly *bear,* to *bear* arms); reversals of letters and words generally disappear; reads selectively to locate information; reading speed increases with development of silent reading skills; distinguishes fiction/nonfiction, fact/opinion, synonym/antonym; recalls prior knowledge and relates to new text; recognizes author's purpose; uses index, captions, subheadings, margin notes; uses encyclopedia, telephone directory; interprets diagrams; reads for both knowledge and recreation

Fourth Grade

Begins to develop different reading styles/rates for different purposes (e.g., skimming); locates and uses references; increases silent reading rate; expands vocabulary; recognizes plot and implied main idea; understands idioms/multiple meanings; paraphrases or summarizes a story or article; selects/evaluates/organizes study materials; discriminates different forms of writing (e.g., folk tale, science fiction, biography); appreciates author's point of view; considerable independent reading expected; can read newspaper, restaurant menu

Fifth Grade

Makes generalizations; recognizes theme; uses copyright page, preface, cross-references; familiar with more literary forms (e.g., autobiography, fable, legend); reasons using syllogisms (e.g., if a = b and b = c, then a = c); can read many popular magazines

Middle School

Understands paradoxes; appreciates elements of style (e.g., imagery/foreshadowing/flashback/symbolism/irony/mood); recognizes biased writings and propaganda; uses appendices, *Readers Guide to Periodicals,* atlas, almanac, appropriate reference sources; recognizes figures of speech such as personification (e.g., *The computer yawned and spit out the disk*), hyperbole (intentional exaggeration, e.g., *waiting for an eternity*), onomatopoeia (word that imitates sounds, e.g., *cuckoo*); can read many adult-level books

THE DEVELOPMENT OF WRITING SKILLS

Kindergarten

Develops ability to hold and use pencils; traces/copies/writes letters, name, and simple sight words; writes short "stories" using dashes for words or invented spellings

First Grade

Uses traditional as well as invented spellings; works on copying letters and words; writes simple sentences; begins to write short poems, invitations, compositions; tries to use words that describe what the child sees, hears, feels as well as how things look, act, feel; capitalizes the first word of a sentence, first and last names, names of streets/towns/the school, and I; adds a period at the end of sentences and after numbers in a list; prints on the line

Second Grade

Writes letters legibly and uses appropriate size; understands how writing should be laid out (e.g., margins); combines short sentences into paragraphs; spelling and grammatical expression continue to improve; uses words with similar and opposite meanings in writing; alphabetizes; capitalizes important words in book titles, proper names, Mr./Mrs./Miss/Ms.; adds question mark at the end of a question; adds comma after salutation and closing of a letter, adds comma between the month/year and city/state; avoids running sentences together with "and"; begins to use script; begins to develop proofreading skills

Third Grade

Uses both printing and script writing; writes short passages expressing a central idea; sequences ideas well and uses expanded vocabulary; identifies/uses various sentence forms (e.g., declarative, interrogative/exclamatory); combines short, choppy sentences into longer ones; uses interesting beginning and ending sentences; avoids run-on sentences; uses synonyms; distinguishes meaning and spelling of homonyms; uses the prefix "un" and the suffix "less"; capitalizes month/day/common holidays/first word in a line of verse/"Dear"/"Sincerely;" adds period after abbreviations/initials; uses apostrophe in common contractions (e.g., isn't); adds commas in a list; indents; spells many words in sight vocabulary (including irregular words such as "eight"); proofreads own and others' work

Fourth Grade

Writes in script; develops interesting paragraphs and a sense of the writing process (outline first, write, proofread); chooses words that appeal to the senses or that precisely explain a point; capitalizes names of cities/states/organizations; uses apostrophe to show possession, hyphen to divide word at end of line, exclamation point, colon after salutation, quotation marks, comma before quotation in a sentence, period after outline items or Roman numerals; uses command sentences; avoids sentence fragments; selects appropriate title; makes simple outline; writes/tells stories that have character and plot

Fifth Grade

Varies type of sentences, including imperative; subjects and verbs agree; uses compound subjects and predicates; ideas are clearly stated in more than one paragraph; keeps to the topic; uses antonyms/prefixes/suffixes/contractions/compound words/words with sensory images/rhyme and rhythm; greater precision in choice of words; uses dictionary for definitions/syllables/pronunciation; capitalizes names of streets/places/persons/countries/oceans/trade names/beginning items in outlines/titles with a name (e.g., President Roosevelt); uses quotation marks or underlining for titles; classifies words by parts of speech; uses subheads in outlines; writes from outline; writes dialogue; recognizes topic sentences; enjoys writing/receiving letters; keeps a diary

Middle School

Develops increasing sophistication in ideas and expression; accurate/effective/appropriate choice of words and phrases; edits to improve style and effect; avoids wordiness and unnecessary repetition; uses complex sentences; avoids vagueness and omissions; develops paragraphs with details/reasons/examples/comparisons; checks for accuracy of statements; connects ideas with transition words; develops paragraphs with topic sentences; adds introduction and conclusion; checks reasoning; uses several sources to prepare a report; makes a bibliography; capitalizes first word of a quote/adjectives of race and nationality; punctuates appropriately; learns to use footnotes; learns notetaking skills

THE DEVELOPMENT OF MATH SKILLS

Kindergarten

Matches/sorts/names objects by size, color end shape; counts/adds up to nine objects; evaluates objects by quantity, dimensions, size (e.g., more/less, longer/shorter, tall/tallest, bigger/same); recites and recognizes numbers 1–20; writes numbers 1–10; understands concepts of addition and subtraction; knows symbols +, –, =; recognizes whole vs. half; understands ordinals (first, 5th); learns beginning concepts of weight, time (e.g., before/after; understands lunch is at 12:00; tells time to the hour), money (knows value of pennies, nickels, dimes), and temperature (hotter/colder); aware of locations (e.g., above/below, left/right, nearest/farthest); interprets simple maps, graphs and tallies

First Grade

Counts/reads/writes/orders numbers to 99; begins learning addition and subtraction facts; performs simple addition/subtraction problems (e.g., 23 + 11); understands multiplication as repeated addition; counts by 2s, 5s and 10s; identifies odd/even numbers; estimates answers; understands ½, ⅓, ¼; gains elementary knowledge of calendar (e.g., counts how many days to birthday), time (tells time to half hour; understands schedules; reads digital clock), measurement (cup, pint, quart, liter, inch, cm, kg, lb), and money (knows value of quarter; compares prices); solves simple number story problems; reads bar graphs and charts

Second Grade

Identifies/writes numbers to 999; adds/subtracts two- and-three digit numbers with and without regrouping (e.g., 223 + 88, 124 – 16); multiplies by 2, 3, 4, 5; counts by 3s, 5s, 10s, 100s; reads/writes Roman numerals to XII; counts money and makes change up to $10.00; recognizes days of the week, months, and seasons of the year on a calendar; tells time to five minutes on a clock with hands; learns basic measurements (inch, foot, pint, pound); recognizes equivalents (e.g., two quarters = one half; four quarts = one gallon); divides area into ⅔, ¾, 10ths; graphs simple data

Third Grade

Understands place value to thousands; adds and subtracts four-digit numbers (e.g., 1,017 – 978); learns multiplication facts to 9 × 9; solves simple multiplication and division problems (642 × or ÷ 2); relates division to repeated subtractions; learns harder Roman numerals; introduction to fractions (adds/estimates/orders simple fractions; understands mixed numbers; reads fractions of an inch) and geometry (identifies hexagon, pentagon); understands diameter, radius, volume, area); understands decimals; begins to learn about negative numbers, probability, percentage, ratio; solves harder number story problems

Fourth Grade

Adds columns of 3 or more numbers; multiplies three-digit by two-digit numbers (348 × 34); performs simple division (44/22); reduces fractions to lowest terms; adds/subtracts fractions with different denominators (¾ + ⅔); adds/subtracts decimals; converts decimals to percents; counts/makes change for up to $20.00; estimates time; can measure time in hours, minutes, seconds; computes area of rectangles; identifies parallel, perpendicular, intersecting lines; calculates weight in tons, length in meters, volume in cubic centimeters

Fifth Grade

Multiplies three-digit numbers (962 × 334); can do harder division problems (102 ÷ 32); adds, subtracts, multiplies mixed numbers; divides a whole number by a fraction; represents fractions as decimals, ratios, percents; adds, subtracts, multiplies, with decimals; divides a decimal by a whole number; understands use of equations, formulas, "working backward"; estimates products/quotients; begins to learn about exponents, greatest common factor, bases, prime factors, composite numbers, integers; understands percent, ratios; understands mean, median, mode; measures area/circumference of a circle, perimeter/areas of triangles and parallelograms; performs metric conversions; uses compass, protractor; reads scale drawings

Middle School

Masters order of operations in complex problems; multiplies/divides two fractions; adds, subtracts, multiplies, divides decimals to the thousandth; converts decimals to fractions, percents, ratios; understands real, rational, irrational numbers and different number bases; calculates square and cube roots; estimates percentages/proportions; calculates discount, sales tax, restaurant tip; understands markup, commission, simple interest, compound interest, percent increase/decrease; understands angles (complementary, supplementary, adjacent, straight, congruent . . .); calculates volume of a cylinder; calculates arc of circle; understands equilateral, isosceles, scalene, obtuse figures; organizes sets of data; graphs coordinates, transformations, reflections, rotations, equations with two variables; solves equations by substitution; begins to learn about conditional probability, permutations, factorial notation, relative frequency, normal curve, Pythagorean theorem; deepens understanding of previously taught skills and concepts

Appendix D

RESOURCE LIST

LEARNING DISABILITIES ORGANIZATIONS

Children and Adults with Attention Deficit Disorder (CHADD)

499 NW 70th Avenue, #101, Plantation, FL 33317
Phone: (954) 587-3700
Web site: http:\\www.chadd.org

Serves children and adults with ADD and their families through support groups, a quarterly magazine, and a newsletter. Over 600 chapters around the country.

Learning Disabilities Association of America (LDA)

4156 Library Road, Pittsburgh, PA 15234
Phone: (412) 341-1515

Provides information and advocacy-related resources; conducts conferences for parents and other professionals. Numerous state and local affiliates.

Learning Disabilities Association of Canada (LDAC)

232 Chapel Street, Ottawa, Ontario, Canada K1N7Z2
Phone: (613) 238-5721

Conducts programs and provides information for children and adults with learning disabilities in Canada.

National Center for Learning Disabilities (NCLD)

381 Park Avenue, Suite 1420, New York, NY 10016
Phone: (212) 454-7510

Offers free information and referral services; conducts educational summits and programs around the country. Membership open to parents and professionals.

Orton Dyslexia Society

Chester Building, 8600 La Salle Road, Suite 382
Baltimore, MD 21286-2044
Phone: (410) 296-0232
Web site: http:\\ODS.org

Free information; referral services for assessment and tutoring. Sponsors annual conference and distributes publications relating to dyslexia. Membership includes parents, researchers, and other professionals.

Parents of Gifted/LD Children

2420 Eccleston Street, Bethesda, MD 20902
Phone: (301) 986-1432

Provides information and a support network for parents; sponsors local and national meetings.

OTHER RELEVANT ORGANIZATIONS

Educational Resource Information Center (ERIC)

1920 Association Drive, Reston, VA 20291-1589
Phone: (800) 328-0272 and (703) 264-9474

A program of the Council for Exceptional Children. Provides free information and referral services. Many good publications.

HEATH Resource Center (Higher Education and Adult Training for People with Handicaps)

1 Dupont Circle, Suite 800, Washington, DC 20036-1193
Phone: (800) 544-3284
Web site: http:\\www.acenet.edu

A program of the American Council on Education. Provides information on postsecondary education for students with disabilities. Many excellent publications including "Getting Ready For College."

National Association of Private Schools for Exceptional Children (NAPSEC)

1522 K Street NW, Suite 1032, Washington, DC 20005-1202
Phone: (202) 408-3338
Web site: http:\\www.spedschool.com.napsec.html

Free information, referral, and research services. Provides information on legal rights. Annual conference for parents and professionals.

National Clearinghouse on Women and Girls with Disabilities

Educational Equity Concepts, Inc.
114 East 32nd Street, Suite 701, New York, NY 10016
Phone: (212) 725-1803

Offers information and referral services, and a national directory of services for girls and women with disabilities.

National Information Center for Children and Youth with Disabilities (NICHCY)

PO Box 1492, Washington, DC 20013-1492
Phone: (800) 695-0285 or (202) 884-8200

Information clearinghouse that provides information on a wide variety of disability-related issues for children and youth up to age 22. Excellent free publications.

National Parent Network on Disabilities (NPND)

1727 King Street Suite 305, Alexandria, VA 22314
Phone: (703) 684-6763

A membership organization for individuals concerned with the quality of life of people with disabilities.

National Rehabilitation Information Center (NARIC)

8455 Colesville Road, Suite 935, Silver Spring, MD 20910
Phone: (800) 346-2742

Offers information about rehabilitation services for adults with disabilities and about obtaining and using adaptive technology.

Parents Helping Parents

3041 Alcott Street, San Jose, CA 95126
Phone: (408) 727-5775

Conducts workshops, training sessions, and support meetings for parents of children with a wide range of special needs.

SUMMER CAMPS

American Camping Association

50000 State Road, 67 N. Martinsdale, IN 46151
Phone: (800) 428-CAMP

Provides listings of summer camps for children with special needs.

Resources for Children with Special Needs

200 Park Avenue South, Suite 816, New York, NY 10003
Phone: (212) 677-4650

Provides information, referrals, parent training workshops, and an annual resource list for parents of children with special needs including a list of summer camps.

BOOKS ON TAPE

Recording for the Blind and Dyslexic

20 Rozel Road, Princeton, NJ 08540
Phone: (609) 452-0606

Provides taped educational books and books on diskette free on loan.

Library of Congress—National Library Service for the Blind and Physically Handicapped

1291 Taylor Street NW, Washington, DC 20542
Phone: (800) 424-8567

Provides books and other resources on tape for youth and adults with special needs.

GOVERNMENT OFFICES

The Children's SSI Campaign

1101 15th Street NW, Suite 1212, Washington, DC 20005
Phone: (202) 467-5730

Provides information on how children who meet disability requirements can get SSI support. Administered by the Social Security Administration.

Federal Student Aid Information Hotline

Phone: (800) 433-3243

Provides free information for students about funding higher education.

Office of Civil Rights (OCR)

400 Maryland Avenue SW, Washington, DC 20202-1100
Phone: (202) 205-5413

Maintains offices for filing formal civil rights complaints (both Section 504 and ADA complaints).

President's Committee on Employment for People with Disabilities

1331 F Street NW, Washington, DC 20004-1007
Phone: (202) 376-6200

Provides information and assistance with employment issues. Sponsors seminars, workshops, and annual conferences.

U.S. Department of Education

400 Maryland Avenue S.W. Washington, DC 20202-1100
Phone: (202) 401-2000
Website: http:\\www.ed.gov

Provides information on education initiatives and loans. Free publications.

EMPLOYMENT

ADA Information Hotline

Disability Rights Section, Civil Rights Division, US Department of Justice
PO Box 66738, Washington, DC 20035-6738
Phone: (202) 514-0301 or (800) 514-0301
Web site: http:\\www.usdoj.gov/crt/ada/adahome1.htm

Answers questions about Title II (public services) and Title III (public accommodations) sections of the ADA. Provides legal, technical, and informational services.

Job Accommodation Network

West Virginia University, PO Box 6080, Morgantown, WV 26506
Phone: (800) 232-9675
Web site: http:\\janweb.icdi.wvu.edu

Provides information and consults about employment issues related to persons with disabilities.

ADULT EDUCATION

The General Educational Development Testing Service (GEDTS)

1 Dupont Circle, Suite 250, Washington, DC 20036

Phone: (202) 939-9490

Provides the GED Test (high school equivalency exam) and information on disability-related adaptations and accommodations.

Literacy Volunteers of America (LVA)

5795 Widewaters Parkway, Syracuse, NY 13214

Phone: (315) 445-8000

Web site http:\\archon.edu.kent.edu\lva\

Publishes a catalog of resources for adults and youths seeking literacy skills. Includes information about addressing learning disabilities.

INDEPENDENT LIVING

National Council of Independent Living Programs

211 Wilson Blvd., Suite 405, Arlington, VA 22210

Phone: (703) 525-3406

email: ncil@tsbbs02.tnet.com

A grass-roots organization run by and for people with disabilities. Provides referrals to independent living facilities.

INDEX

ACKNOWLEDGMENTS

We would like to express our gratitude to the Learning Disabilities Association of Central New York, and to some of the many people who shared their insights with us: Leslie Bogad, Aggie and Sarah DeWan, Sue Loveland, Rebecca Moldover, Paul DeJong, Margie Boudreau, Mary Aitcheson, Teri Hubler, Jennifer Shulman, Tom Haley, and Sandy Smith.